W9-AFK-460

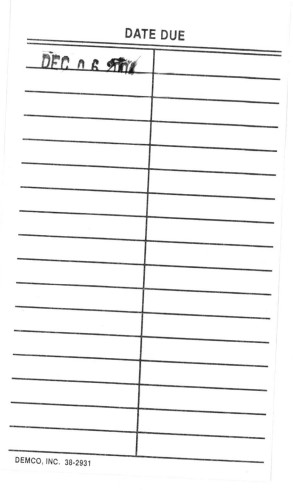

DATE DUE

DEC 0 6 2004

Women's Stressors, Personality & Traits Inner Balance Strategies

☙

Janet W. Kenney, R N, Ph.D.
Photography by Duc Liao

Women's Stressors, Personality Traits & Inner Balance Strategies

Cover and text design by Jeanne Hendrickson

Photography by Duc Liao

Published by Elton-Wolf Publishing

Seattle, Washington

05 04 03 02 01   1 2 3 4 5

ISBN: 1-58619-035-0

Library of Congress Control Number: 2001098424

First Printing February 2002

Printed in Canada

ELTON-WOLF PUBLISHING

2505 Second Avenue Suite 515   Seattle, Washington 98121
Tel 206.748.0345 Fax 206.748.0343
www.elton-wolf.com info@elton-wolf.com
Seattle • Los Angeles • Portland

Dedication
℘

To my three wonderful daughters, Michelle Coon, Noelle Griffith, and Kate Kenney, for all their love throughout my life, and especially for their support of my creative writing projects.

Also, I would like to express my sincere gratitude to Duc Liao, an international fashion photographer, and my daughter, Noelle, for their creative photographs that symbolically represent the topics in this book.

Contents

Introduction 1

Section I Overview of Women's Health

Chapter 1   Women's Inner Balance and Health—
            psychoneuroimmunology (PNI)   11

Chapter 2   Types of Stressors—daily hassles, chronic
            problems, and acute stressors   25

Section II Effects of Personality Traits

Chapter 3   Altruism—caring for others   41

Chapter 4   Assertiveness—taking charge   47

Chapter 5   Confiding in Others—sharing feelings   58

Chapter 6   Emotional Resilience   68

Chapter 7   Hardiness—challenge, control,
            and commitment   76

Chapter 8   Loving and Trusting Relationships   86

Chapter 9   Optimism—positive attitudes   103

Chapter 10 Unhealthy Personality Traits   112

Section III Stress-related Symptoms

Chapter 11 Physical and Emotional Symptoms of Stress   139

Section IV Stress Reduction Strategies

Chapter 12 Acupressure and Acupuncture   151

Chapter 13 Attitude Adjustments   165

Chapter 14 Balance Your Body and Breathing Techniques   179

Chapter 15 Counseling and Support Groups   190

Chapter 16 Dance, Movement, and Music   199

Chapter 17 Exercise—aerobics, stretching, walking   211

Chapter 18   Friendships—sharing and caring   230

Chapter 19   Journaling and Writing   238

Chapter 20   Massage Therapy and Healing Touch   247

Chapter 21   Meditation, Visualization and Prayer   259

Chapter 22   Nutrition, Vitamins, Minerals, Herbs,
              and Antioxidants   283

Chapter 23   Positive Self-talk and Self-esteem   320

Chapter 24   Relaxation, Yoga, and Sleep   332

Chapter 25   Self-nurturance, Joy, and Laughter   350

References   359

About the Author   372

Introduction

❧

*T*oday, life's challenges for women are very complex—life is more chaotic and less natural than in the past. We live in a time of rapid change, and experience greater pressure to adapt, keep up, and compete than in any other time. Stress is an inevitable and unavoidable part of life, yet without stress, there would be no life. It is not only a problem for those living in the fast track, but also for those who suffer from excessive monotony, boredom, or frustration due to lack of stimulation or challenges. Stress may cause some to feel anger or anxiety, or that they have little or no control over their lives and work. Most women find it difficult to achieve a good balance between too much stress and too little. Achieving the right balance is a challenge for many women.

The aim of this book is to enhance your knowledge and understanding of how your thoughts and feelings about yourself and others, along with your actions, affect your physical, mental, emotional, and spiritual, or *mind/body*, balance. The first section of this book describes the physiology of the mind/body interactions, or psychoneuroimmunology (PNI), and typical stressors women experience. The second section explores how some healthy and unhealthy personality traits can either enhance or diminish your immune system and health. The third section identifies common symptoms of stress-related health problems, and the last section explains various stress management strategies to help you achieve a better balance in your life.

Americans are becoming more aware of the need to prevent and reduce stress. Scientific studies suggest that between 80 and 85 percent of all medical problems are linked to stress or stress-related behaviors. The types of situations or events that trigger stress are often different for everyone. There is good stress, or "eustress," that may increase your productivity—up to a point, but the level differs for each of us. Negative stress, or "distress," can cause health problems and disease. Many women are not consciously aware of the origin of their stressors or emotional conflicts that trigger physical and emotional symptoms of potential health problems. We all need to find the proper balance of stress that enables us to perform optimally and live in harmony with ourselves, others, and our environment.

Stressors in themselves are not definitive predictors of disease—many other factors need to be considered, such as your basic personality, your coping skills, and some specific character traits acquired in life. In the last several decades, scientific research has found strong evidence that your thoughts, emotions, personality, attitudes, and beliefs all play a major role in your mind/body balance and affect how you react to stressful events.

The mind/body balance refers to how the dynamics of your mental, emotional, and spiritual being are interrelated with your physical body, each affecting the others. These interactions go in all directions; however the focus is on how your mind and emotions influence your physical health or illness. Your mind/body balance is affected by the way you think, feel, and relate to others, along with the complex interactions, in your daily life and environment. Your mind/body interactions can help relieve your stress and promote healing, or work against you by increasing your stress and contributing to illness and disease. Psychoneuroimmunology is one of the terms used in health care to describe how the interactions of your mind, emotions, and spirit affect your body.

Many excellent books describe PNI or various aspects of mind/body interactions and health. Some of the pioneers and writers in this field are Robert Adler, Herbert Benson, Joan Borysenko, Deepak Chopra, Larry Dossey, Christiane Northrup, Dean Ornish, Candice Pert, Bernie Siegel, and Andrew Weil. They have found that most physical and emotional problems are related to beliefs about ourselves and to our reactions and responses to those around us, our behaviors, and incidents in our environment.

The specific way that stressors or events lead to stressful responses has now generally been accepted by most scientists. Any cue associated with a situation or source of stress may stimulate your neuropeptides and autonomic nervous system to go into a distress mode. The brain and immune system are connected through hormones, endorphins, and chemical messengers, or neurotransmitters, that move through the blood and relay messages from one part of the body to another. These neurotransmitters act as messengers carrying information that creates chemical changes in your body. These chemicals are affected by and continually change as your thoughts, beliefs, perceptions of yourself, relationships with others, and the situations around you change. When you feel joyful and connected with others, every cell in your body responds to that emotion and may enhance immune system functioning. And if you feel depressed, that message is sent throughout the entire mind/body by the neuropeptide system, and may lead to illness.

Unfortunately, many women live in mind/body disharmony inside themselves and with others, and suffer unnecessary physical and emotional distress. If you focus too much on one area of your life, such as your work, then another area, like your family or leisure time, may suffer so that your life is unbalanced. See Fig. 1, *Balancing Your Lifestyle*, and the quiz that follows at the end of this introduction, to identify your level of balance. When your life is unbalanced, stressors can overload your mind/body system. If you deny the physical, mental, and emotional effects of stress on your body, then the sources of your stress are harder to identify, more pervasive, and more difficult to relieve. Denial of emotional pain can both block your mind/body communication and reduce your ability to feel enjoyable emotions.

Although there may not be a general disease-prone personality, some studies suggest that certain character traits or other aspects of one's personality seem to raise your overall chance for good health or risk for disease. Your personality traits probably have the most influence on how you respond to stressful situations and events. If unhealthy personality traits can intensify the effects of stressors, healthy traits may serve as buffers against the body's reactions and enhance health. Various researchers have found that people with certain personality traits are able to handle stressors better, and are less likely to develop various symptoms or health problems, than others without these traits.

Before you can achieve optimal, well-balanced health, it is essential to understand the nature of your personality traits, which are the basis for how you handle life and react to stressors. Some traits may promote your health and need strengthening, or you may want to change or modify unhealthy traits, which may increase your risk for various symptoms and chronic health problems, as described in chapter ten.

Many people accept stress-related symptoms as a normal and inevitable part of their life until their health is greatly affected. Emotional problems can lead to vicious behavioral cycles of stress/muscle spasm/pain/increased stress. These are common reactions to a wide variety of situations that lead to health problems. Your symptoms serve as a warning to you to identify stressors in your life. This is when you need to consciously examine what is going on in your life and body, and then seek help to find effective ways to manage stress and reduce or relieve your symptoms. When any type of symptom occurs, it can exacerbate many chronic health problems and reduce your ability to choose a healthy response. These stress behavioral cycles are a major factor in a variety of health problems. The more distress you have, the less you are able to function effectively or complete all your tasks. This can lead to feelings of frustration and may cause more stress and tension, creating increased distress. Prolonged, persistent stress causes physiological changes in your body that can cause various chronic, repetitive, or disabling illness and disease.

Finding a good balance between too much and too little stress needs to be a priority to survive life's ups and downs. You must look within yourself to deal appropriately with problems in your life and for your personal happiness. Although there are many things in life over which you have little or no control, you can choose various stress management strategies to increase your strength, wisdom, and compassion. Mind/body techniques are gaining in popularity as methods for changing your response to stress by altering your thoughts, emotions, body nutrients, physical health, and self-nurturing behaviors.

There are various stress management methods to reduce stress and promote self-healing and health. Roger Jahnke, author of *The Healer Within: The Four Essential Self-care Methods for Creating Optimal Health,* classified three categories of self-healing, based on one's personal choice and preference.

The first method consists of healthy attitudes and emotional or mental influences to empower you and bring your mind, emotions, spirit, and behaviors into harmony and balance. Stress reduction methods require self-awareness of your attitudes and emotions in response to both daily and chronic stressors. Some examples of appropriate methods are the seven personality traits in Section 2, along with chapters on: Attitude Adjustments; Counseling and Support Groups; and Positive Self-talk and Self-esteem.

The second method includes healthy lifestyle behaviors to improve, support, and maintain optimal functioning of your mind and body. Examples of these methods are discussed in several chapters: Balance Your Body; Dance, Movement and Music; Exercise; Nutrition, Vitamins, Minerals, Herbs and Antioxidants; and Relaxation, Yoga, and Sleep.

The third method consists of self-care activities designed to enhance health and healing by reducing stress and increasing calmness, serenity, and peace. Examples of these methods are discussed in such chapters as: Acupressure and Acupuncture; Friendships; Journaling and Writing; Massage Therapy and Healing Touch;

Meditation, Visualization and Prayer; and Self-nurturance, Joy and Laughter.

Achieving a balance in these areas of your life is a challenge. While many women are able to balance their family, home, career/work, and leisure time effectively, others are struggling to find a balance. When you are empowered by knowledge and inspired to take action, you can become your own best advocate for mastering stress, maintaining your health, and using self-healing methods to nourish and meet many of your needs. Self-knowledge involves recognizing the possibilities for change and ways to improve your life. See Fig. 2, *Optimal Health with Balance and Vitality*, and the quiz that folows, at the end of this introduction, to help you identify your strengths and areas where you may need help to balance your lifestyle. Take this quiz before reading the book so you'll know which chapters to focus on.

Self-knowledge involves recognizing the possibilities for change and improvement in your life, then taking the necessary action. First, you'll need to examine your stressors to see which ones you could reduce or eliminate. Next, consider both healthy and unhealthy traits, which may reduce or accelerate your reactions to stressors, and decide how you might improve your healthy personality traits or decrease unhealthy ones. Finally, choose different ways to manage your stressful feelings—ones that feel right and comfortable to you. You always have choices about how you think, feel, move, speak, and behave in your personal life and relationships.

Over the last twenty-five years, I have taught women's health nursing to graduate and undergraduate students at various universities. During that time, I conducted three major research studies on women's stress factors. Two of my recent studies analyzed the interrelationships among women's stressors, personality traits, and symptoms of women's health problems. I found that women who had medium to high stressors, along with healthy personality traits such as strong trust/love relationships, strong assertiveness and hardiness skills, and the ability to recognize and share their innermost feelings with others, reported significantly fewer health problems than other women. In contrast, women who had fewer healthy traits, and several unhealthy personality traits, including high family altruism, were more likely to report many more health problems than women with healthy traits.

Achieving inner balance, or health, involves reaching a high level of being yourself by discovering feelings, factors, and behaviors that trigger your stress responses. It also means learning new ways to strengthen the inner resources that empower you and bring joy to your life. Your goal is not only to understand yourself better, thus growing in wisdom, but also to use this knowledge to enhance your life. By keeping yourself motivated using various stress management strategies to improve your health, and having faith that you can accomplish anything you try, you'll feel empowered.

Fig. 1   Balancing Your Lifestyle

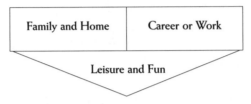

| Family and Home | Career or Work |

Leisure and Fun

Prescription for Balance
- When the homefront is in balance, you perform better at work
- When your career is managed effectively, you're happier at home
- When there is a fair amount of leisure activity in your week, you feel revitalized and your life is enriched.   —Conrad, 1995:17

Family and Home
Achieving balance begins on the homefront, which is the steady center of life. It is the comfort zone where we return for refueling, emotional support, and privacy. Here we can disengage from our work and other activities and bring balance into our lives. You need to prioritize your home responsibilities and delegate some tasks according to age and ability. Your expectations of others must be communicated to them, without demanding. And remember to reward good behaviors and to be flexible—because no one can do a job as perfectly as you—just try to achieve a balance of what is acceptable.

Home Expectations
Number the home responsibilities below that
1 – others expect you to do, and
2 – you expect other family members to handle.

__Grocery shopping   __Housecleaning   __Meal planning
__Meal preparation   __Meal clean-up   __Laundry/cleaners

__Home repairs   __Empty trash   __Yard work
__Car maintenance/repair   __Making beds   __Bill paying
__Help with homework   __Phone calls   __Plan time with spouse
__Bathing children   __Caring for pets   __Medical appointments
__Social engagements   __Run errands   __Parent/teacher meeting

Career or Work

The pursuit of a successful career or work can cause you to let go of other important aspects of your life. While every ego needs to be fed, some people's egos are hungrier than others. You must strive to maintain your values and relationships to meet both your needs and those of your family, and to insure that your daily activities do not get out of balance.

Career / Work Expectations

Check the level of your career/work expectations listed below using a scale of: 1–minimal, 5 – average, and 10 – exceptionally high.

___ Personnel administration   ___ Production
___ Knowledge and skills   ___ Growth and experience

Leisure and Fun

Leisure activities and fun with friends or family members help clear the air of problems, rejuvenate a tired body, and create a more motivated, satisfied person at home and at work. Everyone needs some private time to recuperate from responsibilities. We all need to do something for ourselves to nourish our souls. Without some leisure, it is difficult to see your family, home, and work in a true perspective. Time to relax and have fun doesn't just happen—you have to plan for it. Each person has her own idea of which activities are fun, relaxing, and release stress. Try to find a variety of leisure and fun activities to do during your personal time to provide several outlets for stress.

Leisure and Fun Activities

Check those activities from the list below that you enjoy, and then plan time each day for at least one item in the list.

❑ Reading books   ❑ Exercising   ❑ Gardening
❑ Watching TV   ❑ Taking a class   ❑ Going shopping
❑ Attending sports events   ❑ Cooking   ❑ A hobby

☐ Redecorating   ☐ Handiwork   ☐ Repairing something

☐ Listening to music   ☐ Dancing   ☐ Volunteering

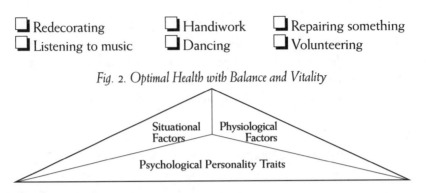

Fig. 2. Optimal Health with Balance and Vitality

Directions and Interpretation

Using the three lifestyle balancing factors below, identify which areas you feel strongest in by writing a number between one and three with a plus sign (+) beside each factor. Number three is the strongest. Indicate the areas you feel weakest or most vulnerable in by writing a number between one and three with a minus sign (-). Number three is the weakest. Compare your plus and minus signs in each area to determine whether you need to strengthen one or more of the factors to balance your lifestyle and improve your overall health.

Adapted from Pryor, F. (1990). *How to manage stress: A woman's workshop.* Shawnee Mission, KA.

A. Psychological Personality Traits

___Altruism—caring for others

___Assertiveness—taking charge

___Caring and sharing feelings/ thoughts

___Creativity and problem solving

___Defined, purposeful goals or visions

___Enjoyable multiple roles

___Emotional resilience

___Hardiness—challenge, control, and commitment

___Loving, trusting relationships

___Optimism—positive attitudes

___Patience and persistence

___Realistic self-expectations

___Self-confidence—belief in own abilities

B. Situational Factors

___Balanced lifestyle—work and leisure

___Communication skills

___Organizational/management skills

___Supportive relationships

C. Physiological Factors

___Affection, love, and touch

___Healthy nutritional patterns

___Recreational and leisure activities

___Regular sufficient exercise

___Rest and relaxation

___Social activities with others

1

Overview of Women's Health

1

Women's Inner Balance and Health— psychoneuroimmunology (PNI)

In the twenty-first century, as more new technology and information flood the market, women's lives will become more chaotic and stressful. Young and middle-aged women are most vulnerable because they are exposed to multiple stressors while trying to meet the demands of their families and balance work-related responsibilities. Older women have greater emotional maturity, experience, and wisdom, which helps preserve their emotional balance during stressful situations. While some women thrive on stress and handle difficult situations easily, others have trouble adapting to change and adjusting to minor or major stressors. They often experience a pile-up of stressors. Women's overall stress is related to their multiple roles, role dissatisfaction, low job mastery, and a sense of vulnerability to illness, all of which contribute to their health problems. Various types of stress create inner turmoil and can wreak havoc on your mind and body. When the demands of multiple roles and stressors become unmanageable, women's emotional and physiological balance may be compromised and their immune system weakened, making them more susceptible to illness. Although women in Western societies live longer than men, women have higher rates of acute and chronic illness than men.

Stressors—things that upset you—are situations or events that you perceive as daily hassles, chronic ongoing problems, and acute episodic events. How you view a difficult situation or unpleasant event determines your emotional reaction and whether it distresses you. Along with poor self-esteem, chronic worry, guilt, emotional dependence and co-dependence can distort your perception and cause you to misinterpret or overreact to daily events. Sometimes disturbing past events trigger inappropriate responses to relatively harmless situations. Also, unhealthy personality traits, such as retained fear, suppressed anger, and buried hostility, can cause exaggerated reactions to stressful events. Exaggerated reactions to stressors can alter your biochemistry and increase your risk for flare-ups or onset of chronic diseases. The ability to effectively handle all types of stressors throughout your life is essential to maintaining your balance.

I believe that health is synonymous with inner balance, a natural process of maintaining harmony and balance within oneself, with others, and with the environment. Many eastern cultures also believe that health equates with inner balance. The Chinese believe in balancing yin and yang, to achieve mind/body health. Deepak Chopra, a well-known Indian physician and writer, advocates the practice of *Ayurveda* to restore health and achieve perfect balance. American Indians also believe that health reflects balance and harmony within ourselves and with others, the environment, and the universe. Likewise, Dr. Meltzer, author of *The Ten Rules of High Performance Living*, believes that any life event, experience, or interaction that throws you out of balance creates disharmony between you and what is happening in your life.

Theories about Stressors

Stressors are major factors that influence and may alter women's health or inner balance. Over the last five decades, theories of the relationship between stress and illness have changed significantly. In the 1950s, Hans Selye first proposed a link between stress and health problems. He identified physiological changes—the fight or flight response to stressors—which he called the General Adaptation Syndrome (GAS). Since then, numerous studies have examined various theories and relationships among different stressors, personality factors, and health problems. In the 1960s, Holmes and Rahe reported that major life changes or events were stressors that could increase the likelihood of major illness. In the 1970s, Lazarus and Folkman theorized that if people perceived a stressor as a threat rather than a challenge, they were more likely to have an adverse reaction. Later, they identified underlying commonalties of stressors, such as perceived personal threats, losses, or dangers, along with acute and chronic problems. Then, in the 1980s, Lazarus and others explored the effect of daily hassles on health problems. From their studies, other scientists found that women's health and illness were affected by different stressors, and were related to age, roles and family relationships, social support networks, and types of employment. While some studies helped explain how various stressors affected women's health, there were conflicting opinions about the interaction and overall effect of different stressors on women's health.

Over the last twenty years, three separate fields, neuroscience, endocrinology, and immunology, combined to form a new field of science, psychoneuroimmunology. Many scientists have found that a multidirectional biochemical system communicates information between the mind and body. Dr. Candace Pert, who wrote *Molecules of Emotion: Why You Feel the Way You Do*, found that biochemicals, known as neuropeptides, are produced by the brain, immune system, and nerve cells in many different systems, and communicate information throughout the mind/body. These neuropeptide molecules constantly exchange, process, and store information as your situations and emotions change. Every system in the body communicates with others via these neuropeptides, which bind with specific peptide receptors across systems. Both internal and external information about oneself are constantly transmitted by the neuropeptides between the body and mind, which are inseparable—communication exists in both directions. The brain directs the flow of neuropeptides among the cells, organs, and systems, but the mind doesn't dominate the body. Each individual's biochemical system is unique, and involves a rapid simultaneous exchange of information molecules in the mind/body.

Since the late 1970s, I have conducted several large research studies to identify the relationships among women's stressors, personality traits, lifestyle behaviors, and their risk for health problems. After years of analyzing the interactions among these variables, I found sufficient evidence to support a more holistic view of women's health. Thus, I designed the Women's Inner Balance Model, which links the psychoneuroimmunology theory of stress and illness with women's personality traits. This model, as shown in Fig. 1, views health as synonymous with inner balance, which is regulated by the interaction among women's stressors, personality traits, and their health problems. Women's stressors include daily hassles, along with chronic and acute stressors. Personality traits that influence your response to stressors and health problems include altruism, assertiveness, hardiness, trusting and loving relationships, optimism, and the ability to confide in others, as well as unhealthy traits such as controlling or inflexible behaviors. Health problems show up as both physical and emotional symptoms, such as muscle aches, sleep problems, headaches, depression, nervousness or being easily upset, and an inability to relax.

Fig. 1. Women's Inner Balance Model: Interaction among Stressors, Personality Traits, and Health Problems

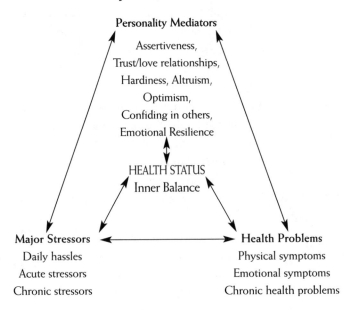

Personality Mediators

Assertiveness,
Trust/love relationships,
Hardiness, Altruism,
Optimism,
Confiding in others,
Emotional Resilience

HEALTH STATUS
Inner Balance

Major Stressors
Daily hassles
Acute stressors
Chronic stressors

Health Problems
Physical symptoms
Emotional symptoms
Chronic health problems

How Stressors Affect Women's Health

The relationship between stress and health/illness is a multi-faceted, complex process. It involves the nature of stressful situations or events, your perception of the situation, and your unique psycho-physiological pattern of reacting to stressful events. Your thoughts, beliefs, emotions, and past experiences influence how you feel about and react to stressors. Stress is your physical, emotional, and behavioral reaction to what you perceive as upsetting—in other words, how you respond to various stressors, such as a change, threats, demands, or losses. When your mind perceives or interprets a situation or event as a major problem or difficult adjustment, you may react as though facing a real danger. Some people thrive on stressful situations, while others view them as terrifying.

Personal, situational, and external factors may also influence your emotional response to stressors. Chronic anxiety, hostility, or depression may accompany stressors and could be the primary factor that affects your immune system and makes you more prone to illness. Stress distorts your perception and your response affects how you perceive your world, interpret your experiences, and respond to people and situations around you. When you perceive stressors or change as small, you usually have a small amount of stress; if you perceive a stressor or change as large, you usually have a greater stress response. Stress alone does not cause illness, but your response to stressors can alter your biochemicals and immune system, and increase your susceptibility to disease. Short-term or acute, and long-term or chronic stressors have different effects on your overall health. If the stress process continues, it can cause biochemical changes within your brain, nervous system, and different hormones throughout your mind/body, resulting in fatigue, exhaustion, and disease. The stage at which stress becomes unmanageable, inappropriate, or persistent, and at which it may generate harmful changes, is unique for each person.

Acute stressors, such as a short-term crisis, are when the body prepares for fight or flight with a surge of adrenalin, triggered by sudden fear or anger. Physiological changes occur rapidly, providing increased energy and alertness, usually lasting a short time or a few hours. Chronic stressors, like constant deadlines, or ongoing relationship problems, that extend over a longer period, can cause persistent physiological changes similar to acute stress, which last over several weeks or months. Dr. Pert found that whenever you deny or repress your emotions, or they go unexpressed over long periods, your normal biochemical systems do not flow freely. There is increased production of two hormones, adrenalin and cortisol, which inhibit healthy functioning of the immune system, increasing your susceptibility to illness. When you are comfortable expressing your emotions, biochemicals can flow freely and restore balance and synchrony to the mind/body systems.

Although the fight or flight response to stress was an accepted theory applied to both genders for several decades, Dr. Shelley Taylor, a psychology professor at UCLA, recently discovered that females respond differently than males to stressors. When stress increases, women are more likely to protect and nurture their children (tend) and turn to their social networks of supportive females (befriend). This "tend and befriend" response may be related to women's need to affiliate and relate to friends who provide protection and support them. Taylor and others believe that two female hormones exert a calming influence and probably create women's particular stress reactions. Other researchers found that testosterone probably takes over in men under stress, and may lead to their acting-out behaviors, while women's reactions involve more emotional conflict, leading to depression.

Physiological Stress Response

Psychoneuroimmunology researchers have found that frequent and persistent stressful situations can alter and impair a wide range of immunological processes, but it is unclear whether these changes actually trigger illness or simply exacerbate existing conditions. Different stressors may produce different responses in the immune systems of different people. A stressor may play only a minor role in producing symptoms, but your mind may amplify the symptoms. Your perception of stressors and your emotional reactions to them play a crucial role in both the onset and progression of disease. In his book, *Stress & Natural Healing*, Christopher Hobbs writes that during the initial acute reaction to stressors, the body's nervous and hormone systems secrete hormones, namely epinephrine and norepinephrine. If you continue to respond to stressors, hormones are constantly released in small amounts that depress the immune system, decrease your energy level and bone strength, and may reduce some brain functions, such as your memory. With constant stressors, exhaustion eventually occurs as the body's strength becomes depleted. In general, acute stressors produce mixed effects on immunity, while chronic stress reactions usually cause elevated cortisol levels, which suppress and interfere with virtually all functions of the immune system. The later immune system response involves a complex cascade of physiological changes that may extend over several days or weeks.

A rich and intricate communication system links your mind, immune system, and other systems. Through it, your perceptions and emotions affect your body's reactions and ability to maintain its chemical balance. Scientists have identified two major stress pathways that effect numerous changes in the immune system. In one pathway, the sympathetic-adrenal-medullary system is activated in response to fear and anger, as well as other acute emotional reactions linked with excitement, fight, and flight. When this pathway is activated, the adrenal glands release epinephrine, norepinephrine, dopamine, and other catecholamines into the bloodstream via neurotransmitters. These hormones interact with the immune cells and cause numerous physiological effects. Some effects are increased heart rate and blood pressure, rapid shallow breathing, elevated glucose (blood sugar) and fatty acids for energy, increased blood flow to the brain and major muscles, and decreased blood to the digestive organs.

In the other pathway, the hypothalamic-pituitary-adrenocortical system is activated during chronically stressful situations or threatening events where one has difficulty coping. When this system is activated, the pituitary gland produces and releases steroids and ACTH hormones, which cause release of peptides, corticotropin, and cortisol. Increased cortisol levels suppress the immune system by reducing the number and function of white blood cells, primarily T-lymphocytes and natural killer (NK) cells.

Chronic emotional stressors, such as recurring family fights, work pressures, or financial problems, can eventually suppress the immune system and predispose women to health problems. Emotional stress, addictions or abusive lifestyle behaviors, derogatory thinking, and other unhealthy habits send signals to the stress center in the brain. Since the brain can't distinguish between an emotional stress signal and a physical one, it releases neuropeptides and stress hormones throughout the body. Any signal that there is trouble tells the brain and other body systems to produce and release cortisol, which alters the immune response.

When you experience chronic, long-term stress, hormones and biochemicals contribute to increased muscle tension that can lead to headaches or muscle pain. Also, when you are under extreme, prolonged, or persistent stress, your body continues to maintain high cortisol levels that depress your immune system, making you more susceptible to colds, the flu, or more serious diseases. Excessive cortisol may increase your blood cholesterol level and elevate your blood pressure, which can lead to hypertension and increase your risk for chronic illnesses and coronary artery disease.

Immune System Response

The immune system is a self-renewing, self-repairing, natural pharmacy that consists of the spleen, bone marrow, lymph nodes, hormones, antibodies, and various kinds of white blood cells. Its purposes are to defend your body against pathological invaders that threaten your health and to repair any damage. The immune system has defined boundaries, such as the skin and mucous membranes, but it must also distinguish between normal cells that need to be repaired or restored, and infections or tumors that need to be destroyed. Cells of the immune system travel throughout your body to wherever they are needed to defend or repair damage. Immune cells also make, store, and secrete neuropeptides to maintain tissue integrity. They also produce chemicals that can regulate your mood or emotions. Normally, when bacteria or viruses gain entry to your body, mucous membranes containing immunoglobulin A kill off most invaders. If bacteria enter the body, antibodies in the blood recognize them and set off a chain reaction whereby different types of white blood cells, or lymphocytes, rush to the location. The white blood cells engulf the invaders and release powerful substances to destroy them.

Whenever you experience a stress reaction, it triggers release of neuropeptides, which are essential to your overall health. The peptides and their receptors enable the immune system to launch a well-coordinated attack against disease. Cells in various systems constantly signal other cells through the release of neuropeptides. During high stress, the neuropeptides trigger secretion of ACTH, which stimulates the production of cortisol and adrenaline. When these hormones are elevated, they reduce the body's natural killer T-cells, which constantly patrol the body and destroy specific targets. Elevated cortisol also causes fewer antibodies to be produced. These changes are sent back to the peptide-secreting cells, telling them how much peptide to produce. This complex system assists the mind/body to make biochemical changes to restore the body's internal balance.

Chronic stress, along with an unhealthy diet, excessive exercise, chemotherapy, aging, and other factors can contribute to immune suppression. When the immune system is suppressed, the natural killer cells become depleted and immune cells may fail to identify and destroy abnormal cells, so that infected or unhealthy cells can cause serious infections and chronic disease. Chronic stress can also influence autoimmune diseases that commonly strike women, such as rheumatoid arthritis, lupus, or fibromyalgia, in which the body's immune system mistakenly attacks its own tissues. Stressors can cause early onset of these diseases or flare-ups in women who already have these diseases.

Effects of Personality Traits on Women's Health

In the 1950s, there was a prominent theory that some people had a "disease-prone personality" and were more likely than others to develop specific diseases. Dr. Hobbs wrote that people with unhealthy personality traits, who were typically impatient, competitive, and hot-tempered, were thought to be more susceptible to stress-related illnesses than those who responded calmly. Impatient people, those who are anxious to get ahead, yet angry at others or at their situation, were described as having type A personalities. These individuals repeatedly responded to stressful situations with increased adrenalin levels, which triggered cascading changes in the immune system, making them prone to digestive problems and cardiovascular disease. According to Kenneth Pelletier, coronary heart disease was linked with people who had type A personalities and reacted excessively to moderate stressors. Individuals who calmly thought through a stressful situation and solved their problems were known as type B personalities, who were less likely to develop stress-related health problems. Cancer was allegedly linked with unassertiveness, inability to express one's emotions, and feelings of hopelessness. Rheumatoid arthritis was thought to be related to perfectionism, compliance, reserve, subservience, nervousness, and anger. With the exception of coronary heart disease, further studies have not supported these theories that specific personality types are linked to specific illnesses.

However, there may be such a thing as a general disease-prone personality type, where some individuals have a higher risk than others of becoming ill. Some evidence suggests that people with depression, anger and hostility, anxiety, and possibly other personality traits seem to have a higher risk for disease. The type of disease an individual develops depends on his or her specific vulnerabilities, which are affected by family health history, lifestyle habits (smoking, drinking, diet, and exercise patterns), environmental exposures, socioeconomic status, and other factors. Studies by Candace Pert at the National Institute of Health suggest that anxiety, hostility, and other emotional states may directly affect the immune system by altering one's hormones and neuropeptides, such as endorphins.

Many contemporary scientists also believe there is compelling evidence that several personality traits and mediating factors influence one's stress reactions and coping ability. Several researchers have spent years studying the effects of various personality traits that may strengthen or weaken one's immune response and affect health. Other scientists have focused on healthy and unhealthy coping styles and their impact on health. Some personality traits that scientists have found helped individuals stay healthy during stressful experiences were altruism, assertiveness, confiding in others, hardiness, loving and trusting relationships, recognizing and expressing one's feelings, and multiple roles. In his book, *The Immune Power Personality: 7 Traits You can Develop to Stay Healthy*, Henry Dreher writes that people with these traits have an "immune power personality"— they handle stressful events with acceptance, flexibility, and a willingness to learn and grow. The terms personality traits and coping styles are often used interchangeably. Other healthy coping patterns are optimistic thinking, hopeful thoughts, and seeking the support or assistance of others when faced with stressful obstacles. Those who have learned to cope with stressful events in healthy ways are less likely to have weakened immune systems.

The Stress Response and Related Diseases

The relationship between stress and physiological changes is now well accepted by most health care providers. Some even believe that about 85 percent of our health problems are stress-related. Dr. Miller, author of *Deep Healing: The Essence of Mind/Body Medicine*, wrote that when you perceive constant pressure, incessant demands, and perceived threats at home or work, you may develop chronic stress, mental hyper-alertness, and persistent muscle tension. Emotional distress from family illness, divorce, conflicting relationships, or bereavement can also contribute to chronic stress. In addition, those who respond to difficult problems with exaggerated emotional reactions and negative, pessimistic thinking often develop chronic distress. Since your nervous system interprets these pressures and problems as immediate threats to your survival, your body, thoughts, and emotions respond in a fight or flight manner. This response creates physiological changes throughout your mind/body system, and can have a deleterious effect on your health if the biochemical changes persist. Scientists have found that with persistent stress, complex neuroendocrine changes occur within and among the brain, endocrine, and immune systems. These changes can increase cortisol levels that suppress the immune system and increase your risk of illness and disease.

Even if you believe you handle stress fairly well, your body may be in turmoil. Stress-related biochemical changes can alter your inner balance, lower resistance to infections, and predispose women to progressive pathological processes. They can lead to symptoms of chronic stress, such as sleep disturbances, headaches, diminished sex drive, diarrhea, back pain, heartburn, muscle spasms, and changes in appetite. Researchers have also recognized that stress contributes to a wide variety of illnesses, including heart disease, strokes, hypertension, bacterial infections, autoimmune disorders, cancer, and depression.

Women's Inner Balance and Health

In her book on healthy living, Joan Lunden emphasizes the importance of balance in your life. She suggests you focus on the connection between your heart and head to achieve a true balance of the things in your life. Joan believes that stress is inevitable since every aspect of our life is ever-changing, unpredictable, and because sometimes we have little control over parts of our life. Therefore, you must look within yourself to find personal happiness. She advises women to develop the courage to try new strategies and find ways to balance their many roles with life's ups and downs.

Likewise, Dr. Meltzer believes that balance is the foundation for vital, healthy living and that only well-nourished souls who have achieved physical, emotional, spiritual, and mental balance will be able to meet the challenges of the new millennium effectively. He states that healthy people have the ability to adapt or respond to expected or unexpected changes in a relaxed, centered way, so that for them stressful life events will become opportunities for growth and healing. You can choose to respond to stress either in healthy or in emotionally destructive ways depending on how you handle challenging and threatening situations. To determine your level of inner balance, you might answer the twenty-three item Index.

The Inner Balance Index

To determine your level of inner balance, rate each topic as to your perception of your life, family, work, and community, and write the number on the right. If a particular item does not pertain to you, skip it. Try to answer quickly and honestly with the first response that comes to mind.

Key: 1–Strongly agree; 2–Agree; 3–Sometimes;
4–Disagree; 5–Strongly disagree

1. My relationship with spouse,partner, or significant other is going well   ____

2. My spouse/partner or friends are a source of emotional support   ____

3. My children are a constant source of pleasure and delight   ____

4. My relationships with my parents are pleasant and rewarding   ____

5. I have several close friends whom I trust and can confide in   ____

6. My close friends, neighbors, and others are usually supportive   ____

7. I frequently spend quality time with these people   ____

8. My career/work/occupation is satisfying and meets my expectations ____

9. My relationships at work with co-workers, boss, and others are usually harmonious   ____

10. My physical work environment is safe and pleasant   ____

11. I attend club, social, or religious activities regularly   ____

12. I am in good physical health and have sufficient energy   ____

13. I exercise at least three times a week to the point of perspiring ____

14. I feel my body weight or size is appropriate for my height   ____

15. I do not smoke too much or drink too many alcoholic beverages ____

16. I get at least seven to eight hours sleep five nights a week ____

17. I do something for fun or enjoyment at least once a week ____

18. When appropriate, I can be assertive and say what I think ____

19. I feel comfortable sharing my feelings when I am angry or worried ____

20. I tend to believe that most things work out for the best ____

21. When things don't go my way, I am flexible and can change ____

22. I feel confident about myself and have control over my life ____

23. When problems arise at home or work, I feel committed to
    work them out ____

Scale: 23–50 = Well balanced; 51–80 = Somewhat unbalanced;
81–115 = Very unbalanced

Every day your life and brain chemistry change according to what you eat, what you do, and what you think or feel. When you engage in behaviors you enjoy, such as listening to your favorite music, meditating, praying, and exercising, your brain produces endorphins, like serotonin, the naturally-occurring opiates similar to morphine and heroin. They can promote feelings of well-being, and reduce or even eliminate pain.

These endorphins cause subtle to profound changes in your mood and intellectual performance. In their book, *Peak Performance Living*, Robertson and Monte write that when you achieve balanced brain chemistry, your mind and body are in perfect harmony and you may feel optimistic, energetic, exuberant, confident, have intellectual clarity, and experience new insights. You may think your self-esteem, confidence, or ability to concentrate are invisible characteristics in your mind, but they are linked to your biochemistry. The neurotransmitter serotonin is linked with these and other positive traits, which create feelings of well-being, personal security, and relaxation, and deep, restful sleep. Serotonin helps you feel less distracted and more focused, thus improving your concentration. Normal or high serotonin levels are associated with balanced emotions and elevated states of happiness and joy. Those with high serotonin levels tend to be leaders of their social network because they are more self-assured and balanced and exhibit less fear and insecurity than others. People with low serotonin levels often crave carbohydrates, experience declines in mood, depression, low energy and fatigue, low self-esteem, and poor concentration, and have more difficulty making decisions than others.

Summary

Although various theories have been proposed to explain the complex relationships among stressors, personality traits, and health/illness, scientists have not reached agreement on how various factors are interrelated in a stress-illness model. Recent psychoneuroimmunological studies found that several personality traits influence one's response to stress and ultimately to illness. These studies suggest that a more holistic model is needed to understand women's psycho-biological processes and the interrelationships among their stressors, personality traits, and health/illness.

This chapter introduced and described the interrelationships among women's stressors, personality traits, and the immune system response which may increase women's susceptibility to various diseases and illness. The Women's Inner Balance Model was proposed, and supported with discussions about how each of the major factors contribute to women's health or illness. Since you are responsible for choosing how you handle your personal problems and distressing situations, whether they are physical, mental, emotional, social, or spiritual, you alone must also decide which strategies are most effective in resolving or eliminating your problems. Managing everyday stress effectively and avoiding chronic stress is crucial to keeping your mind, body, and immune system healthy. You will need a keen sense of balance, willpower, faith, love, and inner strength to accomplish this, so be true to yourself. ℬ

2

Types of Stressors—daily hassles, chronic problems, and acute stressors

*Multi-tasking means we can make five mistakes
in the time it used to take to make just ONE. —Ziggy*

We all experience stress most every day of our lives. The majority of Americans have difficulty achieving a good balance between too much and too little stress. Most people are not aware of how much stress they have in their lives. Underlying stress from too little time, over-crowding, intrusive technology, gridlock and rude drivers, along with too many demands at work and home, has led some people to develop an unrelenting sense of anger, hostility, and alienation that simmers for months or years. Leading social scientists say the nation is in the midst of an anger epidemic, which they attribute to the widespread feeling that things should happen *my* way. Eventually, all it takes is a minor event to trigger an angry, hostile person to go ballistic—in road rage or business and school shoot-outs, along with mob violence.

Materialism and consumerism, along with media advertising, have created a nation of people who expect the good life—and feel they are entitled to it. They believe that "life should be easy" and people should "get out of my way." Leslie Charles, author of *Why is Everyone so Cranky?*, believes that our constant accessibility because of intrusive technology fragments what little time we do have, and adds to our sense of urgency, emergency, and overload. Inadequate time and too much hi-tech equipment such as cell phones, e-mail, and pagers, which can interrupt us anywhere, at any time, are major contributing factors to stress. Many working people feel the need to be constantly doing multiple tasks, so they become impatient over wasted time in traffic gridlock, lines at stores, and automated phone systems. We've become a society with "'hurry sickness," a disease of impatience while everyone around us seems to be moving faster. Hurry sickness can often be seen in drivers who run red lights, weave in and out of traffic, and cut off other drivers. Reactions vary from people who rarely exhibit their hostility to those who have serious impulse control problems, or short fuses.

Stress can arise in any area of life and have a cumulative, pervasive effect on your health. The pressures of living in a fast-paced society that often make us feel rushed, hassled, anxious, or apprehensive can be far less obvious than a major life-crisis. Your chosen lifestyle also determines potential sources of stress. Stress is more likely to occur if you feel your life is out of your control or you are expected to perform in a manner that feels uncomfortable. In other words, if you are unable to shape your lifestyle to meet your own needs, you feel more stressed. When your rhythmic balance of work, leisure activities, and rest is upset, you can easily become stressed if a situation adversely affects your life or your ability to control it. Stress from your job, personal or family life, or simply insufficient time to accomplish your goals may lead to fatigue, exhaustion, work overload, problems with your love relationships, and/or breakdowns in your family life. Under stress, you easily become exhausted, which weakens your immune system and disrupts your biochemicals, so that symptoms of health problems may soon appear.

Today we want and expect more enjoyment from life. We want to enjoy a certain lifestyle, have job satisfaction and intimate, healthy relationships with family and friends. Our search for personal happiness, financial success and security, along with power and personal achievement, without sacrificing our health, has placed tremendous stress on us and our families. Stressors may occur from things in your environment that are mostly out of your immediate control, such as noise, crazy drivers, a demanding boss, or the death of a loved one. Stress can also result from things you can, but often don't control, such as eating unhealthy foods, drinking too much caffeine, or chain smoking, along with holding negative attitudes and emotions, such as guilt, hostility, anger, or cynicism.

Too many people feel trapped in the daily pressures of their materialistic lifestyles. Many cannot enjoy a happy, healthy life because of poor nutritional habits, self-abusive behaviors, and dysfunctional family and personal relationships. Stress is a problem not only for people living in the fast track, because excessive monotony, boredom, or lack of sufficient stimuli or challenges can also contribute to stress. Situations where people feel they have little control over how they live and work also contribute to anger or anxiety, leading to stress.

Stress is also experienced during adjustments or change in personal, social, occupational, or living situations. When situations change, you may feel anxious or threatened by fear of the unknown or by uncertainty as to what the future holds. Some people are afraid of failure or of feeling incompetent, while others view change as a challenge to be met. Whether you perceive change as a threat or challenge determines your response and stress level. Usually there is something better out there, so if you can adapt or respond to expected or unexpected changes in a relaxed and calm manner, you are less likely to have stress and more likely to maintain optimal health.

Definition of Stressors and Stress

Stressors are any situation, event, change, or action that you perceive as a threat, challenge, or loss, and which upset you. Depending on your reaction, they may lead to stress. Stress is your reaction to events or change, rather than the event itself. Stress is triggered by how you respond to stressors—and your reaction may be exaggerated because of your perception, unrealistic expectations, your vulnerability, or inflexibility. You create your own level of stress by how you react to various types of stressors. Hans Selye, the father of stress theory, viewed stress on a continuum between positive, energizing, motivating, beneficial good stress, which he called *eustress,* and *distress,* the negative, disabling bad type. Your perception of an experience or situation determines whether you view it as positive or negative. Negative stress generally occurs when you view change and pressure as burdens and perceive rising demands as threats. You may feel a sense of alienation, frustration, or helplessness, and feel powerless to influence those events.

Stress is not necessarily a negative factor—it can be beneficial, even crucial to your survival and growth. Sometimes stress brings positive, healing effects and promotes increased maturity and strength, like when you fall in love or receive a promotion. You view these events as opportunities. When a situation is seen as a challenge, stress can increase your productivity and happiness, motivate growth and development, increase feelings of accomplishment, and help you meet your goals.

Just because you perceive something as real or true does not necessarily make it so. Your attention may be cluttered by anxiety, fear, worry, and disturbing emotions from past experiences. Dr. Miller, author of *Deep Healing: The Essence of Mind/Body Medicine*, says that past experiences may affect your perception of the present situation, so your stress response may be inappropriate for the present situation. Reactions to negative stressors are not necessarily damaging, and responses are often highly individual. In spite of experiencing life-threatening events, some people maintain good health because they have a strong sense of purpose in their lives, believe in themselves, and are committed to living life well. Those survivors usually have a strong resilient attitude and a highly developed sense of self-control. Christopher Hobbs, who wrote *Stress and Natural Healing*, believes that you can use stress to grow beyond your self-imposed limits, to where what was once unimaginable becomes possible. So how you perceive and respond to any stressor, along with your attitudes and lifestyle, all affect your level of stress.

Women's Stressors

Women's greatest stressors are trying to juggle multiple roles and responsibilities of working and raising a family. Unfortunately, the demands of a woman's occupation do not always coincide with the obligations and pressures associated with childrearing. Many women handle the same career problems that formerly belonged to men, but in addition they are still expected to carry the major responsibility to maintain the home, provide childcare, and meet everyone's social, emotional, and health care needs. Women tend to feel responsible to provide care for others—their children, spouse, friends, aging parents, or ailing siblings. Women with a career and family find that their day is filled trying to succeed in both realms. They may have high expectations or standards for their home and childcare, be unwilling to compromise, or don't want to give up power in their domain. With both parents working, life at home becomes more stressful and demanding as women try to juggle their family and work schedules with their children's needs. Although these women work, they still must purchase groceries, prepare meals, launder clothes, pay bills, clean the house, run errands and chauffeur children, make and meet medical appointments, care for pets, file bills and insurance papers, and make and return phone calls.

Employed, married women with young children report that the less helpful their husbands are with the children and household chores, the more stressed and unhappy they feel about their marriage. Single mothers have the extra burden of work and family responsibilities without any help from a spouse. Because these activities require a huge amount of time and energy, many working mothers have little time left to meet their own physical and emotional needs.

Many women feel driven to "do it all," without realizing the toll such unrealistic goals take on their own health. While women's entry into the workplace has brought them more financial security and economic power, these assets come at a cost. As your responsibilities increase, your stress levels rise, and time for healthy behaviors decreases. In their book, *The Women's Complete Wellness Book*, Judelson and Dell report that women are at greater risk today for stress-related illnesses than they have ever been in the past. When doing it all means sacrificing good health, or when women cannot find time to maintain a healthy lifestyle, exercise, eat nutritious foods, and relax, they should consider doing less for others and more for themselves. Preserving your health is the most important thing you can do for yourself and others, so you will live longer.

TYPES OF STRESSORS
Sociocultural Sources of Stress

Some women have been raised to believe they are second-class citizens who are expected to be subservient, humble, and obedient. This type of socialization is based on the belief that men are superior, dominant, and wiser than women. In order to keep the peace and maintain a good relationship with a man, many women believe they must compromise their needs to meet his. Some women believe they must never appear more intelligent, more capable, or better in any way that would cause a male to feel inferior. A conflicting source of stress for some women is the need to prove themselves—that they are intelligent, socially adept, great hostesses or homemakers, and able to communicate and perform effectively.

Also, many women were raised to believe that they are the care-takers of the world. They feel they must do it all, and if they don't, they believe they have failed in their own and other's eyes. When women try to do it all, they often experience multiple-role conflicts and overload. Some women constantly need approval to reassure them that their appearance or behaviors are appropriate and acceptable, even superb.

The need for others' approval often coincides with continuous attempts at perfectionism, striving to be liked and perfect at all times. Those who constantly seek others' approval may not feel comfortable saying no, and usually have difficulty expressing their anger and strong emotions, because they fear this behavior would be unacceptable. Related to these stressors may be a fear of failure or a fear of success in achieving one's goals. These needs may lead to feeling like an impostor, where one secretly fears her inability to accomplish a specific job. Some examples of these sociocultural stressors are:

- Multiple role responsibilities and conflicts
- Search for control and perfectionism
- Difficulty or inability to say no
- Need for frequent approval of behavior
- Difficulty expressing anger/negative feelings
- Excessive need to please others
- Fear of failure or success in various areas
- Unable to ask for what you need or want
- The "do-it-all" syndrome
- Feel you have little power or influence
- Disbelief in own self-worth and goodness
- Feel guilt from "shoulda, woulda, coulda"

Major Life Events

Life's major stressors, such as the death of a relative or close friend, chronic illnesses, divorce, or financial setbacks, usually take months to recover from, even though they may trigger hidden coping resources within you. Sometimes you can rise to the occasion, summon up your inner strength and manage to function. However, several studies have shown that separated or divorced women and those with a poor quality marriage had lower immune function and greater depression. Also, newlywed couples who exhibited more negative and hostile behaviors had a lower immune system response. Certain events tend to be viewed as highly stressful by most people, most of the time, such as:

- Loss of a loved one, including a pet
- Getting married
- Major illness or injury
- Moving to a new location
- Marital separation or divorce

■ A serious falling-out with a close friend
■ Serious financial difficulties
■ Birth or adoption of a child
■ Loss of a regular job
■ Retirement

Acute, Short-term Stressors

Other major stressors are acute, short-lived events, but they can wreak havoc with your biochemical system. Both acute and chronic stress release many potent hormones, two of which—adrenalin and cortisol—can suppress your immune system and create an imbalance. Examples of some acute stressors include:

■ Experiencing a difficult pregnancy
■ Arguments or problems with spouse or others
■ Adult child leaves or returns home
■ Disagreement over how things get done at work
■ Having a miscarriage or abortion
■ Serious injury or illness of a family member
■ A promotion or demotion at work
■ Preparation for a major holiday or vacation

Chronic, Long-term Stressors

Chronic stressors are those that seem never-ending—they develop from constant daily pressures that become harder to manage and seem to go on forever. You may feel that the situation will never get any better. When you have chronic stress, your body may not be able to turn off the immune response, so increased hormone levels may cause damaging physiological changes. Accumulating, prolonged stress is the leading cause of disease, according to Dr. Meltzer. Domar and Dreher, authors of *Healing Mind, Healthy Woman,* believe that accumulated stress, or a pile-up of numerous small stressors, can sometimes lead to generalized fear, anxiety, and/or depression, which are difficult to attribute to any specific cause. These symptoms may erupt in angry outbursts or you may turn them inward, causing fatigue, depression, or other physical symptoms, which only add to your stress. Thus begins the vicious cycle of stress, illness, more stress, and more illness. These types of problems are dangerous to your health because you are in a perpetual state of stress, which can raise your cortisol levels and affect every cell in your body. Your immune system becomes suppressed, and you are more likely to have frequent health problems. Some examples of situations and events that lead to chronic stress are:

- Crowded living conditions—too little space
- Over-scheduled family calendar
- A demanding, competitive, unrewarding job
- Long daily commutes in heavy traffic
- Work overloads or lack of control at work
- Ongoing personal health problems
- Constant financial problems
- Caring for family members with health problems
- Difficulty coping with own teenagers' problems
- Constant arguments with in-laws or relatives
- Caring for aging parents or relatives
- Difficult relationship with spouse/partner
- Difficult relationship with ex-spouse over children
- Any type of abuse from spouse/partner
- Coping with constant loud noise at home
- Spouse/partner with substance abuse or work problems

Daily Hassles, Irritations, and Annoyances

For many of us, the ability to stay calm and healthy amidst life's constant pressures comes down to the small things—the daily hassles and irritations of everyday life. Some of these hassles include interruptions, broken appointments, annoying phone calls, a run in your hose, bad weather, traffic jams, or deadlines. The way you respond to daily hassles is often a better predictor of your psychological and physical health than your reaction to major life crises. Your reactions and overreactions are the key to your health. Managing stress really means managing the tension, anger, and anxiety you feel in stressful situations so that you can respond in a creative and healthy manner.

When you think of stressors, you probably think of major ones, but numerous small irritations can add up. Usually, you can handle one or two annoyances, but as the number rises, so does your stress level and the likelihood that you'll develop some type of symptom, such as a headache, cold, or the flu. Also, you may overreact to the next stressor that comes along. Unfortunately, life is loaded with daily hassles that can get to you when you're under other pressures or exhausted. It's the little annoyances, petty frustrations, and minor irritations that become the continuous source of stress. Mishandling unavoidable daily irritations and pressures is more harmful to your health and performance than having acute stressors, because how you handle the little things that occur every day can affect your health. Some examples of daily hassles are:

- Getting self and children ready for work/school
- Cell phones interrupting conversations
- Commuting to work during rush hour
- Automated answering machines
- Inconsiderate drivers who cut you off
- Beepers or pagers going off in meetings
- Traffic gridlock and road construction
- Being put on hold for incoming calls
- Loud noise from radios, TV, or leaf blowers
- Listening to awful music while on hold
- Long check-out lines at stores or bank
- Telemarketing phone calls during dinner
- Rude colleagues, salesclerks, relatives or friends
- Long delays on the Internet
- Arguments with children or co-workers
- Being late to work or for an appointment
- Deliveries made "sometime between 9:00 and 5:00"
- Dirty restrooms with no toilet paper
- Waiting for doctors, dentists, and airplanes
- Sorting junk mail and phone messages

Hostile, angry people experience many more daily hassles and personal blows than friendly, agreeable people. Angry people may be looking for things to upset them and are unable to be flexible and roll with the punches. A friendly and agreeable attitude actually helps reduce conflict in your life and invites support from others.

Broad Categories of Stressors

Parenting: Families today tend to be fragmented, with relatives often living far away, which may add to a feeling of disconnectedness and alienation. Your parents may not be close enough to give advice or help with childcare. Many women have to cope not only with raising their own children, but also with the problems of aging and ailing parents. Middle-aged women are sometimes caught in this sandwich stress, since they are usually the primary caregivers. This can be incredibly physically and emotionally draining. And, since nearly 50 percent of all marriages end in divorce, the number of single mothers is rapidly rising, adding another burden to women, who usually have custody of their children.

Work/Career: For many working women, their jobs or careers are their biggest sources of stress. Career women's stress is often related to their high sense of responsibility, loyalty, and commitment to their family and career; their high level of intelligence, competence, and stamina; and their determination to maintain consistently high standards of excellence. Since women with these strengths tend to be the most productive, they are often given the most difficult tasks and heaviest schedules.

Many Americans feel overworked and are frustrated by the long hours they put in—both paid and unpaid. Experts believe that work stress is increasing, given the added pressures of global competition and women trying to juggle the demands of work and family responsibilities. Long hours, a long commute, unrealistic deadlines, a difficult boss, office politics, toxic co-workers, and testy clients are just a few of the many job-related stressors employees experience. More and more work is expected in less and less time, and more people complain of excessive workloads today than in the past, which leave less time for family and leisure. Also, job insecurity, uncertainty, and fear of downsizing, reorganizing, and relocating add to one's stress, along with pressures to perform effectively and efficiently. Women may experience more stress at work than men because they usually receive less pay and are promoted less frequently than their male peers. Many women complain of racial or ethnic discrimination, along with the "glass ceiling" that limits their career advancement, especially if they have children at home. In addition, some women are subject to either subtle or overt forms of harassment, which may hinder their productivity. Also, many women are in monotonous, routine pink-collar jobs in which they lack control over their work, and are underpaid with no chance for advancement. Work stress may contribute to anger, anxiety, feeling a loss of control or lack of self-confidence, denial of feelings, and diminished personal relationships.

Environmental Stressors: Cramped or inadequate housing, violence, noise, crowding, and pollution are the most obvious sources of environmental stressors. The larger a town or city, the more pervasive and uncontrollable are the irritations and pressures upon its residents. The intensity of these stressors and how many occur together depend on where you live and work, the type of transportation you use, and whether you can get away from your environment occasionally. Your personality is often a deciding factor in how you react to environmental pressures— whether you are turned on or stressed out by them. Competitive, ambitious, type A people tend to seek out and thrive on the energy and pace of big cities, and would find quiet towns boring. You may minimize environmental stressors if you live and work in the type of environment in which you feel and function best. Noise is by far the most pervasive stress factor in our environment, from sirens and horns in traffic to loud music or television. Whether the mind blocks it out or not, the body reacts to noise by arousing the sympathetic nervous system, which triggers the stress response. Long periods of constant, unremitting background noise can also impair your ability to concentrate and affect your learning skills.

Nutrition: Chemicals in many foods, drinks, and drugs contribute to stress. Caffeine and other stimulants in coffee, tea, and cola drinks boost the output of stress hormones. Initially you may feel more alert, but later these substances can cause irritability and sleeplessness. Consumption of large quantities of sugar and sugar-rich foods may soon lead to low blood sugar (hypoglycemia), which also causes fatigue and irritability. Excess salt causes nervous tension and fluid retention, and may increase blood pressure. Moderate amounts of alcohol help the body and mind relax, but in excess can be a depressant and impair brain function. The next few pages provide exercises to help you identify some of the major responsibilities you are trying to juggle, along with your major sources of positive and negative stress. You may find these exercises helpful in motivating you to modify the demands you place on yourself and to solicit the assistance of family members or others.

What Responsibilities Are You Juggling?

Using a scale of 1–minimal responsibility to 5–major responsibility, write the number you feel best represents your amount of responsibility beside each item. Skip the item if it does not apply to your life. Add the totals for each column (except recreation), then summarize all three columns to find the total amount of your lifestyle responsibilities.

Home	Career	Recreation	Community
__ Mate	__ School/class	__ Tennis	__ Church
__ Parents	__ Work at home	__ Golf	__ Charity
__ Children	__ Own business	__ Cycling	__ Professional
__ Pets	__ Work for others	__ Exercise	organizations
__ Cleaning	__ Manage others	__ Jogging	__ Political group
__ Laundry	__ Deadlines	__ Boating	__ Youth group
__ Yardwork	__ Commute	__ Dancing	__ School
__ Pay bills	__ Budget	__ Other sports	__ Social group
__ Fixing meal	__ Demanding boss	__ Entertaining	__ Health club
__ Maintain car	__ Work pressures	__ Spectator	__ Ethnic group
__ Buying food	__ Travel	sports	__ Community
__ Buy clothes	__ Other	__ Hobbies	organizations
__ Other		__ Other	__ Volunteer work
			__ Other

__ Total   __ Total   __ Total

__ Grand Total for 3 columns

Interpretation

First, you might wish to circle those items in which you wrote the number 5 so you know what your greatest and probably most time-consuming responsibilities are. Think about how you feel devoting your greatest time and energy to them. Do you feel happy and satisfied about them? Are they responsibilities you'd rather not have, or would prefer to have help with?

Next, look at the Grand Total of your responsibilities from the three columns and use the scale below to determine your level of responsibilities and how you feel about it.

Scale: 20–40 minimal; 41–60 average; 61–80 high;

81+ you're on overload!

Women's Major Sources of Stress

The scale below may help you identify both the sources and amount of your stress. The items include major life-changes, important issues, and worries or concerns that you may have. Use the simple key below to rate each stressor. Skip items that do not apply to you.

Key: 0–no stress   3–moderate stress

1–some stress   5–great stress

1. Relationship with spouse/partner   ____
2. Relationships with children   ____
3. Relationships with parents/in-laws   ____
4. Relationships with friends/neighbors   ____
5. Managing home responsibilities   ____
6. Managing children's schoolwork   ____
7. Household help from spouse/partner   ____
8. Emotional support from spouse/partner   ____
9. Spouse/partner's work or retirement   ____
10. Social life with spouse and friends   ____
11. Pressures from other family members   ____
12. Occupation or career satisfaction   ____
13. Coping with single parenting   ____
14. Own health problems or injury   ____
15. Parents' health problems or injury   ____
16. Loss of spouse/partner, or family member ____
17. Leisure time to relax and have fun   ____
18. Financial status and security   ____
19. Home/neighborhood environment   ____
20. Balancing family and work demands   ____
21. Personal appearance and weight   ____
22. Maintaining a healthy lifestyle—good
    nutrition and exercise   ____

Total score ____ Divide by numbers of items = ____

Interpretation of results

First add up all the items you rated for a total score, then divide the total by the number of items you rated. Your final score should range between 0 and 5.

0–2 = minimal stress   2.1–3.5 = moderate stress

3.6–5 = excessive stress

Your Major Positive and Negative Stressors

To help balance your life and acquire control over major stressors, first you need to recognize and acknowledge stressors that benefit your life and those that detract from feelings of peace and serenity. Listed below are general areas in most people's lives where they may experience either *eustress* or *distress*. Briefly describe the things in your life in each category that seem to be either positive and beneficial or negative and upsetting.

Category	Eustress/Positive	Distress/Negative
1. Health (diet, exercise, rest)		
2. Home environment		
3. Relationship with spouse/partner		
4. Relationship with children		
5. Relations with friends		
6. Relationship with extended family		
7. Occupation/career		
8. Roles and responsibilities at home and work		
9. Outside commitments		
10. Social occasions and events		
11. Exercise and recreation		
12. Leisure / fun time		
13. Personal self-time		
14. Neighborhood		

2

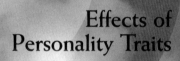

Effects of
Personality Traits

3

Altruism—caring for others

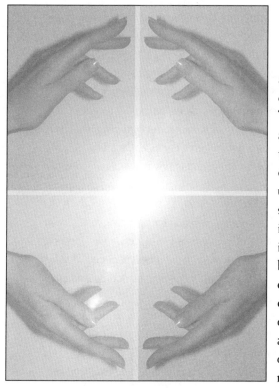

𝒜ltruism, compassion, and service are an intricate part of most religions. Traditional religions have always encouraged followers to be altruistic—to help others, to give of themselves unconditionally, or to be of service to others. Altruism involves a mind-set of wanting to make the world a better place. It flows from compassion and empathy for others, then choosing to act on those feelings. It is a selfless act when you choose to help others, although you often receive more than you give.

Definition of Altruism

Altruism is the giving of your compassion, empathy, and self to others without expecting any gratitude, success, or reward. You do what you can for others, while holding both yourself and another in mutual acceptance and high regard. If you give from your heart, you will feel oneness with yourself and humanity, touching other's lives while being touched by theirs. This relationship between you and others has its own intrinsic rewards.

Personal contact with those you help is essential to experiencing good feelings of joy and euphoria. Caring for others comes from being able to understand another person's point of view and to consider how others feel. While writing checks for charities, raising funds, or collecting clothes may benefit others, these activities do not produce the same physical effects as having personal contact with someone who needs your assistance.

How to Develop Altruism

Each of us has her own feelings about helping others, based on our upbringing, social environment, and life experiences. However, many of us have lost touch with our innate empathy for those less fortunate. You may need encouragement and motivation to engage in activities that bring the pleasures of giving to others. It may require some deep soul-searching to find the altruist within you. Volunteer work can lend meaning, purpose, and social cohesiveness, along with joy, to your life.

One of the first steps toward altruism is recognizing that you must leave your own personal ego behind to develop a healthy helping relationship. If you believe that helping others is reward-driven, it simply feeds your ego. Only when you give with empathy and understanding can you close the distance between yourself and others. Although motivations for helping others are invariably mixed, recognizing one's own reasons for altruistic actions is a healthy form of self-acceptance. Finding your altruistic spirit means connecting with the deepest sources of your compassion. Committed helpers forget their egoistic concerns and give themselves over to another person or higher cause.

According to Dr. Allen Lucs and Peggy Payne, authors of *The Healing Power of Doing Good*, there are four characteristics of altruism. The first, a psycho-spiritual component, ultimately depends on the kind of relationship that develops from helping others in need. Second, frequent contact is important, so you'll need to spend about two or more hours each week to benefit from helping others. Third, you benefit much more from helping strangers than family members or friends, otherwise your altruistic acts may be done out of obligation, nearness, or circumstance. Lastly, in giving to others, you must simply enjoy the feeling of closeness to whomever you help and not expect the recipient to benefit from what you do.

Bridging the gap between yourself and others can spark your sense of being connected to something larger than yourself. You may need to push yourself to connect with other people in an organization by volunteering to do anything that gets you moving and connected to something outside yourself. However, you have the choice to control how, where, and when you wish to work or volunteer. Altruistic people choose activities that provide them with the greatest sense of meaning, affiliation, and connection to something larger than themselves. Their choice reflects their commitment and control. When you find a meaningful type of service, you'll be not only happier, but healthier.

Helping friends and family members can be fraught with potential complications and is not always healthy. Women who always give to others, especially family members, usually put themselves last. They may feel a need to please everyone else, may feel anger at being used, and are likely to have health problems. When you are pressured or coerced to meet someone else's needs, the joy of helping and the health benefits are compromised or even counterproductive. These acts of caring may be motivated by obligation, guilt, or other emotional entanglements. Too much altruism can sap the spirit just as much as healthy helping uplifts the spirit. Researchers found that martyrs—those who would carry out everyone else's orders, or "perfect patients"—were less likely to recover from their illnesses. People who relinquish their will and spirit, who often keep their fears and despondency to themselves, are often characterized by resentment and suppressed anger, with an inability to forgive. They have a strong tendency toward self-pity, coupled with a poor self-image, and lack character or personality traits that might enable them to fight back. When you give more of yourself than you are comfortable with, in the name of compassion, you may feel used and abused. Dr. Dean Ornish, author of *Love and Survival: The Scientific Basis for the Healing Power of Intimacy*, reminds women to give to others only when it comes from your heart, rather than out of fear or guilt, or because someone else thinks it's what you should do. Remember you can only say yes to giving freely, when you can also choose to say no.

People who help primarily for ego gratification will feel powerless and angry when their efforts are not graciously received, or when their actions do not produce the results they desire. They may wonder, why bother to extend myself when those I help don't appreciate it or follow my advice? If you try to change another person's situation and are not successful, you may end up feeling hopeless and worse than if you hadn't tried. Fixing others' problems is the worst possible goal for any helper. When a goal becomes the major reason for helping a person, sooner or later the helper will lose her sense of control because things don't always work out as she wishes. The following guidelines may help you become a healthy helper or altruistic person:

- Go with your heart: what causes or issues are most important to you?
- Determine how you can make a difference: what are your skills or hobbies?
- Decide what kind of help you feel comfortable giving to others.
- Try out different types of situations to see what feels right for you.
- Feel free to stop volunteering if the situation isn't right for you.
- Don't quit just because you have one bad experience or feel rejected.

After you become involved in volunteer or helping activities, keep a journal to explore the meaning of your service to others. Think about your state of mind and feelings with which you approach helping others, and honestly examine both your positive actions and also any selfishness, resentments, or disagreeable feelings and sensations. Record both pleasurable sensations and uncomfortable ones, so you can return to those joyful experiences that you brought to others and yourself. You may find your compassion for others increasing when your heart is open, and may notice changes in both your physical and emotional health and well-being.

Examples of Altruistic Activities

Giving back to others, making the world a better place, doing something more with your abilities and talents by helping others are all altruistic behaviors. Also, practice random acts of kindness, such as helping someone cross a street, offering special knowledge to a friend with problems, holding the door for a stranger, or listening to another's woes—try to make these efforts more frequently, more consciously, and with more loving intent.

Often one of the biggest obstacles to finding volunteer work is figuring out what to do and where to go. Most communities have volunteer organization clearinghouses that are aware of all the opportunities in your area. You may call them or any major volunteer group to find out what is involved and where to go. Some ways to volunteer are:

- Work with others to improve a neighborhood
- Deliver food to the elderly or homebound
- Become a child's tutor in a public school system
- Serve in a literacy program for adults
- Work at a nursing home or hospital as a friendly visitor
- Be a helper at a senior daycare center
- Serve on the board of one of your favorite charities
- Help children at Special Olympics programs
- Serve as a telephone caller for a charity group
- Counsel women at an abuse center

Health Benefits of Altruism

In *Love and Survival,* Dr. Ornish writes that when you help others, you also help yourself. Altruism is healthy for both the helper and recipient because by giving to others with an open heart, you reduce the distance that separates you from others. Helping others unselfishly is the most "selfish" of all activities. When you freely choose to cross the boundaries that separate you from others, you become more socially integrated, joyfully freeing yourself from loneliness, isolation, and suffering. Most acts of community service that bring you into contact with others increase your sense of connectedness with those around you.

Helping others can also give you a sense of meaning and purpose in your life. You may feel a sense of doing something worthwhile with your life and making a genuine contribution to others. When you help others, your self-esteem is enhanced and you feel valued, which can lead to greater inner peace and happiness. Since stress may be related to inadequate self-worth, and can suppress your immune system, helping others with love and compassion may strengthen your immune system. Community service also channels your time and energy. It can distract you from your problems and focus your attention in a rewarding and less stressful direction.

Research shows that participating frequently in volunteer activities to help strangers has strong physical, emotional, and spiritual benefits and seems to be related to a slightly longer life expectancy. Dr. Allan Lucs is a researcher and scholar who has spent his whole adult life helping others. In his book he describes the health benefits experienced by people who consistently helped others. He found that even the smallest acts of kindness toward others can contribute to a sense of calm, self-esteem, and connectedness. Giving to others can trigger the release of serotonin and possibly other brain chemicals, which may generate feelings of increased energy and a general sense of well-being. Many volunteers experience physical pleasure and psychological well-being from helping others. They notice sensations of warmth and energy— feelings that often were directly associated with reduced aches, pains, and other symptoms of illness. Helping others regularly can diminish the disabling effects of chronic pain and reduce the symptoms of physical distress. Pain relief may be related to an increase in painkilling endorphins released during happy experiences.

By engaging in frequent, regular volunteer work, these short-term effects may eventually lead to more subtle long-term benefits, such as long-lasting emotional tranquility, enhanced self-esteem, fewer symptoms of distress or depression, and a sense of optimism. Assisting strangers through a group or organization has been linked to fewer physician visits, extended good feelings from helping, and other positive effects. One study found that women with multiple roles who engaged in regular volunteer work not only lived longer, but were physically and psychologically healthier than other women. Altruistic activities can also ease the tension of healthy people who are overworked and living stressful lives. While chronic stress can suppress your immune system, altruism, love, and compassion may enhance it. $\mathcal{B}$

4

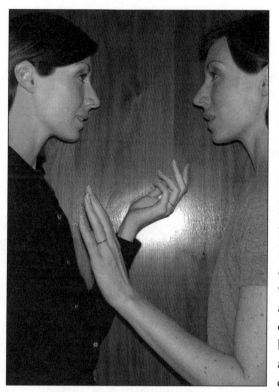

Assertiveness—taking charge

*W*omen have been taught both culturally and historically to be other-oriented, or more concerned about caring for others than themselves. Women are also taught to be passive, submissive, and compliant so people will like them, and never to seek to be the center of attention. Having learned these non-assertive roles well, many women are afraid to be assertive, even though they carry multiple roles and work long hours as wives, mothers, and employees. If women can't voice their needs, rights, and opinions to others, their own personal needs often go unmet, and their conflict and stress can be enormous.

By responding assertively in your interpersonal relations with others, you can reduce or eliminate emotional distress. Whenever you act passively, you may feel anxious and tense, or angry and resentful at not expressing your true feelings. In his book, *Stress Management for Dummies*, Allen Elkin writes that you may feel victimized, taken advantage of, pushed around, or frustrated at not getting what you feel you deserve. If you don't express your views, you may have less self-esteem, power, and control, and feel less hopeful that you might achieve your desires. By being assertive, you resist becoming a self-sacrificing martyr, and are able to monitor and take care of your own physical and emotional needs. It is important to your health to be able to communicate your thoughts and feelings in socially appropriate ways. If you want others to understand you and your point of view, you need to express yourself. Positive outcomes are more likely to result from assertiveness because others will know where you stand, and you are less likely to feel guilty, embarrassed, or stressed out.

Definition of Assertiveness

Assertive people express their opinions, wants, rights, and feelings while still respecting the rights of others and not compromising or demeaning them. They speak from their own point of view, take responsibility for their feelings and actions, and try to help others understand their position, while leaving room for continued discussion. Assertiveness falls on a continuum between passive and aggressive behavior. *Unassertive* or passive people are often shy and reluctant to assert their rights and privileges. They are afraid to let their needs, wishes, or displeasure be known, so when others don't behave as desired, they often feel hurt, anxious, and resentful. They may behave in a self-effacing, apologetic manner so others do not take them seriously. *Aggressive* people say whatever they think, sometimes in subtle, passive-aggressive ways, or directly express their anger in a hostile or abusive manner. They vehemently defend their own rights, yet often violate or usurp the rights of others, leaving others feeling put down or turned off. Others often feel anxious and tense around aggressive people.

Do you know whether you are passive, assertive, or aggressive? The items below may help you identify which type of person you are. How comfortable do you feel about the following:

Key: 1= very comfortable 5= very uncomfortable
___ expressing your needs, wants, and desires to family members
___ handling criticism from parents, supervisors, or friends
___ sharing your thoughts and feelings with others
___ asking for help from family members and friends
___ refusing requests for help from family and friends
___ receiving compliments from friends and colleagues.

If the sum of your responses is less than 15, chances are you are fairly assertive. But if the sum of your responses is less than 18, you may want to think about how your passive behaviors may contribute to your stress level.

How to Become Assertive

Being assertive means standing up for yourself and expressing how you truly feel, yet being considerate of other people's feelings and respecting their rights. You do not attack or blame others, nor do you become meek and withdrawn. Assertiveness is not simply getting what you want, when you want it, disregarding the rights and feelings of others. Assertive people do not dominate, demean, or humiliate others.

You may first learn to be assertive by watching how others behave. Notice how those you admire for their assertiveness act in various situations—watch their posture, eye contact, and use of "I" statements. Use your inner eye to observe how you behave in similar situations, and compare the similarities and differences. Begin trying out assertiveness skills in situations where you feel only small amounts of anxiety, then work your way to more difficult situations. Remember, you are trying to change behaviors that you were comfortable with for years, so take your time and don't be upset if you act passively in some situations for a while.

Assertiveness training is an effective strategy for replacing passive, withdrawn, or inhibited behaviors with positive, expressive ones. Assertive behavior enhances your self-esteem by developing your ability to express yourself comfortably. Women can learn to express their likes and dislikes, speak for themselves without self-consciousness, accept compliments comfortably, disagree openly, ask for clarification, and say no without feeling guilty. This can reduce anxiety and feelings of powerlessness, and promote your ability to cope with stressors and reduce or eliminate internal stress.

Girdano and Everly, authors of *Controlling Stress and Tension: A Holistic Approach*, describe the following seven steps to learn how to become more assertive:

1. *Greet others*, initiating at least two exchanges or conversations each day with someone you do not consider a close friend. Many unassertive people are too shy to greet others or initiate conversations.

2. *Give and accept compliments*, which often increases your number of friends. It is a polite way to show that you notice others and care what they think. Many unassertive people fail to compliment others because they think others wouldn't care. Also, try to accept compliments graciously.

3. *Use "I" statements* to express your thoughts and feelings, both when you agree or disagree. "I" statements let your views be

known without criticizing or blaming the other person. Unassertive people may be afraid to use the word "I" because it may be interpreted as a personal rejection, although this usually doesn't happen among friends.

4. *Ask why* in a calm and pleasant manner to indicate that you want or need additional information from people you believe are superior to you. Or you may prefer to ask, what makes you think that? or could you explain that? so that you sound less threatening or challenging. Learn to feel more comfortable obtaining information and expressing yourself. Often unassertive people are afraid to ask a question because they feel it represents a challenge, yet it does not. It is merely a request for more information.

5. *Express your feelings spontaneously,* not days or weeks later. With practice it gets easier. Unassertive people often repress their feelings, which is unhealthy. It is better to risk hurting someone else's feelings than to keep your feelings bottled up. If she is your friend, she'll agree.

6. *Disagree with someone* when you believe differently. Some people take a disagreement personally, but they need to work that out themselves. A disagreement can be a healthy and positive way to learn new ideas, especially with a friend. Try not to be arbitrary, so make sure you believe in what you are saying.

7. *Use eye contact,* but don't stare at others, since this may be interpreted as a challenge. Maintaining eye contact may feel awkward at first, but continue trying, and do not look down when you break contact. Start with short intervals of two to three seconds, then try to increase the amount of time gradually.

Watch how you say things, since it is not just your words, but also the manner in which you say things and your body language that are important. Use a clear, moderate voice: try not to talk too fast or use a high-pitched voice, and don't mumble or use a sarcastic tone. Be aware of irritating verbal mannerisms and unconscious habits, such as coughing, sighing, giggling, or using meaningless phrases like you know, are you with me, or yeah. The way you walk and stand gives a good impression of how confident you are. Stand up straight, with your chest expanded, head held erect, eyes level with the other person, and arms relaxed, not crossed on your chest. Sit upright, shoulders relaxed, with your hands at your sides or loosely clasped. Try to look confident and at ease.

Remember that as you increase your assertiveness skills, you will also improve your self-concept. Not all assertive behaviors result in rewards—sometimes other people may simply be defensive or aggressive. Don't let their problems hinder you. Feel good about yourself and your new assertive personality.

Examples of Assertive Behaviors
- *Sharing your thoughts and feelings*
  I am so upset about . . .
  I thought we were going to . . .
- *Expressing your needs*
  I would like your help with . . .
  It upsets me when you don't . . .
- *Receiving compliments*
  Thank you for saying so.
  How nice of you to say that.
- *Handling criticism*
  I don't agree with you.
  You seem upset by my behavior.
- *Requesting help*
  Would you please help me with . . .
  I need a favor from you.
- *Refusing requests to help*
  No, I can't do that for you now.
  That's not a good time for me.

Sometimes when you are assertive, you may seem a little cold or be viewed as putting others off. Tact and packaging may be required, such as finding a convenient excuse or a little white lie. Remember that discretion is often the better part of assertion.

In a recent article, How to Talk So People Will Listen, Marlene Pagley described how women tend to be more polite, hesitant, and apologetic in their conversation than men, and as a result may not be heard or understood. She suggests that women need to think of the four C's when they communicate: be clear, concise, consistent, and creative.

- Be *clear* as to what you want and explain your expectations to others.
- Be *concise* by stating your specific desires in as few words as possible.

- Be *consistent* in your message until your listener understands, or use examples.
- Be *creative* and use your imagination to get their attention.

Temoshok and Dreher offer other suggestions for becoming more expressive and assertive in their book, *The Type C Connection:*

- Don't blame others for your feelings or try to change others. Instead, tell them how you feel and what you want from them.
- Avoid passive-aggressive behavior in which you express your anger in indirect ways. Speak and act directly and decisively to defend your integrity or your physical and emotional safety.
- Learn how to say no to resist becoming a self-sacrificing martyr. When you say yes, you lose your right to whine. Passive personalities need to practice when and how to refuse demands to protect their emotional health.
- Refuse to please others simply for the sake of winning their approval.

In her book, *The Dance of Anger,* Harriet Lerner provides ground rules for effective assertive communication. Here are some key excerpts from her guidelines:

- Speak up when an issue is important to you—if you are going to feel bitter, resentful, or unhappy by remaining silent. But, you don't have to address every issue.
- Don't use derogatory tactics—such as blaming, preaching, labeling, ridiculing, ordering, diagnosing, warning, or interrogating.
- Be specific about what you want—don't make vague requests since others can't read your mind or anticipate your needs.
- Avoid telling another person what she or he thinks or feels. You are not in their shoes.

When you feel a person has attacked you, try to understand that person's perspective—where he or she is coming from—so that you won't take her or his attack so personally or seriously. Try to use some judgment before you react. Decide whether a creative counter-attack, or reframing and letting go of the attack, is the best choice for the moment. A thoughtful counterattack may help you and the other person understand each other better. If you think the attack arose from the person's own emotional pain, and that she or he needs love at the moment, you might try to offer support. In either case, it is important to let go of your anger after resolving the problem.

Health Benefits of Assertiveness

Mind/body researchers have established that assertiveness seems to bolster and balance your immune system, while dwelling on anger and grief suppresses the immune system and decreases white blood cell activity. Assertiveness is a behavioral style for effectively expressing and channeling one's anger, honoring both your own need for honest and satisfying relationships, and other people's need to be treated fairly and respectfully. Whether there is a direct link between these emotions and specific diseases is controversial. Recent studies suggest that when women try to appease others, deny their true feelings, and conform to social standards, known as type C behaviors, they are more likely to suffer physical health problems. Women who use these unhealthy coping behaviors usually have inadequate supportive relationships, and tend to internalize their stress and inhibit their emotions. However, when women reverse these behaviors, studies show that their resistance to disease improves.

Several researchers have found that when people are assertive and express their views in daily interactions or confrontations, they are able to handle their stressors more effectively and have fewer health problems. Assertive women tend to use coping skills that ward off depression and enable them to ask for and accept support from loved ones. They are not afraid to be themselves, and to enjoy pleasures in life, which may be the best contributors to their physical health. They also are more likely to recover from existing illnesses quicker because they take charge of finding out what may help them get well. In contrast, those who respond passively suffer silently and internalize their feelings, which alters their immune system and contributes to more illnesses that take longer to recover from.

Assertiveness helps you deal with stressful topics efficiently, resolve conflicts quickly, and put less strain on yourself and on your relationships with others. As you become empowered to change your personal behaviors and learn to be comfortable expressing your views assertively, you may find that you have fewer symptoms of illness, miss less work, boost your immune system, and generally feel better. Another important change is to feel comfortable expressing so-called negative emotions, to reduce their effect on your body when you keep them inside. By learning assertiveness skills, you may increase your feelings of self-respect and self-esteem, which may empower you to recognize, acknowledge, and confidently protect your space. With assertiveness, you will feel more confident to take charge of your life, and can express your feelings and needs in healthy ways, including releasing anger in an appropriate manner.

TAKING CHARGE OF YOUR LIFE

In *The Ten Rules of High Performance Living*, Dr. Meltzer writes that if you love and respect yourself enough and nurture and reward yourself, then you must take charge of your life. If you believe in yourself and what you are doing, you'll nurture the heartfelt belief that you deserve to be healthy and happy. When you love yourself, you believe you deserve a fulfilling life. This means taking control of your thoughts, intentions, actions, and deeds. Since you, and only you, are responsible for your life, you decide when and how to achieve fulfillment or how much you'll suffer.

Definition of Taking Charge

Taking charge means accepting full responsibility for both your successes and failures. You create whatever is happening in your life, and have only yourself to answer to. Taking charge is goal-oriented and empowers you to live out your dreams. Dr. Meltzer believes that the keys to achieving your dreams are your beliefs and expectations, a positive attitude, clear thinking, and self-determination. You have the ability to change the course of your life if you so choose.

How to Take Charge of Your Life

There is a bridge between your belief systems and your vision of a fulfilling life. Belief systems often become self-fulfilling prophecies. Your feelings shape your belief system and you become what you feel. When you value, respect, and feel good about yourself, you can create a positive belief system. If fear dominates the way you think, feel, and believe, you will behave in ways that contribute to failures in your relationships, family, work or career. With a take-charge attitude, you need to believe you can achieve health, success, and personal fulfillment, along with your dreams.

You have the power to take charge of your life instead of feeling like a helpless victim. How you see things determines how you respond.

When you see yourself as a victim and blame others for adverse circumstances in your life, you give away your power and allow others to manipulate you. This creates unhealthy stress patterns. You choose what you think, feel, and do about your goals, career, friends, and lifestyle. Through your choices, you create wellness or illness, happiness or misery, success or failure.

Your self-worth or self-image is determined by how you feel about yourself. How you see yourself, or your opinion of your life, is closely related to your ability to take charge of your life. Your feelings and thoughts about your self-worth determine your actions and behavior. When you sincerely believe that you are a special, worthy woman, you'll have the self-confidence to pursue your dreams and handle life's challenges effectively.

First, you must believe that *you are completely responsible* for your mind, body, spirit, and life. You are responsible for your thoughts, feelings, actions, and behavior. If you blame someone else or outside circumstances, you are saying that others have control of your life. In other words, you are relinquishing your current life to others.

Second, *take charge of your thoughts.* Mind power has everything to do with living out your dreams. You may need to alter your attitude and expectations of yourself and others to achieve your goals. Fritz Perls once said, "other people are not in this world to live up to your expectations." And, in his book by the same title, Richard Carlson writes that Rule number One is "Don't sweat the small stuff," and Rule number Two is "it's all small stuff." Abraham Lincoln believed that "people are about as happy as they make up their minds to be." So, learn to think positively, like an optimist, especially in the face of adversity. As you develop sound, positive thinking habits, you'll begin to feel you can handle anything.

Third, *take advantage of opportunities.* Learn to live in the present: avoid agonizing over problems from the past or worrying about the future—you can't change what's already happened, and you can't control everything in the future. So when opportunity knocks, seize the moment, be patient, and keep your faith that good things will happen. Choose to make the most of each situation. When you have the right attitude, you'll be amazed at how well things will work out for you and others.

Fourth, *set your goals high, but within your reach* to achieve happiness and fulfillment. Plant seeds for success today, so you can enjoy the fruits tomorrow. Remember your thoughts create your actions, so if you are goal- and solution-oriented, you'll take charge of figuring out what hurdles are in your way and how to get where you want to be. Decide on appropriate solutions to any predicaments, then take action.

Fifth, *taking charge of your life includes being decisive.* Indecision prevents you from taking action, and you may feel you've lost control of your life, which can intensify your stress. If you dislike making decisions, what can you do? Write down the problem, then list your options, including "doing nothing." Instead of using linear thinking, where you start at a given point and move directly toward the goal, try lateral thinking, where you consider unusual alternatives, along with their pros and cons. Be ready to compromise. Remember that many decisions can be modified or changed later.

Sixth, *develop the willpower and self-determination* to control the direction of your life—to make the impossible happen. With willpower, you set goals, make choices, and take deliberate actions to achieve your goals. Willpower helps you to focus and carry out your intentions. Dynamic willpower can energize your mind and body to purposefully direct your actions. Self-determination means that you are willing to stand up for what you believe in and to take the necessary risks for your beliefs. Take a stand on major issues at home or work. Visualize what you see as optimal in your life, then go after it with confidence.

Lastly, taking charge of your life means taking responsibility for modifying your behavior, making adjustments to changes, and being adaptable or flexible, especially in the face of adversity. It means making the best out of what life offers. Dr. Meltzer offers the following keys to taking charge of your life:

- Embrace the responsibility for taking charge of your mind and body
- Take charge of your thinking: create the habit of a positive attitude
- Be opportunistic: take advantage of good opportunities
- Be visionary and goal-oriented
- Gain self-confidence and develop self-worth
- Utilize willpower and self-determination to create the habit of success
- Make any appropriate adjustments in your attitudes, beliefs, and expectations to stay in charge of your life
- Learn how to care for yourself in all ways

—Meltzer 1998:55

Health Benefits of Taking Charge

Your belief systems affect how your body functions, including your immune system. Dr. Meltzer believes that positive belief systems have infinite healing powers because they open the channels for creative healing energy to work and have a favorable effect on your neuroendocrine system. Fear, anxiety, inadequacy, and insufficiency are destructive to your immune system because they affect your mind and body, which changes your body chemistry. If you let these feelings control your health, you have essentially surrendered yourself and given away your power. Learn to rely upon yourself for your health, security, and well-being. When you believe in yourself, you will succeed, but if you limit your self-expectations and have chronic self-doubts, you will be disappointed with your life and health.

A take-charge attitude has been linked to improving your chances of recovering from disease. These forms of active coping mean that you believe you can take control of a situation or illness and make decisions about how you'll handle your life. You decide whether to explore various options, obtain more information, weigh alternatives, discuss strategies with relatives and friends, or simply to take good care of yourself. Feeling in control of your life and responsible for your decisions and actions enhances your physical and emotional health and well-being in numerous ways. $\mathcal{B}$

5

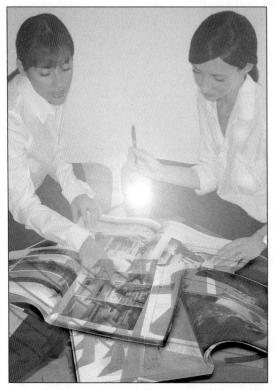

Confiding in Others—sharing feelings

When I express my negative feelings openly and honestly,
sometimes it feels like getting rid of toxic waste.

While it is commonly accepted that expressing our emotions is good for our mental health, few people realize that it is just as important for our physical health. In his book, *Deep Healing: The Essence of Mind/Body Medicine,* Dr. Miller writes that in our culture it is considered socially correct to conceal or suppress our emotions, with the hope that we'll maintain control and not upset others. Although our emotions are central and powerful to our being, women have been taught to hide their true feelings, and are often afraid to express themselves honestly for fear that others will be indifferent to their problems or alienated by their anger. When women express certain emotions, they may be called weak, grouchy, manipulative, bitchy, or a shrew. Many women try to avoid displaying so-called negative emotions, such as anger, fear, or sadness, because they feel embarrassed or are unsure whether their emotions will be tolerated by others.

Our basic emotions are neither good nor bad, positive nor negative. The only bad emotions are those which are stuck inside our minds because we feel we can't express them. Women have learned to deny their feelings, to suppress them, and to go through the motions of pretending to be happy. You may put on a cheery face to avoid upsetting those around you, but repressing your feelings may gradually lead to health problems.

In an earlier study of women's stress and coping, I found that the majority of women of all ages coped best with stressful situations by talking with others about their problems. Surprisingly, many married couples spend only seven minutes a week talking with each other. Mayell reports in 52 *Simple Steps to Natural Health* that the lack of effective, heart-to-heart communication is a common problem in many relationships, marriages, and families, so many women share their reactions to personal problems with other females. And some women are uncomfortable disclosing their personal problems and feelings with loved ones or close friends, yet they are comfortable discussing some of their most intimate feelings with their hairdresser, masseuse, manicurist, or strangers.

For many years, James Pennebaker, a psychologist at Southern Methodist University, and his colleagues studied whether it was healthier and more adaptive for people to share their upsetting thoughts and feelings with others or to keep them to themselves. They report in *Emotion, Inhibition and Health* that people who had major upsetting events were far more likely to develop health problems if they did *not* talk about these experiences than if they disclosed them. So, when women do not or cannot express their thoughts and feelings, they are less likely to understand, organize, and resolve their problems. Putting your problems into words helps you understand them better. Concealing your thoughts and feelings prevents you from resolving difficult experiences. This is unhealthy and may trigger secondary problems and increase your stress. Some women are reticent to discuss their stressful events or personal shortcomings because they feel that certain topics may be embarrassing, threaten their relationships, or lead to humiliation. They consciously restrain, hold back, or work to *not* think, feel, or reveal their problems, which requires psychological energy. Others may experience frequent ruminations or worry about unresolved problems, which contribute to additional physical and emotional problems. Once you acknowledge, express, and resolve your feelings of sadness or anger, you are less likely to feel unhappy or depressed.

Definition of Confiding in Others

Confiding in others is the ability to communicate your heartfelt emotions with someone you trust to understand your feelings. It involves more than just talking. Confiding means you are comfortable sharing your innermost thoughts and feelings with another person, along with your options, plans, or preferences. According to Dr. Pennebaker, self-disclosure means that you don't keep significant secrets from those close to you. But it does not imply compulsive honesty, sharing trivial details, or confessing unnecessary information for the sake of total honesty. You must be willing to risk revealing some of your inner self to form deeper connections and closer intimacy with others. This can help increase your awareness and understanding as you acquire personal insights and accept others' love.

Personality Quiz for Ability to Confide

Answer each of the following statements with true or false:

1. Before I make a decision, I usually try to consider all sides of the issue.
2. I believe in playing strictly by the rules.
3. I rarely, if ever, do anything reckless.
4. I am a serious-minded person.
5. I always try to be fully prepared before I begin working on anything.
6. I very much dislike it when someone breaks accepted rules of good conduct.
7. I rely on careful reasoning when making up my mind.
8. I am a cautious person.
9. Whenever I decide things, I refer to the basic rules of right and wrong.
10. I am not an impulse buyer.

Those who answered true to six or more statements are considered to be more inhibited or restrained than most people. While the trait of inhibition is not inherently bad or unhealthy, inhibited people are less likely to disclose their deepest thoughts and feelings indiscriminately. In society's eyes, inhibition is a socially desirable trait. The problem is that overly inhibited individuals thrive on predictability in an often unpredictable world. When faced with unexpected traumas and events, it is often best to remain flexible, confide in chosen others, and acknowledge your changing moods.

How to Feel Comfortable Confiding in Others

Numerous studies have shown that openly sharing your thoughts and feelings with others can enhance your relationships and make a powerful difference in your health and well-being. Although it seems unbelievable, simply talking openly or sharing your feelings with your partner, relatives, or friends can be a liberating and healing experience, if you feel safe confiding in them. As soon as you realize what you're feeling during interactions with others, it is important to share those feelings. Dr. Ornish, author of *Love and Survival*, found that when you open your heart by confiding in others, you release your emotional defenses and allow yourself to be emotionally vulnerable to others. As your emotional and spiritual heart begins to open, the physical heart often follows, and as healing occurs the doors to success and joy open much wider.

When you begin to express your emotions in a healthy way, you will learn how to protect yourself from repeating painful mistakes. Both experiencing and fully sharing your feelings of disappointment, grief, or joy are healthy ways to learn to accept both the successes and disappointments in your life. Although life is not always fair, a variety of emotional experiences is part of human life. You'll learn that in time all things will pass and you will develop a way to enjoy what you have at the moment and release unpleasant things when their time has passed.

From various studies about the effects of confiding, Dr. Pennebaker and his colleagues found that it was more helpful to deal with upsetting thoughts and problems directly than to avoid thinking about them. Although talking or writing about these thoughts can be helpful, it can also be a painful and anxiety-provoking experience. While dealing with an ongoing problem, you may feel temporarily distressed. Don't expect that by sharing your thoughts and feelings, you will immediately feel better again. After confiding your feelings, you may feel as though you have just relived the event or experience, and feel sad or depressed for several days. You may need some time to come to terms with painful past experiences, but gradually you'll feel better after letting go of your anger or grief. This unique letting-go experience is directly linked to your health. Once you acknowledge and disclose your thoughts and feelings, you can deal with them in more constructive ways with less anxiety, and function on a higher intellectual level. As your anger or grief lessen, you may develop new insights into the relationship between your old feelings and current problems. With a broader insight into your problems and a new outlook, comes a sense of resolution of some problems and a sense of peace.

If you decide you'll feel healthier by expressing your feelings, then you need to determine whether to reveal those feelings to the person who triggered your emotions or to share them with a close friend or trusted counselor. Choose someone who will focus on your feelings and encourage you to express your emotions and experiences. Find someone who can resist the natural inclination to give advice on how to solve your problems unless you specifically ask for their help.

Learning to communicate your heartfelt thoughts and feelings with special others takes time and effort. In his book, Mark Mayell says it also takes courage to honestly examine your true feelings and express them to others, since you may be opening yourself to rejection. Sharing personal confidences is a risk, but one that has important benefits, such as greater self-knowledge and a better understanding of others. But not confiding is also a risk, since it may isolate you from friends and lead to loneliness.

To remain healthy, Dr. Candace Pert, author of *Molecules of Emotion: Why You Feel the Way You Do*, recommends that you aim for emotional wholeness. If you're upset, first you must figure out what's really bothering you. Always tell yourself the truth—seek to be honest about what is upsetting you rather than blaming others, then find appropriate ways to express your emotions. She encourages you to express all of your feelings, regardless of whether you think they are acceptable, and then let them go. When you have a natural release for all your emotions, then you are freed from suffering. When your emotions are moving and your chemicals flowing, you can experience feelings of freedom, hopefulness, and joy in your whole, healthy state.

Steps in Learning to Confide

1. *Awareness of your feelings* is the first step in healing, says Dr. Ornish. When you feel an emotional reaction to a person or event, Dr. Miller suggests that you open yourself to feeling and recognizing all the emotional reactions you are experiencing.

2. Next, you must *decide whether or not to express your feelings*. Sometimes just being aware of your feelings is all that's important, since there are times when it is best to keep your feelings to yourself.

3. *Consider your timing* before starting to confide in someone. If you need someone's full attention, be sure it's a mutually good time to talk without interruptions.

4. *Acknowledge and express your feelings*. When you can accept your feelings without dismissing them as insignificant or judging them as right or wrong, you'll be more comfortable sharing them with others. It may help to practice describing your feelings in metaphors or with an analogy. Any message from the heart is better than none.

5. *Use "I" statements* to express yourself when you share your thoughts and feelings. "I" messages declare your part in the action, let you see the effect of your message, and state your need. It is better to say directly, I feel ..., I think ..., or I need ... Third-person statements such as, You make me feel ..., place blame on others, who then may feel that you are criticizing or accusing them of something, and react defensively.

6. *Learn to actively listen.* The ability to listen and accurately understand what is being offered is vital for effective communication. Listening is the yin while talking is the yang—without both elements, there are just two disconnected messages floating around.

According to David Spiegel, who wrote a chapter on Social Support: How Friends, Family and Groups Can Help, there are several steps you can take to enhance your communication skills and receive the support you desire from others:

1. *Be selective* about whom you confide in. Not everyone needs to be part of your support group. Informing everyone about your problems may increase your stress.

2. *Banish secrets.* Family members often want to protect each other from bad news, but hiding major problems limits them from sharing in the common mission to help. It is best to share relevant changes or problems directly and openly with close family members and friends, so that they may offer empathy or share your joy.

3. *Include your children.* Although children may be young, they sense when they are excluded from something important, and assume they have done something wrong. Explain the situation at a level they can understand to reduce their anxiety and guilt.

4. *Let family and friends know how they can help.* You might just want a supportive, empathetic listener, or someone to handle difficult tasks occasionally. Friends and family usually want to help, so let them know what you need.

5. *Accept emotional support.* A hug and a few tears can go a long way toward helping you feel understood and cared about. If you start crying when talking about your problems and fears, let the tears flow. Others may cry with you and you'll feel closer.

The ways you examine, talk, or write about upsetting experiences are important. Set aside a specific time and location to explore your deepest thoughts and feelings in a self-reflective way, especially if you plan to write about them. If you choose to discuss your feelings, try to find someone who is objective and not personally involved.

Close friends and groups can provide an opportunity to express fears, pain, anxiety, sadness, and other difficult emotions in a sympathetic environment. Some support groups, especially those led by health professionals, focus on helping members vent strong emotions about their situations. Spiegal says that a strong sense of acceptance and control comes from facing your worst fears and moving beyond them. Talking about your problems can be healthy and good for you, but just whining or complaining gets you nowhere. Listening to others' problems can be stressful, too.

When you have a quarrel with your lover or disagree about how to do things, you need to express how you feel, ask for what you want or need, and work things out. A misunderstanding with a good friend needs to be openly discussed. When you feel taken advantage of at work or home, or you do not like your job, consider what you would like to do within reason, and explain to your employer or those with whom you live, what you believe will make your work or life more meaningful.

If you are uncomfortable expressing your feelings verbally, Dr. Pennebaker found that those who wrote their feelings about disturbing, traumatic events in a journal had a better immune system and reported fewer health problems.

Health Benefits of Confiding in Others

In her recent book, Dr. Pert wondered whether our "cultural norm of denial that anything is wrong—and acting according to socially expected behaviors" could be related to women's high rates of depression. She asked, "are we ashamed to admit we might be sad, unhappy, disappointed, and not very satisfied with our life?" Dr. Pert believes that all emotions are healthy because emotions are what unite the mind and body. Anger, fear, and sadness, the so-called negative emotions, are as healthy as peace, courage, and joy. Yet in today's society, when women become overly busy, or caught up in egocentric thinking, they tend to lose touch with their inner selves and become blind to the underlying psychological causes of their health problems. She states that when you deny, stifle, or suppress your primary feelings of disappointment, fear, pain, frustration, or hurt over some insult or injustice, this creates disharmony in your mind/body system, which then acts at cross-purposes rather than as a unified whole. Domar and Dreher, authors of *Healing Mind, Healthy Woman*, feel that if you let your feelings simmer and grow into secondary feelings of resentment, hostility, or anger, you may become chronically unhappy and depressed. When anger is turned inward, not expressed, and buried below your consciousness, it can slowly lead to depression. David Spiegel also believes that since emotional expression creates a specific flow of peptides in the body, chronic suppression of emotions gradually disrupts your mind/body system, placing you at risk for both major and minor diseases.

When you try to block expressing stressful experiences, they may surface through unwanted thoughts, ruminations, dreams, and associated thought disturbances. The harder you try to repress your feelings, the greater the stress on your body. Dr. Pennebaker reported that during times of severe stress, people often try to inhibit their emotions, thoughts, and behaviors. Inhibiting your emotions can become a cumulative stressor and increase the likelihood of stress-related problems. When you try to block the flow of negative emotions, you may also have difficulty feeling positive emotions, such as joy and hope, and may also block your natural coping process and fail to resolve your problems. Withholding your feelings gradually undermines your body's defenses and can affect the immune system, the heart and vascular systems, and even the biochemicals of the mind/body system, according to Dr. Pert. This can make you feel foggy and less alert, and limit your awareness and ability to make appropriate decisions to change your behavior and solve your problems.

After years of research, Dr. Pennebaker reported that different psychological conflicts are often linked to specific changes in your body, but denial may prevent you from seeing the link between these conflicts and your illnesses. Some people use denial to avoid thinking about unpleasant experiences, or to dwell on physical symptoms to block their anxiety and psychological pain. Eventually you may recognize the cause-effect relationship between your psychological conflicts and recurring health problems such as headaches, back pain, diarrhea, or asthma, which are signals of distress. Then you can focus your energy on reducing the cause of distress and begin to resolve underlying emotional issues. You may find your health problems begin to subside as you learn to heal yourself. Being in touch with your feelings and aware of conflicts influencing your body helps your healing process. When you realize your problems are somewhat predictable, you may feel you have some control over them and can design ways to avoid them. Your perceptions of predictability and control over your world are essential to good psychological health.

How you handle stressors may be more important than the traumatic event or situation itself. Confiding in others and sharing your heartfelt thoughts and feelings helps you stay in touch with any negative feelings as they arise so that you do not suppress them. As you learn to effectively express your feelings about being hurt, frightened, or rejected, you'll become more aware of your inner feelings. Expressing your heartfelt thoughts and feelings is essential when things are not going well, but is also important when things are going well. Dr. Meltzer writes that sharing your feelings and problems with others helps you understand, organize, and resolve unsettling situations and events. As you learn to express how you feel and ask for what you need, you'll keep your relationships alive, and feel better inside.

Although heart-to-heart communication may not come naturally to you, both Drs. Pennebaker and Ornish believe that opening your heart through self-disclosure and confiding your deepest thoughts and feelings can have many remarkable health benefits. According to Pennebaker and Trave, if you can express your true thoughts and feelings, you can relate more easily to others, learn from their experiences, and adopt healthier coping strategies. It can provide an emotional catharsis that may help you acquire insight to harmonize and balance your mind/body, lower your overall stress and enhance your ability to resist disease. Furthermore, writing or talking about your feelings can influence your basic values, daily thinking patterns, and how you feel about yourself. You become more aware of your feelings, which enhances your immune system, reduces cardiovascular reactivity, improves your physical health, and may even prolong your life. Self-disclosure is a powerful force to heal the loneliness and isolation that often separate us from others and from parts of ourselves that we have kept hidden from others. Sharing your thoughts and feelings enhances your support system and helps you feel less alone and frightened. Once you express your feelings, then let them go so that they don't fester, build, or escalate out of control, you will feel more competent to handle other problems. Those who can express their authentic feelings, listen to what others have to say, and respond with love and generosity of spirit find that confiding is a rich and rewarding experience.

When your capacity to confide is fully developed, the feelings you lift from your mind don't simply float off into space. They work their way through your mind, and activate your intellectual awareness, which helps you make sense of your experiences. Thus, you will come to understand how your conflicts and problems have changed your life, relationships, and world views. These insights facilitate healing connections. Talking about these events, especially writing about them, is akin to putting back together the fragmented psychic puzzle left scattered after experiencing a traumatic event. By finding your own way to confide your inner truths, you are engaging in a healing endeavor. ∽ß

6

Emotional Resilience

When you are in sync with your beliefs and principles, and in harmony with your emotions, happiness becomes the story of your life. —Meltzer, 1998:68

In the new millennium many women frequently feel very stressed. They need to find a way to slow down and thrive in spite of all the change and chaos that add to their stress. Emotional resilience, the ability to bounce back from trauma and misfortune, is gaining interest after decades in which being a survivor or victim was viewed as a form of heroism. Scientists are beginning to identify some personality traits of resilient people—those who bounce back quickly from traumatic situations and recover readily from distressing events or unfortunate circumstances. They have found that strong, close relationships and feeling connected to and supported by others are important traits of emotionally resilient people. Other relevant traits are intelligence, competence and problem-solving skills, along with an interest in seeking information by asking questions.

Resilient people tend to react to problems by trying to learn rather than feeling like a victim. Self-reliance, flexibility, and a sense of humor are also resilient qualities. Additional traits may include a sense of optimism, adventure, courage, self-understanding, and the ability to work hard and find appropriate outlets for your emotions.

Definition of Emotional Resilience

Emotional resilience is the ability to get through, get over, and thrive after having experienced trials and tribulations, or traumatic events, according to Monika Guttman, author of an article titled Resilience. It also means that you can be challenged and not break down —you have the ability to rise above adversity. Emotionally resilient people know how to balance their daily pressures and demands with fulfillment, personal pleasures, and a lifestyle that protects them from the impact of negative stressors. They have the ability to express their feelings and emotions appropriately and effectively.

How to Develop Emotional Resilience

Richard Carlson, author of *Don't Sweat the Small Stuff—And It's All Small Stuff*, noted that when a major crisis occurs, you know in your heart that you have to respond and get through it, so you muster your inner strength and get support from others. But when small things interfere with your life, you may react automatically and feel annoyed at having to put up with minor inconveniences—that life just doesn't meet your demands. You may think, why should I have to put up with this? When you are tense and tired, there is a natural tendency to magnify your problems in life. Disappointments loom up as disasters, daily hassles feel as though everyone is out to get you, and you're more likely to become upset over trivialities. It's the everyday disruptive events that test your resilience and call on your inner resourcefulness and emotional flexibility. Managing stress really means controlling your emotions, such as the tension, anger, and anxiety, that you feel in some situations, and responding effectively rather than reacting emotionally.

Whenever you experience stressful situations, Dr. Miller, author of *Deep Healing: The Essence of Mind/body Medicine*, claims that your emotions are always involved and affect most of your important decisions and behaviors. You choose whether or not to be aware of these emotions. Only when you are aware can you decide whether your response is appropriate to handle the issue, or whether you should modify your feelings and their influence on the results. When problems arise, you need to face them so that you have more control over your emotional response, as most problems will not go away. Your ability to relax and avoid knee-jerk reactions, along with the ability to elicit other positive emotions and strengthen them, can enable you to make more conscious and rational choices.

If you recognize your reactions to yourself, others, and the situations you find yourself in, then you can examine your feelings and emotions. Joan Borysenko, who wrote *Minding the Body, Mending the Mind*, emphasizes that when you feel good about yourself and can set aside your fear and isolation, you will be able to experience your natural positive emotions of love, joy, confidence, and peace. These emotions are always with you and can be expressed when you learn the art of emotional balance. You can really enjoy the present when all your energy is available to be in the moment rather than ruminating about and dwelling on unfinished business. Therefore, you must learn to let go of your fears, resentments, and regrets, to free yourself from the past, forgive yourself and others. Don't look back, but move toward the future.

In his book, Dr. Miller asks how you can make the right choice in today's complex world, when you only have the following questions:

1. What image do you have of yourself? Do you feel
   able to deal with your problems?
2. What is your view of those around you? How do
   you think others feel about you?
3. What do you think is the relationship between the
   above two questions?

He believes that the choices you make each day are based on how you feel about yourself and those around you, and your interpretation of the relationship between the two.

According to Patricia O'Gorman, a psychologist and author of *Dancing Backwards in High Heels: How Women Master the Art of Resilience*, women use six different styles of resilience. These styles are not value judgments, nor do they indicate the need for a woman to change her style. O'Gorman identified the following styles of resilience.

Balanced resilience—women who are flexible and able to respond easily to change. Their resilience can help them to become more conscious of their strengths and take on more challenges.

Undeveloped resilience—women who are tentative, inexperienced, and prefer to leave decision-making to others. These women often feel alone and incomplete, and need to learn to make their own decisions and feel more comfortable taking on responsibility.

Paradoxical resilience—women who feel like two different people. They are likely to feel anxious in situations where they think they are unskilled, ashamed, or inadequate, but are generally quite competent in their own areas of expertise. These women need to realize that their expertise in one area can apply in other areas too.

Self-contained resilience—women whose identity is defined by being extremely competent, but who tend to isolate themselves from others and constantly feel they must do it all. They need to develop some flexibility and a willingness to let others help them.

Overwhelmed resilience—women who feel shame and self-contempt, and are unable to use resources on their own behalf. They need to recognize their superb survival skills and use them to meet their own daily needs to enhance their self-esteem.

Stellar resilience—women who tend to define themselves by the knowledge that they have survived a traumatic experience. They are vigilant about staying on track in all areas of their life, but need to integrate their past and present so they can be more open with others and let them take charge occasionally.

Daniel Goleman, author of *Working with Emotional Intelligence*, describes some characteristics of emotional intelligence that are similar to those of people with emotional resilience: self-awareness, self-confidence, and self-control, along with hardiness and the ability to accept change. According to Goleman, those who are emotionally resilient view problems as difficult but exciting and view change as a chance to move forward rather than step backward. These personality characteristics or traits probably occur on a continuum, ranging from a small amount in some people to healthy amounts in others. Judith Sills, who wrote the article Emotional Resilience is a Muscle You Can Build and Build, says that resilient people may be born with some of these traits and have learned some from experience. Some traits of emotional resilience, such as a calm temperament, a low anxiety level, or a tendency toward optimism, are passed along in one's genes, while other traits are nurtured during childhood, and some develop as we go through life and learn from our experiences. Over the years, most people become more adept at handling their emotions and impulses.

According to Goleman, there are some personality characteristics or traits you can learn to enhance your emotional resilience, feel more in touch with your emotions, and enjoy life. Six of these traits—emotional self-awareness, self-confidence, self-control, emotional consistency, adaptability or flexibility, and optimism—are described below:

Emotional self-awareness means recognizing your emotions and their effects on your decisions and performance. Dr. Meltzer, author of *The Ten Rules of High Performance Living*, believes that you must know your true feelings and not run away from them. Emotional self-awareness requires an honest appraisal of your underlying feelings, which are felt from your heart. By examining how you feel during the course of the day, you'll know whether your actions are based on positive loving thoughts or negative emotions. You'll soon learn that you feel happiest when you feel loved, nourished, and supported. Tune in to your emotions frequently during the day, otherwise you may become so caught up with schedules, chores, or other trivial details that you'll be a victim of your own emotionally chaotic lifestyle.

Goleman believes that people with emotional self-awareness know which emotions they are feeling and why. They can see the links between their feelings and what they think, do, and say, and they realize how their feelings affect their performance. Your intuition and gut feelings from your memory are your source of wisdom and judgment and become the heart of your self-awareness.

When you deny, suppress, or lose touch with your primary feelings of fear, pain, frustration, hurt, or disappointment, secondary feelings of anger, resentment, and worry may build up. Suppressed emotions can lead to feeling unbalanced, increasing your stress and depressing your immune system, says Dr. Meltzer. It is important to confront your emotions and problems rather than avoid them. Try not to let your anger or resentment carry over to tomorrow. Self-awareness helps you stay in touch with any negative feelings as they arise and not deny them for days or weeks. When you're aware of negative feelings, try to find a constructive way to express them.

Emotional self-confidence is the courage that comes from knowledge of your self-worth, abilities, values, and goals, writes Goleman. A strong sense of your self-worth and abilities helps keep you emotionally balanced when unexpected things happen. Disappointments come and go, and some things may bother or upset you. Dr. Meltzer believes you'll need emotional self-confidence to act appropriately and keep your life balanced. Goleman maintains that a person with strong self-confidence and self-worth presents herself with self-assurance. She exhibits a sense of presence and can state her views even if they are unpopular and stand up for what she believes is right. Also, she is decisive and able to make sound decisions despite uncertainties and pressure from others.

Emotional self-control is the ability to manage distressing feelings and disruptive emotions and impulses effectively. It depends on the brain's emotional centers working in concert with the executive centers, according to Goleman. Self-control is largely invisible: some signs include managing one's impulses, remaining cool while under stress, and confronting problems rather than avoiding them. These traits are the core of emotional resilience. Women with good self-control stay composed, positive, and unflappable even in trying moments, and can think clearly and stay focused, even under pressure.

Emotional consistency is having the courage to live up to your heartfelt emotional convictions every day, writes Meltzer. This means having a positive emotional reaction to whatever happens. Emotional consistency is motivated by your desire to be healthy and happy. You can change emotional setbacks into opportunities for personal growth and development if you expect adversity and problems, because they will occur. When problems occur, take one step backward to think about the problem, then two steps forward to improve your quality of life. You will learn, grow, and become stronger.

Adaptability is being able to respond easily to changes and be open to new ideas and options. Goleman thinks that those who are adaptable can examine new ideas and consider original solutions to problems without feeling threatened. They enjoy exploring different perspectives and thinking outside the box. Resilient people often just take one day at a time, rather than working on how to deal with all aspects of a major problem at once. They are flexible and can handle multiple demands and rapid change smoothly.

Optimism is an attitude of hopefulness and persistence in spite of adversity. Optimistic people look beyond the downside of their problems to find some meaning or challenge in a difficult situation. They put things into perspective to understand what they can control and what to let go of. Optimists have learned to go with the flow and let go of problems they have no control over. They look for the positives, knowing that they are powerless over many things that happen in life. Also, optimists believe that bad news is an isolated event or a difficult situation, "which too shall pass." Problems are seen as temporary and changeable. Optimists continue trying to attain their goals despite obstacles and setbacks. They believe that with persistence and hope, they will succeed.

Another way to strengthen your emotional resilience is to remember that you only have to get through today, so just take one day at a time. Judith Sills suggests that you maintain your usual daily routine by focusing on each task you need to accomplish during a crisis, seeking spiritual support from your higher power or reading inspirational material, and sharing your problems with family, friends, or colleagues. She also suggests engaging in activities you enjoy that will keep your mind occupied, such as cooking, gardening, meditating, or exercising, to escape temporarily from daily pressures. Other suggestions to attain emotional resilience include the following: practice being patient, surrender to the fact that life isn't fair, choose your battles wisely, set aside quiet time daily, practice random acts of kindness, and remember to breathe before you speak. In addition, you need to enjoy each day as it comes, and not be afraid of what it may bring, so that fear doesn't prevent you from enjoying the many positive, pleasant moments in your life.

Health Benefits of Emotional Resilience

In a study of stress, Harvard scientists found that those who coped poorly with stress were four times more likely to become ill than those with good coping skills. For many women, the ability to stay calm and healthy amidst life's constant stressors comes down to dealing with the small things, or life's daily hassles. Your emotional reactions or overreactions to daily hassles are often the best predictors of your physical and psychological health. Research has shown that getting emotionally upset over chronic, unavoidable irritations and hassles is more harmful to your health than your reactions to major crises.

In addition to stressors creating problems, your emotions and moods affect how you respond or react to problems. According to Dr. Goleman, we influence each others' emotions, because emotions are contagious. Your emotions are like magnets—they may attract or repel others. Women are constantly "sending" and "catching" each other's moods or emotions, and they are more susceptible than men. When you are happy, vibrant, and enthusiastic, others may be attracted to you and feel as though good things will happen. If you do not let anything interfere with your loving feelings, you empower your emotional magnet so that your love and joy attract the same feelings from others. In contrast, when others suffer from emotional pain, frustration, disappointment, or anxiety, you may catch their moods and feel dreary, sad, or depressed. If you have heavy, dark feelings and tensions because of fear and self-destructive thinking, Dr. Meltzer suggests that you try to eliminate these feelings, as they can become self-fulfilling prophecies.

Your moods and emotions also affect your brain chemicals, which change as your feelings change, and can affect your mind/body. Dr. Meltzer believes that when you are not in touch with your real feelings, you may become addicted to work or obsessed with drugs, money, sex, gambling, or alcohol, or develop co-dependent relationships. Then you'll need to examine those deep hidden recesses of your soul and the love in your heart to face emotional problems. Dr. Meltzer recommends that you take time to examine your choices and make thoughtful decisions from your heart. No matter what you are going through, you can find happiness if you keep in touch with the love in your heart. Happiness also teaches you to turn your conflicts into opportunities and successes and create your own emotional fulfillment.

When you are relaxed and happy, a glow radiates from your heart and face. Happy, relaxed people make good choices. They reach out to others, have kinder and gentler thoughts of others, and they don't punish themselves by abusing food, drugs, or alcohol. A positive mood stimulates your adrenaline and noradrenaline, which generates enthusiasm for your work and increases your energy. You work best when these hormones are in your system. When you are tired, stressed, or feel threatened, your body produces cortisol, which alters your immune system and is detrimental to your health.

Women are still largely responsible for setting the tone and pace of the home and family life. One of their greatest challenges is to sustain an atmosphere that nourishes the body and mind and helps family members bounce back from adversity. Dr. Meltzer writes that positive loving feelings nourish your whole being—heart, mind, body, and soul. So listen to your heart and body—they will tell you what you need to do. Trust your instincts or gut feelings. By keeping in touch with the love in your heart and appreciating the blessings in your life, you can stay centered and emotionally balanced. Expect to find joy and seek fulfillment in every experience. From the depths of your self-confidence, consistently create positive new emotional experiences.

When you are emotionally balanced, you live each precious moment to its fullest. You can cherish yourself, acknowledge the beauty in others and around you, and appreciate the love within you. To achieve emotional resilience and balance, work toward strengthening your emotional self-awareness, self-confidence, and self-control during difficult situations in your life. These traits—managing your strong impulses, staying calm while under stress, and addressing your problems rather than avoiding them—are the core of emotional resilience. Also, when you make a commitment to yourself to be happy and healthy, you'll enjoy a higher quality of life. ℬ

7

Hardiness—challenge, control, and commitment

Individuals with hardiness believe that they have the power to change things and that change stimulates their growth and development. They feel in control and expect situations to be challenging, so they react to stressful events by increasing their interaction in them through exploring, controlling, and learning from them. Through these actions, Dr. Joan Borysenko believes that women with this trait transform their stressful problems into a different frame of reference which revolves around continued personal growth and understanding.

A sense of control over most situations is vital to your health and well-being. Some women are reluctant to act freely and with certainty, though they may be aware of their options and choices. Many women have been conditioned to give unselfishly and suppress their own desires. They often give to others, deny their own right to take, and become resentful if they feel unappreciated, according to Domar and Dreher. If you think you've lost control over too many things in your life, you are more vulnerable to all types of mental and physical illnesses. You don't always need actual control, but you do need to believe you have some control over those events that affect you.

Women who feel in control of their life can handle an enormous amount of change and thrive on it. A zest for life and a sense of being in control can strengthen your immune system. When you feel you have some influence over your work, relationships, and other situations, you have the perception of control. This gives you the ability to handle daily stressors with fewer physical or emotional health problems.

In the 1970s, Dr. Suzanne Kobasa Quellette, a psychologist at the City University of New York, began to study personality traits that influence how people respond to stress. From her numerous studies, she found that people with the trait "hardiness," which consists of three factors—control, challenge, and commitment—were able to handle stress-related problems and resist diseases better than others. These people view any stressor or problem as a challenge rather than as a crisis, which buffers unhealthy responses to difficult situations.

Definition of Hardiness

In an article on Hardiness and Health, Dr. Kobasa and her associates defined hardiness as the ability to endure stressful events while maintaining peak levels of mind/body health, and to recover readily from devastating circumstances. The three components of hardiness, which are described below, are not mutually exclusive, but inextricably intertwined. Each woman applies a unique mixture of these factors when she responds to specific demands or problems.

Control is the belief that you can influence situations to become more manageable, and your willingness to act on that belief rather than feeling helpless. Hardy people take control of their life and health by using their knowledge, skills, imagination, and choice. They do not feel they have to be at the mercy of events or that they are passive recipients of their fate. People who exhibit control believe and behave as if they have influence over their life. They have a sense of mastery, confronting problems with confidence in their ability to devise and implement effective solutions. Henry Dreher, author of *The Immune Power Personality*, writes that healthy control implies that you feel empowered, while unhealthy control implies a hunger for power. People who don't believe they have control feel powerless, lack self-confidence and initiative, and tend to respond to extreme pressure with helpless resignation.

Challenge is the attitude that many changes in your life are normal events, and the belief that these changes can stimulate your personal growth rather than threaten your security. Dreher believes that individuals with high challenge rise to the occasion because they view change and chaos as challenges to overcome rather than feeling threatened or defeated by adverse situations. Hardy individuals are open and adaptable, which enables them to face stressful events boldly and enthusiastically. People who lack challenge avoid change, risk-taking, and exploration, and seek comfort and security.

Commitment is a strong sense of purpose and meaning expressed by becoming actively involved in life events rather than avoiding them. It is an attitude of curiosity and active involvement in what is happening, investing your time and energy to overcome problems. Dreher says that committed individuals do not give up easily—they are not quitters. They find meaning and have goals and a sense of purpose in their relationships, work, and projects, so despite obstacles they keep moving along to achieve their goals. People with low commitment lack meaning and purpose in life, are alienated from their work and/or relationships, and avoid commitment because of fear, uncertainty, or boredom.

How to Develop Hardiness

Your personality is not a fixed entity, but rather a dynamic sense of self interacting with an ever-changing world. According to Dreher, your personality is not solely based on your genetic inheritance, early experience, psycho-social development, circumstances, or viewpoint. It is a result of all these factors, along with continuously interacting with others in your life. This helps you become a unique, vibrant, and unpredictable person.

Your perception or interpretation of any stressful situation determines how well you cope with problems as they occur. The Borysenkos, who co-wrote The Power of the Mind to Heal: Renewing Body, Mind and Spirit, define stress as "the perception of physical or emotional threat coupled with the perception that your responses are inadequate to cope." Your ability to cope with chaos and change determines whether you will have hope and grow with the situation, or feel helpless and overcome by it. Once you have faced your fears, the most important thing is to learn how to live your life—not only in spite of fears, but in a fuller, more joyful way. Hardy people see change and crisis as a challenge rather than a threat. Even when they cannot control the outer situation, they realize that they always have control over their response to the things happening around them. There is a wise saying, suffering is inevitable, but misery is optional.

Since daily stress is usually unavoidable, concentrate your time, talents, and energy on those things you can do something about and try to avoid the others. Try to control what you can, and ignore that which you can't control. The famous serenity prayer by Reinhold Niebuhr, *God grant me the serenity to accept the things I cannot change, the courage to change the things I can, and the wisdom to know the difference,* aptly describes the meaning of control. In other words, you have a choice to find serenity within you when you cannot change things, to act courageously in your relationships, work, and unique pursuits, and to use wisdom in deciding when to act and when to let go.

Hardy people also thrive on change and crises because they are committed to a set of values that puts their problems into a positive frame of reference. Dr. Meltzer believes that your purpose in life changes as your values change, and they guide you toward maintaining or developing special relationships at home and work. People who are committed to their values and purpose in life, such as being needed or useful and enriching others' lives, are less stressed than those who lack this commitment. Those with a purpose in life are happier, healthier, and feel a sense of freedom.

Some successful hardiness training programs have been developed to teach "transformational coping," a healthy way to think about and handle stressful events, rather than trying to avoid them. When you try to avoid concrete problems with potential solutions, you either maintain an unhappy status quo or make matters worse. In transformational coping, Dreher suggests that you first assess the event as an opportunity to challenge your problem-solving abilities rather than as a danger to your well-being. Next you devise and implement plans (control) to change your environment or yourself to meet the challenge. Lastly, you follow through with conviction (commitment). People who assess an event as a threat or danger rather than an opportunity, such as pessimists, lose themselves in distractions and retreat from their stressful environment because they feel helpless. They may begin to feel depressed, angry, withdrawn, or abandoned. Those with hardiness traits buffer the effects of stress on their bodies by confronting the stressful event. This prevents them from lapsing into anger, depression, or helplessness—which can harm your immune and cardiovascular systems. Also, by becoming involved with your sources of stress, you can alter your environment and relationships to reduce the stress.

In his book describing immune power personality traits, Dreher described four steps used in hardiness training programs: focusing on your problems; reconstructing the situation; taking decisive action; then processing feedback and sometimes resorting to compensatory self-improvement. These steps are described below.

1. *Focusing on your problems.* Often we skim the surface of our awareness of stress and conflict, accepting common labels for our problems instead of looking within to define and fully understand our problems. Focusing helps you shift your perceptions from the usual to the personal, which is a prerequisite for a meaningful personality change. Many women have difficulty getting in touch with their authentic emotions and creative impulses because they have kept them buried under layers of defense and countless adjustments to please and appease others. One purpose of focusing is to recover the feelings and desires that you may have neglected in early life. The other is to discover your essential needs, goals, and emotions related to your present stressful situations.

The first step in focusing is to find a comfortable place, a retreat from daily distractions, and turn your attention inward. Think about your problems and experience your bodily reactions. If no specific event comes to mind, ask yourself, what stands in the way of my being happy and fulfilled? Next, find the word, phrase, or image that best captures these sensations and represents your mind/body state as accurately as possible. It could reflect an emotion (sadness, joy, anger), a thought, or an attitude (indifference, competitiveness). The word, sentence, or picture you choose should label the sensation you feel. This period of moving between sensations and labels helps you develop a better awareness of your stressful problem, so you can begin to understand the causes and effects of your problem. With a better understanding, you can integrate your deeper feelings about a situation with your attitudes, thoughts, and perspectives on that issue. Once you identify the core issues and find appropriate labels, you may feel a sense of relief. Next, ask yourself about your levels of commitment, control, and challenge toward the specific circumstances. Your answers will help you develop a new perspective, understand the dynamics involved in your problem, and use the following steps toward hardiness with greater success.

2. *Reconstructing the situation.* This is an exercise in imagination that frees you to initiate actions connected to control, challenge, and commitment. You use your imagination and intelligence to view the

event objectively from several different angles and to devise specific strategies for effective coping. According to Dreher, there are seven steps in situational reconstruction:

1. Identify the major stressful circumstances or events in your life today.
2. Imagine three ways in which they could have been worse and write them down.
3. Imagine three ways in which they could have been better and write them down.
4. For each of the three "worst-case" events, write down a scenario to explain it.
5. For each of the three "best-case" events, write down a scenario to explain it.
6. Consider exactly what you could have done, or still can do, to increase your chances for the best-case scenarios to occur or happen.
7. After determining what actions would bring about a desired outcome, the final step is to carry them out.

Understanding the purpose of reconstructing the situation is a key to success. When you imagine ways in which the case could have been worse, you gain a new perspective and understanding and can develop a balanced view of your circumstances. Imagining only the worst outcomes leads to heightened stress, decreased self-esteem, and possibly increased health problems. Imagining best-case scenarios is a powerful mind/body approach to hardiness and health. When you feel and see pictures of yourself effectively solving problems, this exercise moves you toward creative possibilities.

The advantage of reconstructing the situation is that you use both the imagining and reality-based parts of your brain. Imagining best-case scenarios without investigating what needs to be changed can become mere wishful thinking rather than success. Instead, the entire process helps you identify a specific plan of action based on the realization of what you can do to attain the best-case scenario. Through this process of self-reflection, you choose actions designed to increase your self-esteem, sense of meaning, and potential for success. But keep your plan based on reality and be careful not to set standards of behavior, performance, or achievement that are beyond your reach.

3. *Taking decisive action and processing feedback.* The purpose of taking decisive action is to reduce your stressful circumstances. By taking action, you learn that you have more control than you thought you had. Action plans are not fixed programs designed to help you achieve your defined ideas of success. They are dynamic strategies to learn more about yourself and what is meaningful to you and to others and to learn what conditions can help strengthen your hardiness. When you take decisive action, you get feedback from observing yourself, from other people observing you, and from the reactions of people toward whom your decisive actions are directed.

4. *Compensatory self-improvement.* Sometimes no amount of focusing or reconstructing a situation leads to a viable action plan. There may be some circumstances that cannot be changed and must be accepted graciously rather than banging your head against a wall. It is equally important to prevent these circumstances from leading you into feeling helpless, a position which leads to depression, self-pity, or self-destructiveness. The article by Kobasa and associates explains that compensatory self-improvement means finding another stressful problem—usually related to the initial circumstance—that you can do something about, then taking decisive action in that area.

Mind/body researchers found that several other stress reduction strategies such as meditation, relaxation, and visualization may enhance your health by increasing your sense of control. People who regularly practice meditation in a disciplined fashion develop a commitment to their own well-being, learn a sense of control over their mind/body, and take on the challenge of expanding their awareness and healing potential. Some of these strategies may help boost your hardiness. But unless you also increase your commitment, control, and challenge, they will not contribute to long-term stress reduction. In a book chapter, Inquiries into Hardiness, Quellette wrote that each of these mind/body techniques is a solitary exploration in self-awareness and healing and may help you build hardiness in only one area—your inner physical and spiritual life. But unless all three factors—control, challenge, and commitment—are integrated into a broad program of change, these strategies won't transform your ability to deal with stress.

However, Dreher states that improving your hardiness does not depend on individual stress-reducing techniques. Instead, it involves a heartfelt decision to examine how your life is going. At some point people realize that there are lots of things that they like and don't like in their lives, and decide to examine what is important to them and where they want to go. Your most profound changes may start with simple questions. Dreher offers the following suggestions to help you develop or strengthen your hardiness. Make three columns on a sheet of paper, then label them with the words Commitment, Control, and Challenge. Under the word Commitment write, "What is important to me and where do I want to go? Under 'Control' write, Where do I have influence? and Where am I avoiding influence? and under Challenge write, What inspires me? and Where have I lost my inspiration? Now scan your mind for the things you like and dislike in your life, including your family life, relationships, occupation, leisure activities, creative pursuits, and friendships, and write your answers in the columns. Let your answers guide you to take the necessary steps to increase your hardiness, by following the four steps described in the preceding pages.

Individuals with hardiness are proactive types who assess problems, devise creative solutions, and carry out their plans of action. Despite chaos and change going on around them, they believe in their own personal power and ability to control parts of their lives, but not in absolute power. Perceiving the difference between healthy and unhealthy control takes practice, but you can learn to distinguish between them. If you think you need absolute, total control over all situations in your life—which is impossible—you may be fighting a sense of helplessness. The need for total control comes from feelings of inadequate self-confidence. Domar and Dreher, authors of *Healing Mind, Healthy Woman*, write that some women try to direct every action and person within their realm for fear that if they don't their hopes and desires may not be realized. When things don't go according to their plans, they tend to blame themselves for their problems, and there may be some truth to this. They may have self-degrading thoughts because they believe that they failed to control situations; this leaves no room for human error.

A woman with a healthy sense of control has a deep-seated belief in her own ability to change stressful situations, or at least change her reactions to them. She has confidence that she can improve the conditions of her life and health, and does not assume responsibility for everyone else's problems, others' behaviors, or for her own diseases. She accepts the fact that many factors are not under her control. Hardy women have a balanced view of their own power. They search diligently for realistic leverage in any situation and take whatever action seems appropriate. In addition, they recognize situations over which they have minimal influence, and know when to ignore or gracefully remove themselves from these, including avoiding traps of co-dependence and terminal frustration. These women have a balanced sense of control which is both internal—they can influence but not command—and external—they know they can change many stressful situations, but they can't run other people's lives.

Health Benefits of Hardiness

From her research studies, Dr. Kobasa Quellette found that hardiness can both affect the way you deal with stressors and soften the impact on your immune system, so you are more resistant to illness. In a study of several hundred women, she concluded that hardier women developed fewer mental and physical illnesses. A study of women with rheumatoid arthritis showed that those with hardiness had a better functioning immune system, more T-cells, and better overall health. Hardiness not only balanced their immunity, it also improved the health of these women with a potentially disabling disease. In other words, people can compensate for genetic predispositions to certain diseases by developing healthy personality traits to cope with stress. In addition, Dreher reports that individuals with hardiness tend to seek and use family members and friends for social support in a healthy manner to bolster their self-worth and self-efficacy, while people low in hardiness sometimes use support to reinforce their position of alienation, passivity, and dependence.

Most research studies suggest that hardiness has a positive influence over well-being, the type of coping methods people use, and the practice of healthy behaviors. In many respects hardiness is the opposite of helplessness: those who feel helpless believe they have little control and often have difficulty coping with many of their problems. People with low hardiness usually feel helpless in stressful circumstances, writes Dreher. They may retreat from situations where they feel threatened and may perceive change as unnecessary, often dwelling instead on their own negative emotional reactions. In addition, Borysenko says they may magnify the effects of negative consequences on their own well-being, become alienated from friends or activities, and feel powerless to change things. These people are likely to become ill when stressful events occur because they feel helpless in the midst of change and turmoil, which suppresses their immune system.

When a major tragedy or catastrophe occurs, hardiness may not allay anxiety or depression during the period. However, once the crisis has passed, hardy women have fewer residual symptoms of anxiety and depression. Periods of anxiety and depression are understandable and perhaps unavoidable when you have no control over certain painful events. Quellette's research suggests that hardiness will increase your resilience after you have weathered the crisis. When women openly express their fears, pain or sadness, they bounce back more rapidly to their usual well-being. ♡

8

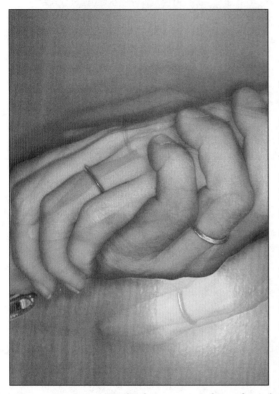

Loving and Trusting Relationships

Love is the most powerful and still the most unknown energy of the world.
—*Pierre Teilhard de Chardin*

A close and loving relationship is the most important of all human needs and the most powerful healing force in the universe, writes Dr. Dean Ornish, author of *Love and Survival.* Everyone needs to love and feel needed and loved by others. Dr. Meltzer believes that in loving relationships you feel cherished, appreciated, valued, and cared about by your partner. Mutual love, trust, affection, loyalty, and respect are the crucial factors in long-lasting, supportive relationships. Studies of various age and ethnic groups have found that good, close relationships, followed by a happy marriage, generate the greatest amount of happiness. Couples in a happy marriage are physically healthier, experience less emotional stress, and are more productive in their jobs than unhappily married couples.

Your happiness, emotional security, and capacity for self-expression depend closely on how well you relate to others. Loving people are happy people because they feel others' love and show it. The deeper your love for others, the more meaningful your life will be. In his book, *The Ten Rules of High Performance Living*, Dr. Meltzer suggests that each night you might ask yourself, "how much love did I show other people in my life?" Do you tell important people in your life, "I love you"? Your love and

faith can open your heart, mind, and body to your healing consciousness. With love in your heart and courage to back you up, you
can accomplish many goals.

Definition—what is love?

Love is a choice about how you feel about and relate to another
person. It is a way of thinking, not a way of feeling, writes Paul Pearsall,
author of *The Ten Laws of Lasting Love*. When you truly think about and
know love, you'll begin to feel it. Love consists of thoughts, words, and
actions that bring out the best in you and others. The essence of love is
the realization that you are what you love. The way you love usually
defines the way you live. Love is first based in caring for another as you
care for yourself. Bloomfield and Cooper, authors of *The Power of 5*, say
long-lasting love is an emotional process that requires time to experience a deepening sense of being together, frequently sharing love and
intimacy, and weaving them into memories of your love story.

Wise Thoughts about Love

Good marriages are made by being the right partner, not by
finding the right partner. Pearsall emphasizes that strong marriages are
more tolerant than confronting, more forgiving than argumentative, and
more compromising than demanding. They radiate a mature and stable
love that can be felt by others. The relationship is primary above all else
and determines every decision, wish, and prayer. Partners learn to think
as one: both are vulnerable, mutually supportive, and interdependent.
Over time, they've learned to think, feel, fear, and grow together. This
requires time, effort, patience, tolerance, forgiveness, and a willingness to
continue learning about each other.

Happy couples relax and enjoy each other's company, which
reduces tension and can help make their relationship last. Bloomfield and
Cooper recommend engaging in daily touching and talking to help syn-
chronize with your partner's rhythms and provide essential cues that help
renew intimate bonds after time apart. Touching and talking are vital to
retain closeness and passion in your relationship.

Joan Borysenko, who wrote *Minding the Body, Mending the Mind*,
believes that our emotions fall into two broad categories—love and fear.
Love is associated with openness, a sense of letting go, and relaxation.
Fear is associated with defense of the body—muscle tension, rapid
heart beat, and a sense of holding tight. Learning to love and let go

is important to reduce stress and achieve peace of mind. However, you cannot give or receive love if you feel unlovable, says Martha Beck, author of the article, Love-your-life Guide. Many women spend much of their lives trying to make sure no one will criticize or reject them. They may say they are doing things for love, when they are really motivated by fear of others' disapproval, judgment, or anger. You need to act on love, not fear of being unloved. Beck writes that truly loving actions always really matter, but actions based on fear of disapproval never really matter.

In the majority of contemporary marriages, partners join together to enhance the "self." This is the expected, efficient, and convenient way to live, states Pearsall. It is well suited to our modern lifestyle of personal growth and self-enhancement, and demands less time and effort. It is a way to fulfill oneself and get through life, along with an efficient way to raise children, advance one's career, and accomplish household tasks. Many couples find this type of marriage is happier, easier, more secure, predictable, and less demanding of their time. In *great* marriages, the self is silent and replaced with "our" way, says Pearsall. This means compromising, letting things go, being open to learning from one's partner, and seeking happiness by making a better life together rather than for oneself. Freedom comes with the opportunity to learn, understand, ask, hope, and discover mutually with someone else. Both partners learn to accept disappointments and chaos, acknowledge their problems and forgive, then combine their mutual talents.

How to Develop and Maintain Healthy, Loving Relationships

There are several major characteristics of couples who maintain lasting, loving relationships—commitment, realistic expectations, good communication, ability to settle arguments lovingly, understand gender differences, and share power and workload equally. Each of these characteristics is discussed, and where possible, the ideal relationship is described, followed by problems and possible solutions.

Commitment and Time Spent Together

Couples who are happy together chose to be committed to each other and their relationship. Their commitment, desire, and belief in their partnership are the foundation for their marriage. When they view marriage as their top priority, they appreciate what

unrealistic expectations of your partner's behavior. You can remove these expectations and share more love by reminding yourself that it isn't your partner's responsibility to satisfy all your needs and guarantee your happiness. His or her task is to give you a safe and warm place to cope with the bad stuff, while they struggle with their own problems.

When one partner doesn't live up to the other's imagined expectations, often that person becomes upset, as if a basic trust has been broken. Bloomfield and Cooper wrote that once trust is lost, a major shift occurs in how you feel about your partner and your relationship. Even your memory gets altered and you may react with dread to almost everything your partner says or does. You may feel constantly on guard against attack.

Your chances of staying married are what you make them, based on your beliefs about your marriage and whether or not you choose to be a loving, proactive partner. One prevailing belief is that marriage is not supposed to be exciting; this allows us to think our life is normal if it is stifled and boring. Page says another belief is that marriage is not supposed to be joyful; this helps you rationalize your own joyless marriage. To have a joyful marriage, you must change your mind-set. The solution is to move beyond your high expectations and find the attitudes, actions, and simple day-to-day pleasures that help create a beautiful and enduring partnership.

Pearsall suggests that you practice the art of discovery by acting as if you've never seen your partner before. Erase your judgments and listen to his words so you can explore the man you are with. Break the bonds of past experiences and cast aside your unmet expectations. Clear your mind, be in the present, and look your partner in the eye. When you talk, try to connect with your partner as if you may never see him again. Engage your partner at a heart level, and find where you can exist in harmony. Then develop a trust to move you through the tough times together.

COMMUNICATION

Good communication is essential to the quality of any relationship and for family harmony. True heart-to-heart communication takes time and effort. It takes courage to look within yourself and honestly express what you feel, and to open yourself to rejection. True communication has important long-term rewards in self-knowledge and better understanding of others. Those who express their authentic feelings, listen to what others have to say, and respond with love and compassion find that communication is a rich and rewarding experience. It is one of the most important factors that influences our health.

Ineffective communication is a common problem in relationships, marriages, and families, and is often the catalyst for all other marital problems. In his book, *52 Simple Steps to Natural Health*, Mark Mayell states that poor communication can create problems in all areas of life and lead to loneliness, family problems, job dissatisfaction, stress, and even illness. The erosion of heart-to-heart communication seems to have increased over the decades. One study found that married couples spend an average of only seven minutes a week talking to each other. No matter what problems couples face, each partner often has different points of view, and those differences must be respected rather than ignored or invalidated. Even though couples don't always agree, honest, open communication between partners facilitates a possible resolution of problems.

Some steps to develop good communication and intimacy between partners are to: identify your feelings; disclose your feelings and needs; listen carefully and acknowledge your partner's feelings; and work toward intimacy—becoming connected. Each step is discussed in the following paragraphs.

Identify Your Feelings

First, it is important to recognize your feelings for what they are, not what you think you ought to feel. Ornish writes that even knowing what you feel at a given moment can be difficult because it requires paying attention to your emotional self. Recognizing your own emotions may give you a clue as to how your partner is feeling, since "hearts tend to resonate with each other."

Disclose Your Feelings and Needs

The key to heartfelt communication with your partner and family members is your willingness to reveal some of your inner self. Once you realize what you are feeling, it is important to share it. Self-disclosure is the starting point for genuine intimacy. Although self-disclosure may be frightening, it can lead to building a real relationship in which partners are free to be who they are, according to Julia Cameron, author of *The Artist's Way*. It means that partners tell each other about all their important feelings and events in their private lives, and don't keep significant secrets from each other. The healing powers of self-disclosure may explain why close, personal relationships predict health. Ornish says to be careful to express your feelings, not your thoughts, and tell others directly and clearly what and how you feel, because "thoughts connect your heads, while feelings join your hearts." If you want or need something, let your partner know. If your partner is doing something that bothers you, tell him why it bothers you and what you would like him to do about it. The experience of sharing openly and honestly with others allows those you love to truly know and understand you.

Women's lives revolve around connecting and nurturing others to foster intimacy. American men often have fewer friends for social support than American women do. Usually a man's wife is his best friend, and sometimes she is the only one with whom he feels comfortable sharing his feelings. Page believes that couples must share their thoughts and feelings or they risk losing touch with what is important in their marriage. One measure of your progress in learning to share your feelings is how much time passes between when you recognize a feeling and when you're ready to talk about it. The shorter the time, the sooner your relationship and own emotional health will improve.

Listen To and Acknowledge Your Partner's Feelings

Besides sharing your own thoughts and feelings, remember to listen with an open mind to what your partner is saying and feeling. Respect each other's opinion, even if you can't find an immediate solution to a problem. Spend time discussing problems and issues you think are important. Also watch for the unspoken feelings that may be expressed in body language, actions, and facial expressions. Sometimes words say one thing, but body language reflects something completely different. Gently probe for buried feelings if your partner seems willing to benefit from expressing them. Don't try to solve or fix your partner's problems or eliminate his or her pain. Someone else can't do that for you and you can't do it for someone else. Your best approach is to listen, empathize, and generally be available.

Acknowledge your partner's feelings with empathy, caring, and compassion. Tell your partner what you think he said by summarizing his words. This can reveal any areas of misinterpretation or misunderstanding and prevent future fights. It is important to understand each other's viewpoints. Stephen Covey, author of *The 7 Habits of Highly Effective*

Families, says that the key to success in life is the ability to understand another person's view and see things from his perspective. He reminds us to "seek first to understand, then to be understood."

If your partner expresses thoughts and judgments, try to avoid the attack–withdrawal–counter-attack trap. When you feel you've been wronged, try stepping into his shoes. Ornish suggests that you ask yourself what your partner is going through that caused his insensitivity, thoughtlessness, or egotism. Don't deny your own feelings, but try to resolve them in a healthy way. If you feel inappropriately judged, you might say, "I'm feeling judged and attacked, and I don't like it."

Work Toward Intimacy—becoming connected

Both men and women desire intimacy and connection in their loving relationships. True intimacy is completely mutual and can occur at any time or age, but it is impossible to be intimate with someone who is not intimate in return. By sharing your innermost feelings and private thoughts, you form stronger connections and closer intimacy with your mate. Long-term intimacy develops as partners share their inner lives, along with a range of feelings and events. Successful couples are well matched in their ability to be intimate. They are deeply invested in each other's spiritual and personal growth. They are completely there for each other, emotionally open, caring, attentive, and accepting. They say what they mean, and mean what they say in a kind and loving way. If a couple continue to share their feelings and their sense of adventure about life, their love will grow. Marital intimacy, commitment, and support provide emotional benefits, says Page. They reduce loneliness and offer a dependable lover and companion. When partners must share events or feelings that may cause the other pain, they time them carefully and are kind and compassionate.

Openly sharing one's feelings on a personal level is very difficult for some people. The decision to become increasingly open, to reveal your vulnerability, and to work at letting go of your defenses is scary. Page writes that some people fear that intimacy will reduce their freedom and autonomy, or they will lose part of themselves. Cameron recognized that in troubled relationships, partners may avoid each other because they don't want to hear what the other is thinking for fear it might hurt them. Others are afraid that if they open up, they risk giving their partner power over them, although others only have power over you if they have something you need. And some people withhold negative feelings due to shame, frustration, or depression. Dr. Ornish feels that if you know who you are, and where your inner peace comes from, you're empowered. However, if there is no one you trust to open up to, defenses that you think will protect you may actually further isolate you from others. Often the behaviors we think will protect us actually weaken us. And if you don't express your feelings and needs, don't expect your partner to read your mind.

Settle Arguments Lovingly

The Golden Rule of Love is: relate first, resolve second. One of the most difficult parts of a loving relationship is handling differences and disagreements without arguments, anger, and hostility. Occasional conflicts are unavoidable between a married couple or partners. Arguments are okay when they are fair, honest disputes about priorities or family policies. Before arguments become a problem, couples should talk about what constitutes a fair fight. Studies indicate that happy and unhappy couples have about the same number and type of problems. Even when two people care deeply for each other, their communication often gets mixed up, leading to arguments or shattering the bond between them. Whether couples stay together or grow apart depends more on how they deal with conflicts than on what they fight about, writes Mayell. How couples handle misunderstandings and conflicts determines whether the problems are resolved, a major fight occurs, or the relationship even survives the ensuing years.

It is more important to be able to deal with emotions that arise during arguments than to solve marital problems. It is impossible to resolve problems in a relationship if either partner feels misunderstood, unappreciated, or ignored. On the positive side, conflict can play a positive role by provoking change and growth in both partners.

Personal relationships can cause serious emotional stress when arguments, intense disagreements, and insults occur on a regular basis. When you argue or disagree with your partner, your first tendency may be to try to win him over to your side. During an argument, Bloomfield and Cooper say all it takes is one "zinger" to trigger instant anger or alienation in a partner. Anger impairs judgment and impedes communication. Everyone has "hot buttons," and when pushed, they set off an emotional reaction. Zingers can affect your partner's emotions like an unexpected electric shock, and should be avoided.

The worst habits that add to problems during conflict are criticism, contempt, and stonewalling. The most damaging reactions are defensiveness, stubbornness, and withdrawal from interaction. When two people become angry, one may be speechless, cry, yell, or even leave the room. In *Working with Emotional Intelligence*, Goleman listed other unfair tactics such as bringing unrelated subjects into an argument, interrupting, or using sarcasm, threats, or jokes. When these reactions, habits, or tactics become the norm during conflicts, one partner may become agitated and mentally disorganized.

The impact of intense emotional episodes depends on attitude and maturity. Some people carry grudges for years over real or imagined insults, while others deal with them, forget them, and go on living a healthy life. In any intense exchange with a spouse, it's normal for some negative thoughts and feelings to arise. Christopher Hobbs writes in *Stress and Natural Healing* that there are many unwanted consequences of holding in negative feelings generated by emotional upsets. Since we are "nice" women, we stuff it, deny it, bury it, or block and hide our anger, says Cameron. Suppressing angry feelings can lead to greater stress and block the flow of energy within your mind and body. Unexpressed anger can poison intimacy in several ways. You may hold it in until you explode and scare your partner. You may distance yourself from your partner rather than risk his anger, or your annoyance may leak out in passive-aggressive behavior such as sulking or lateness.

Anger is often fueled by negative judgments of others, which may lead to isolation. According to Dean Ornish, anything that promotes a sense of isolation among couples leads to chronic stress and sometimes to illnesses such as heart disease. Your approach to others determines whether you experience isolation, chronic stress, and suffering, or intimacy, relaxation, joy, and health. Your thoughts more than feelings are likely to be heard as criticisms, and when others feel criticized, it's very hard for them to hear anything else you say. Ornish suggests that you share your feelings in ways such that others do not feel attacked. Your feelings help connect you to others, whereas your thoughts, especially negative judgments, tend to isolate you and increase your distress. Joan Borysenko says that relief of anger is attained by releasing these negative thoughts and emotions.

Expressing anger directly, yet calmly, is a much more loving act than seething, and you accomplish what you need much sooner.

As long as negative thoughts don't become too extreme, most people are able to handle them. However, men usually have a difficult time handling relationship conflicts, while women have more problems with emotional distance. When negative thoughts become overwhelming or flood a partner, Bloomfield and Cooper believe this is often influenced by how much stress he or she has within and outside the relationship. Men become flooded far more easily than women, and their most common reaction is withdrawal to save themselves from feeling trapped and overwhelmed. One partner may become fixated in his or her perception of the other. If the problem is seen as the other person's, Mayell says that there is little possibility that change can occur. If the angry partner withdraws from the relationship, believing the problems can't be solved, it is almost impossible to reconcile.

In most relationships, women raise the majority of important issues. Consider your timing before starting an important discussion. Inform your partner beforehand what you want to discuss if there are potential problems involved. Don't avoid conflict, because then couples may never discuss issues, which often surface later. Some men try to avoid conflict by sidestepping or withdrawing from a problem when they feel threatened by hearing or expecting criticism, or sense that their partner is bringing up a difficult issue. This doesn't make the problem go away, and women just get more upset by this behavior. Women often interpret withdrawal as lack of caring, which it usually isn't. According to Bloomfield and Cooper, often a man is silent when he doesn't know what to say and is thinking about it. When a man feels threatened or challenged, his attention may focus on being right, rather than being kind or listening. He may not be aware of how uncaring or hurtful he sounds to his partner. And he has no idea that by his response, he is starting a quarrel because he thinks she is arguing with him. He defends his point of view while she defends herself from his barbed comments, which may hurt her feelings. Also, most men try to preserve their independence and negotiating status. They see talking as a kind of display of competition and showing what you know. Women must try to be flexible and handle problems in a calm, clear, and gentle way. They may need to clarify or reframe their dialogues. Try to be pleasantly persistent and let him know you are not attacking him and that you need his help in dealing with issues or conflicts in your relationship. Bloomfield and Cooper say that when you handle conflict con-structively, it can be a positive learning experience for both you and your partner. Constructive arguing means calmly discussing issues and really listening with an open mind. How flexible a couple is in handling their disagreements may determine the health and length of their relationship.

Whenever you experience and express hurt or angry feelings, try to avoid using blame, insults, and sarcasm with your partner, even when he doesn't respond as you had hoped. When you blame your partner, you merely reinforce the message that it's his job to keep you happy. That sets you up for disappointment and victimhood. Sometimes the fear of being alone seems worse than emotional or physical abuse and keeps women in a degrading relationship. You should never accept abuse or ill-treat-ment from your partner. Consider whether you are dealing with human shortcomings and inadequacies, or outright destructiveness, which is clearly unacceptable. For a successful relationship, Bloomfield and Cooper recommend that you say how you feel. The more concrete and specific your complaint, the more likely you are to improve your partner's understanding of why you're irritated, confused, or angry. Deal with one situation at a time, and don't make assumptions or try to read your partner's mind.

Editing or pausing to avoid saying destructive, negative com-ments in favor of something more polite combines courtesy and politeness, and prevents problems from escalating. Another approach is to use an *agreement frame* to establish rapport, share honest feelings and minimize resistance. For example, Bloomfield and Cooper suggest you say, "I agree with your basic idea and here's another angle..." or, "I respect your intense feelings about ...and here are some thoughts of my own." Use "I" statements to reflect your own feelings. These statements should be direct, immediate, clear, and straight. Mayell says that using "I" statements to describe the problem shows that you are taking responsibility rather than placing blame. It establishes your participation in the action, helps you observe the effect of your action, and states a need. It also encourages each person to explore his or her own feelings and put them into accurate words.

When problems get in the way Joan Borysenko recommends walking together to ease communication and allow silent pauses to occur more naturally. This can bring a strong feeling of connection. Don't try to discuss your problems immediately. Unwind a bit first and wait until tempers have cooled down before trying to discuss the situation. This helps restore a sense of control over the situation and will help solve problems. Allow the conversation to follow thoughts, ideas, and impressions as they come. If you and your partner are having problems with your relationship, walking together may be a way to alleviate stress. The tension can be reduced through the exercise.

There are conflicts in even the best and happiest relationships. You can resolve them more easily if you develop effective communication skills, and talk openly about your concerns when they arise, before they become major problems. Maintain a positive mind-set that you can work things out, and develop the ability to stand back and see situations objectively before arguments begin. Talk things through calmly, and try to understand your partner's point of view, so that you can reach a reasonable compromise. In *The Book of Stress Survival*, Alix Kirsta writes that it is not only what you say that affects how well you communicate, but your tone of voice, facial expression, movements, and gestures, which are nonverbal cues that reveal your true feelings. So be alert and sensitive to these cues, and express yourself clearly to encourage empathy. When problems seem insurmountable, remember that you have a choice of actions and attitudes which will enable you to cope more successfully. Emotional maturity, experience, and wisdom are your best tools in dealing with conflicts.

Understand and Accept Gender Differences

Maintaining healthy relationships is an ongoing process of discovery of each other and letting go of old expectations. According to John Gray, author of *Men Are from Mars, Women Are from Venus*, men and women not only communicate differently, but also think, feel, perceive, respond, and love differently. Women often share their feelings to seek acknowledgment, while men want to fix the problems for their partner. Many women expect men to feel and behave like women, but without a clear understanding of our differences, women may become demanding, resentful, judgmental, and intolerant.

Men value power, competency, efficiency, and achievement, according to Gray. They like to prove themselves and develop their power and skills because they feel fulfilled primarily through their successes and accomplishments. Women value love, relationships, communication, and beauty, and tend to spend their time supporting, nurturing, and helping others. Their sense of self is defined through their feelings and the quality of their relationships, so they find fulfillment through sharing and relating with others. Men are motivated when they feel needed, while women enjoy feeling cherished.

Women are generally concerned with living together in harmony and loving cooperation. Gray writes that women are relationship-oriented and pride themselves on being considerate of others' feelings and needs. They express their love by offering assistance to others without being asked. However, a man may feel offended when a woman offers unsolicited advice. He feels she does not trust his abilities or presumes that he can't do something himself, which can make him feel incompetent, weak, and unloved.

Some women need to learn how to win the support of a man and empower him to be all that he can be. A man feels empowered when he is trusted, accepted, appreciated, admired, and encouraged. The secret to empowering a man, according to Bloomfield and Cooper, is never to try to change or improve him, because then he feels controlled, manipulated, rejected, and unloved.

Share Power and Workload Equally

The relationship between partners should be based on a fair balance of give and take, a reciprocal two-way exchange, state Bloomflield and Cooper. In balanced relationships, both partners are secure in the other's love and find each other attractive. They are emotionally invested in the relationship, and try to fill various needs of the other. Pearsall notes that good partners compliment each other's strengths and limitations. Neither partner feels suffocated or emotionally slighted, nor tends to take the other for granted. In a great marriage, each partner knows that one is never complete without the other. They see each other as half of the whole marriage, says Pearsall.

Domestic equality is a good predictor of marital happiness. In a recent survey of almost 1300 women, *Redbook* reported their greatest stressors. The women indicated that the more their husband helped with household chores, the happier they were with their marriage. Almost two-thirds of the women who expressed high rates of marital dissatisfaction reported that their husband "seldom or never did a fair share of the housework." The less a husband helped with household chores, the more stressed and unhappy his wife was with the marriage. Overall, husbands were seen as being good providers, satisfying sexual needs, helping with family problems, and discussing things that were important to their wives.

Establishing a happy, long-lasting relationship is a major challenge for modern couples because extended family members are seldom nearby to offer emotional support. Many working wives and mothers suffer from stress as a result of trying to juggle their work or careers with family responsibilities. To make relationships healthy, women may need to change their expectations of themselves, their partners, and their relationships. What many women seek in an ideal relationship is emotional and intellectual fulfillment, intimacy, compatibility of interests, attitudes, and ambitions. This ideal motivates them to strive for more fulfilling and equally-balanced partnerships based as much on friendship and equality as on romantic love. Yet women may be more critical and less tolerant when they are dissatisfied. Kirsta writes that placing too many demands on a partner or having unrealistic expectations often causes stress and breakdown in the relationship. In *Healing Mind, Healthy Woman*, Domar and Dreher wrote that we all have complex relationships, and partners must accept each other's needs and respect each other's boundaries. There is a delicate balance between intimacy and separateness. Some relationships clearly need more closeness, while others need some distance. Couples may need to work on their relationship by openly expressing their needs, finding mutually acceptable areas of compromise, and achieving a fair balance of give and take, while complementing each other's strengths and accepting each other's limitations.

Health Benefits of Loving and Trusting Relationships

Marriage is no cure-all for one's problems. Although married people are generally healthier than singles, marital difficulties can lead to health problems. In his chapter on Social Support, Spiegel wrote that many studies have found that men and women who were unhappy with their marriages reported poorer health, and dissatisfied women experienced more depression than those who were satisfied with their marriages. Couples who were *least* satisfied seemed to get on each other's nerves more often than happily married couples. This may lead to persistent biochemical changes that could eventually weaken a partner's immune system.

Based on their numerous research studies of the immune system and personality traits, Kiecolt-Glaser and Glaser reported that marital conflict and disruption, including bereavement, separation, or divorce, depress the immune system for a while, and increase susceptibility to disease. Marital strife and poor marital quality were also associated with depression, which is caused by underlying anger, sadness, and mostly fear. Dr. Ornish also found that depression, loneliness, and isolation may predispose you to suffering, diseases related to reduced immune function, and premature death. People can even die of broken hearts and shattered dreams, when they ignore their need to experience love and spend time with loved ones.

A strong marriage is good for one's health. According to Dr. Ornish, love and intimacy are two of the most powerful factors affecting one's health, even more than exercise and a low-fat diet, because they improve health and healing. When people feel loved, good things happen in their bodies that reduce their risk of becoming sick and promote healing. Several studies have shown that men who believe in their wife's love and support are healthier and less likely to develop heart disease than those without a partner's love and support. Another study found that married women had better immune function overall than divorced women. Having a spouse to share your problems in stressful times can help keep you healthy. Love and emotional support provide a sense of purpose, meaning, and belonging in life. Scientific studies indicate that love truly is the healer, and kindness and compassion are the heart of healing. In *The Power of the Mind to Heal*, the Borysenkos reported that the heart, immune system, and hormones all respond in a positive way to the love, compassion, and connection you give yourself, your partner, and others around you.

In healthy love relationships, each partner makes a commitment to care about the other, as well as about him or herself and the relationship. Both partners must develop good communication skills and settle arguments lovingly. Domar and Dreher recommend that each partner value and respect the other for who he or she is. In solid marriages and love relationships, the fundamental needs for approval and appreciation are met by both partners. Share your joys, pleasures, and sense of humor with your partner so that the life and love you share will last much longer. ℬ

9

Optimism—positive attitudes

When you are happy, vibrant, and enthusiastic, good things will come to you. —Meltzer, 1998:80

ife is full of personal tragedies and crises, but most people eventually move on. Many people believe that your health is related to the genes you inherited, along with good eating habits and healthy lifestyle behaviors. This viewpoint fails to take into account how much your personality and perception of stressors influence your well-being. Your attitudes determine how you view and respond to life's events and challenges.

Although optimists experience the same problems and setbacks as pessimists, optimists react to them in a different way and are able to bounce back quickly rather than giving up and becoming depressed. Optimistic, positive thinking is one way to a healthy, happy life. Optimists are future-oriented—they use today to plan for tomorrow. Their outlook is realistic, yet hopeful. They consider the past as history, while pessimists think about what they "woulda, shoulda, coulda" done differently.

Optimism is considered a relatively stable personality trait, that can affect how an individual perceives and copes with various stressors. If it seems that good things happen more often to those who expect them, this is true when it comes to health. There is scientific evidence that several psychological traits, particularly optimism, contribute to good health. Martin Seligman, who wrote *Learned Optimism*, has studied optimism for several decades. He believes it is vitally important in overcoming defeat, in creating an enduring perseverance, in promoting achievement, and in maintaining or improving health. On the other hand, pessimism, fatalism, and resignation have been linked to poorer health. Thus, your attitude can be a self-fulfilling prophecy.

Definition of Optimism

Psychologists classify people as optimists or pessimists by how they explain why bad things happen to them. Optimists expect things to go their way, and generally believe that good rather than bad things will happen to them. They believe they can overcome problems that arise during the day, assuming that these problems are resolvable, and also that the problems are unlikely to be disruptive or to have adverse consequences.

In *Health and Optimism*, Peterson and Bossio suggest that optimism involves three components—mental, emotional, and motivational. When confronted with stressful situations, optimists use different coping strategies than pessimists—optimists believe their goals can be achieved, make plans, and persevere to achieve their goals, whereas pessimists are more likely to get upset and give up.

How to Become More Optimistic

Personality traits such as optimism and pessimism affect your health almost as much as physical factors do. When your world seems to be out of control, you may feel powerless, but you can still choose how you respond to unsettling events. In today's chaotic world, it's easy to be a pessimist, but pessimism is not a fixed and unchangeable trait. Just as people have learned to be helpless, they can relearn how to be hopeful. Seligman's theory of "learned helplessness," based on the belief that when life is out of your control, you may give up, is a form of pessimism. Learned helplessness is a major stumbling block to success—when you invent excuses for why you can't do something, the end result is that you usually can't do it. Your failures and disappointments in life can be a strong force for positive change when you view them with hopefulness. An optimistic explanatory style stops helplessness, whereas a pessimistic style generates helplessness, and pessimists often expect problems even though things are going well for them. Optimists are those who resist helplessness, do not easily become depressed when they fail, and do not give up easily. They may cling to the belief in a positive future against reasonable odds, which sometimes makes it happen—or they just keep trying.

While we all experience periodic low moods that may last for a short while, Seligman believes you can learn how to be more optimistic—and get out of the habit of seeing every problem in a negative, pessimistic way. This negative explanatory style can be changed into a positive style just by believing that you can change your thinking pattern. Seligman recommends developing *flexible optimism*, in which you view problems realistically rather than as something personal, pervasive, and permanent. He says that if your general mental attitude is one of flexible, real-life optimism, or hopefulness, you will reap many benefits. Flexible optimists usually keep one eye on reality and respond thoughtfully and resiliently to one situation at a time. They don't talk about how great things are when they're really bad, and they are usually able to bounce back from setbacks and shake off their failures in one area before moving on to the next problem. Flexible optimists generally exhibit a pragmatic, goal-oriented attitude, even in the face of difficulties. They tend to set realistic goals for themselves that are related to greater, more lasting achievements in their work, relationships, and health.

First, you need to be aware of your own typical explanatory style. Listen to yourself—how do you explain your hassles and problems? You might write down a recent problem you experienced, then identify what caused the problem. In *The Power of 5*, Bloomfield and Cooper suggest asking yourself, "Was the cause something I did, others did, or just circumstances?" according to your perception. Next, consider whether you think the cause will occur again in the future. Is the specific problem an isolated event, or does it influence other areas of your life? The goal of this exercise is to help you examine how you explain problems and setbacks to yourself and others, so that you can catch distorted, pessimistic thoughts and replace them with positive, optimistic ones.

Seligman offers three general ways to handle pessimistic beliefs—distraction, disputation, and distancing. *Distraction* is a simple but effective technique to interrupt habitual negative thought patterns by thought-stopping or attention-shifting. You can reduce ruminations by scheduling some time later for thinking about your problems, instead of obsessing about them while trying to accomplish other tasks. When something disturbing happens, and you find it hard to stop your thoughts about it, either tell yourself you'll review the problem at a specific time later, possibly with someone who can act as a sounding board, or jot down the problems and let them go. If you write down your problems and set aside a time to think about them, they no longer serve any purpose circling around in your mind.

Some people do not have much success trying to suppress unwanted thoughts, especially negative ones. The harder they try to push these thoughts away, the larger and stronger they come back. Instead, Bloomberg and Cooper suggest that you might find by just letting go of your efforts to suppress unwanted thoughts, and by mentally relaxing your mind, your thoughts will gradually move on to something else. In other words, when you stop resisting unwanted thoughts, they lose their power and soon diminish or fade away, and you'll quickly regain mental control.

Disputation is a technique where you find a reason or argument that disputes the logic of your beliefs when problems occur. It means that you change your views about your problems by changing your interpretation of them. Any time you find yourself upset, anxious, or angry, ask what you are saying to yourself. Learn to examine the evidence for accuracy. If your beliefs are accurate, then concentrate on ways to change the situation and prevent it from becoming worse. Pessimists frequently overreact with negative beliefs that distort the truth or are factually incorrect. For example, you may find that you blow things out of proportion, or personalize and blame yourself for something that happened, when in reality it was just bad timing or circumstances beyond your control. Challenge your thoughts instead of assuming your usual negative thinking, then try to think positively about resolving the problem.

Since most problems have many causes, consider alternatives by asking yourself, "Is there any other way to look at this problem?" Think about possible contributing factors, then focus on those that are changeable, specific, and nonpersonal causes. Even if your belief is correct, ask yourself what its implications are, and how likely they are to occur. Last, consider whether your belief is useful or would it be better to let it go. Is there a way to change the situation in the future? How can you go about changing it? You'll feel much better, more in touch with reality, and able to accomplish more this way.

Distancing is removing yourself from unfounded accusations about yourself and others, or from someone whose beliefs about you are contrary to your own. Beliefs may or may not be factual, but just because someone told you that you didn't measure up to his standards or meet her expectations, doesn't mean that he or she is right. You may need to get away from that person or situation and filter the statements through your own self-knowledge before you can objectively handle the criticism to determine if it has any merit. Then you may decide to avoid future encounters with that person, if possible, or to recognize that perhaps he is trying to blame you for his problems or shortcomings.

Optimists tend to use more active, problem-focused coping methods and to deal directly with the sources of their problems. They have more vigor and resilience, so they look for the best way to resolve difficult situations and may seek help from others. The Borysenkos, who wrote *The Power of the Mind to Heal*, believe that optimists are likely to reinterpret a situation positively, instead of using denial or distancing. Pessimists are likely to deny the reality of their problems and drop goals with which stressors interfere, and are often preoccupied with their own emotional distress.

Peterson and Bossio suggest that you try to make sense of bad events, so that you can soften their harmful effects. Search for the meaning and purpose of traumatic circumstances and try to learn whatever you can from the experience. You might ask yourself, "Why did this happen? Why did it happen to me? How can this experience make me a stronger or wiser person?" Your answers may give you a sense of coherence and help you regain control over your life.

Another strategy to develop optimism is first to identify your desired goals in life and then develop your own customized affirmations for success. Make time for quiet, calm, and serenity in order to search within yourself and ask for guidance. Listening to sacred or inspiring music may help you connect with your higher wisdom. If your message feels light and effortless, it's probably the right choice. If it feels dense and heavy, like an addictive craving, it's probably wrong for you. Learn to recognize your inner signals. Create a crystal clear vision—see it, hear it, feel it deep in your heart. Listen to your heart and body, your higher power, and your intuition.

Imagine strong inner images to get the energy and willpower to do things you wouldn't ordinarily do. Then supercharge your intentions with actions and let the universe work to connect you with good opportunities. Every day do one thing to bring you closer to your goals and dreams. Be different—take the steps that will get you closer to the life you envision. Ask yourself, "Will this action take me closer to my vision?" Align your daily actions with your vision. Your drive will become super-charged, powered-up by your desire to create the life you envision. Then, as positive experiences occur, express gratitude for all the wonderful things that are occurring in your life. Universal Law requires that you state your desires as if they have already been fulfilled, achieved, and are present now in your life. You need to act as if you were already there, because the subconscious mind can't tell the difference between what is real and what is imagined.

Your personality traits are like magnets that attract or repel others. Knowing what you want out of life can help you to consciously attract positive people, opportunities, and experiences that move you toward achieving your goals. Keep your attraction magnet focused on higher qualities—joy, love, gratitude, and living your dream. Your joy will lead you to people, places, and opportunities that will take you closer to your life's passion—your mission here on earth. Enlist the support of others who are upbeat, positive, going after what they want, doing something worthwhile for themselves and others. Keep your focus on the present and let your vision move you forward.

Sandra Lamb, author of How To Be a More Positive Person, offers several suggestions to increase your optimism. First, if you are a sedentary person, try to get some vigorous exercise daily to raise your serotonin levels. Second, find ways to get sufficient sleep at night, because inadequate or disturbed sleep can create mood prob-lems, and when coupled with stress or perceived failure, can contribute to pessimistic thought patterns. Third, remember to eat foods that are good for you: mood-altering foods such as caffeine and sugar can cause problems for pessimists. If your blood sugar falls, you'll lack the energy to produce mood-elevating serotonin, which helps you feel good.

In addition, Lamb recommends being good to yourself by engaging in your favorite activities to lift your mood and increase your self-esteem, such as singing, dancing, listening to music, meditating, or reading. Remember to reward yourself each day by doing things you enjoy, like soaking in a bubble bath or watching a favorite video. If necessary, give yourself permission by thinking of reasons to do them, such as, "I've been working hard all day, everything is going well," or, "I've earned a break." Make contact with positive people who make you smile or laugh—they can lift your mood. When good things happen and prospects brighten, a person begins to expect positive things.

If you frequently have problems with negative thinking, you might read the chapter on Attitude Adjustments for ways to neutralize some of your pessimistic thinking, especially self-deprecating thoughts. Build optimism into one area of your life at a time. Start with little challenges and minor predicaments. Learn how to think positively in a consistent fashion and to expect the best results. You might focus on strained family relationships or a difficult area of your work—wherever you'd like to increase your hopefulness and optimism. As you develop sound, positive thinking habits, you will be able to face any difficult circumstance successfully.

Health Benefits of Optimism

Many studies have found a positive relationship between optimism and good health. Positive attitudes and good moods have a tremendous effect on the way our bodies function—the mind/body connection. Dr. Meltzer feels that optimists try to create positive solutions to their daily challenges, which seems to help them manage stress more effectively. Several studies have shown that optimists' tendency to look on the bright side affects their psychological appraisal of stressors, methods of coping with them, and their moods, which may reduce an unhealthy biochemical response. Optimists appraise stressors in a more positive light and their active problem-focused coping may protect them from the effects of acute stress on the immune system. Positive optimistic thoughts give rise to good moods, which foster more positive thoughts, and create a fairly stable way of viewing life events as less stressful. However, optimists may become more stressed than pessimists when faced with persistent stressors over which they feel they have little control, or when the outcome to a problem is contrary to their expectations. But they rebound quickly once the problem is over. Recent studies show that optimists do better than pessimists in work, school, and sports, suffer less depression, achieve more goals, wage more effective battles against disease, and live longer.

Seligman described four theories to explain how optimism contributes to good health. First, optimists are likely to have an immune advantage because they experience events as less stressful than pessimists do. Bob Arnot, who wrote *The Biology of Success*, cites studies that found that optimists have higher levels of natural killer-cell activity and a smaller decline under stress, so that they are better able to fight disease. They also have lower levels of the stress hormone, cortisol. Optimism helps make you more resilient under stress and protects you against certain diseases.

The second theory is that optimists are healthier than pessimists because they take an active role in their own personal health. They are more likely to have an exercise routine, eat properly, seek medical advice when needed, and stick to health regimens. Research shows that optimism is also a major factor influencing your level of fitness, which helps prevent disease and contributes to healing. Optimists also have more hope, even while struggling with illness, which may contribute to healing and living longer. Pessimists believe that, no matter what they do, it won't change their health, so why bother to exercise, eat healthy meals, or give up smoking. According to Seligman, pessimists use denial when ill. They tend to believe that their sickness is permanent, pervasive, and personal. Not surprisingly, studies have found that angry, suspicious and mistrustful people, like pessimists, were twice as likely to develop heart disease as optimists.

Seligman's third theory is that optimists are less likely to encounter bad events in their life than pessimists because they tend to take actions to avoid them. He believes that pessimists are less likely to do anything to stop bad events once they occur. One long-term study of young men and women found that optimists lived an average of two years longer than pessimists, who were more prone to accidents and violence, including car wrecks, household mishaps, and even homicide. Arnot reports that bad moods may contribute to pessimists' health problems since they are more likely to do risky things when they're either distracted or downright reckless.

The fourth theory is that optimists have better health because they enlist social support and tend to sustain deep friendships and love. Optimistic, self-confident people tend to have more friends to whom they can turn during times of stress. Their resilience during crises may depend on their supportive relationships. When trouble strikes, pessimists are more likely to isolate themselves and to take fewer steps to obtain and sustain social support. Pessimists' lack of social support often makes the difference: they are sick more often and their illness usually lasts longer.

Optimism is no panacea—it has its limits. Sometimes it prevents you from seeing reality clearly, or accepting responsibility for your failures. Optimists also may engage in wishful thinking, which can distract them from making concrete plans. And constant optimism may prevent you from exercising caution and sobriety, and from conserving resources. Some studies found that while optimists are more likely to be happy, pessimists are more likely to be right.

But these are just limits—they do not offset the benefits of optimism. If you learn 'flexible optimism,' Seligman believes that you can choose to use it when it is appropriate for the situation, without forcing yourself to always be optimistic. When you have problems and setbacks, use distancing, distraction, or disputation techniques to curtail negative thoughts. Optimism is a tool to help you increase your control over the way you think about your problems and to help you achieve your goals. If you have faith in yourself and believe that you can accomplish anything you try, you will feel empowered.

Both optimists and pessimists have a place in society. We must have the wisdom to listen to the pessimist's keen sense of reality when this perspective is valuable, and also to engage in flexible optimism with our eyes wide open.

One of the most widely used methods for determining optimistic or pessimistic personality traits or dispositions is the *Life Orientation Test*, developed by psychologists Michael Scheier and Charles Carver. You might answer the questions below to determine your own level of optimism.

Life Orientation Test*
> Key: 4–Strongly agree, 0–Strongly disagree

> 1. In uncertain times, I usually expect the best.   4 3 2 1 0
> 2. If something can go wrong for me, it will.   0 1 2 3 4
> 3. I'm always optimistic about my future.   4 3 2 1 0
> 4. I hardly ever expect things to go my way.   0 1 2 3 4
> 5. I rarely count on good things happening to me. 0 1 2 3 4
> 6. Overall, I expect more good things to happen
>   to me than bad.   4 3 2 1 0

Scores range from 0 to 24, with 12 the midpoint. Low scores reflect a more pessimistic attitude or trait, while scores higher than 12 reflect a more optimistic viewpoint.

* Adapted from the test designed by Michael Scheier and Charles Carver (1985).

10

Unhealthy Personality Traits

Many things influence our lives, such as our personal relationships with family members and friends, the type of work we do, and our work environment. When life becomes very stressful, we may blame outside factors and circumstances. One out of every five healthy individuals responds to stress in a destructive manner, declares Dr. Eliot, author of *From Stress to Strength*. And, personality traits such as suppressed anger and hostility, fear, helplessness, perfectionism, pessimism, superwoman syndrome, and others may increase your reaction to stressors, according to Dr. Meltzer, who wrote *The Ten Rules of High Performance Living*. And women are catching up with men as they try to juggle many different roles and responsibilities. Stress is women's number-one health problem, and often this is a very complex problem.

Certain personality traits frequently determine how you handle stressful situations. In your own mind, you know that some of your thoughts, feelings, and behaviors are maladaptive and dysfunctional. Dr. Meltzer writes that chronic worry, guilt, emotional dependencies and codependencies, along with low self-esteem, often distort your perceptions and block appropriate responses. Retained fear, suppressed anger, and buried hostility increase your chances of over-reacting to stressful life events. Other ways you may increase your stress are when you perceive situations or events as threats rather than challenges, try to control yourself and others rather than allowing things to happen, blame others instead of accepting responsibility for your actions, deny or ignore significant events when they need to be processed, and complain instead of problem-solving.

Sometimes your unconscious mind takes over the role of your conscious awareness. Then your emotional responses to stressful events, your ability to think efficiently and be creative, and even your physical health may be controlled by unconscious processes. Some people use such strategies as smoking more, overeating, and drinking alcohol, procrastinating, using recreational drugs, and losing their temper to attempt to handle stressful events and avoid unpleasant emotions. Dr. Miller, author of *Deep Healing: The Essence of Mind/Body Medicine*, says that usually these people are only partially aware of the results of their unconscious behaviors. And some people use even more extreme measures—they give up emotionally and feel completely helpless.

Many people are literally stewing in their own stress chemicals. While appearing cool on the surface, they often explode unexpectedly when confronted by a seemingly minor situation. In *Stress and Natural Healing*, Hobbs wrote that those who are typically impatient, competitive, and hot-tempered are more susceptible to the negative effects of stress than those who respond calmly. Control over your emotional reactions to stressful events is critical to controlling the complications of stress.

You are responsible for getting the most out of life and realizing your full potential. To lead a fulfilling, well-balanced life with good relationships, Alix Kirsta, author of *The Book of Stress Survival*, says you first must understand your own personality characteristics, especially those unhealthy parts that you can change; you also must have enough self-confidence to believe that you can change. If you fail to understand or accept yourself as you are, you may develop personality traits that are unsuited to your true nature and do not meet your needs. Before reading further, you may wish to take the quiz at the end of this chapter to identify your unhealthy traits.

This chapter describes eleven unhealthy personality traits, which often increase your stress and susceptibility to health problems. The traits include: anger and hostility; aggressive and controlling behaviors; denial of problems; fearfulness; helplessness/powerlessness; inferiority complex; isolation and loneliness; perfectionism; pessimism; supermom syndrome; and type A and B personalities.

Angry, Hostile, Resentful Women

Anger is an instinctive, normal, useful emotion when it is based on honest, realistic convictions and expressed appropriately and respectfully. It is the most popular and commonly-used reaction to stress. Bloomfield and Cooper, authors of *The Power of 5*, define anger as the thoughts, feelings, physical reactions, and actions that result from a blameworthy or attack-worthy physical, emotional, or mental provocation—"a demeaning offense against me and mine." Anger can be an appropriate and effective way to deal with a situation, especially when your anger occurs in small doses and is expressed in the right way. Some advantages of anger are that it is activating and mobilizing—you feel you are doing something about what's causing your stress by taking action and solving the problem. Anger can make you feel powerful, as though you're in charge, when you aren't. You may get your way by becoming angry because others may feel intimidated and more obliging than normal, wrote Allen Elkin in *Stress Management for Dummies*. If you think that by acting strong, assertive, and confident by expressing your anger so as to stand up for yourself and not become a victim, you're wrong.

Everyone feels anger occasionally, but some people experience too much anger too often. Dr. Eliot says that anger and hostility are often the result of personality traits such as perfectionism, unassertiveness, aggressiveness, loss of control, denial, and depression. When you use anger as a weapon, it works against you. Anger is not only terribly stressful, but can be like taking a small dose of slow-acting poison—it eventually destroys your relationships and harms your health. The everyday kinds of anger, annoyance, irritation, and hostility that run through the heart and mind of the average person are dangerous. If you're quick to accuse, blame or feel anger when faced with everyday delays and frustrations, this can lead to a heated argument.

Bloomfield and Cooper say that anger has three core components: first there is a feeling that you are being stepped on. You may think, "I'm never appreciated" or, "Why does this always happen to me?" The second component is your bodily reaction—your blood pressure soars, your heart accelerates, your muscles become tense, your brain goes into an active mode, and you feel flooded with feelings of anger or hostility. The third component is the attack in which you lash out to blame or accuse, in words or body language, which may amplify your feelings of hostility. Dr. Ornish, author of *Love and Survival*, believes that loneliness and isolation may cause people to become angry and hostile. Hostile people experience far more daily hassles and personal blows than friendly, agreeable people do. Hostility is an interpersonal experience—hostile people are more likely to provoke and react to social conflict. They are not necessarily aggressive, but tend to be cynical and mistrustful and to take things personally. They are prepared to be defensive even before the conversation and have greater reactivity during mild stress.

Recent studies show that actively expressing anger can work against you, make you angrier and solidify an angry, hostile attitude. One study reported that women were likely to feel ashamed, had feelings of low self-esteem, and felt ineffective if they expressed anger outwardly, while men felt ineffective if they didn't let their angry feelings out. Elkin says that just because you're angry doesn't mean you have to say your piece in the heat of the emotional moment. You're better off waiting until you've calmed down, and choosing a time when your anger is less and the other person is in a better mood.

On the other hand, when anger occurs frequently, is triggered by very minor hassles or perceived slights, and you struggle to suppress your anger, but it simmers for long periods, this can be more destructive than if you express it. Ruminating over past hurts refuels anger and is self-destructive. When anger is intense and prolonged, it can cause incredible amounts of stress, harm your relationships, and damage your overall health. Holding onto a grudge and anger is always easier than forgiving the source of your anger. Although major offenses are harder to forgive, Elkin believes that you can reach forgiveness by trying to understand where the other person is coming from.

A special form of anger is guilt. In *Minding the Body, Mending the Mind*, Joan Borysenko writes that guilt occurs when someone hurts you but you turn your anger inward toward yourself. For example, when someone makes a request of you and you're too busy, but they persist and you feel you owe them, you become angry with yourself for not honoring their request, then you feel guilty.

Much of our stress is due to mental conversations we have with ourselves. When you're upset, you may tell yourself, "I'm angry because—that person made a critical remark, or my spouse doesn't understand me, or someone cut in front of me." The problem is that these automatic thoughts set the blame for feeling angry on something outside yourself. When you blame someone or something else for how you're feeling, you give this person or thing the power to cause your emotional state, say Bloomfield and Cooper. Some women often have distorted thinking, which contributes to misinterpreting what they're experiencing and misjudging others or themselves. You may believe these distorted thoughts which are actually rigid, unrealistic ways of perceiving what's happening to you. Some of the most common patterns of distorted thinking are: always being right; blaming others; believing others should change their bad habits; feeling victimized; thinking things are either good or bad; dwelling on the negative; jumping to conclusions; personalizing everything; resisting change; and pessimistic thinking.

Many stress-related illnesses and disorders are linked to excessive anger. Anger can be harmful to your physical and emotional health. When you frequently lose your cool, you lose your perspective, your health, and may eventually lose your life. Emotionally inappropriate behavior creates changes in the neuroendocrine system, which adversely alters your immune function, and leads to increased susceptibility to diseases. By accepting responsibility for your behavior, you have faith in your ability to change, to transcend your distorted thinking patterns.

According to Williams and Williams, authors of *The Trusting Heart* and *Anger Kills*, anger and hostility are the most damaging stress-related personality traits, and can lead to high blood pressure and/or an unexpected, fatal heart attack. Physically destructive anger, which can lead to a stroke and/or coronary blockage and heart attacks, is anger turned inwards. Hostile people with high levels of cholesterol secrete more adrenaline than those with lower cholesterol levels. Studies have found that hostile people are unhappy people, with more hassles and unpleasant life events. Anger affects those around you: it can strain and damage your relationships with people you love. Elkin writes that angry people lack strong friendships, which means they have no one to talk with about their problems. Anger, together with hostile feelings, can lead to conflict, mental and physical abuse, breakups and divorce, and may endanger your job. And hostile people tend to engage in destructive health behaviors, including smoking, drinking, and overeating.

When you suppress anger, it is still there and can alter your cortisol levels and gradually damage your arteries. In working with hot reactors—people who are often cool on the outside, but simmering inside—Dr. Eliot found suppressed anger was only the tip of the iceberg. Ruminating on angry feelings can increase negative emotions and their damaging physiological effects.

A recent study found that when married couples had angry or hostile behaviors, including criticizing, blaming, denying responsibility, making excuses, and frequent interruptions during a dialogue, they were more likely to have increased blood pressure and heart rate. In *The Dance of Anger,* Harriet Lerner writes that wives had greater and more persistent biochemical changes related to marital conflict, including reduced immune response, than men. The wife may become increasingly stuck in the role of the weak, vulnerable, dependent, or dysfunctional partner, while the husband avoids sharing his own weaknesses, neediness, and vulnerability. Other self-defeating behaviors women may adopt include: submitting to unfair influences, feeling life is out of control, misunderstanding their role in angry situations, protecting their husband's charade by maintaining the status quo, and feeling helpless and powerless to change the situation.

Anger is not an automatic reaction beyond your control—it is a response that can be consciously managed. Bloomfield and Cooper write that there are times when direct confrontation may be the best choice, while other times avoiding conflict may be a better option. Constructively expressing gripes, criticisms, and annoyances is a matter of knowing how to express yourself and choosing the appropriate time and place for the discussion. It also means choosing your battles wisely.

Usually your thoughts and perceptions of events are what make you angry—thus your anger is largely self-created. Your expectations play an important role in determining your level of anger, says Elkins. Unrealistic expectations about your world and the way other people should think and act, as well as demands that they be more like you, add to your anger. When you create unrealistic demands, you end up judging people who don't act in ways you think they should, and they fall short. If your expectations of others are accompanied by shoulds and should nots, you imply that you're perfect and the other is to blame. Joan Borysenko says that when you believe that "Unless someone behaves as he or she should, then it's his fault I'm unhappy," it only serves to reinforce your bad feelings about yourself, which can easily turn into anger. Believing you are right and that nothing can change your mind reduces your ability to see other options and leads to separation from others. You might ask yourself, "Would I rather be right or be happy?"

To improve your relationships, Harriet Lerner suggests you first learn to go inward to explore the true sources of your anger and clarify where you stand by asking yourself: "What about this situation makes me angry? What is the real issue here? What do I want to accomplish or change? What things will I accept or not accept?" Only when you are clearly aware of your hot spots or triggers and your anger and hostility patterns can you effectively choose ways to change your emotions into more healthy and constructive feelings. Second, you must calmly explain to a friend or spouse what has upset you. You need to use good communication skills so that you can clarify what is acceptable to you and settle differences through negotiation and compromise. Bloomfield and Cooper believe that it is important to take full responsibility for how you feel and respond, and that this is easier when you're not feeling like a victim of circumstances. Stop blaming other people for causing your problems. The Borysenkos, authors of *The Power of the Mind to Heal*, recommend that you let go of regrets, resentment, and the tendency to be judgmental or critical of others. This is at the heart of physical, emotional and spiritual healing, so you can open your heart to love. You are responsible for your own happiness, so you must avoid thinking that it is your job to change other people or to tell them how they should think, feel, or act.

Aggressive and Controlling Behaviors

Aggressive women want what they want, when they want it, and will say whatever they think—often in an abusive manner. This often leads to feelings of embarrassment and guilt. However, all their decisions are made from their own point of view. Some women look at control as an end goal, and invest a lot of energy in trying to accomplish their objectives, but often have poor results. Eliot thinks that angry, aggressive women often polarize situations because they feel that others' feelings or perceptions are of little or no importance, which usually results in a negative outcome. Their behavior arouses others' anger, so they often make enemies.

Many women carry around a lot of unnecessary guilt and resentment. Some set impossibly high standards for themselves and others and feel guilty when they or others fail to reach their goals. Although you may not realize it, guilt and resentment affect your behavior and lead to aggressive and controlling behaviors. A woman who is angry with herself may also act aggressively toward others, writes Joan Borysenko. Often women who are most critical of others' behaviors are very critical of themselves. Their constant efforts to correct and control those around them add to their burden and their victims are likely to respond with anger and annoyance, perpetuating the cycle.

Women who desire control or power have a strong need to affect or influence others, a need that is stronger than their need for relationships with others. They need to make other people think and behave as they want, and they tend to believe that it is their God-given-right to do so, since they think they know everything. According to Lunden and Morton, coauthors of *Joan Lunden's Healthy Living*, they seem arrogant and even disrespectful when they try to control others and tell them what's best for them. Because these women look at control as an end goal, they invest a lot of time and energy trying to accomplish their objectives but seldom get positive results. It's a no-win situation.

These personality traits may be associated with more frequent illnesses and poor immune function. Reducing your fears is the first step toward breaking out of aggressive and over-controlling behaviors. Next, you must change your mind-set that is conditioned to fear the consequences if something goes wrong. There's a big difference between blowing off steam and venting your problems. You can blow off steam with anyone, but choose people who can help you when you vent, so that you can solve the problem.

Denial of Problems

One common way to handle negative, unpleasant emotions is denial. Some people completely deny their feelings, no matter what is going on in their lives—they just say they are fine and mean it. Others may be more aware of how these people feel than they are themselves. Dr. Eliot claims that this personality trait is common to all hot reactors—they feel no pain. When they struggle to cope with a difficult situation, they would rather deny their feelings than allow themselves to feel defeated. They believe that discomfort and struggle are part of a normal state of mind, and rarely recognize the symptoms of their own fears, uncertainties, and doubts.

Although the conscious mind is unaware of this emotion, the unconscious is painfully aware. The inability to experience and express unpleasant, distressing emotions has been linked with many psychosomatic illnesses, from headaches to back pain. Since the tension behind the emotion cannot be dissipated consciously by talking about it or taking some action, neurochemical changes occur and are expressed through the body.

Expressing your feeling and confiding in others, whether they be friends, relations, or professional counselors, is a healthy personality trait. Chapter 5 on Confiding in Others—sharing feelings, Chapter 15 on Counseling and Support Groups, or Chapter 18 on Friendships, may be helpful in reducing denial of your problems.

Fearfulness

There are many kinds of fear—fear that you're not good or smart enough, that you aren't attractive, that you won't get your way, that bad things will happen, or fear of intimacy or abandonment. Most of your fears are created by the way you think about common situations, due to imagining the worst-case scenarios. When your belief systems are dominated by fear, Dr. Meltzer asserts that your negative beliefs can create behavior patterns that keep you from accomplishing your goals—they become self-fulfilling prophecies. Fear of failure leads to failure, fear of abandonment may create abandonment, and fear of intimacy often causes a break-down in relationships.

Wishing that life were different is the essence of suffering— avoiding the present while dreaming about a happier life. The only way to avoid that suffering, says Borysenko, is to let go of your impossible desires which prevent you from living in the present. When you desire things you don't have, (the if-onlys) and try to avoid things you don't want, (the what-ifs) you become absorbed in mental preoccupation. Your happiness can't occur until you cease thinking only about your desire, and live instead in the present moment, or reality. When your mind is still, not thinking, wanting, or fearing the present, but is totally absorbed and attentive to the moment, you'll begin to enjoy life.

Letting go of unrealistic desires or unpleasant feelings, emotions, or thoughts is not a process of simply leaving your mind alone, according to Lunden and Morton. It is cultivating your ability to believe that you can live more happily in the present reality. It means gradually reducing or ridding yourself of fearful, distrustful, unloving feelings that you can't express and purposefully seeking to attain your goals, one step at a time.

Helplessness or Powerlessnesss

Women who feel helpless or powerless believe that they have little control or influence over their life and often are unable to regain control. They believe that they are victims of their circumstances. When women are consistently placed in situations over which they feel they have no control, Dr. Seligman, author of *Learned Optimism*, says they develop a sense of helplessness and powerlessness that often extends beyond any specific event. Many women feel that some part of their life is out of their control most of the time. Joan Borysenko found that when women believe they cannot influence most situations in their life, or reach their hopes, dreams, or goals, they begin to believe that they have no power to change their world. If they see only obstacles and frequent disappointments, some women develop chronic stress.

Women with these traits feel they have no right to express their feelings, which contributes to their feeling helpless. They can barely cope with difficult situations because they think their actions and responses don't make any difference. They have little motivation to do anything about their problems, writes Borysenko, and their negative mind-set makes it difficult for them to believe they can do something right to change a situation.

The attitudes you grow up with about yourself may prevent you from assuming as much control over your life as you would like. Women were often taught to give unselfishly to others and suppress their own desires. The more they give to others and deny their own needs and pleasures, the more resentful they become, especially if they receive little appreciation in return, says Kirsta. Many women fear rejection if they state their needs, are unable to express their anger, and need to seek approval from others. These feelings and behaviors prevent them from asserting their needs and taking control of their life.

Some women are aware of various options and alternatives open to them, but feel inhibited from acting freely in their own best interest. Indecision is closely related to one's sense of control and influence and stems from failure to clarify desired outcomes on the basis of one's personal interests, needs, wishes, and goals, writes Elkin. Or, they may not recognize their options for control because they feel trapped. This kind of stress is usually found in people pleasers— those whose self-esteem is completely dependent on the opinions and validation of others. They feel as though someone else is always pulling the strings—especially those affecting their own identity.

They may or may not exhibit outwardly dependent or needy behavior, but Eliot says they lack an internal sense of control.

With learned helplessness, it's almost as if your spirit or life force has left your body. When you feel helpless in a particular situation, you set off mind/body chemicals that tend to support those feelings. This helpless feeling causes your nervous system to flood your brain and body with chemicals consistent with this belief. Constantly feeling helpless can upset your endocrine balance, elevate your cortisol level, an immuno-suppressant hormone, and reduce norepinephrine, which is necessary for feeling happy and content. Rather than the stressful event itself, the inability to feel in control of stress can reduce your immunity. Dr. Miller claims that you may gradually experience increased feelings of weakness, frustration, fear, despair, and loneliness, which may lead to anger. Your behavior and physical strength are also affected, along with your digestion.

Helplessness is associated with many illnesses such as ulcers, heart disease, and cancer. You may experience anxiety, writes Joan Borysenko, when you try to control an unpredictable situation, then depression sets in when the situation seems beyond your control. Although you may not actually be helpless, holding that self-image reinforces your belief, and may produce a self-fulfilling prophecy.

Some women use *behavioral avoidance* to escape from an uncomfortable person, place, or activity rather than trying to deal with the situation. Another way some helpless women handle stress is to use *cognitive avoidance*: they distract themselves with work or leisure activities. When women continually avoid dealing with stressful situations and their emotions, they tend to get more and more stuck in their ways and are unable to make effective changes. Although these avoidance techniques are common, they do not resolve the problem nor reduce women's emotional stress, and may contribute to health problems such as depression and immune suppression.

According to Dr. Borysenko, stored patterns of helplessness can dominate women's lives. It's hard to break the cycle until the person's own wounds are healed. People don't usually hurt others intentionally, but from either ignorance or unconscious patterns. Most of us are doing the best we can under the circumstances. Women cannot grow and change until they examine the roles they have chosen in life. When you feel uncertain and that your life is out of control, you may have feelings of anxiety and upset. Although you'd like control over the unpleasant and unsettling events in your life, frequently you can't control others or events. Therefore, Dr. Miller suggests that you learn how to feel more comfortable with uncertainty and lack of control over some areas of your life. Without the conviction that you have some control over your life, you have no way to handle life's up and downs. Feeling empowered can enhance the effectiveness of the immune system and your healing response. Love and laughter can only be experienced after you let go of helpless thinking patterns that block your expression of them.

Inferiority Complex

Women who feel inferior have a self-deprecating opinion of themselves, usually without any evidence to back it up. They have low self-esteem and self-worth and often lack self-confidence. Your level of self-esteem is determined by how you really feel about yourself. Your self-worth is how you see yourself and is a deep-seated emotional opinion of your value. Since your feelings and thoughts about yourself determine how you act, your self-worth influences your behavior. When you have a negative opinion of yourself, you feel unworthy of love. In time, low self-worth invites rejection and failure, so women may live with the belief that they are losers and often settle for less than they deserve.

Many women depend upon others to feel good about themselves. Equating your self-worth with either your performance or the approval of others is a dangerous course. Then your self-worth is based on relationships with others which reinforce your own passivity and insecurity. The problem arises when you feel you need to do well or absolutely must have success for the approval of others. By making your self-worth contingent on these factors, you are vulnerable to unnecessary stress.

Women with low self-esteem and self-worth often have trouble coping with their problems, and may believe they are incapable of success in most areas of their life. These distorted thinking patterns lead women to believe that they are just no good, so they give up their attempts to improve things and isolate themselves socially. Gloria Steinem believes that women's damaged self-esteem has prevented them from realizing their full potential of personal and political power. If you have low self-confidence and feel you are not in control of your life, Kirsta believes that you are in danger of becoming a victim of persistent, overriding feelings of resentment, anxiety, and fear. Some women with veneers of self-confidence act confident, and *think* they deserve love, care, and compassion, but often they don't *feel* it in their hearts.

Women with an inferiority complex are full of self-doubts, so they are nonassertive and may reveal fears about themselves and uncertainties about what to do. They may feel angry and resentful at not expressing their true feelings. They may think, "Why bother to express my opinions or my needs? They can only get me trouble." When women do not express their feelings over irritating things in life, but carry them around inside until a minor situation sets them off, Eliot says they may explode. While appearing cool on the outside, these women often have increased stress hormones. Some feel victimized, pushed around, taken advantage of, and not in control of their life. Elkin states that when women act assertively, they may feel guilty or anxious and worry about any repercussions from their behavior. They prefer a temporary peace at a high cost to themselves and others.

Women who sacrifice themselves to caretaking responsibilities and have low self-esteem are more prone to various physical symptoms and diseases. Domar and Dreher, coauthors of *Self-nurture*, write that low self-esteem and self-worth are often related to underlying anxiety, fear, and depression, which block some women from achieving optimal health. This can lead to many stress-inducing problems, such as inability to adapt, setting too high self-expectations, and lack of assertiveness. Kirsta acknowledges that low self-esteem contributes to poor self-expression and negative emotions such as anger and aggression, when you are afraid to express your thoughts and feelings.

Some ways to keep an inferiority complex are to always put other's needs before your own, believe that your feelings do not matter, believe that being wrong or making a mistake must be avoided at all cost, believe it is not polite to disagree or express a contrary opinion, and to feel guilty whenever you do something that you want to do.

Healthy women express their own point of view, take responsibility for their feelings, and try to help others understand why they are upset. According to Dr. Eliot, proactive women accept responsibility for their own actions and circumstances. They often find options where others don't see any opportunity for choice. And when they are up against something they truly can't influence, they make an active choice to separate from it or to go with the flow, rather than continue to struggle.

When women learn to nurture themselves, their self-esteem and health improve markedly. Taking charge of your life and building your self-esteem are inseparable, writes Dr. Meltzer. When you believe in yourself, you'll find you can love yourself for who you are, have confidence in your abilities, and value yourself. Ways to improve your self-esteem are to take time each day for your own pleasure, learn to be your own judge of how well you've done, try your best without worrying about other's opinions, and expand your life beyond your caretaker roles. Many times in life you may not perform as well as you'd like and may not get approval from others. Until you raise your self-esteem with dignity, confidence, humor, and enthusiasm, your low self-image may prevent you from enjoying happiness in life.

Isolation, Loneliness, or Antisocial Traits

Loneliness is often rooted in the sense of self as an isolated, separate entity. Some lonely women try to appease others, deny their true feelings, and conform to social standards, which are characteristics of type C behavior, write Temoshok and Dreher, authors of *The Type C Connection*. These individuals usually lack a good social support system, internalize their stress, and inhibit their emotions, all of which contribute to stress and reduced immune function. Anything that promotes isolation from people, groups, or neighbors leads to chronic stress.

Studies of several diverse groups found that people who are lonely tend to have weak immune systems, and low levels of natural killer (NK) cell activity. According to Kiecolt-Glaser and Glaser, in a chapter titled, Mind and immunity, socially-isolated individuals have more stress hormones in their urine, which is linked to illnesses such as cancer and heart disease and to shorter life expectancy, than those with a strong support system. And divorced people who hold the most negative feelings about their separation or divorce and have the most difficulty letting go of a former spouse tend to show the greatest suppression of their immune system. In contrast, other studies found that anything that leads to real intimacy and feeling connected to others can be healing.

How you approach other people each day can determine whether you experience isolation, suffering, and illness; or intimacy, relaxation, joy, and health. The way you listen and talk with others affects how well others hear you. You need to communicate your feelings in ways that are likely to be heard without causing others to feel attacked. Expressing your feelings helps connect you to others, whereas your thoughts, especially judgments, tend to isolate you. Although you may think expressing your feelings will make you feel vulnerable, Dr. Ornish says it will actually make you feel safer.

Perfectionists

Many women strive to do everything and to do it all perfectly. Perfectionists have unrealistic expectations that insure that no situation or person is ever good enough. For some women, extreme perfectionism has less to do with current pressures than with voices from the past, which made them feel unloved unless they performed well. Their high expectations are usually based on beliefs that they or others *should* and *have to* accomplish things perfectly. These beliefs are motivated more by fear of failure, rejection, and ridicule than by true ambition. *Should* implies that you're perfect and the other person is to blame. They believe in the adage, "If you want something done right, do it yourself." Since some women are unable to delegate even the most minor tasks, Eliot says they become angry with themselves or others whenever any detail isn't done just right, according to their standards. They leave no room for the slightest human error. Lunden and Morton wrote that true perfectionists have high levels of self-blame because they set too-high standards for themselves and sometimes fall short of achieving their own goals. This may lead to feeling guilty and defensive, so they perceive themselves as failures.

Perfectionists impose tremendous burdens on themselves, which adds to their stress. First, their behaviors frequently restrict relationships with others, because few people can meet their high standards. Since their standards are unachievably high, they lose their self-esteem when they fail to meet their goals. Second, because perfectionists have so much trouble delegating, their productivity is usually limited rather than increased. And third, perfectionists may reflect too long on decisions without taking any action for fear of making the wrong decision or by being reluctant to take responsibility. They may delay starting a project for fear they won't get it done perfectly. Some become very anxious about every project, fearing that it may not work out right. Others continue to edit, refine, and polish their work over and over again, hoping to achieve perfection, which is not necessarily a quest for their best. It is a pursuit of the worst in yourself—the part that tells you that nothing you do will ever be good enough. Sometimes when you say you can't do something, you may mean that you won't do it because you can't guarantee that it will be perfect. Eliot also found that some people's lives were in such a delicate balance that one minor conflict or mistake could throw everything off. If your sense of perfectionism is beginning to cause you such stress, you need to find the balance between well-done and overdone.

Perfectionism often entails distorted thinking, such as an all-or-nothing belief, over-generalization, disqualifying positive comments, using emotional reasoning, and "should" statements. Another problem of perfectionistic women, report Domar and Dreher, is their reliance on a mental filter: they pick out a single negative detail and dwell on it so exclusively that they envision themselves as complete failures. Perfectionism creates many stress-inducing behaviors, including fear, guilt, procrastination, defensiveness, and failure to delegate, all of which reduce your self-esteem and job performance.

If you are a perfectionist, try not to set too-high standards for yourself as a wife, homemaker, or parent to earn your family's love or to be considered worthy of their respect. Allow yourself to be loved for who you are, for yourself as a person, complete with special qualities and faults, says Kirsta. Domar and Dreher suggest that you remind yourself that every woman has negative tapes from the past playing in her head, and that usually these are only half-truths or outright falsehoods. Cognitive restructuring may help you restore a sense of balance and perspective, and is described in Chapter 13.

Pessimists

Life is inevitably full of personal failures and frustration—defeat and rejection are daily experiences for some. Everyone reacts to these experiences with a momentary sense of helplessness. However, when women feel that they repeatedly fail, they begin to believe that whatever they do will fail. This leads to their feeling helpless, then hopeless. Gradually learned helplessness becomes part of their permanent personal belief system—their explanatory style. Seligman explains that learned helplessness is based on the belief that whatever you do doesn't matter, so you react by giving up or quitting, believing you won't succeed in overcoming your problems. This is the way that pessimists consistently explain the cause of their problems to themselves and others. Pessimists often miss opportunities or lack the enthusiasm necessary to overcome life's obstacles. They often deny their problems, yet are preoccupied with their own emotional distress.

According to Seligman, pessimists use a self-defeating explanatory style to explain their problems. This style consists of three types of mental explanations for bad events: *internal*—"It's all my fault;" *stable*—"I always mess up everything I do;" and *global*—"It's going to affect everything in my life." Those who tend to blame themselves (internal) for their problems are likely to develop symptoms of learned helplessness and low self-esteem when they fail. Peterson and Bossio, authors of *Health and Optimism,* say that when a woman blames unlucky events on her personal flaws (internal), she may undermine her own performance and increase her risk for apathy, depression, failure, illness, and even death. And, women who habitually believe their failures will be long-lasting (stable) and pervasive (global), are likely to develop chronic feelings of hopelessness and helplessness, and are at risk for repeated mistakes, depression, and illness. They project their failures into the future and onto new situations.

If you find yourself thinking, "My life is the pits," whenever a problem arises, you are using a *global* negative explanatory style. Thinking your child gives you a problem about going to school whenever there is a test is a *specific* style. But sometimes pessimism is okay—we live in a difficult world, and few people want to be around perpetual optimists.

People who have negative thinking and disparaging thoughts are classified by some as having type D personalities, characterized by negative emotions and social inhibition. Sandra Lamb, author of an article on "How to be a More Positive Person," wrote that having a type D personality can be a temporary or chronic trait. Chronic pessimists tend to make matters worse—they can turn a molehill into a mountain, and often magnify a single problem into a major disaster.

There are several theories as to why women are more likely than men to become pessimists. One theory is that women are socialized to define their self-worth by their love and social relationships, while men are raised to compete and seek achievement. Because a woman's self-esteem may depend on her relationships with males and friends, loss of these relationships or social isolation may be perceived as a failure on her part. The other theory is that while young men are rewarded for self-reliance and physical activity, young women are encouraged to be passive and dependent. Seligman believes that this socialization process contributes to learned helplessness, and may lead to pessimism, resignation, and giving up because you believe that life is out of your control. As adults, women often find that society depreciates their role of wife and mother, and if employed, women often find their achievements are given less credit than men's. If women have a pessimistic explanatory style, they are more likely than men to develop depression following a helpless experience. For information on ways to become more optimistic, see Chapter 9 on optimism.

Supermom Syndrome

Supermoms have an "I can do it all" syndrome. They believe they can and must do everything by themselves, and some feel they could and should do more. Seldom are they satisfied with their accomplishments. Many women try to meet the needs of significant others while denying their own, according to Kirsta. They may be motivated more by fear of failure or rejection than by true altruism. Some women even neglect their own personal needs because they consider other's needs more important, and feel that they don't deserve to have their own needs met. Often they feel overwhelmed by the dual pressures of career and family life, and stretched in their caretaking responsibilities between their children and elderly parents. Inundated by the media, and sometimes by their families with messages that their self-worth depends upon being a supermom, they extend themselves beyond their capabilities.

Some supermoms feel trapped—they feel they have little control over their life, and are inadequate to meet the challenges. They see others as a source of demands, and share little of their responsibilities at home with family members, believing that "If I don't do it, it won't get done." These beliefs lead to selflessness and low self-esteem, which are major health issues. The constant caretaking and striving of women who never give themselves a break takes its toll on their emotional and physical well-being. This may result in chronic fatigue, exhaustion, helplessness, and depression. Women who take on too much are likely to blow a fuse. Their low-lying anger threatens to erupt at any time. Others just become numb to how bad they feel. Domar and Dreher report that self-denial is associated with some autoimmune diseases and the progression of certain types of cancer. Although emotional suppression, conformity, and self-sacrifice may not cause autoimmune diseases, they seem to contribute to their progression.

In addition, women who always put themselves last and need to please everyone else are less likely to recover from a severe illness. They tend to follow every doctor's order, be the perfect patient, and even relinquish their will and spirit while keeping their fears, dread, and despondency to themselves. Although they often have a strong tendency toward self-pity, unspoken resentment and anger, and inability to forgive, they may suppress these feelings. The author of *Optimal Wellness*, Golan, writes that because of their poor self-image, and a lifelong pattern of rejection, self-condemnation, and depression, many supermoms are unable to develop and maintain meaningful long-term relationships. They lack the personality traits that might enable them to assert their needs.

Most supermoms need to slow down and review their priorities, then try to move, talk, and behave in a more relaxed, slower manner to see if they then experience less stress. To stop being a supermom, you need to consider how much time you spend each week on activities that enhance your own pleasure and fulfillment. You need to nourish your body and soul and believe that you have the right and responsibility to be good to yourself. If you don't take care of yourself, nobody else will. Domar and Dreher claim that self-nurturance is one of the healthiest messages you can give your mind. Supermoms might say to themselves, I can take care of my needs and feel good about myself without anyone else's confirmation. Chapter 25 provides information on how to develop self-nurturance.

Type A and Type B Personalities

The typical type A personality is the hurried workaholic who responds quickly and intensely, actively focuses on the task or outcome, and attempts to get many things done efficiently. They exhibit certain traits—verbal and nonverbal impatience and hostility, interrupting or filling-in a conversation during pauses—and they may fidget, finger-tap, or grimace during conversations. They hold on to things and emotions. They may be unpleasant to others, but their traits may not be as harmful as once believed. They think everyone expects them to achieve, so they feel guilty about relaxing.

Type B personalities appear more relaxed, listen intently, and rarely if ever interrupt. They are likely to hold off action until they think the situation through, and formulate a plan to solve the problem. They focus on the process of getting the task done, pace themselves, enjoy a lunch or stretch break, are able to let go of problems, enjoy reading the funnies, and like to laugh.

When women feel in control of their own future, they are more likely to be healthy. Although type A personalities may go about life annoying everyone else, they may not cause themselves much physical distress unless they have toxic traits such as anger and hostility. So being a type A hard-working personality probably won't give you a heart attack unless you're also angry, mistrusting, or cynical. Dr. Eliot says that these hot reactors often perceive any gap between their expectations and reality as personal defeat—a threat to their identity and self-esteem.

They experience fear, uncertainty, and doubt, and may have unhealthy lifestyle habits such as smoking, excessive drinking, and compulsive overeating. In response to stressful situations, Dr. Hobbs claims that they may eventually develop certain kinds of ulcers or digestive problems. However, many type A personalities outlive seemingly calmer type B personalities.

Although type Bs may be more placid and cool as cucumbers on the surface, some are very hot under the collar. One theory is that calm-appearing people are often unassertive and afraid to say what they really think. Dr. Eliot says that they may become human pressure cookers with stuck safety valves—they literally stew in their stress-induced hormones. Their silent stress slowly causes elevated cortisol levels, which contribute to physical changes such as irritability, hyper-alertness, elevated blood pressure, erratic heart rhythms, increased fat and cholesterol in the bloodstream, and increased gastric acid.

Ways to Change Unhealthy Traits

It is your responsibility to change your unhealthy attitudes or traits to reduce your stress, restore balance to your life, and improve your health. First, you need to understand your current emotional styles and traits. The quiz at the end of this chapter may help you recognize unhealthy personality traits that you can change if you choose to do so. Do you ever overreact, repress, or deny your feelings? You may do fine with some emotions, but don't know how to handle other ones. Also, you may find that you either get stuck in some emotions and can't let go, or may not even be aware that you have some emotional feelings. Second, consider assumptions and views about yourself that may be holding you back. For example, fear of abandonment or fear of intimacy may contribute to your maladaptive behaviors. Third, Dr. Meltzer suggests that you examine the major distractions and frustrations in your life so you will know in what areas you need to lighten up. Otherwise problems in these areas can accumulate and cause more stress. And fourth, Kirsta recommends that you develop the determination and courage to make changes where possible, especially learning assertiveness skills, to help you regain control over your life and attain your goals.

Two emotions that are very difficult to let go of are both variations of blame. When you blame yourself, you feel guilty and ashamed. When you blame someone else, you feel resentment. To let go of your resentment, Joan Borysenko says you need to understand why a person who hurt you did so. Some people are simply unaware of the consequences of their actions. They're not evil—just ignorant. If you don't confront them with the results of their actions when they hurt you, then their opportunity to learn is lost and you end up holding on to the resentment.

No one likes frustrating situations, yet they are an integral part of our lives. When faced with a frustrating situation, you may overreact too quickly, and become too angry too fast. If so, your fuse is way too short. Elkin suggests that you learn to be more tolerant of upsetting situations and work on developing patience. When you are angry, try to acknowledge your anger without resorting to verbal or physical hostility, then discuss the conflict with the other person or sort things out on your own to help you regain emotional control. Those who practice "reflective coping" solve their problems faster and more effectively, get the anger out of their systems, and have better health than those who harbor grudges or explode.

When confronted with a potentially anger-provoking situation, you can say things to yourself that increase your anger, or things that may reduce or eliminate your anger. By consciously and explicitly using powerful self-talk messages, you can begin to regulate your anger. Examples of anger-reducing thoughts are: "Don't take this so personally;" "Let it go— it's not worth the emotional distress;" "I can choose not to get angry about this;" and "Would I rather be right or be happy?" For more information, Chapter 8 has a section on anger management.

After your anger has been settled (or even if it hasn't been), let bygones be bygones so that you can bring closure to the situation and reduce your anger and stress to indifference. Identify your resentments and/or guilt, and replace them with forgiveness. Learning to trust more is one way of feeling less angry and less hostile. Also, try to keep your expectations of others more realistic so they're less likely to disappoint you. Other people often see things differently and may have different priorities than yours. Given the chaotic world we live in, Elkin recommends that you learn to expect the unexpected and see what will probably happen, rather than reacting too rapidly.

Learned helplessness can be reversed by developing skills that enable you to define and defend your own territory and your personal space and improve your quality of life. Some areas to work on are developing self-respect and self-appreciation, the basis of self-esteem, then assertiveness skills and tools for recognizing, acknowledging, and confidently protecting your time and space. Also learn healthy ways to express anger. All of these are empowerment skills, explained in other chapters of this book. According to Dr. Miller, deep healing occurs when you give yourself both permission to feel entitled and assertive and the personal power to use and express these skills when they are appropriate. You must believe that control over your life resides within you, not that you are helpless or a victim of circumstances.

Reducing perfectionism requires several strategies, many of which are described in Inlander and Moran's book, *Stress: 63 Ways to Relieve Tension and Stay Healthy.* First you need to establish your priorities and set realistic expectations for yourself. Look at your agenda for both work and home, and decide how much time you have. Then determine what level of quality is needed to finish a project. Sometimes top quality is unnecessary when less quality will suffice. Once you have set these guidelines, get started and follow through. Schedule adequate time to accomplish projects and correct mistakes before deadlines. Realize that you can't be perfect all the time and that no one expects it of you. Allow yourself to make mistakes and forgive yourself. View mistakes as a learning experience. Place value on quality work finished on time instead of perfect work turned in late. Choose when to be perfect and when to do your best under the circumstances.

Reducing a lifetime of unhealthy traits can be very difficult. Most of us can reduce some of our unhealthy behaviors and become stronger, once we realize how our behaviors affect our life and relationships, along with their impact on our health, says Kirsta. You have choices about the way you speak, move, and handle your daily life and personal relationships. The process of changing yourself involves considerable courage and resolve, because it does not happen easily or quickly. You can begin by assessing both your positive and negative qualities, accepting your strengths and faults, and then try to achieve a balanced integration. Learn to care for yourself as lovingly as you care for others. Get in touch with your mind/body needs, reject negative thoughts, and learn to use effective communication skills to maintain positive relationships. Replace chronic worry and pessimism with a more optimistic, positive attitude. Accept your frustrations as part of life and getting things done—life isn't always going to be the way you want it. The benefits of making these changes are greater self-confidence, self-esteem, minimal stress, and improved health.

Quiz to Identify Your Unhealthy Personality Traits

Rate how often you feel each statement below, using the following key:

1–Seldom, 2–Occasionally, 3–Frequently, 4–Often, 5–Almost always

1 ___Feel angry, bitter, or resentful toward parents, spouse, friend

2 ___Find that it is difficult to establish relationships with others

3 ___Have feelings of low self-esteem or feel inferior to others

4 ___Are unable to forgive yourself for your mistakes

5 ___Have difficulty forgiving others for their behaviors

6 ___Are unable to ask others for what you need or want

7 ___Feel uncomfortable confronting others or saying no

8 ___Have difficulty expressing your anger, sadness, or fears

9 ___Try to please others as often as possible

10___Blame others for your problems or events that upset you

11___Feel you are unable to relax or slow down

12___Are unable to have fun or do not allow yourself to have fun

13___Find you are unable or unwilling to examine your emotional feelings

14___Feel you are out of touch with your genuine feelings and needs

15___Have unusual and overwhelming fears that limit your activities

16___Feel you have little power or influence over your life

17___Feel as though you are a victim of life's circumstances

18___Find that you rarely touch or are touched by others

19___Feel isolated or unconnected to family members or friends

20___Believe that whatever can go wrong, probably will

21___Feel very unsure of yourself in new situations

22___Become sad or uncomfortable when someone criticizes you

23___Have difficulty sharing your feeling when someone hurts your feelings

24___Feel physically ill when you argue with someone

25___Feel trapped, with no control over your life

26___Become annoyed or upset when problems arise at home or work

27___Feel uncomfortable when asked to say what you think

28___Try to control your own and others, behaviors

29___Try to ignore strong feelings about others or your work environment

30___Try to deny or ignore the effects of significant events at home or work

Unhealthy Behavior Traits

For each behavior, write the number you rated each statement on the line below the number trait, then add all the numbers for each trait and divide by the total number of items to determine your average score for that trait. If your average score is 4 or more on any trait, you probably have a tendency toward this unhealthy trait and may need to learn how to reduce these behavior patterns to enhance your health.

Angry, hostile and/or resentful of others
  1   8   10   18   25   26
___   ___   ___   ___   ___   ___   Total___Avg___

Aggressive and controlling toward others
  2   5   10   18   28
___   ___   ___   ___   ___   Total___Avg___

Use denial to avoid dealing with problems
 13   14   29   30
___   ___   ___   ___   Total___Avg___

Feel fearful about situations and relationships
  6   8   15   21   27
___   ___   ___   ___   ___   Total___Avg___

Usually feel helpless and powerless
  6   7   16   17   25
___   ___   ___   ___   ___   Total___Avg___

Have an inferiority complex or low self-esteem
  3   8   9   21   22   23   27
___   ___   ___   ___   ___   ___   ___   Total___Avg___

Are lonely, isolated from others, or anti-social
  2   3   18   19   23
___   ___   ___   ___   ___   Total___Avg___

Are a perfectionist

3	4	9	10	11	22
—	—	—	—	—	—

Total ___ Avg ___

Are a pessimist

12	15	16	17	20
—	—	—	—	—

Total ___ Avg ___

Are a supermom or workaholic

9	11	14	25	26	28
—	—	—	—	—	—

Total ___ Avg ___

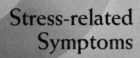

Stress-related
Symptoms

11

Physical and Emotional Symptoms of Stress

There is abundant evidence that difficulty handling life's daily hassles and stressors contributes to various physical and emotional symptoms. In a landmark study by Harvard scientists, people who coped poorly with stress were sick four times more often than those with good coping skills. Researchers estimate that stress-related health problems cost the United States economy up to $250 billion a year. Every week an estimated 95 million Americans suffer from a stress-related problem such as accidents, absenteeism, or substance abuse, and take medication for their aches and pains. Some scientists estimate that over 80 percent of all illnesses are stress-related, and 85 percent of all industrial accidents are linked to stress-related behaviors.

There is also strong evidence that stress affects the biochemicals of your immune system, leading to a wide variety of physical and emotional responses. Stress responses can affect your heart function, hormone levels, the nervous system, metabolic rate, memory and thinking, and physical coordination. They can also raise your blood cholesterol, blood pressure, and uric acid levels and increase the risk of developing many illnesses, including heart disease, cancer, immunodeficiency diseases, and even the common cold. To be effective, the immune system needs to be in a state of constant readiness to fight off the many viruses and other invading germs you encounter daily with increased environmental toxins. When your body is overloaded and the immune system diverted by high stress and toxins, it fails to function effectively, so you may experience suboptimal health and have vague complaints of fatigue and other symptoms. When your stress level reaches overload, some common symptoms you may experience include fatigue or chronic tiredness, disturbed sleep patterns, frequent upset stomach, headaches, backaches, skin rashes, loss of energy and judgment, over-dependence on alcohol and drugs, and altered eating patterns.

We all have unique responses to stress, and everyone has one or two target organs that are more vulnerable to stress reactions. Some women get angry or irritable, develop an ulcer or gastritis, have diarrhea, a spastic colon, or tense muscles. Others develop headaches, depression, anxiety, or fatigue. And some exhibit high blood pressure, arthritis, an allergy, or autoimmune disease. However, why one person's stress leads to stomach cramps while another gets a headache, is unknown.

Many times the organ or part of the body that responds to accumulated stress can actually symbolize an internal emotional conflict. This theory, the "disease specificity model," was first proposed by psychiatrist Franz Alexander in the 1950s. According to Alexander, many individuals with stomach ulcers will say that something is eating at them. Those with asthma or breathing difficulty may be trying to get something off their chest. And some with difficulty urinating may be pissed off. Those with constipation may fear letting go of something, while some with arthritis may have stiff or rigid attitudes. People with acne, herpes, or other skin eruptions may be "sore" at someone or want to break out, and those with high blood pressure or night sweats may be burning up over something.

Dr. Janet Kenney and Ano Bhattacharjee, coauthors of a research article, analyzed the interrelationships among stressors, per-sonality traits, and symptoms of health problems of 300 women. They found that women with high stressors and unhealthy personality traits such as low trust/love relationships, low assertiveness skills, inability to express their feelings, low hardiness, and high family altruism, were much more likely to have numerous physical and emotional symptoms of health problems than women with the opposite traits.

For many women, the ability to stay calm and healthy amidst life's constant pressures comes down to how they handle the small things—the daily hassles and irritations of everyday life. Some of these hassles include frequent interruptions, broken appointments, annoying phone calls, financial anxiety, bad weather, traffic jams, or deadlines. Your reactions and overreactions to daily hassles are the key to your health and are often a more powerful predictor of psychological and physical health than your reaction to major crises. Managing stress really means handling the tension, anger, and anxiety you feel in stressful situations so that you can respond calmly and creatively.

One troublesome symptom of excessive mental stress and tension is distortion of your sense of time. Dr. Larry Dossey, who wrote *Recovering the Soul: A Scientific and Spiritual Search*, calls this hurry sickness. Many women frequently have such thoughts as, "There's never enough time," and "What else can go wrong today?" If you have these feelings frequently, it can be an early warning sign that your stress has reached an intense and potentially harmful level. Some signals of distress from hurry sickness are

1. trying to do more and more in less and less time, but falling behind.

2. feeling your muscles tightening, especially in your neck and back.

3. feeling increasingly fatigued in mind, body, or emotions.

4. finding that you make frequent mistakes or careless errors, or that you have diminished coordination in your speech, writing, or movement.

5. feeling increased irritability, frustration, impatience, or hostility, and wanting to distance yourself from others.

6. noticing that your mind wanders with distractions and that you have difficulty concentrating or are more forgetful.

7. feeling blue, sad, or empty, despairing or pessimistic, with an increased sense of vulnerability, and

8. feeling a surge of anger, aggression, or hostility at other people.

—Bloomfield and Cooper, 1995:25

Symptoms of stress vary greatly from one person to the next. The best way to guard against illness from too much stress is to recognize the early signals and know how far you can push yourself without incurring more serious symptoms. The key to reducing stress is to recognize your signs and symptoms, identify what possibly causes your reactions, and take action soon to reduce your level of stress. You need to consciously examine what you are thinking about, feeling, saying, seeing, or hearing and exactly *how* you are doing it. It is important to recognize certain mind/body signals that tell you it's time to slow down and relax more. If you can identify ways that your body and mind react to or show stress, you can treat and reduce your symptoms. This means that you need to be sensitive to your body's subtle changes and emotions and recognize all the signs and symptoms as soon as they occur.

Early Warning Signs of Stress

Absenteeism	Indecision
Anxiety	Indigestion
Backache and pain	Lack of creativity
Blame others often	Lack of joy in life
Boredom	Loneliness
Compulsive overeating	Loss of appetite
Constipation or diarrhea	Loss of sense of humor
Difficulty concentrating	Memory lapses or loss
Difficulty with others	Muscle aches and pain
Dry mouth or throat	Nail-biting, fidgeting
Easily distracted	Palpitations, racing heart
Fear of making decisions	Restlessness
Feel trapped/overworked	Sleeping problems
Feel unappreciated	Teeth grinding
Forgetfulness	Use or increased use of drugs,
Headaches	alcohol, or cigarettes

Physical Symptoms of Stress

You may not know when your body is tense, or you may be so used to being tense that you may not even notice it. Muscle tension can creep up on you slowly and often imperceptibly, although you don't feel the tension until you notice a headache or soreness in your neck and shoulders. These muscular responses to stressors can cause severe problems. The natural response of someone who is worried is to tense the neck and scalp muscles. In *Deep Healing: The Essence of Mind/Body Medicine,* Dr. Miller wrote that if muscle tension lasts for long, it can produce tiny areas of injury in the muscle fibers, which are detected by local nerves and experienced as pain. The problem is that additional muscle tension gives rise to more pain, which produces more tension, and so on, until the muscle goes into a spasm. This vicious pain/spasm cycle continues unless it is interrupted by a muscle relaxant, a pain killer, or a deep relaxation technique. It is important to become aware of body tension before it builds up and creates pain.

Common Physical Symptoms of Stress

- Headaches (tension, sinus, migraines)
- Sleep problems (insomnia, early wakening, restless sleep, frequent awakenings, nightmares)
- Frequent colds or common flu
- Allergy problems (eyes, nose, hives, rashes, itching, acne, psoriasis)
- Gastrointestinal problems (frequent upset stomach, indigestion, heartburn, loss of appetite, diarrhea, or constipation)
- Muscle tension, aches and pains (neck, shoulders, or lower back, or joints)
- Chronic fatigue, weakness, malaise, lethargy or listlessness
- Shakiness or trembling
- Excessive sweating, cold, clammy hands

Emotional Symptoms of Stress or Mood Signals

Stress affects your mood in a variety of ways. Some mood changes take place on the surface, while others are deeper and more pervasive. Irritability and impatience are hyperactive states, relatively superficial signs of underlying anxiety and aggression. Despite well-known gender gaps in stress responses, men are more likely to become antisocial or alcoholics, while women often ruminate and become depressed or anxious when they are upset about their problems. Restlessness and frustration, if persistent, can be more serious, and can develop into full-blown hostility or anger. This can be caused by feeling a lack of control or fulfillment at work or home. Apathy and boredom are "flat" feelings, often associated with inadequate activities that keep you interested. They can be just as stressful as the more common emotions of stress. Most serious symptoms are disheartening emotions such as guilt, shame, depression, and chronic fatigue, along with a sense of helplessness or hopelessness, which are often related.

Signs and Symptoms of Emotional Stress

- Nervous, tense, or irritable
- Anxious, easily upset, or worried
- Feel alone, lonely, isolated from friends
- Feel used and/or abused by others
- Unable to rest or relax
- Feel overwhelmed with responsibilities
- Feel guilty about something
- Feel sad, depressed, or unhappy
- Frequent sudden mood changes
- Frequently feel angry or very annoyed
- Feel overwhelmed and can't cope
- Fear of failure or success
- Frequent crying spells, sadness
- Feel pressure to succeed
- Afraid, scared, or fearful of life
- Fearful of intimacy with others
- Dissatisfied with work or life
- Feel life is out of your control
- Disinterested in work or life
- Disinterested in having sex, low libido
- Anger, hostility, impatience
- Intrusive or racing thoughts

Behavioral Signs and Symptoms of Stress

Any unusual behavior pattern that indicates you are not acting like your usual self may be a sign of an adverse reaction to a stressor. Some characteristic type A or workaholic behavior patterns include leaving important tasks undone until the last minute, then panicking and feeling unable to complete them, allowing insufficient time to get to work or to important appointments, or trying to do two or more things at the same time. Stress can also impair your ability to communicate well, according to Kirsta, author of *The Book of Stress Survival*. You may talk too fast, too loud, or too aggressively, swear more, interrupt others or talk over them, not listen to what others have to say, and argue for the sake of it. These are typical ways that stress can alter your patterns of relating to others. Other behavioral signs include trying to do without sleep, nodding off during meetings, losing your sense of humor, and reacting nervously or irritably to everyday sounds.

Outbursts and overreactions can occur when you lose your perspective on problems that you would normally face calmly. You may not be able to discriminate and judge even everyday situations or events accurately, or control your reactions to them calmly. While an occasional outburst, whether of anger or tears, may be a valid, healthy way to release pent-up tension, frequent outbursts may indicate serious problems.

Another behavioral symptom that suggests that you are losing your ability to handle stress effectively is consistently acting and feeling out of character. An inability to feel or express any emotions or a sense of being on automatic pilot—acting more like a robot than a human—indicates that you've lost contact with your surroundings and yourself. Common symptoms include difficulty making decisions, frequently changing your mind, memory blocks or loss of short-term memory, being at a loss for words, and lapses in concentration. You may also experience anxiety and inhibition when faced with everyday challenges.

Common Stress-related Diseases and Conditions

Cardiovascular: heart disease such as atherosclerosis, coronary artery disease, angina, myocardial infarction, fatal heart attacks, peripheral vascular disease, arrhythmias, and essential hypertension.

Central nervous system: fatigue and lethargy, insomnia

Endocrine: diabetes mellitus, amenorrhea.

Gastrointestinal: stomach ulcers, irritable bowel syndrome, diarrhea, nausea and vomiting, ulcerative colitis.

Genitourinary: diuresis, impotence, decreased libido, infertility, recurrent, non-specific vaginal infections, and flare-ups of STDs, such as (HPV) human papilloma virus and genital herpes.

Immunological: autoimmune diseases such as systemic lupus erythematosus, multiple sclerosis, myasthenia gravis, rheumatoid arthritis, Graves' disease, and fibromyalgia.

Muscular: muscle contractions, shoulder aches, chronic back pain, and any chronic pain.

Neurological: headaches (tension, migraine, cluster), epilepsy, and strokes.

Psychological: major depression, chronic anxiety disorders, mood disorders.

Pulmonary: asthma (hypersensitivity reaction), hay fever.

Skin: eczema, neurodermatitis, acne, psoriasis.

Other: overeating, obesity, and substance abuse (alcoholism, drug abuse, etc.). Some types of breast cancers and allergies may also be stress-related.

Research on the relationship between stress and development of cancer has found conflicting results. In humans, some studies have found a relationship between stress reactions and susceptibility to breast cancer, along with the rate of breast cancer recurrence, while other studies found none. One study found that even though psychological issues remain unresolved, a woman with breast cancer's emotional response (or non-response) may influence her immune system's ability to fight this disease. These conflicting results may relate to certain characteristics of stressors, such as their chronicity, intensity, predictability, and controllability, which could influence the immune system.

Cardiovascular diseases cause over 240 thousand deaths of American women annually, six times more than breast cancer, and may be stress-related. Other studies have also found that people who experience major life changes, marital discord, and bereavement have altered immune system functioning. The stressful pressures on married career women with children may also gradually take a toll on their health. More research is needed to discern how stress affects the immune system and influences health.

The Stress-symptoms Scale

This scale gives you a way to measure your stress level by indicating the number and severity of your stress-related symptoms and behaviors. To use this scale, simple rate the frequency with which you've experienced each of the symptoms listed below in the last two weeks, using the following key:

0 – Never   1 – Sometimes   2 – Often   3 – Very often

Physical
____ Aching neck or shoulders
___ Acne or psoriasis
___ Allergies: eyes, nose, skin
___ Cold, clammy hands
___ Chronic fatigue, lethargy
___ Constipation or diarrhea
___ Excessive sweating

0 – Never   1 – Sometimes   2 – Often   3 – Very often

____ Frequent colds, flu
____ Headaches
____ Hives, rashes, itching
____ Increased perspiration
____ Indigestion/heartburn
____ Joint aches and pain
____ Loss of appetite
____ Muscle aches and pain
____ Nightmares
____ Problems sleeping/insomnia
____ Pounding, racing heart
____ Restlessness
____ Shakiness or trembling
____ Teeth grinding/jaw clenching
____ Upset stomach

Mental

____ Difficulty concentrating
____ Easily distracted
____ Feel lost for words
____ Inactivity or boredom
____ Indecision
____ Intrusive/racing thoughts
____ Loss of sense of humor
____ Memory lapses or short-term memory loss
____ Procrastinating

Emotional

____ Afraid, scared, or fearful of life
____ Angry, annoyed, impatient
____ Anxious, easily upset
____ Dissatisfied with work or life
____ Disinterest in work or life
____ Fear of failure or success
____ Fearful of intimacy with others
____ Feel alone, lonely, isolated
____ Feel guilty about something

0 – Never   1 – Sometimes   2 – Often   3 – Very often

____ Feel helpless, or hopeless
____ Feel life is out of your control
____ Feel pressure to succeed
____ Feel sad, depressed, or unhappy
____ Feel overwhelmed and can't cope
____ Feel used/ abused by others
____ Feelings of doom
____ Forgetfulness
____ Frequent crying spells, sadness
____ Frequently running late
____ Frequent sudden mood changes
____ Loss of sexual interest, low libido
____ Nervous, tense, or irritable
____ Overwhelmed with responsibilities
____ Unable to rest or relax

Behavioral
____ Arguing for the sake of it
____ Being too aggressive
____ Compulsive overeating
____ Frequent outbursts or crying
____ Hair-twisting or pulling
____ Increased use of drugs, alcohol, or cigarettes
____ Interrupting others or talking over them
____ Nodding off during meetings
____ Not listening to other people
____ Overreactions to everyday sounds
____ Swearing frequently
____ Talking too fast, too loud
____ Teeth grinding, nail-biting

Total Score ____

Scoring the Stress-symptoms Scale
____ Your score   ____ Your comparative rating with others

0–19	Lower stress than average
20–39	Average amount of stress
40–59	Moderately higher than average stress
60 and above	Much higher than average stress

4

Stress Reduction
Strategies

12

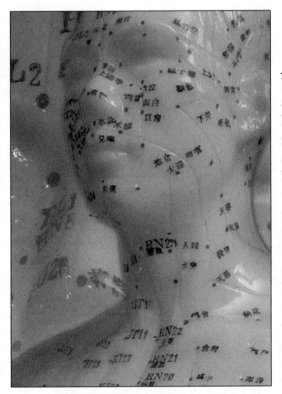

Acupressure and Acupuncture
Lyn Matthew, LMT, OBT and Janet Kenney, RN, Ph.D.

Some cultures strongly believe that harmony in all areas of life is essential to health. Many Asians strive to maintain mental, physical, and spiritual harmony and balance. Those who practice Oriental medicine believe that by keeping an energy force, called Qi (chi), flowing freely through the body's meridians, you can maintain balance and health. They also believe that everything was created in terms of opposites, and is in a process of continual change between two general poles, called Yin and Yang. Although these are opposites, both are necessary for harmony to exist in nature and in every individual.

In Oriental medicine, the life-force energy which travels along the meridians has a different name in each culture. The Chinese call it Qi (pronounced chi), Japanese call it *Ki*, and it is known as *shakti* or *kundalini* in India. The mind, body, and spirit are each infused with emotional aspects that affect one another. Physical symptoms affect the emotions and psyche, and, likewise, emotions affect the body's physical systems. During good health, energy is added through food and oxygen and moves easily along the meridians. Any physical problem reflects disharmony in the whole person.

Acupressure, an ancient healing art deeply rooted in traditional Oriental medicine, is considered by many to predate acupuncture. Some believe it is one of the most effective methods for relief of tension and other health problems. Practitioners trained in acupressure can help many people, while others want to learn to use their own hands for self-treatment. Some people prefer to use acupuncture to alleviate their symptoms and/or health problems.

Definitions of Acupressure and Acupuncture

Acupressure refers to bodywork techniques that use finger or manual pressure to stimulate energy points. The pressure stimulates the body's recuperative powers by releasing obstructions and balancing the flow of chi along the meridians.

Acupuncture or meridian therapy involves stimulating energy points along the meridians using a variety of methods. This may include inserting and manipulating fine needles, applying heat by burning an herb, or using a weak electrical current. The goal of both therapies is to keep the energy patterns balanced and restore the flow of chi through-out the meridians by stimulating various acupoints located along the meridians and other areas of the body.

The Oriental Medical Model

Traditional Chinese medicine recognizes many patterns of disharmony. According to Tom Williams, author of *The Complete Illustrated Guide to Chinese Medicine,* the three most commonly-used methods are the Eight Principles, the Five Element Patterns, and the Channel Patterns. This chapter focuses on the Five Elements theory, which emerged from observations of the natural world. The first recorded reference to the Five Elements occurred between 476 and 221 BC, writes Giovanni Maciocia. The Five Elements—earth, metal, water, wood, and fire—each symbolize different inherent qualities and states of all aspects of existence. They are broad categories for organizing phenomena both within the body and in nature. The Elements contin-uously interact and influence each other in a well-defined integration to bring harmony to everything. Each Element serves to "nourish" one other element, and to "control" another element. Thus, there are two basic models of physiological relationships among the elements and internal organs in which the Elements are related, a nourishment cycle and a control cycle, as shown in Figure 1.

Each Element is also represented by two Organs, grouped in complementary pairs, one Yin and one Yang, representing polar qualities. Yin and Yang serve as regulators for physiologic harmony of each Organ. Yin Organs function structurally to store all vital substances, and Yang Organs perform vital functions. Qi energy, which constantly flows through the Organ-meridian systems, has Yang qualities, and is generally strong and active.

The way each Element responds serves as a guide to understand the flow of Qi energy. Acupoints are fixed points on each meridian on the skin's surface, which act as entrances and exits for Qi. Stimulating one or a combination of key acupoints restores harmony and balance to the affected area. Interactions among the Elements and the Yin and Yang Organs are shown in Figure 1, and their actions depicted in Table 1.

Fig 1. The Five Elements of the Creation Cycle. From Maciocia (1989), The Foundations of Chinese Medicine. *New York: Churchill Livingston.*

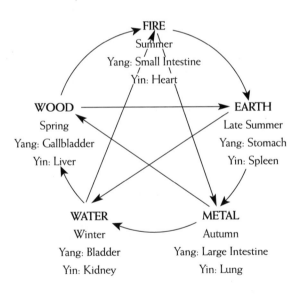

The symmetrical circles connecting the five Elements represent the Generating-Nourishing sequence, while the arrows linking the Elements indicate the Controlling and Over-acting sequences.

Early Chinese physicians discovered an energy network that transverses just below the skin surface along the meridians and communicates between the external environment and the internal organs and structures. This invisible, flowing energy force, Qi, is responsible for the functioning of the Organ-energy systems, and life itself. This energy force actually vibrates within and around the body like a magnetic field, and also exists in the environment as a natural force within the air and weather.

Table 1. Interaction of Elements with Yin/Yang and Meridians, and Effect of Conditions Relating to Emotions, Activity, and Foods

ELEMENT	EARTH	METAL	WATER	WOOD	FIRE
Season	Late Summer	Autumn	Winter	Spring	Summer
Yang Meridian	Stomach	Large Intestine	Bladder	Gallbladder	Small Intestine
Yin Meridian	Spleen	Lung	Kidney	Liver	Heart
CONDITIONS					
Emotions in Balance	Concern Confidence	Empathy Happy	Courage	Assertive Patience	Joy
Emotions out of Balance [1]	Worry	Sadness Grief	Fear	Anger	Bitter
Body Activity [2]	Sitting	Lying	Standing	Reading	Walking Running
Food Flavor [3]	Sweet	Pungent	Salty	Sour	Bitter

1. Emotions which are unbalanced cause stress.
2. Too much or too little time spent in this body position can bring an imbalance and stress in the associated meridian.
3. Too much or too little of each flavor can bring an imbalance and stress in the associated meridian.

Meridians

The Chinese divided the body into twelve regular meridians which run to and from the head, hands and feet, and two control meridians. Blood and energy flow through the meridians, or channels. Each meridian carries bioelectrical energy waves or Qi through their pathways to provide energy and nourish the internal organs. Meridians are named according to the Organ with which their energy is associated. The meridian's main function is to maintain good balance and flow of energy for health. Each meridian is related to a season of the year and each is related to two body organs, one yin and one yang.

EARTH		EARTH		FIRE
Stomach (yang)	→	Spleen (yin)	→	Heart (yin)
7 AM–9 AM		9 AM–11 AM		11 AM–1 PM
				↕
WATER (yin)		WATER (yang)		FIRE (yang)
Kidney	←	Bladder	←	Small Intestine
5 PM–7 PM		3 PM–5 PM		1 PM–3 PM
				↕
CONTROL MERIDIAN		CONTROL MERIDIAN		WOOD
Pericardium (yin)	→	Triple Warmer (yin) →		Gallbladder (yang)
7 PM–9 PM		9 PM–11 AM		11 PM–1 AM
				↕
METAL		METAL		WOOD
Large Intestine	←	Lung (yin)	←	Liver (yin)
(yang)		3 AM–5 AM		1 AM–3 AM

Table 2. Regular and Control Meridian Cycle

Qi or chi energy circulates throughout the entire body along the meridians within a twenty-four hour period. For two hours a day, each meridian has a high tide of energy that flows from one meridian to the next. The Regular Meridians nourish the organs of the body. There are two Control Meridians: the Pericardium Meridian protects the heart physically and emotionally, and the Triple Warmer coordinates and oversees the working of the body and serves as the body's thermostat. When an obstruction occurs, the flow of energy slows down and is restricted or made to go faster than the normal cycle. The best time to treat a meridian is at its associated time of day, as shown in Table 2.

Energy flows freely throughout the body when the meridians are open and balanced. The flow of energy along the meridians can be obstructed by many different types of stressors from either internal or external sources. Accidents or falls, trauma, psychological or emotional stress, air pollution, sitting or standing too long in one position, repetitive motion, excessive exercise, eyestrain, and other factors contribute to blockage of meridians. When the flow of energy is reduced or blocked in a meridian pathway, an imbalance occurs. An imbalance of energy flow can cause various symptoms along the pathway such as numbness, pain, pressure, stiffness, chills, heat, or discoloration, to mention just a few. Too much or too little energy flowing along the meridians can cause illness, and cessation of energy causes death. A few relationships between posture, movement, emotions, and blockage of meridians are shown in Table 1.

Some very simple examples may help explain the basic premise of the Five Element theory and how an obstructed meridian may contribute to meridian imbalances leading to health problems (see Table 1). A neighbor who has a foul temper and constantly yells angrily about petty issues most likely has an imbalance in the wood meridian. A man dies of a heart attack after jogging excessively. Did he have a fire element imbalance? Perhaps you wake up at 4:00 AM and can't get back to sleep again. There could well be an imbalance in the lung meridian of the metal element. This concept is highly simplified, and these are just a few examples of a topic that is considerably more complex than shown here. There are many more associations for each meridian.

How These Therapies Work

In Asian cultures, many healers believe that a life-energy force radiates from all living things. In *The Power of the Mind to Heal*, the Borysenkos say that some Western physicists have also suggested that a universal energy connects all things and transcends time and space. This energy-force communicates between the skin or external body to the circulatory, nervous, muscular, digestive, genitourinary and all other systems of the body. Within the body there are over 1,000 acupoints, which work in harmony to maintain the flow of energy and balance. Some health practitioners can actually see or feel pockets of blocked emotions and energy held in the body that cause a reduced flow of energy and impair health. Many practitioners of Oriental medicine consciously use their own life-force energy to diagnose and heal their clients. And some practitioners can even observe and clearly 'feel the energy' move as they work to break up blockages within the body.

The balance of this vital energy is considered a key aspect for both physical and emotional well-being. When life stressors are overwhelming or out of control and one's emotions are unbalanced, the vital energy system becomes weakened or blocked and affects selected parts of the body. Imbalances can lead to body aches and pains, swelling, fatigue, colds, flu, and other illnesses. Muscles may become tense and blood circulation blocked. By stimulating key acupoints, muscle tension is released, the circulation of blood is restored, and energy begins to flow freely again.

In most forms of acupressure or acupuncture, the therapist initially assesses the condition of the meridians by looking at the body, asking questions, listening, touching, palpating the pulses, looking at the tongue and meridians, along with the *hara* diagnosis. The Oriental Medical Model includes an even more complex way of assessing the body's energetic system based on Chinese Medical parameters relating to the balance and circulation of yin/yang, along with many other methods. The therapist determines the state of meridian imbalances and develops a therapy plan. When reduced or blocked meridians are released through touch or other physical methods, there is a clearing of the internal pathways, which many people experience as increased energy. Various Asian and alternative modalities are adept at using techniques that release blocked emotions and provide some kind of emotional energy release or catharsis in healing.

The Chinese also believe that people can intentionally move this energy, Qi, internally along the meridians through the practice of breathing exercises, mental concentration, and meditative movements known as *tai chi* and *yoga*. Qi can also be directed externally—moved from one person to another. The ability to control the flow of Qi is called *Qi Gong*, meaning "the manipulation of vital energy." Besides acupressure and acupuncture, yoga is also considered a mental control method of balancing the body's vital energy. It is also believed that Qi energy is used in telepathy, clairvoyance, and psychokinesis—the ability to move objects without touching them, wrote the Borysenkos.

ACUPRESSSURE

According to oral tradition, the earliest text on Oriental Bodywork Therapy is Qi Bo's classic on medical massage. Qi Bo was a Chinese master who lived more than 5,000 years ago. Throughout much of China's history, Oriental therapy was a highly-regarded healing art. The ancients used their hands to heal and maintain health.

Over the centuries more than 660 acupressure points have been identified on the body. Of these, 365 acupoints (called *tsubos*) are located along the major meridian pathways, although they are not obvious to the untrained eye. They are unique in that each acupoint provides access to the internal base energy system. The acupoints are close to the skin's surface. They appear as depressions at junctures of muscles, in places where nerves emerge from muscles, at the trunks of muscles and nerves, and in spaces between wrinkles on the skin. Often a tender sensation occurs when the point is pressed.

Acupoints on the skin are sensitive to bioelectrical impulses in the body and conduct those impulses easily. Western scientists have mapped out and shown the existence of this system of body points through the use of sensitive electrical devices. Stimulating acupoints with manual pressure, needles (acupuncture), heat or laser, releases endorphins, which are the neurochemicals that reduce pain. As pain is unblocked, the flow of blood and oxygen to the affected area is increased.

When a muscle is chronically tense or in spasm, the muscle fibers contract. This can be triggered by fatigue, trauma, stress, chemical imbalances, and/or poor circulation. For example, a person under stress may have a headache that can be relieved with pressure on certain acupoints, as discussed later in this chapter. As specific acupoints are pressed, the muscle tension softens, enabling the fibers to elongate and relax, so blood flows freely and toxins are released and eliminated. The increased circulation brings more oxygen and other nutrients to the affected areas, increasing the body's resistance to the imbalance of illness and tension. When blood and energy circulate freely, there is a sense of harmony and well-being.

Today there are dozens of forms of Oriental bodywork, each with its own diverse heritage and techniques. There are styles from China, Japan, Korea, and other countries. They all have a similar foundation in theory and philosophy and include manipulation along the energy meridians of the body. *Shiatsu* is a form of Japanese acupressure, which means applying pressure on acupoints to balance the flow of chi in the meridians to promote and maintain health.

There are many styles of Shiatsu, including Zen, Five Element, Tao, Setei, Japanese, Macrobiotic, and Anma, which is a vigorous therapy similar to massage and given on a table. The other forms of Shiatsu are traditionally given on the floor. The client is fully clothed and lies on a futon or padded surface. The Japanese form applies pressure to meridian tsubos using hands, fingers, forearms, elbows, knees, and/or feet to balance the meridians and organs and to clear the mind and emotions. Some clients are given exercises or may be instructed in the use of self-acupressure to assist their healing between appointments.

TuiNa is the traditional form of bodywork therapy used in China. "Tui" means push and "Na" means grasp. The therapy deeply affects the flow of Qi in the meridians and utilizes soft tissue manipulation, acupoints, and structural realignment to treat disorders.

When selecting a practitioner, check for bodywork certification from an accredited school, institution, or organization. The national organization representing the traditions of Oriental bodywork in the United States is the American Organization for Bodywork Therapies of Asia. To locate a therapist in your part of the country, call 856-782-1616 or access the organization's website, www.healthy.net.aobta.

ACUPUNCTURE

Acupuncture or meridian therapy is a principle or method by which some health problems and pain can be relieved and wellness promoted through insertion of fine needles into acupoints, often accompanied by different manipulations. Acupuncture is based on many theories. The most popular are the Eight Principle Patterns and the Five Element theory. According to John Pirog, author of *Meridian Style Acupuncture*, acupuncture is like opening and closing holes of a flute to alter the amount of energy flowing through the meridian. Originally bronze medical needles were developed for acupuncture.

Currently two types of acupuncture are available—Meridian Style and Modern Style, writes Pirog. In Meridian style, acupoints are located according to tenderness and tissue changes. Mild needles are used with a mild stimulus. Insertion is shallower and there is less manipulation of the needle. All painful acupoints must be stimulated with needles. In Modern style, Chinese acupuncturists select acupoints according to a standard anatomical reference. This type of acupressure uses fewer needles and a stronger stimulus. Insertion is deeper and thicker needles with manipulation are preferred.

Acupuncture practitioners consider two different environments—the internal that is within you and the external, which surrounds you. The internal environment includes the functioning of your organs, body fluids, and sex and reproductive functions, as well as your thoughts and emotions. The external environment includes the atmosphere—its weather and seasonal changes, including wind, rain, heat, cold, dryness, and dampness. How well your body handles changes in your internal and external environments determines your health, diseases, and your life. Ill-effects from either environment can harm the body. Disorders can show up in symptoms classified as stagnant, deficient, or excessive.

The pattern of symptoms determines whether there are deficiencies in Yin or Yang that need replenishing, or harmful excesses that must be eliminated. Yin and Yang are closely connected, and acupuncture can help balance abnormal states of energy transversing the meridians. Stimulating acupoints with needles performs these functions and adjusts your body for increased balance and harmony.

During an acupuncture treatment, you will usually change into a hospital gown and lie down on a padded table. Extremely thin sterile needles are inserted along ten to twenty specific energy pathways known as *acupoints*. Some people compare the sensation to a mosquito bite, although the hands and feet are usually more sensitive than other areas of the body. The needles contact and regulate the inner energy force called Qi, and you may feel a tingling or a mild to moderate heaviness. The needles are usually left in place for twenty to thirty minutes, and may be stimulated by twirling, heat, or applying a small electrical current. Some acupuncturists use laser stimulation to the acupoint, which is painless and as effective as needles. After a session you'll most likely feel relaxed, and shouldn't return to a stressful situation or heavy work.

Most people require between seven to ten treatments, although those with chronic problems may require more. While some individuals notice an immediate improvement after the first treatment, others may not notice any effect until after many treatments. The usual frequency of treatments is between two and four times a week. An acupuncturistwho has been trained in China for four years has considerably more expertise than one trained for a year in the United States.

In 1997, a National Institutes of Health consensus panel found clear evidence of acupuncture's value in relieving muscle pain. Later, other investigators discovered that acupuncture works by calming pain-induced brain activity by 60 to 70 percent. Oriental doctors believe that by stimulating specific energy pathways, energy is balanced and the body's pain-killing endorphins are released into the cerebrospinal fluid. Acupuncture has also achieved good results in relieving dry mouth caused by Sjogren's syndrome, jaw pain from temporomandibular joint syndrome (TMJ), diabetic nerve pain, stroke rehabilitation, asthma, and chronic lung disease. Some people find it helps relieve chronic headaches. It can also temporarily relieve ringing in the ears, or tinnitus.

Complimentary Therapies

Both acupressure therapists and acupuncturists may use three complementary treatments to their therapy: moxibustion, cupping, and gua sha.

Moxibustion is a method of burning herbs on or above the skin at specific acupoints or along meridian pathways to increase energy in the body, treat disharmony, warm chi and blood in the channels, and increase the body's resistance to illness.

Cupping is a treatment of disease by suction of the skin surface. A vacuum is created in small heated jars which are attached to the body surface. The vacuum draws up the tissue into the cups, pulling body congestion up and out. It is used in areas of swelling or pain.

Gua Sha is a treatment affecting circulation, pain blockages, and release of toxins. Using a smooth edge jade or scraper, the skin is rubbed with deep strokes to increase circulation and release toxins.

Self Acupressure

Prepare by dressing in loose, comfortable clothing. Allow enough time so your self-treatment can be relaxing and unrushed. Wait at least an hour or more after eating before giving yourself a treatment. Find a comfortable, relaxing position. Play relaxing music, dim the lights, and clear your mind of all thoughts so you can relax and enjoy the moment. You may use acupressure daily for continued good health and well-being.

Acupressure points can be easily identified by locating certain anatomical landmarks on the body. Some points lie under major muscle groups and some near bone structures that are easily identifiable. Beginners are encouraged to obtain an acupressure book with specific illustrations of acupoints and a good guide for specific disorders (see the references at the end of this book) or enroll in a basic acupressure course at a local massage school.

Once the appropriate acupressure point or points have been located on your body, place your finger or thumb on the point at a 90° angle. The point will respond to a slow firm pressure. Hold the point for at least a minute of pressure. Ideally you should hold for three minutes or until you feel a regular pulse in the point and soreness is released. Do not exceed fifteen minutes of pressure on any one point. Always use stable pressure to calm and relax the nervous system and promote healing.

While holding an acupoint you may feel pain in another part of the body. This indicates the two areas are related. Press both points. When you feel a pulsation on both the points you are holding, the circulation has increased. When the pulsation is very faint, hold the points longer until they balance with a strong pulsation. If you are unable to feel anything, hold the point for three minutes and release until your sense of feel increases.

While giving yourself acupressure, close your eyes and use abdominal breathing. Take slow deep abdominal breaths while holding the point and feel the balance between pressure and pain. Deep breathing purifies and revitalizes the body. Hold the breath briefly and allow the energy to circulate throughout the body, and exhale. This helps the acupoints release and allows the healing energy to travel throughout the body.

After several sessions of giving yourself acupressure, you will begin to feel deep relaxation and as the meridians begin to balance, you may feel tingling in your fingers and toes, signifying restored circulation and harmony in the body. Often when toxins release, there is a flood of heat to the body area of the acupoint. Continue to hold the acupoint until your normal body temperature is restored. In contrast, you could feel the point cool during your treatment as the body relaxes. Keep a blanket or sweater handy in case you feel cool. After the treatment, drink plenty of water or warm herbal tea, take a leisurely Epsom salts bath to open the pores to release bodily toxins, and pamper yourself. Get a good night's sleep.

Always consult a reference guide for contraindications, especially during pregnancy. Remember—acupressure is not a substitute for medical care nor a sole treatment for life-threatening diseases or serious medical conditions. Always consult your physician when in doubt. Acupressure is best used as a wellness treatment or for superficial conditions.

Examples of Self-acupressure

Stress headaches are common in our culture. Using the fingers on specific acupressure points can assist in relieving tension in the head, neck and shoulders. Tension constricts blood vessels and reduces the supply of oxygen to nerve cells in the brain. The following self-acupressure-point treatments have been known to help release tension headaches. This and treatments for other problems are described in Michael Gach's book, *Acupressure's Potent Points*.

1. GB 20 on the lower back of the head in the two hollows at the base of the skull.Press the right point with the right hand and the left point with the left hand. This point is also good for stiff neck and eye strain.

2. GV 16 is on the center of the lower back of the head in the hollow above the vertebral stem. Hold with your finger. This point also relieves a stiff neck.

3. Bl 2 is on both sides of the nose, where the nose meets the eyebrow ridge. Hold both points with right hand on right side and left hand on left side of nose. This point also helps to relieve eye pain and fatigue.

4. ST 3 is just under the cheek bone, about a finger and a half lateral to the nose. Hold the points with both hands, right hand on the right side and left hand on the left side. This helps relieve sinus problems and jaw tension.

5. LI 4 is in the webbing between thumb and index finger at the high spot of the muscle. This point is forbidden in pregnancy. Hold the web between your thumb and index finger, one side at a time, and press your thumb toward the bone.

6. LV 3 is on top of the foot in the valley between the big toe and second toe. Hold this point with your finger. This point is also good for eye fatigue.

7. GB 4 is on top of the foot, one inch above the webbing of the fourth and fifth toes in the groove between the bones. Hold the point with your finger.

Other Types of Acupressure and Acupuncture

Ear acupuncture is based on auricular therapy that recognizes the ear as a complete representation of the human body. The ear is viewed as an upside-down embryo. The body is treated by pressing selected points on the ear. Iridologists believe that the entire body is represented in the eye and evaluation of health is through an eye examination. Reflexology theories assert that all organs and body systems are reflected in the hands and feet. Reflex zones represent pathways of energy throughout the body. By massaging the zones, toxins are released and energy balanced. Korean Hand Therapy is based on the theory that the hand consists of a complete representation of the meridian system. Imbalances are detected by rolling an instrument across the hands and fingers, and are treated by giving pressure to specific areas on the hand.

Acupressure and acupuncture are ancient healing arts of Asia, deeply rooted in the traditions of Chinese Medicine. Acupressure is a form of bodywork employing manual pressure to the body to release obstructions and balance the flow of Qi in the meridians. By stimulating various acupoints located along the meridian pathway, Qi is restored. Balance of Qi energy is the key to physical and emotional well-being. Acupuncture is a meridian therapy using the insertion of needles into specific acupoints, often accompanied by manipulation to restore the flow of Qi. Traditional Chinese medicine recognizes a number of imbalances and the oriental medical model includes a number of complex assessment techniques to determine the patterns of deficiency and excess.

To obtain information on a licensed acupuncturist, contact the
National Acupuncture and Oriental Medicine Alliance (253-185-6896),
or www.acuall.org or www.acupuncturealliance.org
American Association of Oriental Medicine
Oriental Medicine Alliance

To obtain a listing of certified Asian bodywork practitioners, contact the
American Organization for Bodywork Therapies of Asia
(836-782-1616), or www.aobta.org
American Association of Oriental Medicine (610-266-1433)

If you prefer a physician, you may request Western physicians or
Western medical doctors who practice acupuncture by contacting the
American Academy of Medical Acupuncture
(800-521-2262) or www.medicalacupuncture.org

13

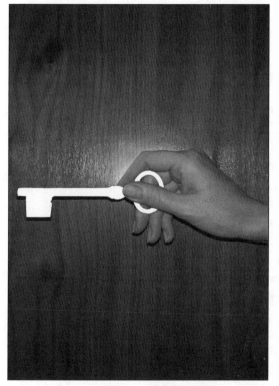

Attitude Adjustments

I can respond to all situations, secure in the knowledge that my higher power and angels will guard and guide me to retain my inner balance.

*W*ould you believe that most stress is self-created? Feeling stressed is a two-part process: first you need a situation or event to trigger your stress, then you perceive that situation as stressful. Thus, not only can a situation cause stress, but your perceptions and expectations about the situation can also increase the amount of stress you feel. You may also have "automatic thoughts," which are often negative and occur almost outside your awareness. Usually these automatic thoughts are very fast, unconscious, and very believable. When women are under stress, they often have irrational negative thoughts that may cause self-doubt, anxiety, fear, and trembling, along with negative emotions, especially depression. Some women even experience increased pain from muscle tension. Although you can't change some stressful situations, you can learn to change your thoughts and reactions to various types of stressors.

This chapter explains women's typical stressful, unhealthy thought patterns or attitudes that have a powerful effect on their health and behaviors, and the use of cognitive restructuring to release negative thoughts. Unhealthy attitudes and behaviors, such as a negative mind-set, catastrophizing, worrying, unrealistic expectations, need for others' approval, or being controlling, overly serious, a superwoman, are described, along with solutions to reduce these attitudes. In addition, a section on how to develop a passion for life concludes this chapter.

Definition of Attitude Adjustment

Since your attitudes and beliefs about yourself or any potentially-stressful situation determine how much stress you experience, you can change your physical and emotional reactions by changing your attitude. Attitude adjustment refers to changing your perception or perspective of yourself or about a stressful situation so that you feel in control of the situation or able to handle the problem, without letting it get out of hand.

Use of Cognitive Restructuring to Adjust Attitudes

Another name for attitude adjustment is *cognitive restructuring*, developed by Dr. Aaron Beck and popularized by Dr. David D. Burns. This technique has been used in mind/body health to change our unhealthy thoughts, which can affect our emotional states, and in turn influence our physical health. All of us have certain tapes that play in our heads: unfortunately, 90 percent of most women's tapes are negative, write Domar and Dreher, authors of *Healing Mind, Healthy Woman*. Cognitive restructuring can help you learn to identify negative thoughts, question their accuracy and validity, and replace them with more realistic thoughts. It is a way to erase old negative tapes and 're-record' new ones that are fairer and more truthful. When you eliminate negative thought patterns, you can free yourself from many factors that add to your emotional and physical distress.

Many women have deeply ingrained cultural messages about how they are supposed to behave. Some women believe they should be subservient both at home and in the workplace. They have been taught to care for others first, to be unselfish, and that they are not expected to be intelligent, powerful leaders. Some women have also been plagued by negative thoughts about their abilities and self-worth for years, even decades. Women who think they are worthless, and unintelligent, and that they will never succeed in their careers or relationships are likely to become seriously depressed and anxious. Sometimes you can see that these negative thoughts are false and cruel, but other times you feel vulnerable and repeatedly hear these tapes, especially type A women who constantly strive for perfection. Negative tapes can be restructured by first acknowledging your automatic thoughts and then recognizing the

lies at the heart of these long-accepted beliefs. Knowing the source (parents, teen peers, colleagues, friends, or the media) of a negative tape can
yield profound insights. However, some tapes are internal representa-
tions of your own worst fears that you may be found inadequate,
unattractive, or unlovable. Whether you know the source or not, it is
important to restructure these messages.

Cognitive restructuring involves a search for inner truths. Alice
Domar, a mind/body physician, described a process she uses with her
clients. Prior to restructuring an automatic negative thought, you must
first honestly face that thought, discover its origins and effects, then test
its logic. You begin by identifying one common negative thought pattern
that repeatedly plays in your head, then ask yourself these four questions
about that thought:

- Does this thought contribute to my stress?
- Where did I learn this thought?
- Is this thought logical?
- Is it really true?

—Domar and Dreher, 2000:92

By using your intelligence and self-awareness in responding to
these questions, you will uncover surprising truths about your negative
thoughts and their influence on your mind-body. Once you see the false-
ness and cruelty of a negative thought, Domar and Dreher suggest that
you work with a supportive friend or support group to help you transform
your distorted thinking. Sometimes we hold on tightly to narrow views,
fears, insecurities, and self-serving hopes in our minds, thus blocking our
ability to change and to accept a new way of thinking. If you can learn
to open your mind and release anger, frustration, or negative thinking,
you'll gain control over your thoughts and feelings. Cognitive restructuring
reveals the distorted thinking that often underlies a negative mind-set,
catastrophizing, excessive worrying, unrealistic expectations, seeking
others' approval, being a control freak, or trying to be superwoman.

Which Attitudes Need Adjusting?

Negative mind-set—Negative thoughts are stressors, not just
responses to stress. Your thoughts influence the emotional way you
perceive events and influence certain chemicals in your brain. Do you
ever wake up in the morning dreading the day, fearing it will be a
nightmare? When you do, your brain will access its "horrible day"

files, and when you have that mind-set, you'll find it difficult to solve any problems that arise. By giving yourself those negative messages, you put yourself into a weak mode of self. No matter what happens during the day, you'll focus on the damages, defects, and failures. Always looking on the negative side, believing that the glass is half full, can lead to feeling depressed and physically empty. An all-or-nothing attitude such as, why bother to exercise since I'll never look like Jane Fonda? or overgeneralizing with beliefs such as, if I quit smoking, I'll just gain weight because that's what happens to everybody, leads to false assumptions and dysfunctional thinking which distort reality and reduce healing.

Solution: To stop the downward spiral, remind yourself that negative thoughts can be self-fulfilling, and a bad mood doesn't necessarily make for a bad day. Concentrate on how you met similar problems or challenges in the past, so that you change your thinking into a more competent mode of positive problem-solving. When you replace negative thoughts with constructive ones, things will go much better because you have adopted a take-charge attitude to make things work for you.

Catastrophizing—Whenever you feel stressed, there's a good chance that you're distorting or exaggerating the situation. Allen Elkin, author of *Stress Management for Dummies,* calls this type of thinking "catastrophizing" and "awfulizing." It occurs when you make a mountain out of a molehill or think of the worst possible things that could happen as a result of a stressful situation. With a little effort, you can turn any typical hassle into a major tragedy or catastrophe and elevate your stress level. The body cannot tell the difference between events that are actual threats to your survival and those that exist only in your mind. How you react to a situation determines whether it adds to your stress and illness or promotes your health.

Solution: Awareness of this unhealthy trait is the first step toward reducing it, so you can respond to what is really happening in the present. Learn to control negative catastrophic thinking to reduce your stress and suffering. Small hassles or frustrating inconveniences such as being stuck in traffic, being late for an appointment, or broken appliances, should be viewed as such, and not blown out of proportion. Ask yourself, will I remember this situation or event in the next hours, three days, or three months? Remember to take one day at a time. Although life's problems can be temporarily huge, if you take the long view and remember that brighter days are ahead for those who persevere, you'll have less stress. If you challenge and dispute your own assumptions and exaggerated thinking, you can look at the situation differently and regain control over your emotions. Don't assume that the worst will happen; ask yourself these questions:

- What can I do, if anything, to improve the situation?
- How have I successfully handled this problem in the past?
- How important is this problem in the bigger picture of life?

Can't-stand-it-itis—Do you have "can't-stand-it-itis"—where various situations, circumstances, or hassles you dislike drive you crazy? When you say and believe you can't stand, hate, or despise something, Elkin says your emotional stress rises more than if you merely disliked that same thing. Even though you may not like some hassles and frustrations, you don't have to go ballistic and explode with inflated rage about the situation. This only leads to becoming more angry, upset, and distraught.

Solution: When you recognize that can't-stand-it-itis is contributing to your stress, you need to step back and challenge your thinking. You might ask yourself:

- Can I really not stand it, or do I really mean I do not like it?
- Is my overreacting helping me in any way, or making things worse?
- Couldn't I really stand it a bit longer, especially if I was paid to do so?
- How can I cope with this now and in the future?

Worry-wort—Are you a "what-if-er?" If you tend to take a problematic situation or event and think what-if something could happen, then Elkin claims that you make it into something that probably will happen. If your doctor said you were at risk for heart disease, would you then assume you'll die from it eventually? This way of thinking adds unnecessary stress to your life. Dr. Joan Borysenko, who wrote *Minding the Body, Mending the Mind*, believes that worrying, consciously or unconsciously, creates tension that reduces your mental focus, so you tend to worry more. It becomes a self-sustaining cycle. Some women are advanced worriers, who spend time worrying about past memories or future problems they envision. Others may think that by worrying about a possible problem they can prevent it from happening. "Worry is interest paid on a debt before it becomes due."—(Borysenko, 1987:119). Though many unpleasant things happen in life, most things you worry about never happen, yet you may worry about the possibility of their happening.

Solution: Learn to accept that life is unfinished: live in the present—do not worry about the past or future, because it will take care of itself. Another way to look at life's circumstances is to believe that everything happens for a purpose, but you may not know the reason or outcome yet. So if you go with the flow, and calmly wait for a situation to sort itself out before becoming alarmed, you may be pleasantly surprised. Some people believe there are no coincidences—that all things in life were meant to happen, so it doesn't help to push-the-river or try to control situations that are beyond your control. To stop this type of thinking, ask yourself:

- What are the chances of this terrible event really occurring?
- Am I being a worrywart or over-concerned about this happening?
- Does my worrying about a potential problem help me in any way?
- When I am older, is this something I really should have worried about?

Unrealistic expectations—Your expectations of how an event or situation will turn out, such as an argument with a partner, or a vacation, often determine how stressed you become. If your expectations of how others should think or behave are unrealistic, you may be very disappointed and overreact, creating more stress than you need. If you believe that, life should be fair, or that, people shouldn't be rude, you'll be sadly disappointed. If you expect everyone else to be totally honest and completely fair, you'll be upset because your expectations won't always be met. When these forms of rigid demands and inflexible expectations are unmet, you may become upset and angry. In truth, you are judging and finding fault or blaming others for their behavior because people often don't and won't follow rules and guidelines for polite, considerate living.

Solution: You need to adopt more realistic expectations of others because things often don't work out as you would like, and people don't always behave as you hope they would. Remember that other people usually see things differently than you and may have other priorities than yours, so they often do things that you wouldn't do. Seek to understand others before you try to influence, diagnose, or prescribe for them, otherwise your words will go unheeded. If you set realistic expectations of others and upcoming events, you won't be disappointed. Try to give up rigid demands and expectations of others, and be more flexible—learn to go with the flow, and you will have much less stress. Remember it is not necessary *to* always be right. You might say to yourself:

- People have the right to be wrong, and often they are.
- Just because others don't meet my expectations, I won't take it personally.
- I will not get my hopes and expectations up about an upcoming situation/event.
- I would really like it if people were nicer and more considerate of others.
- Why should people act the way I want them to?—They don't, and often won't.

Need for others' approval—Do you frequently equate your self-worth with your performance and/or the approval of others? Elkin calls this self-rating and it usually leads to much unnecessary stress. The basis for this stress-producing thinking is that you believe you have worth, are a terrific person, and have a right to feel good about yourself because you have accomplished great things, or you have marvelous traits, or some important person approves of you or what you have done. The problem arises when you feel you must do well, must succeed, or need others' approval. However, there are many times in life when you will not perform as well as you would like, and will not get the approval you seek from others. By making your self-worth contingent on any or all of the above, you are vulnerable to their approval and to unnecessary stress.

Solution: Learn to be your own judge of how well you performed, and consider the circumstances under which you had to meet a challenge. Were you short on time, did your computer break down, or were you under too many other pressures? Believe in yourself and your ability to handle problems, stressful situations, and to deal with life effectively. Most of us do the best we can under the circumstances we're faced with, and we realize, then accept the fact, that we can't be perfect all the time. So ask yourself:

- Do I really need to have others' approval to feel good about myself?
- Do I really have to be better than others to feel good about myself?
- If I don't expect others to be perfect, why should I expect it of myself?

Control freak—Do you become stressed when you feel that things are out of your control? When you feel uncertain about the future or that things are out your of control, your anxiety and stress may increase. While we would all like to have control over many unsettling, unpleasant, and unexpected events in our lives, usually we don't have that choice. How can anyone control traffic gridlock, long waits for a doctor, lousy weather, or crazy drivers? But you do have a choice as to how you respond to unexpected, unpleasant events by becoming more comfortable with uncertainty and lack of control.

Solution: Take active control of those things in your life that you can, and learn to accept those that you can't control. When faced with difficult problems that seem out of your control, consider the wisdom offered in the serenity prayer:

Lord, grant me the serenity to accept the things I cannot change,
to change the things I can, and the wisdom to know the difference.

So, the next time you are faced with a situation that is out of your control, you might decide to surrender to the flow, take the path of least resistance, or concentrate on changing those things you can and trying to avoid those you can't change. Ask yourself:

■ How much control do I really have in this potentially
   stressful situation?
■ Is it really worth getting upset about the situation—can
   I ride it out?
■ What can I do to distract myself or get through this situation?

Rationalizing—Do you ever try to explain away a problem by inventing excuses for your own or others' behaviors? Rationalizing is a process of explaining events that satisfies you intellectually by conforming to your perceptions. You may invent feelings or even identities for others. The selected pieces of information you choose to explain others' behaviors are frequently projections of your own thoughts or feelings. Whenever you find a solution that sounds like common sense but doesn't feel right in your head and heart, Joan Borysenko says that you're probably rationalizing.

Solution: When you feel uncomfortable about your own or others' behaviors, try to stick with the facts as you know them. Try to gain a sense of perspective of what is happening to you. A blame-free perspective helps you gain insight with a calm awareness. Perhaps you need to look for what is motivating your own or others' behaviors, and stay in touch with reality. Be open to new explanations for events and try to understand others. Learn to accept responsibility for your own behavior and don't try to explain away your faults or others' problems.

Too serious—Do you take life and yourself too seriously? When you do, your stress level rises. Life is filled with daily hassles, inconveniences, and other frustrations that can drive you crazy if you let them. Try to keep an appropriate balance between fulfillment and stress by lightening up your life. You can learn to reframe problems or laugh at them.

Solution: Try reframing a situation so that it comes out with an unusual ending. My daughter and I were almost hit by a crazy driver who suddenly made a right-hand turn from the left-turn lane at a red light. Thankful that we weren't hit, we laughed at his audacity, then two blocks later we saw that a cop had pulled him over. Justice has its own rewards! Humor also helps defuse many difficult situations and can reduce the potential stress and pressure you may feel. A great sense of humor, combined with a sense of the absurd and a bit of whimsy, can make your life less stressful. If you look for and see the humor in daily events, you'll maintain an even balance, and maybe help those around you feel less stressed. Stephen Covey, who wrote *The 7 Habits of Highly Effective Families,* believes that a sense of humor is a gift because you need the ability to see the irony and paradox in things and to reaffirm what is important.

Another way to lighten your life is to mingle with others who make you laugh—their sense of humor can be contagious, so you can talk about your own stressors in a more comical way. Look for funny cartoons or humorous quips, then share them with others, or stick them on the refrigerator. My favorite one is a bumper sticker: "Ever stop to think, and forget to start again?" It keeps others from tailgating my car.

Superwoman—Do you ever feel frazzled, as though you are on a never-ending merry-go-round? Are you running around in circles until you're exhausted, but can't seem to stop? Do you often feel like you're running in too many directions at once, but not accomplishing enough? Then you may be trying to compete for the superwoman award.

Have you ever seen other women who move from one activity to another exuding ease and graciousness and who never flaunt their busy schedule? While being better organized isn't always the answer, doing things more effectively can help. Crucial to a balanced life is knowing who you are, how you operate, and what your own sense of purpose is.

Solution: Don't let yourself become overwhelmed by tasks and obligations, but learn to see them in perspective. Accept only those tasks that you can handle, and don't waste time worrying about what you can't do. Only you can determine what you will do with your life, when and how. You begin this by determining what your life is all about—your grand design—your reason for living. Next, you need to identify your goals—what you hope to accomplish. Your purpose encompasses all your goals, so strive for those goals by focusing on your life purpose. You choose how you will live.

Women learn to handle stressful situations by association and repetition, but it is very difficult to change habitual patterns of thinking and reacting. When faced with a potentially stressful situation or event, try to step back emotionally and distance yourself so that you can realistically assess the situation. If you tend to overreact to any situation, it may be helpful to examine possible errors in your thinking such as those discussed above. Consider whether it is really worth getting so upset about something. Try to adopt a no, sweat attitude, whether you're in a traffic jam or running late for a meeting. Tell yourself, "Don't sweat the small stuff." You may correct your perception and thoughts by challenging and disputing their reasonableness—can you tolerate the situation a little longer? Do you need another person's approval to feel good about yourself?

Remember that just because someone says something, that doesn't make it true. Try to put the situation into a realistic perspective to reduce your stress and regain your balance. Use a relaxation technique, such as counting, breathing, meditating, or visualizing a good outcome to help you relax and avoid catastrophizing. Give yourself time to figure out how best to handle the problem, how to cope, or how to remove the source of stress. As a problem arises, you can fix it, eliminate it, or change it. Letting go of a problem helps you release the negative thoughts that have control over your life.

Another way to handle problems is to focus on the positive things in your life. Truly believing that things are great in your life sends that message to those around you. When you exude vitality, warmth, and joy for life, you believe others will perceive you that way and respond in a positive way. When you're comfortable and happy with yourself and show it by how you treat others, it affects everything you do and everyone you touch.

PASSION FOR LIFE

Several doctors, including Harold Bloomfield, Daniel Goleman, and Viktor Frankl, have emphasized the importance of having a purpose in life. A passion for life is more than a vague feeling of hopefulness or joy for living. It is a deep, inner commitment to a life that motivates you to pay attention, to extend a helping hand, to care deeply for the well-being of others or for mother earth. Goleman and associates, who wrote *The Creative Spirit*, call this a "creative spirit"—a high-powered force of life that may increase in strength with age, as you focus on what truly matters to you.

When you find a path with your heart, it can lead you to a plan of action that calls for you to respond with passion—to act on the basis of a positive emotional and intellectual commitment to someone or something. According to James and James, authors of *Passion for Life*, when you devote positive energy and enthusiasm to an activity or cause that has personal meaning, you expand your horizons and move beyond your self-centered activities, so that you act in ethical, loving, and compassionate ways.

Many people have only a vague idea of what is important to them, and their lives are based on an imprecise understanding of their values. When we are unsure of our personal values or don't know which values are most important to us, we may suffer inner conflict. Perhaps you need to ask yourself, "Am I getting what I really want out of life?" You can decide by listing the ten things you love to do most, and then ask yourself:

- When was the last time I did this?
- Do I prefer to do this alone or with others?
- Would those closest to me approve of this?
- Do I plan to do this in five to ten years from now?
- Does it involve either physical or emotional risk?

—S. M. Simon, 1974

Once you complete this exercise, reflect on which pursuits would bring you the greatest feelings of joy, fulfillment, or balance. Next identify any inconsistencies between your ideal values and your current lifestyle, then figure out how you could change your life and begin doing activities that you value. Set goals that turn you on and develop your vision for accomplishing those goals. When you spend your days living in harmony with your values and goals, you become more energized, focused, and feel at peace.

How to Attain a Passion for Life

We will never reach a better life until we can imagine it for ourselves and allow ourselves to have it. Carefully consider what you want to create or a goal you wish to reach. It may be an immediate need, or perhaps something of such significance or value that it will outlast your lifetime. To accomplish this, first take a few minutes to relax quietly and explore how you want to be remembered at the end of life. Envision the specific kinds of qualities and actions you truly wish for if you could do some things differently between now and then. Or envision a complete outcome—the end goal you are striving for. It might be more energy or physical fitness, a closer loving relationship, greater joy in your family, a safer neighborhood. Adopt realistic expectations and consider the steps you must take, one at a time, so you don't add more stress to your life. Next, describe what you currently have, your abilities and resources, in relation to what you want to obtain. Be honest and acknowledge both your strengths, knowledge, and skills and your limitations, such as available time and family or financial pressures. Then ask yourself whether you are devoting some time daily to living the kind of life that will help you reach your goals. Do your priorities reflect movement in your desired direction? If not, you may wish to make some specific changes to move you in the direction of your heartfelt values and purpose. Compare your current reality with your specific outcome image. The image should be precisely what you want to create out there, up ahead. This comparison can help create a healthy tension inside your mind that draws you toward achieving the goals you are seeking.

Once you've begun, you'll acquire some knowledge about what is working and what isn't. With increased experience and wisdom from each effort, you can efficiently and accurately evaluate the merits and weaknesses of each action. Each action builds momentum -gradually adding energy and force to each new result you want to create. Set your sights on goals you hope to achieve which will fill you with joy, happiness, and fulfillment. Once you've planted the seeds for success, practice using a positive attitude each day to enrich your life. Your thoughts create your actions, so expect the best. One way to keep an appropriate balance between stress and fulfillment is to lighten up your life.

In his book, Stephen Covey describes several principles for healthy attitudes toward life, which can enhance your health. Habit 1 is to *be proactive*, which means taking the initiative to act based on your principles and values rather than reacting to your emotions or circumstances. Being proactive is the most important action because it determines whether you choose to be responsible or a victim. Proactive people have developed and use four traits that determine what happens to them and how they respond. The first trait, *self awareness*, is the ability to step back and examine one's own thoughts and behavior before taking actions to make changes. The second trait, *conscience,* is your moral or ethical inner voice that tells you deep inside how you are treating others (harmful or helpful), and enables you to evaluate whether your own life is right or wrong. The third trait, *imagination,* is the ability to envision or imagine, based on past experience, a better way to solve problems both for the present and future. And the fourth trait, *independent will,* is the power to put aside your own present desires for something far greater and more powerful in the future—for the greater good of all.

Covey's Habit 2 is to *begin with the end in mind,* which means creating a clear, compelling vision of what you want in life that will guide other decisions in your life. Your vision or goal gives you the power and purpose to rise above daily stressors and hassles and to take actions based on what matters most to you, whether it is an event, a season, or a special project. Without a vision of your future, you just let life happen and may be swept along in the flow of society's values and trends, living without purpose. If you don't take charge of where you are going, someone or something else will.

Habit 3 is to *put first things first* and deals with how to make those things that matter most happen. Many people feel that there's a real gap between what really matters most to them and the way they live their daily lives. This habit means that you walk your talk—that your life really reflects and nurtures your most cherished values and determines how you spend your time. You may need to spend time with those who are most important in your life and carefully plan or create your own future together.

And, Habit 6 is to *synergize* by learning to value—even celebrate—the differences between other people's thoughts, views and feelings, and your own. Through synergy, you learn to create a shared vision and values and find new solutions and better alternatives. You may feel vulnerable to others' different views, and it takes self-confidence to be humble enough to listen to and accept others. However, when you have these characteristics, you cease being a law unto yourself and can learn from others and exchange insights. Synergy is the highest, most productive and satisfying level of human interdependence.

Benefits of Healthy Attitudes and a Passion for Life

Those with healthy attitudes about life, others, and themselves are less stressed and more relaxed, and have a strong immune system to ward off diseases and infections. Healthy, positive attitudes stimulate energy, help keep you focused, and increase your ability to work well.

Healthy attitudes also give you a more realistic perspective about life, so that instead of exaggerating worst case scenarios, you're less likely to react inappropriately and increase your stress. Also, by merely describing sensory experiences or desired visions, there are subtle, instantaneous responses in the motor cortex of the brain. Your desired suggestions can lead to images which may produce immediate physical changes.

When you can laugh at yourself and your circumstances, you lower your stress level: your blood pressure and heart rate decrease, and your brain may release endorphins that can create a calm feeling. Laughter also enhances your immune system and helps defuse a difficult situation. It reduces your production of stress hormones and increases production of T-cells and interferon, which can help you resist diseases. By not taking yourself too seriously, others are less likely to pick on you in a demeaning way, so your self-esteem remains intact.

Mary Wollstonecraft Shelley, the British novelist, said, "Nothing contributes so much to soothing the mind as a steady purpose—a point at which the soul may fix its intellectual eye." A meaningful life is a continuous process that includes purposive goals as well as actions to achieve them. While acknowledging the importance of each day is an excellent way to illuminate your purpose, power and values, it also is a time to reflect on your day. You may wish to:

- write down the high points of your day.
- consider all the things you are thankful for.
- review how you overcame a difficult experience and acknowledge your resilience.
- recognize how those things that happened helped you become who you are.

According to Viktor Frankl in *Man's Search for Meaning*, when we are motivated by a meaningful purpose in our lives, we engage in activities and experiences that are significant to our lives. When we are determined to reach value-oriented goals, make a cause our own, or reach out lovingly to another person, and are prepared to make sacrifices because we see a reason for our efforts, then we have an inner happiness or satisfaction that comes from these experiences. Thus, the concepts of meaning and happiness are interwoven.

B

14

Balance Your Body and Breathing Techniques
Your posture reflects how you feel about yourself and your environment.
Standing tall with your shoulders back shows that you feel confident and balanced.

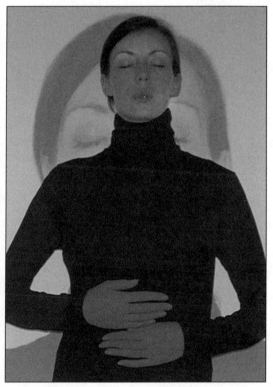

Balance Your Posture

*F*or a long and active life, few things matter more than good posture. It is very important to sit, stand, and move correctly and with ease. Your body depends on movement to sustain its vitality and to preserve its natural, graceful motion. When you lift up your head and relax your body alignment, you can help prevent or reverse the physical aging process. As you age, your moving posture takes cues from previous habits which are etched into your memory each time you stand, turn, bend, and walk. Research suggests that how you sit and stand may exert a powerful influence on how rapidly you age and on your mood. Alix Kirsta, author of *The Book of Stress Survival*, says that the way you stand and walk gives a clear impression of how confident you are. Standing tall with your head held erect, chest expanded, shoulders back, and eyes level implies that you recognize your own strengths and capabilities. Walking with a relaxed, poised body, and a firm, rhythmic stride shows that you know where you are going and can get there at your own pace.

Tension and stress are daily realities that we tend to ignore, but we often absorb them into our physical form and posture. Your levels of tension and stress may increase when you are unaware of your body. Through inattention or neglect, you may let your body sag, bulge, stiffen or spread, or you can stand and move with grace and vigor.

According to Bloomfield and Cooper, who wrote *The Power of 5,* your body shows your emotions by giving up the fight against gravity, sagging when you feel low. When you are depressed or tired, you may stand with rounded or drooping shoulders, so that you not only look old, but tend to feel that way too. Slouching or hunching over in your chair while working at a desk creates ten to fifteen times as much pressure on your lower back as sitting up straight, and it restricts your breathing and impedes circulation. A slouched stance, concave chest, and downward gaze convey a lack of confidence and a desire to remain unnoticed.

Definition of Good Posture

Great posture begins with your head and neck position, which strongly affects the placement and comfort of your shoulders, chest, and back. The best posture isn't forced, but released. Standing or sitting upright with a relaxed posture facilitates physical and mental balance. You make the choice every waking minute whether or not to consciously maintain good posture.

The Body Scan

Prior to balancing your body, doing a body scan can help you identify areas with tension. The longer a muscle area stays tense, write Bloomfield and Cooper, the less aware you are of this tension, and the greater the tendency for that muscle tension to lock-in to your body. The body scan begins by finding a comfortable position, lying or sitting. Then close your eyes and, with sensory awareness, start scanning your body from the top of your head to your toes. Think about how your head and face feel. Next, examine your neck and shoulders, then think about your upper, middle, and lower back. Lastly, think about your buttocks, thighs, calves and feet. Look for any sensations you feel, such as comfort or discomfort (pain), tension or relaxation, and heat or cold. Consider what's happening in your body and where. Whenever you notice tightening or stiffening of a body part, such as your shoulders or legs, you should release that tension—shake the muscles, shift your position, and take several deep breaths to relax. The ability to read your body's reactions and tension takes practice, or biofeedback training. With some practice, you'll learn to perform a body scan in less than a minute and be able to quickly identify areas of tension. This exercise helps you develop awareness of your stress, and to think about ways to release your tension.

How to balance your posture

Many variations of posture exercises originated in China, along with self-healing techniques and other methods for relaxation, stretching, and exercise. The preliminary posture, as described by Roger Jahnke, author of *The Healer Within*, can enhance your health. In the standing position, your spine and pelvis are upright, and your knees are slightly bent to allow the pelvic bowl to be upright. Relax your shoulders and move them down and back. Your arms are at your sides with the palms facing back. Adjust your head so that it is directly on top of your spine and shoulders. Lengthen your neck gently upward, then nod as if to say yes—this adjusts the chin gently downward to lengthen the back of the neck. Repeat this exercise a dozen times a day while taking a few deep breaths, exhaling deeply, then relaxing. Imagine or feel your internal energy circulating. The preliminary posture can be performed anywhere—while waiting in line, driving a car, or riding a bus.

Posture Exercises

Think tall: While sitting or standing in the preliminary posture, breathe naturally and comfortably. Lengthen your neck by moving your head upward. With your chin slightly in, flatten your lower back and broaden your shoulders. Now gently lean your head to the left, then to the right, returning to the most central, balanced spot you find. Next move your head slightly forward then backward, then find the precise center again. Try to think tall as you lift your head to float upward, but don't strain your neck.

Sit tall: Whenever you sit down, it is important to find the most balanced, comfortable position that supports your lower back. Let your chest and shoulders come forward as you bend at the thigh/hip joints to ensure that your buttocks and lower back are centered squarely and as far back in the chair as possible. Then smoothly bring your upper body against the seat back and hold your head up. Your back should be upright, yet relaxed, providing support for the lower lumbar area. The edge of the seat must not cut into the back of your thighs. Place your feet flat on the floor or keep one foot elevated on a chair rung or small stool.

Women commonly cross their legs and hold the inner thighs together. Loecher and O'Donnell, who wrote *Women's Choices in Natural Healing*, say that this can lead to back tension and problems because it twists the lower spine and pelvis. After you sit down, keep each knee lined up with your foot. Ideally, you sit with your feet apart, resting on an adjustable footrest or flat on the floor. Keeping your legs together can distort the balance between the hip, knee, and ankle joints, causing strain. If you must cross your legs, do so at the ankles.

If you sit for long periods at a desk, choose adjustable seating for the best support and comfort. Your chair must fit the length, size, and contours of your body. The chair height should precisely match the position of the desk or countertop. Armrests can relieve about 25 percent of the load on your lower back and provide stability and support when you change positions. A badly designed chair or desktop that is too high or low can affect your posture and compound the effects of physical strain and tension. If you're at a computer, typing all day, avoid back and neck strain by having your hands near chest level so that you don't drop your head to see the screen or keyboard. Remember to get up, stretch, or walk around for a couple of minutes every half hour so that your muscles don't become fatigued and tighten.

Healthy posture for walking: Walk tall by thinking about holding your head and neck up high and letting them ride lightly on your shoulders. Draw your shoulder blades back toward your spine and downward. Extend your neck and let your head rise, centered and at ease. This helps decrease tension in your shoulders and neck. Keep your hips and lower back in a stable position and raise your pelvis by tucking the buttocks together and slightly under as you walk. Imagine a straight line coming from your bellybutton that points upward toward your shoulders so that your pelvis is in a more level position that makes walking easier on the spine. Tighten your abdominal muscles and walk with your heel coming down lightly on the ground first, then gently push off with your toes. Your feet should land softly to reduce the amount of pounding and shock waves generated throughout your lower body. Simply focus on landing each foot softly and smoothly, and you can walk as fast as you desire. Keep your feet pointed straight ahead and don't hyper-extend the leg.

Use the "heterolateral" walking pattern by moving your left arm forward as your right leg advances and your right arm forward as your left leg steps out. Release tension as you walk by using breathing techniques.

Each time you exhale while walking, think about releasing any tightness that is holding your body rigid. This can help prevent stiff walking, stress walking, and heel pounding.

The flowing motion: Assume the preliminary posture first and rest for a moment. Jahnke describes the movements for this exercise. As you inhale slowly, turn your palms forward and slowly swing your arms forward and upward to shoulder level as you gradually lift your weight onto the balls of your feet. Your elbows are slightly bent. Let your mind drift free of concerns. Now as you exhale, turn your palms downward, lower your arms slowly to your sides, and gradually let your weight down so that your feet are flat on the floor. When your hands pass your legs, allow them to continue to swing toward your back slightly and lift your toes as high as possible. Try to inhale and exhale fully, as you develop a gentle rhythm. Gradually you will gain a sense of ease, a flowing sensation as you gently and smoothly turn your palms at the top and the back of the arm swing. Once you get the flowing motion going, you may rest in the rhythm and flow as the movement goes on its own. You may feel as if you are floating within an energy field. The flowing motion can be modified for sitting or lying down. You may start with one to three sessions per day of between ten and twenty repetitions; or more if you wish, thereafter, one or more sessions per day of twenty to fifty repetitions is recommended.

Bending correctly: While standing, if you need to pick something up, be sure to bend your knees so that your hips, knees, and ankles are doing the work, not your back. When you bend at the waist, it puts a great strain on the back muscles and can lead to back problems.

Neck-toning exercise: This exercise is used to improve your neck strength and resiliency, and relieve tension. Throughout each movement, maintain your best posture. Place both hands against your forehead, then slowly and smoothly push your head against your hands, while using equal pressure to push back with your hands. Gradually increase the resistance, but do not use your maximum strength to push your forehead. Hold for two to five seconds, then release and relax. Next interlace your fingers and place your hands behind your head, then gently and smoothly push your head backward against your hands while using equal pressure from your hands to push forward. Hold for two to five seconds, then release and relax. Do ten to twelve of these exercises several times a week.

Health Benefits of Good Posture

The preliminary posture and other exercises have several benefits. For one, you must relax enough to adjust your posture. Simply shifting to the preliminary posture has a health-enhancing effect on the brain because you have to relax and concentrate on arranging the body parts. This adjustment optimizes the functioning of all your organs and glands because it is the posture in which they were designed to work best.

The flowing motion exercise and others require gentle activity of many body muscles, which increases your energy and gently accelerates the circulation of oxygen and nutrients in the blood. The relaxed pace of this exercise lowers the blood pressure and brain waves are decreased into the alpha range, which is associated with self-healing responses. The movement of the arms increases the lymph flow in the chest and shoulder area. When this is combined with significant expansion of the upper rib cage, it triggers elimination of metabolic by-products from intracellular spaces. These exercises have a strong effect on your biochemistry and enhance functioning of your immune system.

BALANCE YOUR BREATHING

Breathing is the foundation of all relaxation and meditation techniques, along with some exercises such as stretching. Taking slow, deep breaths helps your body start to relax and reduce your pace to match your breathing. When you concentrate on slow, calm, deep breathing, you clear your mind and loosen your muscles. Lunden and Morton, authors of *Joan Lunden's Healthy Living*, suggest that you let each inhalation empower you, and release tension and stress as you exhale.

Take several very deep breaths during the day to improve your health. Deep breathing exercises send soothing messages throughout your body. They are excellent ways to reduce tension and stress and induce the relaxation response, according to Dr. Herbert Benson, author of *The Relaxation Response*. Deep breathing initiates relaxation and causes the blood capillaries to expand, which allows a greater volume of oxygen and nutrition-bearing blood to move more effectively toward tissues that need healing. Your breathing is remarkably linked to the power of healing.

Many people tend to use shallow chest breathing that delivers less oxygen to your lungs and the rest of your body. This type of breathing reduces your vitality for healing and may contribute to an under-supply of oxygen. Inadequate oxygen may make you feel dizzy, shaky, or groggy, and may cause fatigue, depression, stress, and anxiety.

Definition of Breathing

Conscious breathing is a technique employed by many ancient and New Age modalities. In many Indo-European languages, the words for "spirit" and "breath" are the same—recognizing that breath is actually the movement of spirit in matter. Breath is considered the primary link between mind and body in yoga and other holistic traditions. Breathwork is also an excellent relaxation technique. The simple practice of observing your breath is also a powerful form of meditation and a way to harmonize your body, mind, and spirit.

How to Balance Your Breathing

While several variations of breathing are described below, *diaphragmatic* or *abdominal* breathing is considered the most calming and revitalizing form of breathing. This exercise relaxes the mind and body and centers your awareness. Lie down on your back in a comfortable position, bend your knees, and place your feet about eight inches apart. If you have back problems, place a pillow under your knees. Relax with your eyes closed. Gently place one hand over your chest and the other over your lower abdomen so you can feel each breath, or you can put a book on your abdomen. Slowly inhale through your nose, first filling the lower part of your lungs, then the middle and upper parts of your chest. The abdomen expands with each breath as the diaphragm lowers and fills the lungs with air. Try to make your hands rise upward as you inhale, using your abdominal muscles. As you slowly exhale through your mouth, make a whooshing sound, and press your hand downward on your abdomen. Make your inhalations and exhalations of equal duration—you may count slowly to three on each. Do not force or hurry your breathing, for this is a quiet, deepening and centering exercise. Keep your breathing steady, slow, and full. Let your exhalation come out of its own accord, and continue for up to five or more minutes. Continue to focus on making your abdomen move up and down as you breathe, and allow your chest to follow your abdomen's motion naturally. To insure that you are doing abdominal breathing correctly, check if the hand on your abdomen rises more than the hand on your chest. If you're doing chest breathing, the hand on your chest rises more. Try to practice this exercise daily for ten to twenty minutes.

If you are a shallow breather, deep breathing can initially result in hyperventilation, dizziness, anxiety, or nausea. You may need to begin by practicing only four or five deep breaths several times a day for a week to become accustomed to a greater oxygen supply.

Breathing Exercises

A simple breathing exercise is to focus on exhaling. While sitting comfortably with your eyes closed, focus on your breathing. Begin with a deep breath, then as you exhale, concentrate on feeling your body sinking down and loosening up, becoming more relaxed with each exhalation. When your mind concentrates on your inner rhythm of breathing, your body will gradually match that rhythm and slow down.

The Essential Breath is the basis of most health enhancement breathing methods. It is the natural breathing pattern known as abdominal breathing, which Jahnke describes. He suggests that you begin by adjusting your posture—sit or stand erect, so that your lungs, chest and abdomen can expand freely. As you inhale through your nose, feel your abdomen expand as you fill the lower portion of the lungs first. Then feel your ribs and chest expand as the upper lobes of the lungs fill to capacity. You may feel a sense of satisfaction when your lungs are completely full. When you slowly exhale through your nose, allow yourself to relax deeply. Repeat the same sequence. When performed optimally, you reach a point of fullness, rest naturally for a second, and then gradually move into a long, slow exhalation. When you have taken several slow, full breaths and have reached your optimum fullness, you may experience a flowing feeling or warmth spreading throughout your body as you drift into relaxation. To enhance a relaxed feeling, you may imagine that as you inhale, the air carries with it a sense of peace and calm. Quietly say to yourself, "Taking in peace and calm." Then as you exhale, imagine all the toxins, tension, and anxiety leaving your body, and quietly say, "Letting out tension and anxiety."

The Remembered Breath is the same as the essential breath, except that it is done every time you remember to do it. When you remember to take a deep full breath, you must adjust your posture and focus your attention on breathing and relaxing, says Jahnke. The point is to become conscious of using the Essential Breath frequently throughout the day. Also, learn to rest in the rhythm of the movement, and allow your breath to be natural as you go deeper into relaxation. Soon you begin to feel carefree and light, and may become aware of a soothing floating sensation and a feeling of lightness.

The Holding Breath exercise is another simple technique. First exhale completely through your mouth, making a whooshing sound. Then, close your mouth and inhale deeply and quietly though your nose to a count of four. Hold the breath for a count of seven, and then exhale through the mouth for a count of eight, making the whooshing sound. This can be done in any position. If you are seated, keep your back straight. Do this exercise at least twice a day, and whenever you feel stressed, anxious, or off-center, but don't do more than four breaths at one time. With practice, this exercise will become a powerful means of inducing a state of deep relaxation.

The Vigorous Deep Breathing exercise can also be used to relax the mind and body. While sitting upright, comfortably relaxed with your feet on the floor, take moderately forceful and deep breaths through both nostrils, first filling the lower, then the upper lungs. Then forcefully exhale through the mouth. Take a breath every four to five seconds at first, then increase to one full breath every two to three seconds in the last minute. The increased oxygen brings energy and mental clarity, while the decreased carbon dioxide may cause a lightness and near euphoria. Do not do this exercise too vigorously or for too long, especially if you are prone to fainting. When you finish the vigorous breathing, take in a very deep breath and hold it for as long as possible, then slowly release it before returning to your normal breathing pattern. Sit for a while with your eyes closed and feel all the sensations in your body and ease yourself into the calmness you created. Practice this for one to three minutes. Initially you may experience some tingling sensations or light-headedness, as this is a form of hyperventilation. However, this technique can be very energizing and relaxing.

The Dynamic Breathing exercise emphasizes exhaling forcefully to discharge tension and clear mental stress. Stand upright with your feet slightly apart and breathe in deeply through your nose until your lungs are fully expanded. Then sharply expel the air through your mouth, using a "shoo" or "hoo" sound and extending this sound for as long as possible, while you drop your upper body forward toward the floor, bending at your knees. Relaxing and dropping your upper body forward as you exhale compresses the chest cavity and ensures that you expel all the air in your lungs. Concentrate on exhaling fully as you lower your body then relax for a couple of seconds before inhaling. When you are completely relaxed, slowly rise again, inhaling to a steady count of eight as you expand and fill your lungs and begin the exercise again.

Yawning is usually associated with boredom or the need for sleep, but it is also another way that your body tells you it is under stress. Yawning helps relieve stress, especially when you allow yourself to fully yawn. When you fully yawn, more oxygen enters your lungs, revitalizing your blood and body. By releasing that plaintive sound that comes with a good yawn, it also releases tension. The next time you feel a yawn coming on, go with it. Open your mouth wide and inhale more fully than normal. Take that breath all the way to your abdomen, and then exhale fully through your mouth, completely emptying your lungs. Enjoy the feeling of exhilaration.

Health Benefits of Breathing Exercises

If you are stressed and tense, breathing can help return your body to a more relaxed state and enhance your emotional and spiritual health. When you practice abdominal breathing, you enhance the oxygen exchange—taking in generous amounts of oxygen as you inhale, and eliminating carbon dioxide as you exhale. These deep breathing exercises accelerate several profound self-healing processes. They pump the lymphatic fluid within your body as the diaphragm compresses the abdominal organs. They also trigger relaxation that reduces constriction of blood vessels and expands the capillaries. Dr. Candace Pert, who wrote *Molecules of Emotion: Why You Feel the Way You Do*, says that this reduces your blood pressure, and initiates the release of numerous neuropeptides for natural restoration. Changes in the rate and depth of breathing produce changes in the quality and kind of peptides that are released from the brain. By consciously changing your breathing pattern, the peptides are rapidly diffused throughout the cerebrospinal fluid to restore internal biochemical balance. Since many of these peptides are endorphins, the body's natural opiates, your pain may diminish. Relaxed breathing also slows the brain wave frequency toward the alpha, or self-healing range. When you start abdominal breathing, you may find that you are more relaxed and in control of your emotions and mental abilities; you will feel less anxious, less depressed, and less stressed. You may also sleep better and have more energy. Individuals who practice breathing techniques daily are able to sustain wellness, can adapt to greater stress, and have greater endurance, writes Jahnke. All of these changes are powerful healers that enhance the immune system.

According to Lynch, author of *Dr. Lynch's Holistic Self-health Program*, the best way to learn the effects of deep breathing is to try it out in different situations. The more comfortable you are with a technique, the more you believe in it, the better it's going to work for you. Check your breathing when you are concentrating on complex work or are agitated or upset. If you are breathing deeply through your nose, you will have greater concentration and more energy and will release useless tension. Deep breathing has an amazing calming effect—nature's tranquilizer. Also, counting your breaths clears your mind and is a form of relaxation you can practice anywhere. ℬ

15

Counseling and Support Groups

$\mathcal{M}$any women need validation that what they think and feel is normal and inevitable when they experience tough times. Seeking help with your problems, whether that means professional help, talking with a close friend, or taking time out for yourself, is an essential part of your mental and emotional health. Some women like to discuss their problems with a close friend, yet others would rather not share their distress with others because of the unsettling thoughts and feelings that are recalled. Also, though you may just need someone to listen to your problems, some friends may offer inappropriate advice.

Many counselors specialize in the types of problems with which they help women, and often can provide a different perspective to help you gain insight into ways to handle your problems. Individual or group counseling usually offers empathetic support, understanding, and insight into your dilemmas. Counselors actively listen in a nonjudgmental way as each person expresses and explores her problems. They respect you as a person who is capable of making wise choices and decisions. They demonstrate genuine feelings for you through open, honest, direct communication, and show consideration of your feelings.

Social support groups are a very effective means for people to learn successful ways to handle their problems. Some groups provide social and emotional support as their primary goal, while others focus on problem-solving and offer vital information. Most support groups offer understanding and compassion and can provide valuable assistance, especially during major crises such as illness, traumatic experiences, or loss of a loved one. A support group whose members have similar problems is a great place to find emotional release as well as practical advice.

Definitions of Counseling and Support Groups

Counseling may be done with an individual or group by a health care provider who has had special education in counseling. Counselors first try to understand how a client views or perceives a problem, then validate with the client their understanding, and may use a variety of techniques to guide or motivate the client to cope with or handle the problem. Many counselors focus on identifying each woman's feelings about a problem and use reflection to verify their understanding. Sometimes just explaining your problem can help you clarify it and acquire greater insight into factors affecting your problems and how to reduce your stress. Often a counselor will guide you in resolving your problems, offer advice about areas to think further about, or suggest ways you may not have thought of to reduce your problems and stress.

Support groups offer various kinds of assistance with emotional and/or physical health problems, which helps women feel less alone with their problems. Whether the group deals with general stress or specific emotional problems or illnesses, when you are with others with similar conditions, you're more likely to feel understood. Some groups encourage members to share their thoughts and feelings and offer emotional support, while other groups focus on teaching or providing information to empower members.

Know When You Need Help

It is not easy for most people to admit to themselves, much less to others, that they have an emotional or health problem. In our society, some people still think that seeing a mental health professional or seeking a support group means they are "crazy" or weak, and unable to cope. Women may have a very hard time finding and getting appropriate help, write Judelson and Dell, authors of *The Women's Complete Wellness Book*. When you have a chronic health problem, usually it is better to talk with someone outside your immediate circle of family and friends. Alix Kirsta says that the closer you are to someone, the harder it is for her (or him) to offer objective advice as they know you too well and tend to be emotionally involved. Also, family members and friends may lack the professional expertise to help you with your problems.

When you are in emotional pain and nothing seems to help you feel better, when life seems too difficult to handle, or it is too hard to get through the day, then it is time to seek help. Obtaining help for mental or emotional problems from a professional counselor or support group is a sign of strength, according to Judelson and Dell. It shows that you recognize when you need to take care of yourself, and are wise enough to seek appropriate resources to maintain and improve your well-being.

Therapists

Psychiatrists are doctors who specialize in mental illness and are licensed by the state. One in three psychiatrists is board certified, but this may not indicate their level of clinical skills. If your emotional problems are not related to a medical problem, and you have tried counseling, support groups or self-help measures for several weeks, you may consider seeing a psychiatrist for help with stress. Psychiatrists offer three kinds of treatment—psychodynamic or psychoanalytic therapy, cognitive/behavioral therapy, and medications for mental illness or disorders.

Psychologists have completed at least four years of graduate education in psychology, generally hold a Ph.D., and usually have specialized in clinical or counseling psychology. They must be licensed to practice in your state. Although they cannot prescribe medications, they do offer individual and/or group counseling.

Other *mental health professionals* include clinical social workers and mental health nurse practitioners, both of whom have a master's degree in their respective fields and may be state certified. Professional counselors and family therapists may or may not have completed graduate education, and are not required to be licensed in all states. You should check out the credentials and length of experience of any counselor you choose.

Types of Counseling and Support Groups

Psychotherapy is a form of counseling used by some psychiatrists to make conscious what is buried in the unconscious, often since childhood. This is a long, slow process in which each person gradually comes to discover secrets held in her unconscious which influence her present thoughts, feelings and actions. The therapist may encourage free association of one's thoughts, and usually avoids interfering in the process. Since the unconscious often contains unpleasant information, it must be revealed slowly so the patient won't object, get too upset, or think the process is stupid. Exploring one's dreams is also considered helpful because unconscious material often reveals itself in a disguised form in dreams, which may need to be disentangled. This therapy is often recommended for those who deny emotional issues behind their stress. In *Stress: 63 Ways to Relieve Tension and Stay Healthy*, Inlander and Moran state that the therapy focuses on the subjective meaning of your experiences to explore, illuminate, and transform the way you view yourself and others. It can provide insight into your emotional conflicts and feelings and help to clarify specific issues that cause you stress. It may also help you learn to manage and resolve the emotional issues that cause your anxiety.

Cognitive/behavioral therapy is based on the principle that because all behavior and perception is learned, it can be unlearned. Your therapist begins by examining your thoughts and behaviors that are believed to cause your problems. A good therapist will review each and every one of your complaints in detail, then decide what can and needs to be changed. The therapist may have you examine your perception of issues that trigger your stress. This therapy may help you change your behavior and attitudes, reduce distorted thinking patterns, correct self-defeating thoughts, and think more rationally.

Supportive therapy can be combined with *insight-orientation* to reassure you that your stress is temporary, while helping you identify factors contributing to your stress. This type of therapy may enhance your self-esteem and help you develop a more positive outlook. Supportive therapy may also teach you stress management techniques, such as deep breathing, positive self-talk, and progressive muscle relaxation to reduce behaviors that increase your stress.

Some counselors specialize in family and emotional problems who deal with a wide variety of personal and relationship problems. Other counselors treat people for drug addiction, alcoholism, depression, loneliness, or post-traumatic stress. If you don't know a good therapist, ask your primary care provider to suggest one or seek referrals from a local health or mental health agency. Be sure to look for someone with a background in treating your type of problems.

Before you begin any type of therapy, first discuss the specific goals you hope to reach with the counselor. Your goals should be realistic and reachable within the time frame both you and the counselor set so that you can evaluate your progress. Whatever type of counseling you choose, it should be a collaborative process between you and your therapist. You need to take an active role in identifying and learning how to resolve emotional conflicts that contribute to your stress. Some stressed-out people benefit from as few as four sessions, while others may need six to eight sessions or more to unlearn old patterns and develop healthier ways to handle their problems.

If you can't tolerate one-on-one counseling, or can't afford private counseling, you may find that group counseling will work for you. A trained mental health professional serves as the group leader or facilitator. The group may vary in size from six or eight, to as many as twenty people, and usually meets for ninety minutes a week. Some groups break into smaller subgroups so that people can share their experiences or practice certain methods together. Try to avoid profit-making groups that advertise with enticing brochures and request high fees for attending meetings.

Counseling groups can be single or mixed focus. Single focus groups deal with one issue or condition, such as grief, and members rely on those who've been in the group longer to share their knowledge and personal experience and inspire new members with their progress. Mixed focus groups help participants solve different types of interpersonal problems. Their strength can be in diversity, whereby members gain insight through experiencing the group dynamics and sharing different perspectives on various problems.

How Counseling and Support Groups Work

Women tend to deal with the physical aspects of maintaining their health and forget the emotional side. When you think about maintaining a healthy lifestyle, do you focus primarily on eating nutritious foods and exercising, and ignore your emotional needs—your thoughts, feelings, and spiritual being? Your emotions are a relevant part of your self-care because they are half of your mind/body system. When you become aware of your emotions by listening and directing them through your whole system, Dr. Candace Pert, author of *Molecules of Emotion*, wrote that you can access the healing wisdom within you. Although expressing emotions is good for your mental health, few people realize that it is equally important for your physical health. Domar and Dreher, who wrote *Healing Mind, Healthy Woman,* say that women who experience and openly express a full range of their feelings appear to have more psychological and physical resilience.

To effectively express your feelings, you must first acknowledge all your feelings, not just the positive ones. Anger, grief, and fear are all normal emotions that are vital to your survival. Anger helps define your boundaries, grief is used to deal with your losses, and fear protects you from danger. The more you deny your feelings, the more likely you are to express them through an explosive release of pent-up emotion. That's when emotions can be damaging to both yourself and others. When you deny these feelings, Dr. Pert claims that they cannot be easily and rapidly processed in your mind and released. Stifling negative emotions, write Domar and Dreher, may lead to depression and hopelessness that can become chronic states as a result of your inability to express and integrate your emotions. If you acknowledge, express, and resolve feelings of anger, grief, fear, and sadness, you are less likely to become depressed or feel hopeless. So express all of your feelings, regardless of whether you think they are acceptable, and then let them go. When you release your emotions, Dr. Pert says that they move through your system, your chemicals flow, and you will feel freedom, hopefulness, and joy.

When you are in emotional pain or are suffering a major life problem, you may isolate yourself from others and think that something is wrong with you. You may attribute your suffering to the belief that you are somehow inadequate, or different from others. When you feel the most vulnerable, you may be afraid to turn to a support group for help. You might think, "I don't want to talk to strangers," or "I don't need to hear other people's problems now." When you are in emotional pain, it is crucial that you reach out to others, but fatigue, shame, depression, and feelings of failure can make you socially withdrawn at the very time when you need contact the most. You may even believe that strong people stand alone, while weaker ones depend on others. Some women feel they have to put on a strong front daily to avoid upsetting those around them. Judith Sills, author of Emotional Resilience Is a Muscle You Can Build and build, suggests that you try to move beyond these feelings and attend a couple of support group meetings to see for yourself. If you join a support group of women with similar problems, you may recognize that your pain, difficulties, symptoms, or struggles are shared by others, which can change your perspective. Regular contact with others who face similar problems helps members know that their experiences are normal in many ways. In the right atmosphere, Domar and Dreher feel that most group members offer compassion to others that can affirm the difficulties of your own experiences.

Members of specialized support groups know what and how you feel because they have been where you are. Who could help you more to deal with your problems and enhance your self-esteem than someone who has already walked in your shoes?, asks Sills. Some support groups are emotion-focused—they help women cope with their feelings about a stressful situation. These groups encourage members to understand how their *thoughts* about a situation affect their *feelings*. When you experience an event as upsetting, you have processed it in your mind, then assigned it some personal meaning. According to Antoni, who wrote Stress Management: Strategies that Work, if your perceptions of an event are distorted in some way, your emotional feelings may be exaggerated. By adjusting your perceptions, you may begin to understand your stressful situation better.

Emotion-focused groups, especially those led by health professionals, focus on helping members vent strong emotions about their situation. In these groups, women have an opportunity to express their fears, pain, anxiety, sadness, and other emotions with a sympathetic audience. Meetings may become a place to deal with difficult problems. David Spiegel, author of a chapter on Social Support, encourages members to be more direct, open, and assertive about what they want and what they don't want from those people closest to them.

Other groups may be problem-focused to help women learn to identify and improve situations that can be changed. Group members learn to be more aware of incidents that tend to increase their stress, and develop strategies to prevent or lessen their negative response, writes Antoni. A good support group will not blame you for your problems, but will help you face, understand, and cope better.

Positive group support is one of the best, longest-lasting ways to learn stress management skills. Support groups, in which everyone shares the same types of problems, offer more effective emotional support, claims Antoni. In good support groups, there is a sense of warmth and security that comes only from caring people who understand your situation because they've been there too. They encourage participants to share their feelings, listen with empathy, offer unconditional acceptance, reassure others of their worth, and provide helpful information.

There are groups for many different kinds of common problems, from various diseases to divorce support, widowhood, infertility, and parents without partners. The best way to find a support group is to ask your health care provider, or see if there is a community directory of specialized groups. Some national organizations for specific health problems can provide contacts in your area. Sometimes one resource leads to another, until you find the right one for you. Also you may ask friends if they have suggestions about where to seek information. Some support groups are conducted by a health care professional, while others are provided by volunteer members who have joined together to provide support for others with similar problems.

Health Benefits of Counseling and Support Groups

There is growing evidence that counseling, social support, and self-help groups enhance our ability to handle problems better. The goal of counseling is to help you deal more effectively with whatever is bothering you and learn to handle your problems better. Groups provide a safe environment in which to learn about your problems, ventilate feelings, and learn from others' experience. Spiegel writes that some research studies have found that groups seem to enhance their members' sense of control over their lives and their ability to cope with their problems, and also have positive physical effects.

Support groups can be an economical, immediate way to reduce stress. They can reverse the isolation people feel in modern society, act as pseudo-families where all players are equal, and encourage members to air and share their vulnerable emotions. Inlander and Moran say they offer a nonthreatening safe haven, where you can vent anger, voice fears, and begin to let go of negative emotions by sharing painful experiences with those who have felt similar emotions.

In support groups, members learn to recognize different types of support and benefits to coping with stress. They may learn how to acquire greater support from their current support networks. The group itself may also serve as a model of good social support by offering members a safe place in which to learn and share their feelings and experiences.

Stress reduction may actually help protect you against some diseases or live with them longer. Support groups offer not only companionship but can also increase longevity. Dr. Dean Ornish, author of *Love and Survival*, found that support groups were an integral part of any program to reverse heart disease. From his perspective, illnesses of the heart are based on an isolation from one's feelings, from other people, and from God or a greater force in the universe. Dr. Ornish believes that you can be alone and peaceful, or with a group and still feel isolated. He found that loneliness and isolation might significantly increase the risk of many illnesses. While no one has shown that exercising, improving your diet, or quitting smoking can increase the survival of breast cancer victims, weekly group support sessions, which enhanced love and intimacy, did increase longevity. Women with breast cancer who were involved in support groups did significantly better and lived twice as long as those who did not attend support groups. Thus support groups can enhance the quality and length of life of people with serious health problems.

When you take advantage of help from counselors and support groups, you can live more fully. Both forms of therapy can enhance your physical and emotional abilities by helping you acknowledge and handle the emotional costs of your problems, while enriching your life. You may also benefit from participating in a support group if you are seeking information about your problems and want to learn better ways to cope. $\mathscr{B}$

16

⌘

Dance, Movement, and Music

Use music to relax, dance or move, so you'll feel younger, calmer or more energetic.

*A*lthough we may not understand why we feel or behave in certain ways, our biological predispositions and life experiences shape our personalities and life-styles, and influence our movement patterns and body images. Even though our psyches may forget or repress parts of our life stories, our minds and bodies do not forget. Thus, unconscious feelings and unresolved issues may motivate and determine our behavior.

During periods of chronic or acute stress, we often experience symptoms of distress when our mind/body systems are out of synchrony or balance. One way to enhance your inner balance and reduce symptoms is through dance, movement, and music. According to Don Campbell, author of *The Mozart Effect,* healing is the art of balancing the mind and body, feelings, and spirit with an everyday routine to keep oneself well nourished and in harmony. A guiding principle of these various forms of movement and music is the unification of mind, body, and psyche. Another basic principle is that when you change a body pattern, you directly affect corresponding mental, spiritual, and emotional realms. By fully engaging in various forms of dance, movement, or music, you may express feelings and body sensations that have been constrained by your stressful life patterns, or reactions and personality behaviors.

These forms of stress management bypass conscious control of your body and move you into unconscious areas that need to begin healing.

DANCE AND MOVEMENT
Definition of Dance and Movement

Dance, movement, and tai chi are all ways to enhance the mind/body connection and promote physical fitness, inner balance, and emotional well-being. Since our life experiences reside in our mind and body, the reality of who we are and who we have been are reflected in our movement. Self-expression through dance, movement, or tai chi can serve as a dynamic and creative process for relief of stress and can promote inner growth as well.

These modes of expression may combine breathing with gentle, flowing movements and balance to create harmony and a meditative state. They may transform parts of yourself that can't be reached by other methods, claims Sandy Lieberman, who wrote an article, Dance Therapy. Some instructors emphasize the benefits of coordination and posture, while others encourage elements of free improvisation that help you express underlying emotions.

Types of Dance and Movement Exercises

Dance. For centuries, dancing has been used to stimulate and relax, and as a form of communication and self-expression. Dancing can be done either individually or in a group. There are no specific rules about what to do, since different things work for different people. The structure can be minimal, wherein you improvise moves with freedom to explore your unconscious impulses—spinning, swaying, leaping, or flowing endlessly in space. Or you may prefer a structured format, such as ballet, ballroom dancing, or dancercise classes.

If you are self-conscious, you may wish to begin at home with solo dance. Start by dancing on your own to your favorite type of music. Be sure you won't be disturbed by anyone. Avoid doing formal steps, just close your eyes and let your body move gently in a way that feels natural to you. Begin slowly to warm up your muscles, and then follow the rhythm of the music and your feelings. Slow, improvised dancing can help you learn to like the way your body moves, so it becomes a source of satisfaction rather than a problem. You may want to intersperse slow, flowing movements with bursts of physical activity. Using free-form dance movements with music, or learning routines can improve your balance, stride, posture, and body image. It also contributes to your flex-ibility through your range of movements along with warm-up stretches. When you feel blue or depressed, try swaying or moving rhythmically to slow music like dancing. Although your troubles won't go away, just mov-ing may help reduce your blues or stress.

If so desired, you may join a dance class, where you can gain strength and control and feel your body sensations. Ballroom dancing offers an excellent, low-impact aerobic workout and a way to meet new people. Debora Tkac, editor of *Everyday Health Tips*, says it may feel good to touch a partner's hand and look into a smiling face. When you hold hands, you may feel your partner's spirit and energy. If you dance regularly, you increase awareness of your body, develop self-confidence, and become more sure-footed.

Square dancing is a group form of movement with many ben-efits, where you not only enjoy physical exercise, but also must keep mentally alert to respond to the caller's instructions. It's a fun way to socialize and interact with others. When you hold your partner's hands, you'll feel their energy and a natural urge to be in harmony with them.

Aerobic dance combines many different types of dance steps, calisthenics, hopping, and jumping, all set to music. Alix Kirsta, author of *The Book of Stress Survival*, writes that you'll strengthen your abdominal muscles by doing leg raises, kicks, and balancing with your legs and arms outstretched. Aerobic dance moves for twenty to thirty minutes give your cardiovascular system a good workout.

Other types of structured dancing may be more vigorous, with continuous aerobic movement that uses lots of muscle groups. You might consider taking lessons in ballet , belly dancing, or modern dances such as the tango, rumba, fox trot, swing, or line dance, which increase your strength and control and can help you get in touch with your body. Jazz and modern dance are great for self-expression and may help you feel more emotionally balanced. Jazz dance helps relieve stress, energizes, increases flexibility, tones muscles, improves your body image, boosts self-confidence, and helps you develop better balance and coordination. You may also lose weight with more vigorous forms of dance.

Dance can give you pleasure as well as improve your health. It helps you stay active and fit by limbering and strengthening your muscles. More vigorous dancing can be like an aerobic workout. You'll increase your respiration and circulation and improve your metabolism and neuromuscular coordination. It is a wonderful form of expression, which requires only time, space, and music.

When you focus on moving your body, dancing can lift your spirits and may help solve your emotional problems. According to Jenny Sutcliffe, who wrote *The Complete Book of Relaxation Techniques*, dance therapy is based on the theory that moving the body can sometimes help people express and work out troubled feelings better than words. It is a highly personal activity that can unlock repressed anger and emotions and release physical and emotional stress, tension, and self-consciousness. Dancing provides an extraordinary feedback effect on the whole body, increasing sensation and stimulating the endorphins, the body's pain-relieving hormones. This creates a feeling of well-being and relaxation.

If you choose dance as a means of relieving stress, remember it's important that you enjoy what you are doing. Try to move as much of your body as you can without straining, and dance for fifteen to thirty minutes each day. You might rent a dance video for suggestions and the music. As you become less self-conscious, perhaps you'll join a dance class or club and try dancing with a partner. But always remember that you are dancing for yourself, not to impress others.

If you decide to take classes, find an instructor who includes warm-up exercises and cool-downs, observes how you move, and has a well-ventilated room with inspiring music. The dance instructor or therapist must create an environment where you can establish a trusting relationship and feel safe enough to relax, says Lieberman. Only then will you feel secure enough to risk being seen by others, and can begin the growth process.

A dance therapist may offer guidance as needed or requested to explore your feelings, sensations, or impulses to move. Lieberman recommends talking together afterwards to help you understand and integrate the experience. This can enhance the therapeutic experience when you verbally explore your movement, feelings, and images to increase self-awareness, empowerment, and integration of your mind and body. Some studies have shown that dance therapy can change how people feel and improve their depression and anxiety. Their body image may also improve.

Movement. Movement therapy combines breathing with gentle, flowing movements and may create a meditative state for some women. It appeals to women who like to achieve a meditative state of mind by moving their bodies. Movement meditation allows a woman to draw in *Qi* or *Ki* energy from the Earth, which many healers regard as the essential life force. This energy moves up and down along the body's meridians.

To use this form of movement, take several deep, cleansing breaths through your nose and blow your breath out through your mouth. There are various positions you can use. One position is a relaxed, squatting stance with your knees slightly bent and your hips and pelvis loose. Another is sitting cross-legged on a floor mat. Close your eyes and center yourself by visualizing your feet as connected to the soil. Visualize the center of the Earth from which you draw female energy, and concentrate upon and honor the Earth. Focus your awareness by gently moving your body in an undulating, snakelike swaying motion. Or see yourself as a flower opening up or as an animal gently moving across the ground. Dance, if you like. You may use sound or music to focus your attention on the movement and on the vibration. Allow yourself to get lost in the sense of movement and the beauty of your body as it moves. Feel the areas of your body that are tight and let the movement loosen them up.

When gentle movement is integrated with full, relaxed breathing and deep relaxation of the mind, the body enters a restorative, healing state. Movement exercises or therapy can help you learn to relax and relieve tight muscles from stress and tension. The exercises also increase your flexibility in the areas and muscles you move and enhance your immune system, mind/body connection, and inner balance.

Tai Chi. Tai chi is an ancient Chinese martial arts discipline that originated as a self-defense method, but is now performed in a slower form. The principles of tai chi are to achieve harmony so that energy may flow freely through the body, and enhance physical and emotional awareness, coordination, and strength. Tai chi focuses on a combination of the body's gentle, fluid movements and balanced postures performed in synchrony with slow, carefully controlled breathing, writes Kirsta. It involves many dance-like postures, done in a series known as forms or sets, and looks like swimming in the air or karate done in slow motion. This helps people relax and can relieve tension and anxiety.

This meditative exercise uses a full range of motion and slow, flowing body movements designed to promote physical strength, mental clarity, and emotional serenity. In *Stress: 63 Ways to Relieve Tension and Stay Healthy*, Inlander and Moran state that the discipline of proper alignment helps your body work more efficiently to enhance health. Tai chi helps create a mind/body connection, which is a good way to fire up your soul at the beginning of the day and recharge your soul at sunset, before dinner. It is also used to improve flexibility and balance and to strengthen muscles. Some say that the art of tai chi is to remedy imbalances in one's life and to strengthen one's inner energy. Those who practice it feel relaxed, harmonious, and refreshed.

Research shows that the controlled movements of tai chi can be helpful for people with arthritis and can reduce stress. The slow graceful movements make it an ideal exercise for those with hypertension, arthritis, or any other body imbalance. It promotes longevity and produces exactly the same physiological response as passive relaxation techniques like meditation. However, these optimum benefits may not occur until after four to six months of daily practice. Because it's slow and doesn't stress the joints, tai chi is a good exercise for all ages, and may reduce seniors' risk of falling. Although it involves real work, it doesn't make your heart pound, sweat pour off, or your muscles ache.

If you are adventurous and prepared for a long-term commitment, you may wish to join a tai chi class. The key to learning and understanding the real art of tai chi is to find an experienced instructor. Most martial arts programs begin with stretching exercises that enhance flexibility. It only takes a few weeks to learn several simple stretching positions or movements, but several years to become skilled in tai chi, since it is a highly precise discipline that must be taught properly to be fully enjoyed.

A license is not required to teach dance exercises and movement therapies, but tai chi is best learned from a knowledgeable, trained instructor. Contact your local YWCA, health clubs, or spas to find out where these therapies are offered in your area.

How These Methods Reduce Stress

During dance, gentle flowing movements, or tai chi moves and positions, you can become fully immersed in your physical movement, release negative emotions, and enhance the natural self-healing resources within you. Although some of these methods provide minimal movement or activity compared to more vigorous exercises, they still stimulate your circulatory, nervous, lymphatic, and immune systems. These exercises also enhance your respiration and oxygen metabolism, according to Roger Jahnke, author of *The Healer Within*, and when they include full relaxed breathing and deep mental relaxation, the mind and body enter a restorative state of inner healing. Some people believe that any form of movement is the essence and secret to a healthier, longer life.

MUSIC

Most sounds that we are exposed to in our environment are not conducive to relaxation, and neither is most music, because it was specifically composed to have the opposite effect. Music is a potent and powerful energy force that comes in a wide variety of forms and expressions. It can evoke different moods and feelings, transform your attitude and awareness, and increase your vitality or induce relaxation. Music can take the listener through rich emotions, thoughts, feelings, and memories. Think of how your whole sense of being changes when you hear a favorite song from the past.

Although music can cross all class and racial barriers, its appreciation is still a matter of personal taste and tradition. The right music depends on your cultural background, preference, and mood. In her book, *The Whole Mind*, Lynette Bassman writes that music also has different effects on different people at different times. Sometimes music will calm a stressed person, while energetic music may recharge a depressed person's body and soul.

Today, music can be a source of entertainment or mental and spiritual awakening. Music can stimulate the mind, body, and heart into the present or restore hidden memories very quickly. Once you recognize the effects of different types of music on your attitude and emotions, you will learn to manage your life by choosing the right music for the right time.

Definition of Music

Music is a universal language that is present in various forms and dimensions throughout your life. Bassman says that music has the direct power to affect the mind, body, and spiritual systems simultaneously and to move these systems toward wholeness and balance. Music is also a "memory magnet" that can recall specific human emotions, feelings, thoughts, and experiences. Music therapy involves working with the effects of sound and music on the mind, body, emotions, and spirit.

How to Use Music to Reduce Stress

The music you listen to influences how you feel, think, and behave every day of your life. Most people enjoy listening to music without being fully aware of its effect on them. Music affects people in different ways. Sometimes music is relaxing, while other times it is stimulating, and occasionally it can be overstimulating.

To fully utilize the powers of music, you need to learn to really listen. Find some time to devote exclusively to the art of listening to music. Dim the lights, turn off the phone, and close your eyes as you listen to music for fifteen minutes each day. You'll be surprised by the new dimension created when you actively focus your attention and simply listen to music. You may find yourself carried away to special places that evoke incredible images, impressions and memories.

Experiment to find the type of music that helps you relax, whether it is New Age, jazz, or a violin concerto. You may prefer music that energizes and revitalizes you. Listen to your favorite pieces on a headset whenever you feel the need to relax or be energized. You may choose to rest, walk, work, or relax at the end of the day when you listen.

Your voice is also a musical instrument—everyone can sing even if they are off-key. Singing is a wonderful way to discharge feelings or give yourself an uplift. Sutcliffe recommends singing around the house, in the shower, while walking, or working at home. Bassman says the voice is a very useful way to release stress, balance your brain waves, and actually massage your body from the inside out. Lower sounds allow the body to begin to relax immediately, while higher, elongated sounds recharge your brain and wake you up.

Playing music at home or at work can help to create a dynamic balance between the more logical left side of the brain and the more intuitive right side. If you pay close attention to the beat, pace, and pattern of music, you can learn which music keeps you energized and refreshed or relaxed throughout changes in your day or cycles in your life. According to Campbell, if you choose some of the new electronic forms of deep listening, which combine environmental music, brainwave synchronization, and minimalist structure, you may discover the importance of slowing down to stay in touch with yourself. New Age and ambient music was created to act upon the body and emotions, restore serenity and peace, and enhance spaciousness in our lives. It helps reconnect us with the rhythms of nature rather than the fast-paced chaos in our crowded world.

Effects of Different Types of Music

You can choose music to slow you down or increase your energy. Classical and Baroque music evokes more ordered behavior, while brisk, repetitive, or marching music can quicken your pace. Bright, up-beat tempo music seems to make time pass more quickly. Light, easy-paced background music helps some people to concentrate, while it may be very distracting to others, writes Campbell.

To relax. Baroque composers of chamber music such as Mozart, Vivaldi, Pachelbel, Handel, and Bach can provide relaxation, enhance concentration, and help you feel refreshed. Also, New Age music by Steven Halpern, Brian Eno, or Don Campbell creates a background environment that provides a sense of space and leisure and can induce a state of relaxed alertness. Some people prefer Gregorian chants that are soothing and simple, with no rhythm or harmony. Others enjoy more flowing rhythms of jazz and blues music to prevent the downward spiral of many mental conditions such as depression.

To evoke order and stability. Slower Baroque music by Bach, Handel, and Vivaldi imparts a sense of predictability and order that is mentally stimulating for study or work.

To energize. Try something rhythmic that moves with a fast beat. Latin beat in salsa music is very energizing, and rock music will energize some and induce stress in others.

To evoke sympathy and love. Romantic music by Chopin, Schubert, Tchaikovsky, and Liszt emphasize expression and feeling. Beethoven's *Ode to Joy* starts off slow, sad, and angry but gradually moves toward a glorious, victorious ending.

To focus. Haydn and Mozart's classical works enhance concentration, memory, and spatial perception. Vivaldi's *The Four Seasons* is good for concentrating, since the slower sections of the piece are optimal for deep concentration and the faster sections prevent mental fatigue.

To enhance well-being. Big band, pop and top 40 hits, along with country and western music, can inspire light to moderate movement and engage the emotions.

To transcend and release pain. Religious and sacred music, such as hymns and gospel music, can create feelings of deep peace and spiritual awareness which are useful in transcending problems and enhancing serenity.

Music can also be used with imagery and meditation, according to Debora Bassman. It helps you move deeper into the unconscious mind/body system. In guided imagery, the listener can learn to regulate different parts of the body and be guided by the music. The music allows your inner pace to be better regulated and to enter a dreamlike state. During meditation, music holds the thread of the experience together and helps induce feelings of relaxation and well-being.

Health Benefits of Music

Music has been shown to have the power to enhance your well-being and restore your health. Health is when all your systems are engaged in an ongoing process to maintain harmony and balance in your mind, body, and spirit. Recent studies show that music has many possible therapeutic uses and benefits. Music is often used for relaxation and stress reduction, which help the mind and body to access and expel deeply locked-in feelings. Don Campbell claims that you can repattern and recode the body's emotional chemistry when you hear music that evokes specific meanings and memories in the brain. Deeply focused listening to music can transform and balance your mind, body, and spirit.

Since our bodies are 70 percent water, they are excellent conductors of sound and vibration. You hear sound with your ears, but every cell in your body also literally feels the vibration of sound. Muscle strength, flexibility, and tone are also influenced by sound vibrations. Harmony is a complex system of vibration and resonance that pervades all forms of life. When you are around harmonious vibrations and sounds, Sutcliffe believes that you'll feel better. Disease symptoms can cause any affected organ or system to be out of harmony with the rest of the body. Excessive noise may raise your heart rate and blood pressure by releasing adrenaline and norepinephrine. Don Campbell says that persistent disharmony and noise, whether from traffic, the radio or television, or someone yelling, can make you stressed, depressed, and pessimistic—all of which can depress your immune system.

Music affects both the left and right hemispheres of the brain. Vocal music is affiliated with the left hemisphere and instrumental music with the right. According to Sutfcliff, the right side controls emotion and is the creative side of the mind, so the right type of music is needed to treat different types of problems such as depression or stress.

The harmonics, rhythms, and vibrations of music affect your entire being. They create responses in various parts of your brain that not only control your emotions and balance, but also resonate with the basic rhythms of the body. The right music can take you from a highly tense state to a relaxed, yet alert state in less than a minute. Music affects your heart and respiratory rate, and blood pressure. The heart rate responds to musical variables such as frequency, tempo, and volume, and tends to adjust to the rhythm of sound, writes Campbell. Fast-paced, rhythmic music increases your heart and blood pressure, and primes your body for action. The use of strong, rapid music, at about ninety beats per minute, gives strength, especially when combined with physical exercise such as walking or dancing. Any music with a rhythm faster than your relaxed heartbeat entrains the brain and heartbeat into a faster rhythm, making relaxation impossible. It also triggers beta waves in the brain that increase your ability to respond and act quickly. And conversely, your heartbeat often determines your musical preference.

Some types of music increase the production of endorphins, the body's natural painkillers. The body's healing chemicals can be stimulated by the joy and emotional richness found in music and can boost your natural immunity to disease. A few studies have found that stress-related hormones like cortisol decline when some people listen to soothing, ambient music, or music of their choice.

By slowing the tempo of music or listening to music with longer, slower sounds, Don Campbell says you can usually deepen and slow your breathing. Soft, soothing music calms your mind, reduces muscle tension, and lowers blood pressure. Listening to calm music may give you a feeling of lightness, open your heart, and give you a sense of inner peace. Several studies have found that listening to relaxing music can slow your mind down and shift it to alpha brain wave patterns. The slower the brain waves, the more relaxed and peaceful you feel. Music with a rhythm of about sixty beats per minute can move your consciousness into the alpha range of eight to twelve cycles per second and enhance your alertness and feelings of general well-being. Instrumental pieces, performed on the flute, harp, piano or string ensembles, tend to be more soothing, especially if they have a slow, easy rhythm. However, if you don't like slow tempo music, it may be annoying and you won't relax. Music and melodies must resonate with the listener to be effective.

Relaxing Music—my favorite CDs

    Aeoliah, *Angel Love*

    Aeoliah, *Angel's Touch: Music for the Heart Chakra*

    Steven Halpern, *In the Key of Healing*

    Erin Jacobsen, *Feather on the Breath of God*

    Ann Warner, *Angelic Favorites*

    Check Hallmark Music for titles such as *Music For a Stress-free Day*

Videos

    Tai Chi For Beginners by David Carradine

    Tai Chi For Seniors

Internet

    www.angelfire.com/az/angeljoy

    www.oreade.com

    www.serenitymusic.com

    www.stevenhalpern.com

17

Exercise—aerobics, stretching, walking

Numerous health reports recommend that women engage in some type of physical exercise daily because of its many health benefits. In the past decade, over 55 percent of American women were overweight and many were relatively sedentary. Less than 50 percent exercised for thirty minutes twice a week or more. In 1998, the Centers for Disease Control and Prevention (CDC) reported that in 1998 only 25 percent of adults met the recommended amount of physical activity, and that almost 30 percent reported no physical activity at all. The CDC recommends thirty minutes of moderate exercise, like walking, five times a week, or twenty minutes of vigorous exercise, such as running, three times a week. Many women sit for long hours at their jobs and then became couch potatoes in the evening. Without daily exercise, as women grow older, their body fat increases, and muscles in their arms, legs, shoulders, and abdomen become weak and atrophy. Regular physical exercise, thirty to forty-five minutes daily, reduces women's risk for many serious chronic illnesses such as cardiovascular disease, diabetes, hypertension, obesity, and osteoporosis.

In the 1990s, the typical approach to fitness included jogging, high-impact aerobics, jazzercise, and Tae Bo or kickboxing. Other popular exercises were walking, weight lifting, bicycling, and using exercise machines. However, several studies found that many vigorous exercises were no more effective in enhancing physical fitness than low-intensity exercises. Low-intensity exercise is also preferable because you are less likely to damage your bones, joints, and connective tissue. Health benefits are still gained, while the risk of injury from more vigorous and intense exercises is eliminated.

Regular exercise helps build strong, well-toned muscles, dense bones, and more flexible joints, and improves overall endurance and energy. More vigorous exercise helps balance the body by working the muscles you're less likely to use the rest of the day. It can alter the body's metabolism as fat is burned more effectively, which promotes weight loss and results in a leaner, healthier body. Aerobic activity burns off excess adrenaline and increases your serotonin, which can lift your spirits, improve concentration and relaxation, and enhance your mood. Physical activity can also reduce anxiety and tension, depression, and stress. Mastering a specific activity may improve your self-image and in turn raise self-confidence. Regular exercise also boosts the immune system. Those who are physically fit live longer and enjoy a better quality of life.

There are dozens of exercises, activities, and sports to choose from depending on your lifestyle and personality. It is not necessary to invest in special equipment, join a gym, or sign up for exercise classes. There are many inexpensive ways to engage in daily physical exercise to promote cardiovascular conditioning, muscle strength, and weight control. Many regular daily activities include moderate exercise such as climbing stairs, doing housework, carrying packages or small children, actively playing, and gardening.

Definition of Exercise

Physical fitness means having the energy, vitality, strength, and endurance to meet the challenges of your daily life. Muscles are a collection of long, slender cells organized as bundles of fibers which are attached to adjacent bones. According to Mayell, editor of 52 *Simple Steps to Natural Health,* as muscles contract during exercise, they pull the bones closer together, while nearby muscles must stretch and relax. When muscles are exercised, blood flow increases through them and helps build new cells. With continued exercise, muscles become stronger and build bulk. Although we all have about the same number of muscle fibers, some people increase the size and strength of their muscles through strengthening exercises.

Frequency, Intensity, and Time (FIT)

FIT is an easy way to remember the criteria to gain maximum cardiovascular benefits from your exercise.

Frequency refers to how often you exercise. Three to five days a week is recommended for good cardiovascular workouts or aerobic exercise. You should alternate days of aerobic exercise with strength training to help your body recover.

Intensity of physical exercise refers to how physically demanding an exercise is. The intensity of exercise you need to improve your physical condition varies with age, general health, body weight, level of fitness, and other factors. Low-intensity exercises require more time to increase your aerobic capacity than high-intensity exercises. High-intensity activities provide greater conditioning in shorter time, but have a higher risk of joint and musculoskeletal injury than do low- or moderate-intensity exercises.

The exercise level that provides the best workout for aerobic fitness is called the target heart rate. For beginners, the heart rate should be at least 60 percent of the maximum, and after several weeks of regular aerobic exercise, try to increase to 70 to 85 percent of your maximum heart rate (MHR). This provides you with optimal exercise as you progress from novice to veteran. To determine your MHR, subtract your age from 220.

Age	Avg. max heart rate	Target heart rate (60–80 percent max rate)
20	200	120–160 beats/minute
30	190	114–152
40	180	108–144
50	170	102–136
60	160	96–128
70	150	90–120

Set a pace for your exercise program and initially don't push yourself too hard. Slow down if you have difficulty breathing, feel faint, or have prolonged weakness. Remember to warm up and stretch before and after exercising. Generally, low-impact activity involves movements in which only one foot leaves the ground at any time. These activities are better tolerated by women and less risky. High-impact exercise, jumping or running, is when both feet leave the floor together. Most aerobic programs offer high- and low-impact classes. You can still get a high-intensity cardiovascular workout in a low-impact class because your heart rate is elevated. Moderate-level physical activity expends approximately 200 to 300 calories in a thirty-minute session. Examples of calories burned per hour by activity level for persons of different weights are shown below.

Activity	100 lbs	150 lbs	200 lbs
Walking, 2 mph	160	240	312
Walking, 4.5 mph	295	440	572
Bicycling, 6 mph	160	240	312
Bicycling, 12 mph	270	410	535
Swimming, 25 yrds/min	185	275	358
Running in place	440	660	960
Jogging, 7 mph	610	920	1,230
Running, 10 mph	850	1,280	1,664

Time or duration refers to how long you exercise. Daily exercise of thirty minutes or longer provides greater fitness gains as well as increased caloric expenditure. This is more beneficial than two hours once a week. The number of calories used during exercise is based on the intensity and duration. A longer duration training improves fat metabolism and weight control, and lowers blood lipids. Any activity that involves large muscle groups (thighs, upper arms) and is performed continuously for twenty minutes at your target heart rate is aerobic. Some fitness instructors recommend choosing an aerobic exercise to burn fat, and doing it at a moderate intensity for a minimum of forty-five minutes, at least three times a week. This stimulates your muscle mass, increases your metabolism and burns fat.

Purpose of Physical Exercise

The best approach to physical fitness includes exercises to achieve strength, flexibility, endurance, balance, and coordination. While most people are attracted to one or more of these aspects of fitness, your weekly activities need to include some form of each type of fitness to maintain good physical balance.

Flexibility of your body is enhanced by exercises and activities that stretch your muscles, such as gymnastics, stretch classes, tai chi, some forms of dance, and swimming.

Strengthening activities include those that tone or build major skeletal muscles, like weight lifting, resistance machines, and rowing or cross-country skiing machines.

Endurance is enhanced by activities that boost your heart rate and breathing for twenty minutes or more, such as jogging, aerobics, bicycling, and using exercise machines.

Balance and coordination are improved by tennis, racketball, and sports that require quick movements and hand-eye coordination, like martial arts or rock-climbing.

Below is a list developed by Mayell, of common activities rated by the degree to which they promote the main attributes of physical fitness.

Activity	Strength	Endurance	Flexibility	Balance/ Coordination
Bicycling	low	high	low	medium
Hiking	high	medium	low	low
Jazz dancing	low	medium	high	high
Rowing	high	high	low	medium
Running	low	high	low	low
StairMaster	low	high	low	low
Swimming	medium	medium	medium	low
Tennis	medium	medium	low	high
Walking	low	medium	low	low
Weight lifting	high	low	low	low
Yoga	medium	low	high	medium

Flexibility Training

Stretching exercises are essential to keep your body flexible, the spine aligned, muscles fluid, and the joints lubricated. Stretching is especially important as you grow older, because if you become less active, you lose elasticity in the connective tissue and muscles you don't use. Stretching regularly helps keep your body limber, and you stay active. If muscles are used incorrectly, or aren't used, they become tight. By doing simple stretching exercises daily, or before and after other forms of exercise, it is easy to maintain or increase your muscle flexibility. Physical exercise and stretching can improve your balance, coordination, and agility, and help prevent injuries like falls and fractures. With range-of-motion exercises, stretching also improves your endurance and posture.

Types of Stretching Exercises

There are several forms of exercise geared specifically to improve your flexibility.

Calf stretch: Place the balls of your feet on a step or curb, then let your weight down on your heels, so they are below the step/curb. Hold this position for thirty seconds. You may need to hold on to something unless you have good balance.

Quadricep stretch: You may stand straight holding on to something for support, or lie on your stomach or side. Keep one leg straight and bend the other knee (top one if on your side) behind you. Grasp your ankle and pull your heel toward your buttocks as you exhale. Move your hips forward for a greater stretch or under till you feel tension in the front of your thigh. Hold for twenty to thirty seconds, then repeat the stretch with your other leg.

Hamstring stretch: Sit on the floor, extend both legs straight out in front, then bring one foot toward the other knee. Bend forward over the extended leg as you exhale, and stretch your fingers toward your toes until you feel the tension in the straight leg. Hold this position for twenty seconds, and then repeat with your other leg. Another hamstring stretch is to place one heel on a chair or raised surface. With both legs straight, slowly exhale as you lean forward from the waist over your raised leg, and stretch your arms forward until you feel a slight pull in back of your thigh. Hold for twenty seconds, and then repeat with the other leg. Do several repetitions.

Arm stretches: Stand or sit straight up, raise your arms away from your sides as you inhale, and lace your fingers together over your head, palms up, as you slowly raise your arms upward. Stretch your arms as high as you can and hold for twenty to thirty seconds. Or you can hold a light weight in each hand, raise your hands, palms down, out at your sides to shoulder height twenty times; or move your arms forward in front of you from the shoulders and back beside you ten times. Another exercise is to raise one arm and bend it behind your head to touch your other shoulder. Use your free hand to gently pull the elbow downward behind your back, and hold for fifteen seconds. Repeat this stretch with your other arm, and do several repetitions.

Chest stretches: With your feet spread about shoulder-width apart, raise both arms away from your sides to above your head, palms upward and fingers linked, then stretch your arms upward and back of your head. Hold for fifteen seconds, and then relax. Repeat these stretches several times. Another good exercise is to stand facing a wall slightly more than an arm's length away. Feet should be parallel and about eighteen inches apart. Place your palms on the wall with fingers at shoulder level, and point your fingertips toward center at a forty-five degree angle. Let your body fall forward, keeping your back straight, elbows bent and raised. Push yourself away from the wall by straightening your arms. Repeat this exercise ten to twenty times.

Hips: Lie on your back with your right knee bent, foot flat on the floor, and your left leg extended straight out. Extend your arms out to the sides, palms up. Bring your right knee to your chest, while pressing your lower back and other leg against the floor. Move your right knee across your chest to the left as close to the floor as possible. You can use your left arm to press your knee down, while keeping your right shoulder on the floor. Look over your right shoulder and hold for thirty to forty seconds, then switch legs and repeat this stretch.

Stretching exercises should be performed slowly and carefully to avoid pulling muscles, or damaging connective tissues in joints. Stretch muscles only to the point where you feel a slight tension; if you experience pain, you have stretched too far. Hold each stretch at a challenging position for twenty to thirty seconds, or until you feel the muscles relax. Use slow, deep breaths into your diaphragm as you stretch, focus on relaxing your muscles, and think positive thoughts. Avoid rapid, jerky movements, or holding your breath while stretching. You may choose to practice on a padded mat or thick carpet.

Yoga and tai chi (a slow martial arts workout) are good stretch exercises that include concentration and meditation techniques which benefit both the mind and body. Popular and easy to learn, they increase your flexibility. Pilates is a good stretching exercise that concentrates on using fewer repetitions and more controlled movements for a strong, lean look. Your own body weight is used in resistance exercises to build-strength, endurance, and balance. The six original principles of Pilates are control, centering, coordination, breathing, precision, and fluid motion. Control and centering strengthen the stomach muscles and create good posture and body alignment. Some tai chi and yoga exercises are discussed in Chapters 16 and 24. Classes and personal trainers at many gyms and yoga centers can help you learn these exercises. An experienced teacher is the best way to learn; however, books and videotapes are also helpful.

Benefits of Stretching Exercises

Regular stretching exercises increase your flexibility and provide many health benefits:

- Bring fresh, oxygenated blood to muscles to warm them up.
- Increase the flow of lymph fluid that removes wastes from the body.
- Reduce the build-up of lactic acid in muscles, which can cause muscle cramps.
- Reduce the possibility of sprains, strains, and other injuries.
- Enhance body mobility, full range of joint motion, and relaxation.
- Return muscles to a relaxed, more extended state after use.

Strengthening and Toning Exercises

The goal of strengthening or resistance exercises is to increase the strength, endurance, and flexibility of skeletal muscles, so that they are able to do their job without strain. Muscle strength is the maximum force the muscle produces in a single voluntary contraction and is developed through various resistance exercises. Muscle strength is increased by contracting targeted muscles against some type of resistance. Muscle tone is the inherent tone during a relaxed, steady state. Good muscle tone is needed to exert sufficient pressure on bones to keep them strong and to reduce the risk of osteoporosis. Cardiovascular fitness also improves if strengthening is part of an aerobics program.

While many types of physical exercise will improve the health of your musculoskeletal system, specific exercises are designed to strengthen the abdomen, chest, upper arms, thighs, and lower back. These exercises can be done at home, in a gym or exercise class, or under the supervision of a trainer or physical therapist.

Isotonic Strength: Isotonic, or dynamic strength, is the maximum weight a muscle can support at one time. The most common form of isotonic exercise is weight lifting. Weight lifting machines or free weights can be used to target specific muscles. For women one to five pound free weights are adequate. Multiple repetitions of isotonic exercise with lower weights build strength and muscle tone, while increasing the weight gradually increases muscle size and strength with fewer repetitions. Women who prefer to maintain muscle tone, rather than build bulky muscles, should use lower weights. As with all exercises, good posture and proper breathing techniques are important.

Isometric Strength: Isometric, or static strength, is the exertion of maximal forward muscle contraction against an immovable object. Isometric exercises are often used in physical rehabilitation or along with weight lifting, but have limited use today.

Types of Strengthening Exercises

During your daily activities, you use many muscles when you walk, climb stairs, or carry groceries. If you engage in aerobic exercise or play a vigorous sport, you work your muscles even more. Muscle toning and building exercises can be done at home on an exercise machine or at a health club. The following suggestions are important:

Do simple resistance exercises using two small handheld weights, or dumbbells. When working with weights (or on a resistance machine), the quality of each movement is more important than the amount of weight lifted or number of repetitions. Use slow and controlled movement of the weights in both directions to build muscle more efficiently and avoid injury to the joints and tendons. Mayell recommends that you not allow the weight's momentum to control the move, and never hold your breath during strength-training exercises: always exhale during the exertion phase of each repetition.

During weight lifting, make the two sequences of lifting and lowering of equal duration and emphasis. These slow actions complement each other and are more effective at strengthening muscles than if you jerk the weight up or allow gravity to pull it down quickly. Don't hold your breath—exhale as you lift the weight, and inhale as you lower it. Try to do eight to ten slow repetitions over the course of a minute or so. Use enough weight that you feel the pull as a challenge. Work each muscle group to the point of momentary fatigue, or at least do one or two sets of each exercise per workout.

Mayell suggests the following exercises to strengthen the muscles in your upper body, back and abdomen.

Shoulders and arms: In a sitting or standing position, you can use an overhead press to work these muscles. Hold weights with elbows bent in front of your shoulders, palms facing each other. Slowly raise the weights overhead by straightening your arms, then gradually lower your arms to the starting position. Do ten repetitions, rest, then ten more.

Deltoids: The deltoids are the triangular muscles of the shoulders that raise the arms away from your sides. In the lateral raise, stand with your arms at your sides, palms facing your body. With your elbows locked straight, slowly raise the weights to your sides in an arc to shoulder height, and then return your arms to your sides. In the front raise, hold the weights at your sides with palms facing back. Raise the weights to shoulder height in front of you, and then slowly lower them. Repeat both of these exercises ten times.

Biceps: The biceps are the large muscles on the top of your upper arm. The best exercise for strengthening the biceps is the curl. With your arms down in front of your thighs, and palms forward, slowly bend your elbows as you exhale, and bring the weights up to your shoulders. Keep your elbows, upper arms, and body stationary. Lift, don't swing your arms, or arch your back. Slowly lower your arms to your thighs as you inhale.

Triceps: These large muscles are at the back of your upper arms. Use one weight to do a triceps curl by holding the weight with both hands, arms extended straight overhead. Bend your arms at the elbows and slowly bring the weight down behind your head to neck level as you inhale. Then slowly raise your arms to the extended position as you exhale.

Forearms, wrists, and hands: Do wrist curls one arm at a time in a sitting position. Rest your forearm on your thighs with your wrist and hand hanging unsupported over your knee. Hold the weight palm up, with your fingers curled around it. Slowly lower the weight and let it roll slightly down the hand onto the fingers, then pull your wrist back up, letting the weight roll back onto the palm.

Back and arms: The upper-back row is done by holding the weights with your arms out straight in front of you, elbows locked and palms down. Keeping the arms and weights at shoulder level, slowly bend the elbows to bring the weights back toward your shoulders, then push the weights away from you as you exhale, to return to the starting position.

Chest: The fly lift strengthens the pectoral muscles and expands the rib cage. Lie on your back and hold a weight in each hand, palms up, with arms extended to your sides. Keeping your arms straight, slowly lift the weights over your head as you exhale, then slowly lower them to just above the floor while you inhale. Pull them slowly up again before returning to the starting position.

Abdomen: The abdominal muscles are the weakest muscle group for most people because they are not normally strengthened by sports and activities. Many people experience lower back pain as they age, and need to strengthen their abdominal muscles. The abdominal muscles support the upper body, prevent lower-back problems, and balance muscles that support the spine. Some exercises to strengthen the abdominal muscles are:

1. The abdominal crunch or sit-up is the most common abdominal exercise. Lie on your back with your knees bent and feet on the floor. Concentrate on tightening your abdominal muscles, not your neck. As you exhale, slowly raise your head and shoulders slightly off the floor and hold for ten seconds, and then inhale as you slowly lie back down. Begin with ten repetitions, and add repetitions as you build up your abdominal muscles.

2. Leg raises also strengthen the abdominals. Lie on your back with one knee bent and foot flat on the floor, while the other leg is stretched out. Place your fingers under the small of your back and keep your lower back pressed on the floor during leg raises. As you exhale, lift the outstretched leg about six inches off the floor by contracting your abdominal muscles. Hold the leg up until you feel fatigue, and then as you inhale, slowly lower the leg. Do about ten to fifteen repetitions with one leg, and then switch to the other leg.

3. For a more strenuous abdominal exercise, lie on your back, bending your knees toward your chest, while you extend your arms, palms down, straight out by your sides. Contract your abdominal muscles and press the small of your back into the floor. Point your toes, then straighten your legs toward the ceiling and raise your arms two to three inches off the floor. Hold for ten seconds. Slowly lower your legs to your chest, then relax your arms and legs. Do ten repetitions of this exercise.

4. The bicycle is another exercise to strengthen your abdomen. Lie on your back and bring your knees to your chest. Raise your buttocks off the floor as you extend your legs, and use your hands to support your elevated buttocks. With your feet up high in the air, move your legs as if pedaling a bicycle, while tightening your abdomen.

Upper and lower back: Sit with your right leg out straight. Cross your left leg over and rest it outside your right knee. Bend your right elbow and rest it just above your knee. Next, with your left hand resting behind you, slowly turn your head and look over your left shoulder and rotate your upper body toward your left hand. Hold for fifteen to thirty seconds, and then repeat the sequence on the other side of your body.

Buttocks: Squats and lunges are considered the best exercises to tighten and reduce the gluteal muscles, as well as most of the major muscle groups of the lower body. To squat, place your feet about a foot apart, even with your shoulders. Then as you exhale, slowly bend your knees so that your thighs are parallel to the floor. Keep your back straight, and slowly rise to a standing position. Begin with ten repetitions, and increase gradually. You may add hand-held weights after you have mastered good form.

Lunges can be done several ways, stationary or walking, and with or without weights. You may alternate legs after each repetition or complete several repetitions on one leg before switching to the other. For a stationary lunge, step forward with either leg, slightly farther than an average stride. Keep your torso erect, then bend your knees and lower your hips straight down. The extended leg should be bent so that your thigh is parallel to the ground and your knee is perpendicular to the floor. Stop short of your back knee touching the floor, and then bring your front leg back to the starting position. Alternate legs and lunge forward with the opposite leg. Begin without weights and do fifteen repetitions, then gradually increase the number of lunges or add weights.

Upper legs and thighs: Lie on your right side with your right elbow bent and your head resting on your hand or bicep. Place your left hand on the floor by your chest, and slowly raise the left leg about eighteen to twenty-four inches off the floor, keeping it straight, hold for five to ten seconds, then slowly lower your leg to the floor. Begin with two sets of fifteen leg raises for each leg, and gradually increase the number each week. You may wear ankle weights for added resistance.

Lower legs and feet: To strengthen the muscles in your calves and toes, stand beside a desk, chair, or rail at waist height and hold on with one hand. Align your knees and feet. Bend your knees slightly and raise your heels off the floor, straighten but do not lock your knees. Bend your knees again slightly as your return your heels to the floor.

Judelson and Dell, authors of *The Women's Complete Wellness Book,* offer some safety guidelines when doing strengthening exercises. Always skip a day between lifting weights and strengthening exercises to rest your muscles. Stretch and warm up your muscles gently before doing any resistance training and again after each session. To improve your strength, repeat a movement ten to twelve times, and then allow a brief rest period between sets. Challenge yourself, but listen to your body and respect it. Limit yourself to three sets for each different exercise, and use an exercise mat or carpet for floor exercises.

Benefits to Strengthening Exercises

Strong, well-toned muscles work more efficiently and act as shock absorbers which protect your connective tissues and joints. Other benefits of strengthening exercises are to:

- Keep your muscles strong and flexible, which increases your stamina.
- Increase your bone density if you use weights or resistance training.
- Raise your metabolic rate so that you burn calories faster.
- Pump blood more effectively through the body.
- Reduce fat and lower your risk of chronic diseases.
- Enhance a leaner body image and improve self-esteem.
- Help support the back and prevent pain and injury.

Endurance Training

Endurance is the ability to perform well over a long period of time. Only one in five Americans gets regular endurance exercise, which is crucial for overall fitness of your cardiovascular and respiratory systems. Endurance training with cardiovascular and aerobic exercises enhances the function and capacity of the heart and lungs, and improves the muscles' ability to use oxygen and produce energy aerobically. Recent studies found that aerobic conditioning, especially running, can increase mental functioning by 20 to 30 percent. It also prolongs survival of existing brain cells, possibly due to the increased flow of oxygen and nutrients to the brain during exercise.

How Endurance Exercises Improve Health

Endurance exercises involve alternately contracting and relaxing large muscle groups to put stress on muscle fibers. Muscles become stronger as tiny tears repair themselves. During exercise, the body's fat and carbohydrates are converted to energy. As the body develops a greater need for oxygen, the heart beats faster, increasing the blood flow and the cells' ability to store oxygen. With increased training, the heart and muscles become more efficient, pumping more blood with each beat and using oxygen from the blood and energy stores, resulting in greater endurance and cardiovascular fitness.

Researchers have found that walking thirty minutes a day can reduce depression, heart disease (lowers bad LDL cholesterol and raises good HDL), hypertension, diabetes, arthritis, and obesity. Dr. Candace

Pert, who wrote *Molecules of Emotion,* says that early morning exercise turns on the fat-burning neuropeptides in your mind/body: just twenty minutes of mild aerobics elevates your heart rate and breathing to burn fat for several hours. It can also produce an alert calm feeling after the initial exhilaration, which may reduce your appetite.

As exercise continues, the use of oxygen increases until the amount of oxygen available in the blood is depleted, or anaerobic— without oxygen. Lactic acid can build up in the blood and muscles when energy is used up faster than it can be produced, which is detrimental to your health. To avoid this, exercise at a level where you can breathe comfortably. Remember to always do warm-up stretches before and after exercising to avoid injury, and rest muscles to rid them of lactic acid buildup.

Types of Endurance Exercises

Endurance exercises involve repeated use of large muscle groups during sustained, uninterrupted, vigorous exercise for at least twenty minutes to build cardiovascular strength. These exercises include brisk walking, bicycling, jogging, running, jumping rope, swimming, some types of dancing, cross-country skiing, or using a StairMaster.

Walking is a natural activity that clears the mind and calms the soul. Brisk walking improves the body's oxygen uptake and cardiovascular strength. Twenty to thirty minutes of brisk walking three times a week can be as effective as other vigorous exercises. Walking can protect your heart and blood vessels against disease, strengthen bones, help relieve back pain by strengthening and toning muscles that support the spine, reduce weight, and release tension. Wear comfortable clothing and good sneakers or walking shoes. Follow your natural stride. Stand tall, keep your head held high, and chest raised. Relax your neck and shoulders, and keep your abdominal muscles contracted. As you step forward, roll the foot from heel to toe without locking your knee. Bend your arms at a 90° angle, and swing them parallel to your body, back and forth naturally with each stride. Every few minutes, do the short-shirt pull by crossing your arms in front at the wrists, as if you're going to pull your shirt off. Raise your arms as you inhale, fully stretching overhead. Lengthen your torso as you reach to the sky, then exhale and return your arms to your sides while continuing to grow taller through your spine.

Walking can help ease depression and fatigue. After stretching, you may begin walking at a comfortable pace to clear your mind of mental pollution. Exhale and visualize releasing soul smog—whatever thoughts and tensions are bothering you. Then slowly and deeply inhale clean, refreshing air. Repeat five times. When you walk at a slow pace, says Alice Magnum, who wrote the article Walk Your Way to Great Health, your thoughts go inward to get in touch with your feelings. When you walk at a moderate pace, your thoughts shift to thinking about taking action to resolve your problems. And when you use a brisk pace, or action-walking, you think about what you specifically need to do and how you'll do it to solve problems or accomplish goals. Consistency, not intensity, is what is important about walking.

Bicycling can be on a stationary bike, or outdoors, where you can enjoy nature while you work out. If you cycle regularly, get a bike with a spring seat and high handlebars so that you can sit with a good lumbar curve. English racers, ridden with the torso almost parallel to the ground, relieve spinal compression, but you must be slim and strong to handle this type of bike. Wear a helmet and light-weight clothes, and remember to carry water and stop to drink and relax your muscles every hour.

Jogging and running build cardiovascular capacity efficiently, burn calories quickly, and help release feel-good endorphins. However, these exercises put a great strain on the joints, so knee injuries are common among runners, as are muscle pains, tendinitis, and hip injuries because this exercise repeatedly jogs your entire body. Stretching exercises before and after running, along with good running shoes, and running on a track or dirt trail instead of asphalt, may reduce your chance of injury. According to Crabby Road, "My last good run was in my pantyhose."

Swimming is an excellent nonimpact aerobic exercise that stretches the joints, tones the muscles, and works the cardiovascular system. Cool water offers an additional benefit of improving the circulation, digestion, and nerves. Wear goggles to avoid getting chlorine in your eyes, and don't swim underwater for prolonged periods. The best workout is when you do a variety of strokes, including the crawl, breast, and backstroke.

Dancing in many forms, such as rock and roll, ballet, swing or square dancing, along with aerobic dancing, is a terrific way to exercise, express yourself, and have fun. Music provides inspiration and energy as the rhythm often echoes the heartbeat. Vigorous dancing increases flexibility, makes you feel young, and lifts your spirits. It enhances cardiovascular fitness, oxygenates the body, strengthens and limbers the muscles, and releases feel-good endorphins. Although slow dancing does not provide a vigorous cardiovascular workout, it is a great exercise as long as you keep moving, vary your motions, and enjoy the natural expression of body motion. Try a variety of different dance exercises, or join a dance class and decide which form of dancing you like best.

Aerobic Conditioning

Safety guidelines are important for women who engage in aerobic exercise. Begin and end each session with a gentle warm-up that stretches your muscles and uses the full range of joint motions to prevent injury. If you have been inactive, start endurance exercises such as walking slowly, then gradually increase the amount of exercise to reduce the chance of injury. Some studies found that when sedentary people suddenly exert themselves too strenuously, they risk having a nonfatal heart attack. If the exercise is enough to make you breathe a little faster and feel a little warm from the exertion, then you're gaining in endurance and fitness.

While exercising, your breath should flow steadily with each repetition—inhale through your nose and exhale through your nose or mouth. Keep your feet moving throughout the session to avoid muscle cramps in your legs and feet. Work at a level that does not raise your heart rate to more than 85 percent of your maximum rate. Most authorities agree that twenty minutes or more of aerobic exercise, three or more days a week, keeps your circulatory and respiratory systems fit, but rest a day between sessions so that your muscles can recover and regenerate. According to the Physical Activity and Health report, the cardiorespiratory benefits from physical exercise over several short sessions are similar to the same amount and intensity of exercise over one long session.

Benefits of Regular Endurance Exercise

There are many benefits to engaging in vigorous exercise. You may notice more energy, high spirits, better self-esteem, and less physical and mental fatigue. Exercise serves as an antidote to emotional and physical stress: it stimulates production of opioids, which block release of stress hormones, and enhances release of endorphins, the mood-elevating brain chemicals. It is also a prerequisite to efficient metabolism, which helps you burn calories and fat. Aerobic or cardiovascular exercise can:

- Build and strengthen muscles, bones, and joints.
- Improve cardiovascular and respiratory fitness.
- Increase your stamina and help you feel more energetic and alert.

- Make you look slimmer and trimmer.
- Help you maintain your ideal weight and correct body-fat percentage.
- Boost your brainpower and improve short-term memory.
- Relieve tension and strengthen your stress-coping mechanisms.
- Improve your self-image and boost your self-confidence.
- Give you a sense of euphoria or exhilaration from release of endorphins.
- Strengthen your immune system, protecting you against infections.
- Reduce your risk of developing various chronic diseases.

How to Develop a Regular Exercise Program

Many people think they are too busy to exercise, but with regular exercise, you actually will have more time because you will be more productive, alert, and energetic. Daily exercise should be as important a priority in your life as good nutrition and relaxation. Schedule a regular time to exercise daily, set realistic goals for yourself that you can achieve, and make a commitment to continue an exercise program that works for you. Make fitness part of your daily routine, and reward yourself for progress toward achieving your goals.

First, consider your lifestyle, body type, and personality type. How much time is available and how flexible is your schedule? Pick the time to exercise first, and then select an exercise that you can realistically do during that time. A consistent routine is beneficial. Can you get up earlier to exercise or would you prefer to work out during your lunch hour, or while watching your favorite TV program? Many people like to exercise at the same time every day, whether it's early morning, at lunchtime, or in the early evening. Early morning is a great time for the conscious mind to reenter your body. Gentle stretching or yoga, a brisk walk, or dancing to radio music while preparing breakfast can help wake up the body. If you only exercise on the spur of the moment, focus on those types that really engage you and require no scheduling, preparation, or equipment, like walking.

Your body type and current level of fitness should also be considered. If you are out of shape, you should tailor your fitness program so that you can work up to more strenuous exercises rather than getting worn out or discouraged too soon.

Your personality type influences your choice of activities. Some people enjoy competitive sports like tennis, bowling, basketball, or volleyball, while others prefer solitary activities, like exercise machines or swimming. Do you like to exercise indoors or outdoors? What types of facilities are available—athletic clubs with running tracks, or public parks with special areas for running or sidewalks for roller-blading? Find a safe environment in which to exercise, and choose activities, clothing, and equipment that will protect you from injury.

Second, set realistic goals for yourself and remember that fitness takes time and dedication. Develop a game plan to keep you on track and focused. Routines are helpful initially, but try to build a repertoire of activities so that you won't become bored. Keep your workout moderate in intensity and spread your exercises over several days each week, rather than one day of a vigorous workout. Consistency and frequency of exercise are more important than duration or intensity. Try to do at least a light twenty-minute workout on scheduled days even if you're exhausted. Less vigorous aerobic exercises are almost as beneficial as more strenuous ones. Women who walk three miles a day, three to four times a week, achieve the same benefits whether they walk briskly or at a normal pace.

Third, think of exercise as cumulative during the day, so that every five minutes you exercise contributes toward a goal of thirty minutes a day. Know your limits and don't overdo it as you will feel tired, sore, and frustrated. Start slowly and work up to greater challenges over time.

Fourth, vary your exercises, and choose ones that provide a balance between working your upper and lower body. Challenge yourself with new exercises or increase your routine so that you will not feel that you are wasting your time. Switch back and forth among a number of different exercises to move different muscles, balance your body development, and prevent injury from overuse of muscles. Work with a trainer to learn new exercises to improve undeveloped muscle areas, and expect some soreness afterwards.

Fifth, find ways to enjoy yourself and make your exercise program attractive to both your mind and body. To spice up your exercise, try working out with a friend or family member, take a hike, walk, or bicycle with your partner. Take a class and enjoy the camaraderie of others, the music, and the instructor's inspiration. Get outdoors in good weather to enjoy nature and the stimulation of new sights, sounds, and smells. Any exercise program has moments of boredom, frustration, and even discomfort. If you don't enjoy exercising after a few weeks, try to find new activities that you'll truly enjoy.

Sixth, stay motivated by telling your family and friends about your goals so that they can support your commitment and achievements. When you reach your goals, change your routine or learn a new activity to meet new challenges. Remember to reward yourself for achieving your goals by pampering yourself with a beautifying treatment or a massage.

Videos

Ann Smith *Stretching for Seniors.*
Jodi Stolove *Chair Dancing*

Web Sites

elmos.org/health/fitness
exercise.about.com
fitnesslink.com

18

Friendships—sharing and caring

With kindness, with love and compassion, with this feeling that is the essence of brotherhood, sisterhood, one will have inner peace. —The Dalai Lama

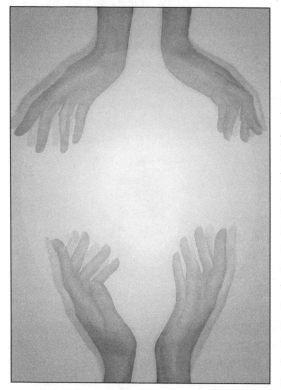

People suffer from a scarcity of deep friendships in modern urban living. When you are in real trouble, you find out who your true friends really are—those that you can count on when the going gets tough are a real treasure. With women's busy lives, the places outside the family where people formerly sought friendships, such as work or church, are beginning to break down. Friendship matters much more to women than to men. When women seek help and receive it, they may establish a connective bond with others. Women need to connect with others, to share their feelings and show that they care about each other. When friends trust each other, they are comfortable expressing their true feelings. Most women need a variety of friends upon whom they can depend. Many women know that their close friends make the difference between living a lonely life and a lively one.

According to Goodman and O'Brien, authors of *I Know Just What You Mean: The Power of Friendship in Women's Lives*, contemporary women depend on their close friends to be there for one another during the good times and bad. A special female friend can be a lifeline. As women reach significant birthdays, they sometimes realize how important a special friend is to their life.

Females have a very different reaction to stress than males, one that revolves around nurturing and seeking the support of others. In times of stress, women turn to their social network of supportive females for comfort and socialization. This may help explain why women are less vulnerable than men to stress-related illnesses and their close relationships with each other prolong their lives, writes David Spiegal, author of the chapter Social Support: How Friends, Family, and Groups Can Help. Your close friendships are probably one of your most important stress buffers. Having a few close friends is associated with a lower risk of dying at any given age.

Friendships and relationships greatly affect our physical, emotional, and spiritual health. While intimate relationships with family and lovers seem to have the strongest effects on your health, strong connections with friends, coworkers, neighbors, and others are as much a protective factor as lowering your blood pressure, losing weight, or quitting smoking. Positive, supportive friendships help you resist disease, enjoy life and live longer. Dr. Dean Ornish, who wrote *Love and Survival*, believes that the loneliness, isolation, alienation, and depression so prevalent today are often emotional and spiritual diseases of the heart. Anything that creates a sense of isolation leads to chronic stress and may increase your risk for various illnesses. They increase the likelihood that you may engage in unhealthy behaviors such as smoking and overeating, which can lead to illness and suffering. You need to cultivate close, positive friendships because when you spend time with loving friends, you'll enhance both their health and yours.

Definition of Friendship

Friendships occur on various levels, from acquaintance to those in which you feel a strong connection with the other person. Genuine friendships are based on authenticity and trust. A friendship is expected to be one of equality that provides mutual benefits. Close friendships are never dull—they provide both emotional and intellectual stimulation. For women, the essence of friendship is talking—sharing your thoughts and feelings openly and honestly. Getting through the tough times, and offering encouragement when friends desperately need it, is the main work of friendship. Friends listen to your joys, concerns, trials, and tribulations, and make you feel good—about yourself and about life. Friends accept you for who you are and make it easier for you to be yourself around them.

Friends can offer different types of support that are important to your emotional and physical health, writes Antoni in the chapter Stress Management. Some types of support include: *emotional* support—shows caring and compassion that makes another person feel loved and valued; *positive regard*—conveys agreement with a person's beliefs and feelings; *informational* support—provides advice or knowledge that may be helpful; and *physical* support—offers physical assistance.

How to Strengthen Friendships

Your friendships are very important—they help keep your body, mind, and spirit in balance. However, you cannot enjoy friendships and reap their benefits without working to maintain them. Loving friendships are built, not found. There is no such thing as the perfect person, so look for the best combination of kindness, sincerity, and compassion. You want friends who play a role in your life, who share interests and want to spend time together. First you must find someone with compatible interests, and second, you must be willing to invest your time and energy to stay connected. Sometimes you may blame your over-scheduled lifestyle for not maintaining good friendships. Perhaps you've forgotten that to be a good friend you must give of yourself to others and work to maintain the friendship. Make time for your special friends, even if you have to rearrange your schedule. How you spend your time shows what you really value more than anything else. If you really value your friends, then you'll find time to be with them. Share simple moments, such as having lunch with special friends once a month, or doing something special together, not just activities like movies or sports. Communication is the heart of all good friendships. Communicating your feelings helps you connect with others, whereas sharing only your thoughts, especially if they are judgmental, may lead to isolation and distress. Dr. Ornish reminds us that feelings join our hearts, and thoughts only connect our heads. Good communication begins by being a good, active listener. One of the ways we affirm our connection with friends is eye-to-eye contact. In *Stress Management for Dummies*, Allen Elkin says to remember to verbally acknowledge what you've heard, use facial expressions, and comment on things you feel are important to convey empathy and understanding. Try to avoid giving advice when friends are venting what is going on in their lives. They may just need a "sounding board" to share some concern or express their feelings.

It's important to have friends in whom you can confide your pain and problems, along with your joys, hopes, and dreams come true. When something is really troubling you, tell someone you trust instead of trying to cover it up. Also, you need to be interested in their pursuits, family, and work. Make merry with those who rejoice and weep with those who mourn, but don't burden others with your minor aches and pains or small disappointments. Friendships based exclusively on bad news are as stifled as those based on only good news, write Domar and Dreher, authors of *Healing Mind, Healthy Woman*. If you share *only* your bitching-and-moaning complaints, your friendships are based on seeking sympathy and compassion for your unhappiness. In all your close friendships, you ought to be comfortable expressing a full range of emotions. However, refuse to gossip or talk of others' vices, as it can be very destructive—your friends may worry that if you talk about others, you'll talk about them.

Some women do not have solid friendships because they don't feel entitled to them. Their low self-esteem, fears, excessive shyness, embarrassment, or feelings of inadequacy often prevent them from reaching out to others, especially when they are most in need of friends. If your self-doubts are overpowering, you may lead a very lonely life. Also, many women have wonderful friends and families, but when they experience a major crisis, they don't turn to them because they don't want to burden them with their problems or pain. They keep their friends at a distance with stoic attitudes and fail to communicate with them. And sometimes when women are highly stressed, Domar and Dreher say that they prefer to hibernate in solitude. They may lack the energy to get out and connect with others. It's hard to put on a happy face when you're upset, angry, or distressed, so many women would rather be alone with their problems.

The Borysenkos, who wrote *The Power of the Mind to Heal*, believe that to overcome your feelings of inadequacy or not being lovable, first you must heal the wounds of your past that separate you from your inner self. Then you need to rebuild your self-respect and love for yourself before you are able to be your true and genuine self with others. When you are comfortable with your own self, you will be able to relate in more meaningful ways with others. You may begin by reviving past friendships, then move on to forging new ones.

In a wonderful article, titled Love-your-life Guide, Martha Beck wrote:

> If you tend to act on the fear of being unloved, rather than love itself, remember:
> at age 20, you're obsessed with what people think of you.
> at age 40, you stop caring about what people think of you, and
> at age 60, you realize that people never were thinking of you— they were busy worrying about what you thought of them. So why not just cut to the 60s part now?"   —Beck, 2000:48

Stephen Covey, author of *The 7 Habits of Highly Effective Families*, writes about three primary laws of love, yet these laws apply equally well to friendships. He believes that acceptance rather than rejection, understanding rather than judgment, and participation rather than manipulation, are the basis for ongoing love and friendships.

Friendship begins with liking and accepting yourself, warts and all, and forgiving yourself for past mistakes. The Borysenkos say that you need to believe that you are as precious and as wonderful as any other person on earth. The more accepting you are of yourself as a special, unique person, the more likely you'll see others in the same light. To learn to accept and love yourself, first you need to recognize your critical self-judgments, your anger, disappointments, and distrust of others. In *Minding the Body, Mending the Mind*, Joan Borysenko writes that you may need to explore and express your feelings with a clear awareness before you can move beyond those feelings toward forgiveness of yourself and others. Don't try to bury your anger or fear or force yourself to forgive anything that still upsets you—it does not help your efforts.

Next, try to stop judging yourself and others, and recognize the perfect inner core of yourself and others. Let those inner resentments and judgments go so that you can move toward forgiveness. Don't look for perfection in yourself or friends. Nobody is perfect and good friendships survive in spite of either one's imperfections. In *The Power of 5*, Bloomfield and Cooper suggest that you reserve judgment of your friends until you know all the facts—there are two sides to every story. Everyone has different viewpoints, and those differences must be respected rather than ignored or invalidated. If you can communicate in a caring, trusting, less judgmental way, you can reduce your arguments with friends. Judelson and Dell recommend that you allow yourself and others to be who they are, and accept them as they are, not as you want them to be. You can't change others, but you can change the way you react, and that may lead to change in their behavior or attitude. Friends let each other be themselves, and listen to their lives. By letting go of your resentment and plans to retaliate, you may find that your anger lifts, easing your pain, and also helps you forgive others of any grievance you hold toward them. As you learn not to judge others, and to accept and appreciate them for who they are, you begin to accept yourself. Joan Borysenko says that by letting go of our incessant need to judge and to find fault with ourselves and others, we can attain happiness and serenity.

Forgiveness is an excellent way to heal the heart and restore the body. Forgiving others doesn't necessarily mean that you accept their actions or behavior. By accepting others' behaviors, you're not necessarily approving their weaknesses or agreeing with their opinions, you're simply affirming their intrinsic worth. You're acknowledging that they think or feel in an individual way. You're freeing them of the need to defend, protect, and preserve themselves. Stephen Covey writes that when you deeply accept and love people as they are, you actually encourage them to become better. In *Optimal Wellness*, Golan states that forgiveness cancels the demands, expectations, and conditions that block your love, and releases you from the self-damaging feelings of anger, bitterness, and hostility.

Acknowledge your anger—all of it. Think about how you were hurt, your response, and how you feel about it right now. Anger depletes your energy and leads to a tendency to view the world in a negative way. Decide to forgive the person. Forgiving is not forgetting—it is letting go of anger and hurt, and moving on with your life. Some decide that because their anger is causing so much emotional pain they'll try anything to relieve it. Also, resolve not to act negatively against the person who hurt you. Give yourself time. Forgiving with your head and heart doesn't occur overnight. Sometimes it takes weeks—even months or years—to get over being disappointed and angry. Studies show that hanging onto your anger and resentment increases your risk of a heart attack fivefold. It also increases your risk of cancer, high blood pressure, high cholesterol, and many chronic illnesses. Forgiving may take time and probably won't come easily.

You have the choice to radiate love and joy, or anger and fear, as the prominent emotions in your life. When you are happy, loving, and vibrant, good things will come your way. Send your loving vibrations to all your friends and loved ones and feel the love from them return every day. The more love and compassion you radiate, the more you will get back. The feeling of loving and being loved and cared for by friends goes a long way in protecting you from the negative effects of stress. Surround yourself with friends who will be there when the going gets rough, and give them the feeling that you will do the same for them.

Health Benefits of Friendships

According to Domar and Dreher, women need social connections to stay healthy and to enhance their recovery from illness. They seem to benefit more from relationships with female friends and relatives. There is a vital link between the strength of your relationships and support systems and your emotional and physical resilience under severe stress. Social support is related to greater resistance to communicable diseases, lower prevalence and incidence of heart disease and faster recovery, along with lower mortality. Those with inadequate psychosocial resources seem to be more prone to illness and mood disturbances when faced with increased stress levels than individuals with friends who provide stability, predictability, and control. Scientists such as Kiecolt-Glaser and Glaser have conducted numerous psychoneuroimmunological studies. They report that women who experienced stressful situations and had high levels of social support had better immune function than those with less support. They also found that stressful personal relationships and inadequate social support can adversely affect your immune system and contribute to illness.

When meaningful relationships are strained, some people experience neck and back pain, headaches, irritable bowel syndrome, and other disorders. Some scientists learned that positive social relationships, especially good communication, can strengthen your immune system, lower your blood pressure, and reduce heart rate. Other scientists have found that your friendships and social relationships can affect not only your cardiovascular system, but also your biochemistry and your immune system's ability to fight off disease. They found that how you relate and speak to others has a direct effect on your body—the more hostility and negativity you feel during an argument, the greater the impact on your immune system. If you can resolve conflicts and communicate without attacking your loved ones, you can protect your immune system.

Research indicates that the quality of your supportive relationships—the strength of love and connectedness you feel—is the best predictor of good health. Friends who are supportive and caring give each other emotional comfort, and may help protect you from the consequences of stress. They act as buffers and can lessen the impact of stressful events on the body. People who feel that others care about them are more likely to take good care of themselves.

Your immune system is also very sensitive to loneliness and isolation, which can keep you from enjoying life. Feeling lonely and unloved, with few human connections, may increase your risk of disease, flood your brain with anxiety-causing chemicals, and contribute to premature death from all causes. Domar and Dreher suggest that when you feel isolated, it's usually because stress, fatigue, and/or depression prevent you from reaching out to your friends and loved ones.

Your attitudes toward others and life in general also affect your friendships and health. When you feel separated from life—whether through loss, depression, or protecting your vulnerability by means of angry cynicism, hostility, or criticism—your heart can close down. The Borysenkos claim that when you judge and criticize others, you separate yourself from those you're blaming and from life itself. Your whole body becomes constricted as your heart closes others out. The tendency toward criticism and anger lies at the very heart of physical, emotional, and spiritual illness.

Friendships help people feel less alone and frightened and more competent to deal with illness. Learn how to establish and maintain strong, positive relationships to promote both your physical and emotional health. Women need a good emotional support system, otherwise they are at much greater risk for illness and death. Dr. Ornish claims that anything that promotes a sense of love, trust, and connection with others is good for your health. ℬ

19

Journaling and Writing

*What lies behind us and what lies before us are tiny matters,
compared to what lies within us.* —*Ralph Waldo Emerson*

One of the most mean-
ingful and effective ways to
improve your mind/body
health is your willingness
to express your feelings,
thoughts, mistakes, secrets,
hopes, and fears. Some
women prefer to confide
in loved ones, while others
choose to write in a journal to keep their feelings
confidential or for later
analysis. Anyone with an
interest in exploring how
they've come to their present
state and how they may
further develop, is a good
candidate for journal writ-
ing. Bloomfield and Cooper, who wrote *The Power of 5*, believe that those
who confide their feelings, concerns, and problems in a private diary—
writing as little as five to fifteen minutes a day—often experience marked
improvements in their health, attitude, and immune function.

Journal writing lets you express yourself and get to the heart of
what might be keeping you uptight and bothered. It can provide a
soothing, relaxing way to get in touch with your feelings and sort out
stressful conflicts in your life. Debora Tkac, editor of *Everyday Health Tips*,
says that writing about your conflicts and feelings can help you analyze
your thoughts and beliefs or serve as a catharsis. It's a great way to get what's
bothering you off your chest. When certain negative feelings are never
expressed, they can lead to illnesses, some of which are life-threatening.

To manage your stress effectively, you need to become aware of when you are feeling stressed and be able to identify sources of that stress. A journal or stress diary can help you do that. It shows the times when you experienced stress and what situations or circumstances triggered your stress. Your journal serves as a cue to remind you that you should take some action and use one or more strategies to reduce your stress.

Definition of Journal Writing

Journal writing means describing in writing any feelings, thoughts, and experiences that you may feel uncomfortable talking about. It helps you figure out what you're feeling about events in your life. It is a way to work through your problems. According to Julia Cameron, author of The Artist's Way, writing also helps you identify what you think and what you believe you need. You can complain, enumerate, identify, and isolate any problems or concerns. Gradually you may "hear" potential solutions and begin to take action to solve those problems.

How to Begin Writing a Journal

First you need to find a quiet, private, comfortable place to write each day, where you can relax without being disturbed. Some people like to write in a diary, while others find that carrying a small, compact note-book around and making notes frequently during the day works well. Or you may prefer to use your laptop or personal organizer. The form and format are less important than the fact that you use it on a regular basis. Learning to let yourself write—to express your feelings and thoughts—begins with small steps. Mistakes and stumbles are a normal part of taking early steps. It may be necessary to go slowly and gently. You are trying to heal old wounds, not create new ones. Progress, not perfection, is what you are seeking.

Write about whatever comes to your mind, no matter how frag-mentary, and try not to filter or edit. Nothing is too petty, too stupid, or too weird to be included. Just let your thoughts flow and capture them on paper. Write about different kinds of feelings in different kinds of ink: you might use red ink for traumatic events, blue for adventurous solutions, black ink for conservative, practical solutions, or purple ink for romantic fantasies, such as escaping to a tropical island in the Caribbean.

Writing helps you discover who you are, sort through your problems, keep a log of what's been going on in your life, and express your feelings about those things. When you write, focus on the issues that you are currently living with, and explore both the objective experience (what happened) and your feelings about it. In his book, *Opening Up,* Dr. Pennebaker advises really letting go of your deepest emotions. Writing gives you a way to release your anger, fear, sadness, and other painful feelings. It may enable you to find meaning when you feel lost in your problems. You can help heal yourself through writing, so you don't keep things all bottled up inside. You may not feel so alone or lost. Describe what you feel about your experiences and why you feel that way. Don't be concerned about temporarily feeling worse. You may feel sad or depressed immediately after writing, but these negative feelings usually dissipate within an hour or so. In rare cases, they may last longer. When you are writing, you may enter into a withdrawal process from life as you know it. Withdrawal is a positive process that you need to go through to step back from your problems and regain a new perspective that is both painful and exhilarating. As you express your feelings, you often go through a period of mourning. In dealing with the loss of your "nice" self, you will find that a certain amount of grief occurs. As you begin to explore your inner self, you may mourn the one you left behind, says Cameron. Without this mourning of your past, you may not be able to repattern your future. You must allow yourself to feel the pain, and use the pain to illuminate future possibilities. Slowly you'll begin to focus away from feeling immersed in your problems and to develop a different view or new perspective, which will empower you toward greater self-awareness and self-confidence, so that you can make valid choices. Writing can also bring you joy and a way to express it.

It is most important to write about your feelings and emotions as you experienced them, even those from dreams or nightmares. Ask yourself, "How did I feel?" Even if the feelings are disturbing or uncomfortable, force yourself to write them down anyway. This is good practice to become more aware of both your waking emotions and those you experience in dreams. Sometimes writing a tiny fragment of an event or thought may start a process of deeper recall which may surface into your memory later. It is important to write each day, no matter how brief or fragmented your thoughts are—just start writing. Remember, journal writing is an exercise or a pathway to develop a strong and clear sense of self. Writing provides a paper trail that helps you understand your inner self, where you can see your own world and eventually meet your creator.

Some topics that you may choose to write about include:
- Tragedies or traumatic events in your life.
- Unhappy or unsettling experiences.
- Things you would like to tell your parents, but don't.
- Some of the things you dream about.
- Things that scare you the most.
- The kind of people you would most like to be with.
- Tow you feel when others criticize you.
- What behaviors by others really bother you.

One of the main obstacles facing many writers is self-censorship. This happens when you sit down to write something and start worrying about who's going to read your journal, whether you're doing it right, and even where to begin. One way to avoid self-censorship is to remember that you're writing for therapeutic reasons. Concentrate on the process, not the product. Try to suspend judgment and self-criticism, and allow your thoughts and feelings to flow freely as you write. Write as if your body were speaking to you and telling you what it is feeling.

Sometimes you may find that your writing is blocked because your thoughts and feelings deal with an area of your life you'd feel safer avoiding or would prefer not to deal with. You may not be happy, but at least you know what you are unhappy about. Fear of discovering your true self is often fear of the unknown—what will happen to you and others if you change? So rather than find out, you decide to stay blocked. This is usually an unconscious response to internalized negative beliefs.

Many negative beliefs and thoughts come to us from our parents, religion, culture, and our fearful friends. Once you have cleared away most of your strongest negatives, you may find you are still left with more subtle but equally undermining ones that are the core negatives you have acquired from your family, teachers, and friends. Julia Cameron says that you still need to confront these negative beliefs because they are just beliefs, not facts. Usually, these core beliefs are personal areas where you feel very vulnerable. They undermine your sexuality, your lovability, and your intelligence—whatever vulnerability they can latch onto. Your writer's block doesn't consciously see that, and only knows that you are irrationally afraid of some dire outcome, if you even mention it. You know in your head that you shouldn't stop writing because of your fears, yet if you don't address these irrational fears, then your mental block stays intact. Dr. Pennebaker, the leading researcher on the benefits of self-disclosure, believes that it is safe to write about upsetting experiences. You can be completely honest with yourself, and no one else will judge you, criticize you, or distort your perceptions.

Some people like to keep a diary of distortions in which they write down their automatic negative thoughts every day. According to Domar and Dreher, who wrote *Healing Mind, Healthy Woman*, these records are a powerful testimony to how much you suffer when old tapes or mind chatter run through your head. They suggest that you use your diaries to challenge and restructure these thoughts by writing down your new thoughts and reminding yourself to live by them.

People who write about personally upsetting experiences report that it is important that their journals be kept anonymous and confidential. Nobody but you should see your journal, because writing is a private act. You can't do anything wrong when you are writing in a journal because it is yours alone. Because there is no beginning, middle, or end, you can write whatever you want. You don't have to fit any form or style. You can never make a mistake about what or how you write about your thoughts and feelings. Writing also has advantages for people who have trouble expressing themselves to others. By writing rather than talking about a problem, you are able to look back at what you've written and examine what you were thinking. Writing about something can be seen as the first step toward going public with it—without taking a risk. Writing about yourself is a transition between keeping it to yourself and telling it to someone.

There is a recognizable ebb and flow to the process of discovering yourself through writing. As you gain strength, some of your self-doubts may return, says Julia Cameron. This is normal, and you can deal with them. Remember that if you give in to them, you may remain stuck and feel like a victim all over again. Gradually you'll discover the joy of journal writing and you'll surrender your need to control the result. The process of writing, not the product, will become your focus as your healing occurs.

One of the most important things you'll discover, yet may be reluctant to believe, is the possibility that the universe is cooperating with your new and expanding plans for self-healing. When you change, the universe further expands that change, a process that Carl Jung called *synchronicity*—the coincidence of events in time and space as meaning something more than mere chance. When you act on faith in the process of self-discovery, the universe shifts to enable you to give up former self-concepts in your quest for your new, emerging self. Self-discovery is the process of finding the river and saying yes to its flow, rapids and all. You may be surprised by new adventures and by saying yes instead of no to new opportunities.

It is hard to believe that your writing and inner-mind work may trigger outer change. When your prayers are answered, you may assume that it is a coincidence, because it's hard to believe that God is involved and helping with your own inner healing. You may find it easier to accept answered prayers as a coincidence or luck than as examples of synchronicity. It may be difficult to accept the hand of God as activated by your own hand when you commit your soul to healing, writes Cameron. In healing yourself, you don't need to change any of your beliefs, only to examine them. More than anything else, restoring your inner balance is an exercise in open-mindedness. God knows that the sky's the limit. Life is what you make it: whether you conceive of an inner god force or an outer God doesn't matter, but relying on that force does.

Health Benefits of Writing and Journaling

Although there is no quick fix or instant solution to your concerns or problems, journal writing can become an insightful, spiritual process that helps you resolve your problems. According to studies conducted by James Pennebaker, people who write about traumatic events not only feel better emotionally, but their physical health also markedly improves. Pennebaker and his colleagues found that college students who wrote about their issues and problems had an increased lymphocyte response, and a stronger immune system for six weeks after the experiment. Compared to control groups who wrote only about trivial events, those who wrote about disturbing, traumatic events made significantly fewer visits to the doctor and reported fewer symptoms of illness for months afterwards. The benefits of writing occur in the process of expressing your deepest thoughts and feelings surrounding a personal upheaval, and then letting them go.

Since the unexamined life is not worth living, an unlived life is not work examining. So as you write, begin to explore your own private fears and villains, along with your champions, dreams, hopes, and successes. You'll learn ways to recognize and resolve fears, remove emotional scars, and strengthen your confidence. As you learn to recognize, nurture, and protect your inner core, you will be able to move beyond pain and constriction. Writing can help you get to know yourself better and what your self-worth really is. This experience will make you excited, depressed, angry, afraid, joyous, hopeful, and ultimately freer. Remember that unexpressed feelings may lower your self-esteem and can actually lead to various problems, such as drug abuse, violence, and self-abusive behaviors.

Writing down your feelings may help relieve emotional stress caused by losing a job, suffering marital problems, being angry with a friend or family member, or enduring other traumatic experiences. Women who write about their feelings often report that they released grief, fear, or anger that had been frozen in their mind and body. The floodgates opened, and they discovered emotions or conflicts they did not know had plagued them for years. This is especially helpful for those who have trouble talking about a problem, worry, or very emotional issue, or who have no readily available listeners. Some experts believe the simple act of disclosure is what helps relieve stress.

Think of your writing and exploration of life as a journey with a difficult, varied, and fascinating view. Over time you'll see recurring patterns of interest, concerns, and responses to situations that help you understand the way you live, your habits, and change those you wish to. Gradually you'll move to a higher level of thinking as your writing and insight provide you with the power for expansive change. It is very difficult to constantly complain about a difficult situation without being moved to constructive action. Writing helps lead you out of despair into undreamed-of solutions. Julia Cameron believes that anyone who faithfully writes daily will be led to a connection with a source of wisdom within. You may be surprised by the wisdom and insight that you possess about yourself. Many women acquire new insights into themselves and glimpse new ways to cope with the stress of their problems. Some report that the writing exercise sparked a lasting improvement in their emotional and physical well-being. You even may experience a heightened sense of autonomy and confidence.

The quality of your life is in proportion to your ability to stay focused or pay attention. In times of pain, when the future is too terrifying to contemplate and the past too painful to remember, Cameron suggests you pay attention to the present—it may be the only safe place since each moment taken alone is always bearable. The reward for your attention is always healing. More than anything else, attention is an act of staying connected to the work around you. Candace Pert recommends journal writing to stay connected since it provides a literal structure to your internal world. Writing gives you an awareness of what your thinking and lifestyle patterns are, so that you can change them if necessary.

As you begin to trust and have faith in your inner wisdom, you'll lose your fear of intimacy because you no longer confuse others with the higher power you are getting to know. Gradually, you'll give up your dependence on any other person, place, or thing. Instead, you will place your dependency on your inner source that meets your needs through people, places, and things.

You learn by going where you have to go. Action is often what you need to move you from stagnation to inspiration, from problem to solution, from self-pity to self-respect. The success of your healing depends on your ability to move out of your head into action, which means taking risks. Most women are good at talking themselves out of taking risks—they are skilled spectators on the probable pain of self-exposure. You learn by doing and moving that you are stronger than you thought. You'll learn to look at things with a new perspective, to solve your problems by tapping your own inner resources and listening for inspiration, not only from others but from yourself. Seemingly without effort, your answers will often come while you are doing other things.

Findings from a published study suggest that those suffering from a chronic disease showed measurable improvements in their health by writing about stressful experiences. Even if you don't suffer from a chronic disease, writing down your thoughts, feelings, relationships, and experiences can be insightful and therapeutic. Other benefits of journal writing are that:

- Sometimes it's easier to write down your problems than to say them out loud.
- Writing can help you believe in yourself and raise your self-esteem.
- When you write, you can hear your own uncommon voice.
- As you write, you can think about and seek answers to your questions and find new questions to ask yourself.
- You can discover your dreams, unfilled hopes, and expectations, or set goals.

With practice, you will learn to hear the desired voice of your internal self. You'll tune into the voice of your current thoughts and feelings. Once you believe that it is natural to heal through writing, Cameron says you can begin to accept a second idea—that God will give you whatever you need for self-discovery and healing. Be willing to see the hand of God and accept it as a friend's offer to help with what you are doing. When you accept God's help, you will see useful bits of help everywhere in your life. There is also a second voice, a higher harmonic, adding to and augmenting your inner healing voice, which shows itself in synchronicity. Learn to accept the possibility that the universe is helping you with what you are doing. 𝓑

20

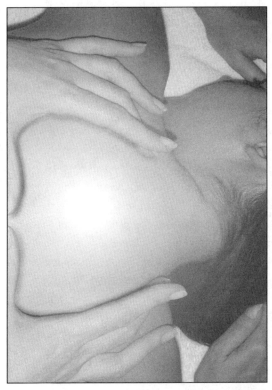

$\mathcal{M}$any different types of bodywork enhance the mind, body, and spiritual balance. Massage and healing touch are two types commonly used. Massage, an ancient form of touch therapy, has become very popular in recent years. Originally Chinese practitioners developed various forms of energy-based massage, with the focus on manipulating points along the meridians that direct the flow of energy, or Qi (chi). Therapeutic massage is the third most often chosen type of alternative therapy sought by adults in the U.S. Massage therapy is part of the mind/body connection, and shows how the power of the body can affect the mind. In the U.S. today, massage encompasses an ever-growing variety of practices. There are more than one hundred different kinds of massage therapies, all of which manipulate the body's soft tissues. And, currently there are over 100 thousand practitioners engaged in some form of bodywork in the United States.

MASSAGE
Definition of Massage

Massage is a general term that includes various forms of bodywork therapy. While some techniques do not use the word "massage," they can usually be traced back to our need as humans to touch and be touched. Western forms, such as Swedish massage, generally focus on the musculoskeletal system and use various hand movements for gliding, kneading, creating friction, chopping, or cupping the body's muscles, bones, and joints. Oriental forms such as Shiatsu focus on balancing the body's system of energy channels. The aim of any form of massage is to ease away muscular tension, dispel tiredness, and reinforce depleted or unbalanced energy. Common practices include use of the fingers, hands, elbows, knees, and other body parts to touch and rub a person's body. Many massage therapists use a combination of techniques and strokes from both Western and Eastern traditions.

How Massage Works

Many therapists believe that massage not only touches the body, but also reacts with the mind. You store some memory of experiences in the brain, but deeper, older messages are stored in the body and must be accessed through the body. Your body is part of your subconscious mind, which cannot be healed by talk alone, according to Dr. Candace Pert. When someone touches you, there is a response throughout the entire mind/body. Some specially trained therapists can simultaneously release the emotions through various kinds of bodywork while enlisting the power of the mind through talk, thus creating an effective healing method. David DiDomenico, who wrote the chapter Massage and Mental Health, says that each woman's response or reaction to touch varies according to her prior experiences with physical contact, body image, perception of the therapist, expectations, physical condition, and the pressure used by the therapist.

An effective massage requires a relaxing environment. The room should be warm, quiet, and possibly filled with soft music. You can sit in a chair if you want someone to work only on your neck, shoulders, and upper back. For a complete massage, you need to lie down on a firm and comfortable massage table or carpeted floor. Beds are usually too soft and the wrong height.

You should be in a comfortable, relaxed position, and think about your breathing. The masseur or masseuse should wash his/her hands, then briskly rub them together to warm them. A good masseuse is able to identify the prime tension spots, commonly found on the neck, shoulders, and back, by feeling tense muscles that are rock hard, like tight, knotted cords. Hard, fibrositic nodules of tissue may also be detected, whereas relaxed muscles feel like putty, firm but flexible. An oil or lotion helps the masseuse to glide her hands easily over your skin, and may enhance your sensations. Allow the masseuse to lift and move your limbs as necessary. You will become aware of subtle feelings of pleasure and discomfort.

Four common strokes besides rubbing are used in Western massage. Anyone can perform them, write Loecher and O'Donnell in *Women's Choices in Natural Healing*.

Gliding, or *effleurage*, is a gentle stroking motion toward the heart used at the beginning of massage sessions to warm and relax the muscles. Gliding stretches and relaxes the long muscles of the calves, thighs, and back. It can be done with the pads of the thumbs or the whole hand with the fingers together and extended. The masseuse's hands are relaxed and molded to the shape of the muscle being worked. Gliding strokes toward your heart are done with more pressure, then circle away from the heart with a lighter stroke using just the palms or fingertips.

Kneading, or *petrissage*, works your muscles by rolling, squeezing, and compressing them to loosen individual fibers. It is a deeper, more penetrating stroke than gliding and is generally done on the large muscles of the back, buttocks, and legs. The masseuse uses the whole hand, including the heel, to push and pull, and the fingers to pick up and squeeze muscles. Circular movements are used, beginning from the depths of the muscle to the surface, being careful not to pinch the skin.

Friction is similar to acupressure in which the thumb pads or fingertips are used to apply pressure to specific trigger points or tender areas. The masseuse slowly applies deep pressure for up to thirty seconds, then makes circular or rotating movements for ten seconds or more before releasing the pressure. Friction can be done anywhere, but is most often used on the back or buttocks to release muscle cramps and relax muscles. Gliding strokes may be used afterward to increase relaxation in the area.

Chopping and cupping, or *tapotement*, are a succession of quick pounding motions done in an alternating staccato rhythm with the hands. The outer edge of the palms and little fingers are used in chopping, and in the cupping movement, the palms and fingers are cupped. This movement is usually done after relaxing the muscles through use of guiding and kneading. The striking and tapping strokes invigorate the muscles. Chopping and cupping are most often used on the calves, upper legs, buttocks, and back.

Get a Back Massage from a Partner. If you have a partner who is willing to learn how to give you a relaxing massage, you've got it made. You need a warm, quiet room and possibly some soft music. Lie face down on a firm, comfortable massage table or carpeted floor where you can fully relax. Your partner begins by briskly rubbing her/his hands together, then pours a small amount of warm oil or lotion on the palms. The partner stands or kneels at your head and places his or her hands gently on your upper back. Both hands slowly move down the sides of the spine until they reach your buttocks, then the hands separate in a curving movement, pulling slowly up your sides and along the shoulders. This movement should be repeated rhythmically until the entire back is oiled and you feel relaxed. Next, your partner moves to your side to massage different areas of the back more intensely, especially any tight, knotted muscles or small nodules. Concentrate on releasing your strain and muscle tension in these areas, such as the spine and lower lumbar region. To relax each shoulder blade, your partner should place one hand under your shoulder and with the other hand, work in a deep, pressing, circular movement around the shoulder blade, using the fingers. Begin at the top of the shoulder and work down around the blade.

To relax the base of the spine, your partner should use alternate hands, and work in a broad, circular motion around the base, using a shallow, kneading movement. Next, one hand is placed over the other at the base of the spine, and the palms are pressed firmly as the hands move up the spine to the neck. Then, the index and middle fingers are placed on each side of the spine, one hand following the other, and with a rocking motion the hands are pressed down as the fingers move down the sides of the spine. Lastly, using both thumbs, trace small, deep, rotating movements up either side of the spine, starting at the base. Finish by pressing the thumbs briefly into the hollows at the base of the skull. Sweep the hands down to the base of the spine and begin again.

A sitting massage can be done by a partner with some gentle gliding strokes across the tops of the shoulders toward the neck. Wrap the fingers of each hand lightly over the edges of the shoulders and sink the palms into the muscles while gliding over them. Then do some gliding strokes by laying the thumbs on each side of the spine and push them toward upward toward the neck.

Variations of Massage

Ayurvedic Shirodhara massage is a therapeutic treatment that helps you look and feel wonderful. Ayurveda is a Sanskrit word derived from two roots: "ayur," meaning life and "veda," meaning knowledge. It originated in India more than 5,000 years ago and is a process that balances the mind, body, and spirit. The Shirodhara massage is used to help reduce stress and expand one's consciousness by dripping warm, herbal-infused oil onto the forehead for about twenty-five minutes, then massaging it into the scalp, and finally applying cleansing herbs. This may be followed by a soothing hand and foot massage.

Shiatsu is a Japanese form of massage that emphasizes stretching movements and gentle pressure applied by fingers and other body parts. It is also known as acupressure, an Asian method that primarily uses the thumb to apply deep pressure to energy points on the body. Massage therapists use their hands, elbows, and sometimes even their feet to apply pressure. It may seem awkward or even painful at first.

Swedish massage is a complementary type of therapy from which a variety of other massage therapies sprang in the nineteenth century, including medical massage, sports massage, and pregnancy massage. Long strokes and kneading on bare skin are used, usually with a massage oil or powder to reduce friction. This promotes relaxation and circulation.

Self-massage on your lower body is an easy way to try massage. The front and inside of the thighs and calves can be massaged by sitting with one leg fully extended and the other bent with the knee up. Mark Mayell, editor of *52 Simple Steps to Natural Health*, suggests using the following steps:

1. Mold your hands to the shape of your upper leg and make gliding strokes from the knee to the upper thigh. Apply deeper pressure as you stroke toward the heart and lighter as you move away from the heart. Reach under the knee to make similar gliding strokes up the calf.

2. Place a hand on each side of the thigh just above the knee. Roll the muscles back and forth, move the hands farther up the leg, and repeat until you reach the groin.

3. Use both hands to knead the outside of the hip from the knee to the upper thigh.

4. Grasp the inside of the thigh with the hand on the opposite side of the body from the bent leg and roll out the muscle with your thumb. Use your thumbs to make circular friction around the knee and ankle joints.

Another way to get a massage is through the use of a handheld massager. With the flick of a switch, you can massage your shoulders, back, neck, and other areas that are tense. Dr. Scholl has a new massager with four heads for use on the spine too, with low and high frequencies. My favorite is a recliner with both heat and selected variations for the area you want massaged. Another popular item is the chair cushion massage with heat and various types of massage for the back and legs. Some types of the chair massager offer different intensity levels and range in price below one hundred dollars.

Health Benefits of Massage

Over time and with repetitive movement, muscles and connective tissues which hold you together often become shortened. Christopher Hobbs says that this can inhibit your range of motion, distort your posture, and may lead to pain. Massage has been used to relax muscles, diminish spasms, invigorate, and create a sense of well-being.

Many women are ashamed of their bodies, and your perception of your body and its ability to function is often revealed in the initial meeting with a therapist. Some women are embarrassed at being overweight, out of shape, scarred, or excessively hairy. It is important that the therapist respect these issues and work with the woman to help her feel comfortable with her body. Body image can be clarified and improved with continued massage therapy by a good practitioner, writes DiDomenico. A woman's awareness follows the hands of the therapist as she/he moves over familiar and unfamiliar areas of the body. Gradually, a woman may develop a greater awareness of her body and gain a more complete picture of herself.

Massage offers significant physical, psychological, emotional, and spiritual benefits. The most important and best known aspect of massage is its relaxing effect, helping women let go of tension. Some women express feelings of vulnerability to massage as they relax muscles that are chronically tense in defensive patterns. As women learn to let go, some report that when they catch themselves tensing up their shoulders or elsewhere, they can release their muscle tension. DiDomenico reports that through this process they develop a clearer awareness of their muscle tension and attain a higher form of control over their body, as well as the ability to relax. Many women have an enormous amount of unnecessary muscle tension that uses up their energy and causes fatigue and discomfort, further distorting their self-image.

There are a number of demonstrable physical effects on the body from massage. It stretches and relaxes constricted muscles, increases range of motion, and promotes flexibility. Massage also slows the pulse rate and promotes relaxed breathing. It increases the circulation of blood and lymph, and the intercellular fluids that transport substances to and from the muscles to the blood. Nutrients, oxygen, hormones, and antibodies must reach every muscle cell, and toxic waste must be carried away. Increased efficiency comes with good circulation, which can be enhanced by vigorous massage. It can help prevent muscle cramps by eliminating the buildup of lactic acid following physical workouts. Massage can also relieve various musculoskeletal problems such as tension headaches, backache, arthritis, digestive disorders, and some-times breathing problems. Some women feel reassurance, comfort, and caring from massage in a way that words cannot express.

Many women find that massage reduces stress and anxiety, calms the nerves, and even improves their self-esteem. Massage can relieve pain by stimulating the release of endorphins. It can also reduce stress hormones and depression, and boost the body's immune system. By releasing muscle tension through a pampering or invigorating massage, you can ease emotional tension. One study found that a thirty minute neck and back massage reduced depression for some people. Other researchers found that people who had a forty-five minute massage once a week had lower levels of stress-related hormones and were more alert, less restless, and able to sleep better.

HEALING TOUCH

Touch is something all humans need in order to feel connected and cared for. It relaxes the whole body and reduces stress, which enhances your immune system and helps you to be healthier. For older people, who are often alone and may receive little touch, or for the chronically ill, touch is very important.

Therapeutic touch was first developed in the early 1970s through the combined talents of Dora Kunz, a natural healer, and Dr. Delores Krieger, a nurse with experience in meditation and teaching. According to practitioners, therapeutic touch enhances the body's abili-ty to heal itself, helps reduce anxiety, and induces feelings of relaxation.

Myotherapy or neuromuscular therapy, also known as trigger point therapy, involves using deep thumb or finger pressure on tight cords or bands of muscle to release muscle cramps or spasms.

Definition of Healing Touch

Touch therapy is a physical technique designed to help people release the psychological walls surrounding them and open themselves up to full communion with others. The special value of healing touch is that it merges the outer dimensions of your soul with that of the other person, allowing an intimate exchange of warmth, joy, sympathy, and spirit. In the process, it recharges your emotional and spiritual batteries.

In therapeutic touch, the practitioner does not actually touch the person, but uses his or her hands to manipulate the energy field surrounding the person, an all-body halo that extends several inches from the skin surface. Healthy people have symmetrical or balanced energy fields in which energy flows evenly through them. People with physical or emotional problems have asymmetric or unbalanced energy fields, and the practitioner aims to balance these fields by reordering the energy field so that the body can heal itself efficiently.

Myotherapy or trigger point therapy involves different systematic movements and techniques designed to relieve pain in muscle trigger points and to relax, revitalize, and rehabilitate muscles. Therapeutic Swedish massage movements may be combined with traditional acupressure during myotherapy.

How Therapeutic Touch Works

There are various theories about how therapeutic touch works, since the practitioner does not touch the person. One is that the practitioner exchanges energy with the person in an intentional and focused way, enabling her to help herself heal. Another theory, based on quantum physics and psychology, believes that in the process of changing the electromagnetic field surrounding the women, healing occurs. The goal of therapeutic touch is to rebalance a person's energy field and to stimulate her own natural healing responses. Healing touch is based on the belief that each person is composed of layers of energy and that each layer vibrates at a different frequency. In their hands, practitioners are able to detect kinesthetic cues, which indicate congestion, clamminess, cold, heat, or emptiness.

During a therapeutic touch session, you may lie down or sit in a chair. There are five phases. The practitioner begins by centering herself, tuning out everything around her, quieting her mind, and becoming compassionately focused on the process. Next, she performs a "hand-scan" assessment by moving her hands from your head toward your feet about two to six inches above your body. This initial assessment is performed to identify areas of imbalance in your energy field. Imbalances feel more tingly or slightly cooler than other areas, and areas with insufficient energy may feel empty or congested to the practitioner. She may use smooth flowing motions over your face, then down the sides and back of your head to your shoulders, comparing the sensation she feels on each side and between the front and back. She will continue working downward, over your torso, pelvis, and both legs, looking for any signs of energy imbalance. You will not feel anything.

When the practitioner senses problem areas, two different kinds of hand movements can balance the energy fields. One gesture is referred to as "clearing" or "unruffling," in which the practitioner uses gentle brushing motions of her hands down and outward from the top of each unbalanced area in a rhythmic, flowing motion to clear congested energy. The other gesture is where the practitioner holds her hands over specific parts of your body, such as energy centers, for one to several minutes, either lightly touching or just above the skin. The purpose of this gesture is to facilitate the transfer of energy from the "universal source" through the practitioner into the woman. This is known as *directing, modulating,* or *sending* energy to a specific area for healing. Near the end of the session, the practitioner uses grounding to help return the woman to a fully alert state, by gently massaging part of the body. The last phase is evaluation of the session, during which the woman is encouraged to describe how she feels from the treatment, and to rest. This allows the new energy received from the practitioner to be integrated into her system.

Myotherapy, or trigger point therapy, aims to release tight muscle bands, tendons, or other body tissues causing pain, and may include stretching muscular adhesions or distortion in the fascia to facilitate neuromuscular reeducation and restore the body's balance. When muscle fibers, fascia, ligaments, or tendons become weakened, over-stretched or inflamed, tiny tears can occur in the soft tissue. As the tissue heals, it contracts, becoming twisted and knotted, restricting the blood supply. Often the muscle fiber may shorten to protect itself from further injury—in effect the muscle learns to avoid pain by limiting its movement. This can decrease the range of motion of the joint, muscle, and tendons, and trigger points may develop. There are two hundred paired muscles in your body, any one of which can develop myofascial trigger points. The therapist applies deep, sustained pressure on sensitive spots, called trigger points, within muscles to release the muscle spasm.

The most tender muscles are usually on the same side. Pressure applied to this side will give the most relief, but equal attention should be given to both sides of your body.

Variations of Healing Touch

One effective touch method that can be used by anyone without training is called *Abrazo*, pronounced ah-BRAH-zoh. Abrazo is the Spanish word for "embrace," and means to clasp another person in your arms and hug him or her. For this embrace, your right arm goes over the other person's left arm, and your left arm goes under the other person's right arm. Both persons tilt their heads slightly to the left so they are looking over each other's right shoulder. The embrace is often accompanied by patting the other person's back with your right hand.

Self-directed acupressure or trigger point therapy. If you experience trigger point pain in your muscles, you may find that acupressure or direct pressure therapy can provide relief of pain from tension and muscle aches. First your muscles must be warm and relaxed. A warm shower or a heating pad on the affected area can relax the muscles so that you can differentiate the tense bands from relaxed ones. When you find a tight band or cord of tense muscle, or a tender point, press your thumb on it with moderate pressure or squeeze it with light to moderate pressure until you locate the spot of maximum tenderness with minimum pressure; this is a trigger point.

In most parts of the body, you use your thumb to press the muscle gently against the underlying bone. Simple direct pressure can help relieve trigger point areas. You may place a tennis or squash ball behind your back while you lie on the floor so that you can lean against it to reach points on your back. Gradually you'll learn to recognize when trigger points are aggravated—you'll sense your muscles becoming tense from poor posture or an uncomfortable sitting position. Take immediate action to relax the affected area by rebalancing your posture and relaxing tight muscles. Keep the area warm after treatment to provide longer-lasting relief, and go through several gentle range of motion stretches.

Reflexology is a form of touch therapy which stimulates the essential life force (chi) to flow to all parts of the body through the meridians or energy lines. Practitioners believe that your body is divided into energy zones and that every tendon, ligament, organ, muscle, bone, and brain cell falls within these zones. Because specific areas on the soles of your feet correspond with parts of your body, gentle pressure applied to these spots can relieve pain and stress. Reflexology may work in the same way acupressure does, stimulating the body to produce endorphins, which create feelings of well-being, relieve pain, and reduce inflammation throughout the body. Pressure on a reflexology point could stimulate nerves which then trigger the release of neuro-chemicals in the brain, just like acupressure.

Reflexologists usually work the entire length and width of each foot or hand during a session, but will pay extra attention to areas that correspond to parts of your body where you have problems. The right foot corresponds to the right side of the body, and the left foot to the left side. Theoretically, the big toe relates to the head, including the brain. The sole of the foot relates to all parts of the body, including organs and glands, while the heel relates to the pelvic area, including the bladder, reproductive organs, and sciatic nerve. The earlobe also corresponds to the head and brain, so pulling it helps clear the mind. Typically, a session lasts thirty to sixty minutes. Long-term problems may require several sessions.

Health Benefits of Healing Touch Methods

Research has shown that this healing method helps reduce anxiety, enhances the immune system, speeds wound healing, induces feelings of relaxation, decreases perception of pain, diminishes depression, and may increase one's sense of well-being and emotional and mental clarity. There are specific techniques for different clinical conditions, and each person's response varies, but most people feel more relaxed and experience a decrease or elimination of physical symptoms.

Trigger point therapy may be used to relieve muscular injuries and emotional stress and strains, along with poor posture, improper body mechanics, or poor nutrition (inadequate vitamin B1, B6, and B12) that can contribute to health problems. The process is designed to help reorient the body's reaction to stress due to injuries, physical strain, repetitive motion, residual tension, mental fatigue, and muscular inflammation.

Reflexologists claim that their technique primarily relieves stress and tension, improves circulation, and enhances nerve function. Stress-related health problems, such as back, shoulder, or neck aches, headaches, chronic indigestion, and anxiety may be relieved. Finger pressure on specific areas of the hands or feet is used to balance, strengthen, or relax the internal organs, the spine, and the central nervous system.

When the Abrazo hug is used enthusiastically and whole-heartedly, it raises one's awareness of the common bond between souls, brings a warm glow of goodwill and love, and also satisfies our deep craving to be accepted and cherished. It helps you express your own feelings in a much more meaningful way than words. As simple as it is, the Abrazo can change your life and that of your family and friends, because it works both ways. Try it, and you'll love it. ℬ

21

Meditation, Visualization, and Prayer

When you set aside time for affirmations, meditation, prayer, and re-creation, everything else in life flows more easily and gracefully. —Adapted from Joan Borysenko

Many women experience hectic lives from constantly switching among their roles of wife, mother, and employee. They may live in a state of perpetual motion which prevents them from enjoying each moment and often leads to stress-related health problems. Some women need a psychological buffer to escape from the stress of daily hassles and chaos in their lives. They long for inner peace, serenity, and happiness rather than constant problems and sensory overload in the fast lane.

In *Love and Survival,* Dr. Dean Ornish claims that our true nature is to be peaceful, and peace of mind comes from just "being" until we are disturbed by other people and problems. Many people expect to find peace, joy and well-being from outside themselves, but this is a misperception.

Meditation, visualization, and prayer are often rated the best safeguards against stress. They are distinct yet complementary practices that draw upon deep levels of human experience that reveal our heart and soul's relationship with our spiritual being. Meditation and prayer are gateways through which you can find inspiration, healing, and renewal for your spiritual journey and your mental, emotional, and physical needs. The principles that link meditation and prayer together are inward attention, inquiry or searching, and attunement to a deeper—or higher—level of awareness or Presence. They involve relaxation and intentional guidance of the thoughts and images that cross your consciousness. This guidance is often called suggestion, and gives you the option to think about something in a certain way, visualize a decisive image, repeat specific words, or perform a particular behavior. The goals of using suggestion are to achieve physical, psychological, and spiritual harmony. These stress-reducing methods are simple ways to reduce the clutter and chatter in your mind and gently return you to the present to reevaluate your life. They can temporarily remove you from daily stresses and help you relax so that you can regain your inner peace, strengthen your inner balance, and understand your self-healing powers.

Many experts in mind/body healing believe that both meditation and prayer are forms of focused intention which can produce relaxation with concurrent shifts in brain wave frequency and body chemistry. Some healers believe that meditation is a combination of prayer and self-healing through the ritual of self-discipline. When you pray you talk with God; when you meditate you may listen to your own thoughts. The Buddhists believe that meditation is essential to cultivate wisdom and compassion, and for understanding others. Upon receiving the Nobel Peace prize in 1989, the Dalai Lama said,

> Peace starts within each one of us. When we have
> inner peace, we can be at peace with those around us.
> When we feel love and kindness toward others,
> it not only makes others feel loved and cared for,
> but it helps us to develop an inner happiness and peace.

MEDITATION
Definition of Meditation

Meditation is the process and practice of opening one's mind to alternative states and levels of consciousness which reside inherently and latently in your psyche. The process begins by focusing your attention on one thing, usually the sensation of inhaling and exhaling each breath, or on a "mantra," a special sound or phrase you repeat to yourself. Any distracting thoughts that enter your mind during meditation are gently disregarded. Meditation enables you to communicate with your heart and nourish your soul. You may experience increased awareness, empower your inner joy, reach your higher loving self, and achieve harmony with your inner spirit.

Eastern philosophers believe that meditation creates a balance and flow of energy through the body. They use meditation to find inner peace, balance in their lives, and harmony with the universe. Others use meditation to calm an overactive mind distracted by changing sensations, thoughts, and feelings, or to take a break from endless mental distractions. Some use meditation to learn to observe things as they really are in the present, and to develop mastery of the mind over life's changes and experiences through increasing insight, wisdom, and compassion.

How Meditation Works

Although there are many different forms of meditation, most share similar goals: to achieve relaxation, quiet the mind, and focus one's awareness. Some forms are used to heal physical, emotional, and spiritual dis-ease, or to achieve union with the Divine and complete enlightenment. When you are comfortably relaxed and free from distractions, your personal thoughts and feelings continuously generate neuropeptides and hormones that travel throughout your body. Meditation is just another way of entering the body's internal conversations, consciously intervening in its biochemical interactions. By shifting the mind from a "shoulda, coulda, woulda" type of thinking, you promote self-regulation and healing on many levels. Meditation provides a chance for your body to catch up with the powerful transforming effects of your natural information flow instead of always running through life. During meditation, as you relax and gradually transcend your usual level of consciousness, pathways to the brain that deal with unconscious thoughts and experiences open up. The two basic components of traditional meditation are passive disregard of intruding thoughts, and the silent repetition of a sound, called a mantra, to minimize distracting thoughts and assist you to resume a focused awareness. Mantras usually are one- or two-syllable words, such as *Om* or words chosen to soothe, such as peace, love, or serenity. Meditation is associated with deep relaxation, where the mind is calm and alert and stimulates the brain to produce an evenly balanced pattern of alpha and theta brain waves.

Steps for Meditating

The common ways to practice meditation are to find a quiet, comfortable place to relax without distractions, to focus on your breathing, and to direct your awareness to becoming one with your body. Although various thoughts may distract your attention, you gently return your focus to breathing or to the repetition of a particular word or phrase (mantra). Refocusing on your breathing or mantra may be difficult at first.

1. Select a quiet place to relax, away from noise, bright lights, and distractions. Some people use a headset with their favorite soothing music to help them relax. If possible, try to meditate in the same place and position every day.

2. Find a relaxing position where you will be comfortable throughout your meditation, without falling asleep. You may sit on a chair, sit cross-legged on the floor, assume the lotus position, sit against a wall with legs stretched out, or lie down. There is no one correct position, but your spine must be straight and your head upright.

3. Completely relax every part of your body: let go of all tension. You may close your eyes and do a body scan (see Chapter 14) to find any tense parts. Prepare to look within yourself, quiet your mind, and focus on your spirit.

4. Slowly breath in and out. Inhale through your nose and exhale through your nose or mouth. Listen to your breath: breathe loudly enough that you can hear yourself and learn to feel it. Take long, slow, deep breaths and feel the air coming in as you inhale, and visualize it flowing out as you exhale.

5. Focus on your breathing pattern and try to maintain it. Concentrate on your breathing to block out other thoughts. You may silently count as you inhale, or repeat a phrase such as, breathe in, breathe out. The words distract the mind while the sound and experience of breathing in and out provide a calm and steady focal point.

6. If your mind wanders with distracting thoughts, let them come and go, and gently refocus on your breathing until your mind chatter stops. Regaining your focus in an easy, gentle way enhances your sense of inner balance. Do not worry about achieving a deep level of meditation; just allow your relaxation to deepen at its own pace. With practice, you will become adept at focusing on your breathing, counting, or using positive affirmations without mindless thoughts distracting you. This may take a while to master.

It is important to practice daily meditation. You will need discipline to meditate consistently and achieve maximum benefits. Start with ten to twenty minutes if possible, but if you can only meditate for five minutes, then do that. During your meditations, your mind may wander a thousand times. Just keep bringing it back, gently and firmly. Many people find that meditating upon awakening, before your thoughts turn to everyday events, is helpful: others prefer to meditate before bedtime.

When you first begin to meditate, do not expect too much too soon. With continued practice, you may be guided on a gentle journey through relaxation techniques that include deep methodical breathing and basic visualization skills. Usually it takes a few weeks to feel the benefits from meditation, and then you may wish to increase your time. As long as you try to relax and stay focused on the present, you cannot fail. With continued practice, your relaxation, awareness, and concentration deepen, leading toward greater relaxation, inner calmness, and sustained awareness. You may develop new insights about yourself and how you relate to your world. When you achieve a deep level of meditation, your alpha brain waves indicate that you have reached the most balanced, relaxed, and harmonious state of your body.

Variations of Meditation

Over the years, several different forms of meditation have been developed. During meditation, you may use selective awareness, which is the power to choose what to focus your attention on and what either to ignore or to put off for another time. Thus, you can change your perspectives and behaviors on many things, and so change your life. Some forms of meditation encourage practitioners to become receptive to a higher purpose or wisdom. Examples of several variations of traditional meditation are described below.

The One-Breath Meditation

One-breath meditation is a simple, effective, on-the-spot way to stay calm and give your body the energy-giving power of deep breathing. It can increase your energy and alertness when you feel fatigued or stressed from the chaos or problems in your life.

In *The Power of 5,* Bloomfield and Cooper suggest that whenever you feel the need to calm down or to increase your energy, take in a deep breath of air. Be aware of your breath coming in, feel the sensation, and relax your shoulders, straighten your spine, and let the air expand your chest. Visualize yourself taking in oxygen-rich air that will increase your vitality and strength by reaching every cell in your body. Imagine a bright light filling every part of your body and soul. Hold the breath for a few moments and feel it lift your spirits, then as you exhale through your mouth, visualize releasing all the tension from your muscles and thoughts. Take several deep breaths as described above until you feel relaxed and energized.

The Mini-meditation

Many people are constantly on the run and never seem to find time to meditate. The mini-meditation is an abbreviated form which is useful when you find yourself having to wait for something. You can use the one-breath meditation described above while sitting in traffic, waiting for an appointment, standing in line at a bank or store, sitting during a TV commercial or boring meeting, or while riding as a passenger in a car or bus.

Meditation for Mental Relaxation

Mental relaxation helps remove you from daily stresses and problems by mentally visualizing a peaceful, natural setting where you can relax, shut out thoughts, and let yourself float. By using deep cleansing breaths, you can slow down, calm your mind, and immerse your body, mind, and spirit in this peaceful setting. Feel your tension drift away, relax, and feel yourself come alive. Practice this form of relaxation for ten to fifteen minutes.

Active Meditations

Some people prefer more active meditations when they feel distracted. You can do a walking meditation in which you repeat a sound or phrase while walking slowly. You can do tai chi, or dance. Whatever you choose, if you do it with focus and awareness, it becomes a form of meditation. Meditation can even be used while you're exercising, making it an active or moving meditation: focus on your movements and breathing. The more relaxed you are while exercising, the more efficiently you will build muscle.

Heartfelt Meditation

In *The Ten Rules of High Performance Living*, Dr. Meltzer recommends using heartfelt meditation. This form embraces a relaxed physical body, a pure, loving heart, deep breathing, and a calm mind. With your body in an effortless state, open your heart and take slow, deep cleansing breaths. With every breath, fill your heart with love. As your heart space expands, calm your mind, and feel the unconditional love for yourself and others. With love from your heart, close and relax your eyes, gaze upward at the point between your eyes, then look within yourself. You choose how you wish to feel, so put a smile in your heart, your soul, and your eyes to recharge your spirit, and focus on the light of your soul. You may use creative visualizations to enhance your meditations and see your dreams come true.

Creative Meditation

Creative meditation relies on the power of guided visual imagery. Begin with a relaxed, traditional meditation, then imagine the kind of events you wish to experience in your life. Guide your imagination to visualize an optimal situation, circumstance, or lifestyle. Dr. Meltzer suggests that you creatively visualize the relationships or situations you desire at home, work, or leisure by directing your mind to see, feel, and savor the experience, whether it is an adventure, situation, or change in relating to others. As you relax and let go, you will transcend your busy mind and flow with inner joy and peace as you float within your visualizations. You must practice your vision for ten to fifteen minutes daily to experience the full benefits and a change in your soul.

Self-healing Meditation

This form of meditation uses your self-healing powers to change, strengthen, or reduce a physical, emotional, or spiritual area or problem in your life. During meditation, you may use a mantra or an affirmation which has special meaning for you to help you concentrate on the phrase and nothing else. Mantras or affirmations are usually statements of strong intent and belief which you repeat either silently in your head or quietly out loud, over and over, to clear your mind of other thoughts. With knowledge and choice, you may decide to use healing affirmations. These affirmations invest and validate the power of your spirit to heal. When used repeatedly, they open up your body's internal channels of communication, allowing the self-healing process to occur. If you choose a life of joy, trust, and satisfaction, then a positive physiological response occurs throughout the body, especially the immune system. Self-healing meditations can be used to cleanse your digestive system, restlessness, or spiritual blindness. They enable you to center on your heart and live peacefully in the present. As you listen to your inner voice and affirmations of your goodness, you'll feel love in your heart and may uncover secrets in your soul. You should focus on healing affirmations that are strong declarations of purpose, conviction, belief, and self-acceptance. Affirmations can open your heart and heal your soul. Some examples of affirmations are given below, and longer ones are given at the end of this chapter.

- My body, mind, and spirit are working in harmony to keep me well.
- I love life and will enjoy life to the fullest.
- My faith will restore my soul and make me whole.
- I expect to be happy and share my joy with others.

Kria Shakti

This is an active form of meditation which involves the principles of creative visualization and affirmations. As with traditional meditation, you find a quiet place where you can relax in comfort. In your mind, you then create a special private place where you meet and converse with your chosen spiritual beings, who serve as your guides. You bring questions, problems, or concerns which you wish to know more about to this place and seek nurturance from your spirits and from affirmations of your self-worth.

Mindfulness Meditation

Mindfulness or insight meditation is based on ancient principles of Tibetan Buddhism. It is a philosophy as well as a meditation practice in which you experience what happens in the here and now by focusing your mind on the present moment. It is considered a "way of being," and may become a way of life rather than just a method to attain calmness and stability. Jon Kabat-Zinn, author of *Full Catastrophe Living*, was the founder of the Stress Reduction Clinic at the University of Massachusetts Medical Center. He designed a mindfulness program to help patients with chronic pain focus on their thoughts, feelings, and body, then respond in a conscious way to reduce their pain. Mindfulness can change the experience of pain: when you become mindfully aware of pain, resistance diminishes, and you become an observer. Pain or tension intensifies when you bring it to your awareness, but the sensation often changes and may diminish or disappear during this meditation. An analogy of mindfulness is to see yourself as surfing the mind, riding the thought waves, and going with the flow, not resisting the impact or direction, but allowing yourself to float freely. An integral part of this meditation is acknowledging the present reality as it actually is, pleasant or unpleasant, painful or comfortable. You learn to work with rather than against change to establish mental and physical calm. It involves going into the body and accepting what is found and felt there, so that old traumas and destructive patterns can be released. When you face, accept, and even welcome your tension, stress, and physical pain, as well as related mind states such as fear, anger, or frustration, you can transform that reality and your relationship to it. How you look at things determines how you deal with stress. If you don't face the present, you may become stuck in the past and have difficulty changing things in the future.

First, find a comfortable, relaxed position and become aware of your breathing pattern. Feel your breath as it flows into your body and watch it flow out again. Feel your body as it lets go of each breath. As you focus on your body, you may feel it relax by itself as any tension in your mind or body flows out with each breath. Now focus your attention on your present thoughts, feelings, and sensations. As thoughts or feelings cross your mind, intentionally but nonjudgmentally observe where your thoughts go, and identify how you feel, then gently return to the present. You may become more aware and more accepting of how things are at this moment, just by feeling your breath flow in and out. Awareness of your thoughts and feelings may help you understand your daily stressors and pressures and reduce your reaction to them. You may relax some just by holding any discomfort or distress you feel in awareness for a moment without struggling. If you have discomfort or distress, perhaps it's how you see and deal with it that are most important. As you stay in touch with the moment, you may notice a tiny shift in your awareness which may lead you to see things differently, so that you feel less stuck with your discomfort or have more options for handling your problems. You may also acquire a deeper insight into what motivates you, how you feel about your world, and how your fears and aspirations affect your reactions. With practice and experience, the need to transcend one's present state gives way to a feeling of unfolding immanence and wholeness in each moment. You may move beyond the present and choose to explore a broader universe.

The key to mindfulness meditation is the quality of your awareness of each moment, not *what* you focus on. It is important to be nonjudgmental—like a silent witness or a dispassionate observer—so that you won't censor what crosses your mind. The goal of mindfulness is to be in a relaxed state of attentiveness both to what is happening in your mind—inner thoughts and feelings—and to your body's sensations and perceptions at the present moment. Try not to avoid or resist unpleasantness, but attempt to clearly see and accept the present moment. As you fully accept the present, you become open to experiencing life more completely and can respond more effectively to life's ups and downs with grace, humor, and wisdom.

There are two ways to practice mindfulness meditation, formal and informal. Formal practice includes the *sitting meditation* and the body scan, which are designed to focus on breathing and on a specific area in the present moment. In the sitting meditation you use the cross-legged Buddha position, with your head, neck, and back erect, although you may sit on a straight-backed chair. Your posture should reflect an inner attitude of a fully awakened mind and dignity. Initially, you focus on feeling the air you inhale and exhale or on feeling your abdomen expand and contract with each breath. Once you master this, you may focus your awareness on changing sounds, sensations, or thoughts.

In the *body scan,* described in Chapter 14, you slowly and systematically direct your focus to various regions of your body, from the top of your head to your feet, noting any physical sensations as you move along. Although it is best to lie down for this exercise, it may be accomplished in a sitting position.

During mindfulness meditation, there are probably several different pathways that have a positive influence on your mental and physical health. Relaxation and focusing your awareness play different yet complementary roles. As you enter your mind/body conversation without judgments or opinions, you release peptide messenger molecules which regulate your breathing while unifying all your systems. Also, by relaxing and focusing on painful sensations, you learn to distinguish and separate your physical discomfort and the negative emotions that may generate discomfort. Gradually, your perception and reaction changes to a more neutral feeling about the discomfort, and you learn to accept pain as a more normal sensation with which you can live.

The informal practice of mindfulness meditation is simply to remind yourself to be in the present moment during daily activities and to "check in" periodically during the day. This can be performed spontaneously when feeling stressed, or during routine activities, such as while driving, walking, showering, or eating. The beauty of informal mindfulness is that it does not take extra time, only shifting from one's mental automatic pilot to being fully aware of the present moment and what you are experiencing.

Health Benefits of Meditation

According to Dr. Ornish, one of the greatest benefits of meditation is that it enables you to live for today and embrace each moment. Meditation can free you from your preoccupation with the past and future and can assist you to focus on and experience life's precious moments. It releases tension and helps you become more accepting of yourself and others—it teaches you to be your own best friend. Through meditation, you can develop an inner peace, and the more inner peace you experience, the better you function emotionally and the more you enjoy life. Researchers have found that meditation provides a deep level of relaxation which can calm the mind, reduce stress, and help you manage anxiety, depression, and other emotional problems. Meditation can ease you into relaxed wakefulness and provide the space and time for you to release unhealthy emotions, enabling a healthy flow of your mind/body biochemicals. It enhances your breathing, quiets your mind, and may counteract negative emotions from stress. It may relieve psychological symptoms of stress such as anxiety, irritability, hostility, confusion, anger, and fear, along with the physical problems of fatigue, high blood pressure, cravings, and chronic pain. You may experience an inner sense of clarity, peace, joy, and well-being that can help prevent some illnesses. People who meditate regularly approach life more calmly and rationally. They are able to make better choices and can recognize and resolve the problems that trigger their tension and anxiety.

Any time during the day, whenever you begin to feel tension or anxiety creeping in, take a meditation break by focusing on your breathing or on silent affirmations and visualizations. These actions will help rest your mind, relax your muscles, and make you feel more peaceful and calm. They also lower your heart rate and blood pressure and increase your circulation, all of which may reduce many physical and emotional symptoms of stress. Stress often contributes to shallow, irregular breathing, which leaves your body starved for oxygen and triggers physiological changes that can affect your mood. Meditation can improve your mood to a more positive outlook. Researchers recently found that regular use of transcendental meditation and murmuring a mantra might reduce the risk of heart attack and stroke by decreasing the fatty deposits and thickness of artery walls of those with hypertension. In Deepak Chopra's book, *Ageless Body, Timeless Mind*, he describes how many of the physiological effects of stress speed up the aging process; meditation can slow and possibly reverse these effects.

When you meditate daily, you may find that it revitalizes your energy, rejuvenates your hormones, purifies your emotions, and cleanses your soul. Relaxation can also accelerate self-healing and optimize your performance, productivity, and endurance at work or play. When you focus your awareness, you achieve greater concentration, which helps you perform more effectively and efficiently.

The more sustained and concentrated your meditation, the more healing occurs as you become in touch with your inner self, which nourishes your soul. This kind of emotional intelligence can be achieved only by acquiring inner wisdom. In addition, when meditation is combined with other spiritual practices, it may lead to transcendental interconnectedness with a higher power in the universe. The feeling of being spiritually centered and touched by a higher wisdom provides a feeling of calm and the courage to deal more effectively with stressful situations.

Although meditation is simple in concept, it is difficult for some to master. But you don't have to master meditation to benefit from it. However, you must meditate regularly for it to make a difference in your life. It is the *process* of meditation, not how well you perform it, that makes it so beneficial. As with any new exercise or diet, the results are not immediate: change and the benefits of meditation occur gradually and can be long-term if you meditate regularly.

Mindfulness meditation is far more than feeling relaxed or reducing tension. The goal is to nurture an inner balance of mind that helps you to face difficult situations with greater stability, clarity, understanding, and even wisdom, so that you can act or respond more effectively. The stressed-out feeling can melt away when you use mindfulness to be fully present in the here and now. Studies by Dr. Jon Kabat-Zinn have shown that mindfulness meditation can dramatically reduce pain and improve the mood of those who live with chronic pain by helping them exist in the present rather than in constant fear that their pain is killing them. He found that patients who used this meditation reported fewer medical symptoms and psychological problems such as anxiety, depression, and hostility. They felt more self-confident, assertive, and motivated to care for themselves and had more confidence in handling stressful situations. In addition to feeling more in control of their lives, they had improved attitudes about themselves and their world and felt a greater sense of meaning in life. Dr. Kabat-Zinn believes that mindfulness meditation enhances some people's sense of wholeness and feeling connected with the world.

VISUALIZATION OR GUIDED IMAGERY

In the early 1970s, Carl Simonton and his wife taught cancer patients to visualize the immune system's cells fighting off cancer cells, with hope that it would help them strengthen their immune systems. Their work received much publicity and sparked interest in the use of visualization. Some visualization techniques are used as part of various anti-stress and self-improvement systems. Doctors, dentists, athletes, artists, and teachers are also beginning to find that these techniques are helpful in specifically stressful situations.

Some people prefer a visual approach to meditation. The way you focus your mind during visualization or mental imagery is an important factor in your health. Visualization can empower women so that they don't feel like victims of circumstance, with no control over their destinies. Without a good, strong vision of yourself, your relationships with others, and where you hope to succeed in the future, you may be living unconsciously and unintentionally, relying on lower levels of consciousness to take over and do their reflexive best. When you do not make choices consciously, the unconscious parts of your mind choose for you, according to your belief structure.

Definition of Visualization

Visualization is a form of suggestion—a mental image or picture in the mind's eye of something you desire. In *Stress and Natural Healing*, Christopher Hobbs explains that you should intentionally or consciously choose thoughts and images of actions, behaviors, or areas in your life you wish to change, and think about them in a positive way to achieve your desired physical, psychological, or spiritual image. Visualization or guided imagery is an inner representation of a flow of thoughts you can envision, hear, feel, smell, and taste. It is the language of the arts, the emotions, and, most importantly, the inner self. Visions are a window on your inner world—a way of viewing your own ideas, feelings, and interpretations, and of transforming and liberating those ideas from distortions that may unconsciously direct your life and shape your health.

How Visualization Works

Many mind/body methods rely on three things—motivation, belief, and expectation. *Motivation* is a clear vision or positive image of one's goal, then believing in that goal long enough—imagine it happening—and having the confidence to follow it through. Believing in your ability to achieve your ideal image acts as both a filter and amplifier—it determines which choices you think are available to you. If your mind is open and the image of your goal is sufficiently clear, you can develop the power to change your body's chemical reactions so that your mental image will begin to happen in physical reality. It works with the universal law of manifestation—that before something comes into being you must have a picture of your goal. Your vision, which may include dreams, daydreams, memories, and reminiscence along with plans, projections, and possibilities, is a powerful factor in the way your mind codes, stores, expresses, and recalls information and experiences. Dr. Miller explains in *Deep Healing: The Essence of Mind/Body Medicine* that thoughts are electrical and may be produced and changed by shifts in electrons and electrical fields. Thus, consistently visualizing an image in your mind causes your cerebral cortex to secrete minute quantities of chemicals called neuropeptides—epinephrine, serotonin, dopamine, endorphins, and enkephalins. These chemicals of emotion travel through your circulatory, endocrine, and nervous systems, which create corresponding changes in many organ functions, including your heart rate, temperature, blood pressure, and immune system.

You have the innate wisdom and skills to heal yourself, but may have forgotten how to access this power. According to Dr. Miller, when you create a healthy image of yourself and hold it in your mind during a relaxed state, the image functions as a model that will happen in physical reality *if* the channels of communication are open and the goal is sufficiently desired. Your inner images are revealed by what you say, how you behave, and the presence or absence of health and healthy behaviors.

Using Visualization

Your awareness is selective, intentional, or unintentional, but your thoughts are chosen according to specific patterns you have learned during your lifetime. Initially you may choose images which are pleasant and very familiar, so you'll have greater success using this strategy. You have the capacity consciously to choose an image to focus on that will determine how you think, see, feel, believe, and act. So prior to using visualization, you need to determine what you want to achieve and how to reach your goals. Usually a clear inner vision does not occur immediately: you may need to take time for vision quests where you can experience peace and solitude. Dr. Hobbs suggests that you take a few days of vacation or employ daily mini-vision quests while walking or praying, to identify and clarify the goals you wish to achieve. During these quests, consider what characteristics represent your ideal self image—happy, optimistic, bright, creative, or open to new ideas. Examine how you would relate to others—confident, friendly, flexible, receptive, or outgoing. Seek your higher wisdom for inspiration for a new direction in your life or for better health. Develop these ideas, then apply them to your vision of yourself to determine whether your vision goals are realistic.

Visualization techniques are generally used with relaxation or meditation. You begin by sitting or lying down in a comfortable position, closing your eyes and relaxing your body. Concentrate on emptying your brain of distracting thoughts and focus on the sound and rhythm of your breathing. While in this relaxed state, focus on the predetermined image you have designed to help you in a special way, or allow your mind to conjure up images that give you insight into a specific problem.

If you need to relax and get away temporally from daily stress, you could take a mini-mental vacation. You may imagine yourself in a pleasant situation, such as soaking in a hot, soapy bath with soft music and candlelight, walking in a quiet forest, lying under a tree with warm breezes blowing across your face, or in your most comfortable chair. To enhance your image, try to use all five of your senses. Focus on colors, shapes, smells, sounds, and sensations. Allow yourself to become totally absorbed in the sensual aspects of your image. Picture yourself walking along a soft, white, sandy beach where the water is crystal clear and the lapis-colored waves are washing your feet. A gentle breeze caresses your body and hair. Feel the warm sun on your body, the sand between your toes, the mist in the air, and cool water on your feet. Then imagine that you are floating face-up in the sea—feel the buoyancy of your body as you gently ride the waves. Smell the sea around you and taste the salty water. Feel the sun spread a gentle warmth over you as your body becomes warm and heavy while floating.

Another relaxing mini-mental vacation might include imagining yourself on a Caribbean trip, lying on the beach, soaking up the sun's rays or snorkeling for tropical fish. Or you could imagine floating peacefully in a beautiful swimming pool, gently rocking with the waves, or perhaps you prefer fishing by a trout-filled stream, or skiing down a mountain covered with powdered snow. You may imagine yourself at a sports event, replay scenes in your favorite movie, or recall details of a pleasant trip you've taken. Guided imagery can help keep you focused and interested in your image and insure that unwanted, intrusive thoughts stay out of your picture. These trips can last for five to twenty minutes and be in technicolor, with music, smells, and sensory experiences.

If you need to improve your health, visualize your inner healer in your mind's eye as an army of nurses and doctors, white blood cells, or a glowing mist of healing energy—sense it any way you choose. You can visualize light and energy coming into your body to heal you, or the immune system attacking abnormal cells and increasing your healthy cells to help the body heal itself. Imagine these healing forces circulating throughout your energy channels, or meridians—the life energy flows up the front and down the back. Place your hands over areas of your body that need healing and visualize the energy flowing to those areas. As you visualize those areas becoming strong and perfect, you may feel energy or warmth passing from your hands into those areas. With experience you may feel waves of warmth, tingling, or a flowing feeling. As you inhale, gather healing resources and send the energy to the area you imagine with each breath. As you exhale, focus on circulating those resources internally, affirm their power to increase your health and vitality, and feel your inner healer sending the toxins out of your body.

If your heart needs healing, visualize healing resources moving there to nourish and support the heart's function. If you have an infection, think of your white blood cells as fierce warriors or Pacman characters attacking the diseased cells, destroying them, and encouraging the growth of healthy new cells. Imagine diseased cells carried in the lymph fluids along with any toxic wastes, and flush them out of your system forever. Then visualize a fresh supply of oxygen-rich blood bathing, nourishing, and strengthening the new healthy tissue. If you have headaches, visualize fresh air filling your head, or a cooling sensation releasing the tension across your forehead. If you have tension in your neck, back, or shoulders, visualize your muscles relaxing and lengthening as blood brings fresh oxygen to them, then imagine the pain flowing out your hands and feet. Practice this for five to fifteen minutes.

If you need to protect your body and spirit from stressful encounters or from being polluted by other people's thoughts and negative emotions, you may try using the White Light or Egg-of-Light exercise described by the Borysenkos in *The Power of the Mind to Heal*. With this technique you visualize either a bright white light surrounding you or a bubble of loving light two to three feet around you. You begin this exercise by taking a full relaxing breath, then focusing on your breathing and noticing how your body rises lightly as you breathe in and relaxes as you breathe out. Next, imagine a great star of loving light in the space above and in front of you. Let this light cascade over you like a waterfall and run through you like a river, from the top of your head down through every cell in your body. Visualize the river of light washing away any fatigue, illness, or negativity out the bottoms of your feet. Imagine that the light is removing any darkness around your heart, so that the light within you shines more brightly and extends two to three feet around you in all directions like an enormous, luminous egg. Then, make a firm mental declaration that any loving and encouraging thoughts will penetrate the egg and reach your heart, while any negative thoughts will bounce off and return to the sender as blessings of love and kindness. Declare that your own loving thoughts will reach the intended person.

If you decide to use visualization techniques, first master relaxation, then set small goals before you try more complex forms of imagery. An experienced instructor can help you with specific problems. Self-help tapes are also available, but results may take longer if you work alone. Practice fifteen to twenty minutes twice a day for three weeks, so that you can see whether using imagery is helpful. The more adept you become at holding your ideal image, the more you will see changes in your life. Your ideal image can become a driving force in your life, motivating you to make choices consistent with your image, and you will notice physiological and emotional changes in your mind/body too. Develop a technique to end your image gradually, as you'll feel slightly drowsy. You might count backwards, then inhale and open your eyes as you say to yourself, "I feel alert and relaxed."

Benefits to Using Visualization

Visualization is an important component in balancing yourself physically, mentally, emotionally, and spiritually. The techniques are simple to learn, and with consistent practice the effect is cumulative, gradually improving your healing and health. Visualization is one of the best methods of mind/body healing because it is a simple, natural way to relax and reduce stress. Three major benefits of visualization are the ability to create physiological changes, enhance your emotions, and acquire psychological insights. Visualization directly affects your physiology by stimulating changes in your heart rate, blood pressure, oxygen consumption, local blood flow and temperature, respiration, brain wave rhythms and patterns, and levels of various hormones and neurotransmitters, all of which strengthen your resistance to illness and promote healing. Strong, powerful visions help some people adjust their internal functions and turn on so-called voluntary physiological controls, which activate the body's healing abilities.

Imagery also influences your thoughts and emotions. During meditation, you may see connections between stressful situations and physical symptoms—how various parts are interrelated in your whole life. You can overcome apprehension, fear, and nervousness by replacing negative thoughts, and you can face pain and challenge difficult situations with positive images. Visualization can help you feel peace and serenity, feel empowered, reduce your stress, and promote sleep by imagining your body feeling warm and heavy. With continued practice, stress and anxiety will be replaced with feelings of calm and balance which can help redefine and shape your life. Gradually, you will maintain a sense of inner serenity, even in times of chaos, and speak and act with the feeling of power and wisdom.

PRAYER AND SPIRITUAL BELIEFS

The role of prayer and spiritual experiences in healing has recently received increasing attention. In his book, *The Faith Factor,* Dr. Dale Mathews cited numerous studies linking religious commitment and health. Research has helped rekindle national interest in the effects of religious experiences on healing. In the Christian tradition, prayer has come to mean communion with a higher power, and is focused on divine grace and the light of spirit. Prayer occurs in almost limitless forms based on the diverse spiritual traditions of the world's multicultural religious traditions. Each tradition has developed forms of prayer that are expressed uniquely for a variety of purposes. The role of spiritual belief in healing has also become more acceptable among health care providers. While organized religion provides the structure and ceremony that lend support and a calming effect in times of stress, spirituality doesn't require a formal worship setting. Some people find their spirituality by communing with nature during walks in quiet places. These may be reflective times to contemplate something beyond life's mundane stresses.

The Borysenkos believe that although we are whole many of us need to remove the fears that prevent us from knowing who we really are. The Buddhists imagine a higher or spiritual self as a sun that perpetually shines even though clouds of pain and illusion may temporarily hide it from view. Whether you call this sun the inner physician, your intuition, essence, or higher self, your task is to discover and live within that place of wholeness to feel peaceful and spacious. Many people never imagine how powerful God really is, and they unconsciously set a limit on how much God can help them. For you to accept God's generosity, you must recognize that His power is unlimited and that everyone has equal access to it. When you are open to God's love and to the infinite possibilities unfolding in every moment, you become a little kinder and a little lighter, and can facilitate your own healing so that you don't succumb to the inevitable hurts and stresses of life. Larry Dorsey, author of *Recovering the Soul: A Scientific and Spiritual Search*, describes prayer as "an attitude of the heart"—an intentional act of turning toward a divine presence for the purpose of dialogue, praise, thanksgiving, confession, petition, inquiry, or struggling with a problem.

Definition of Prayer

You don't have to believe in God or invoke a higher power to pray. Every loving thought and attitude is a kind of prayer. Even the respect, hope, and encouragement of health professionals are prayers that allow the power of their minds to help us heal. During prayer, you take time for spiritual renewal so that you can reach and be nurtured by the original source of all your energy and vitality. Dr. Hobbs believes that deep meditation and prayer open a pathway to a higher wisdom or greater power than the conscious mind can fathom by quieting the mind and allowing the body to heal itself.

How to Pray

All types of prayer appear to aid in healing. Dr. Larry Dorsey, author of *Healing Words: The Power of Prayer and the Practice of Medicine*, found that some people direct their prayers to God the Father, by asking that someone be healed, while others send non-directed prayers of their love or feelings of empathy for an ill person. The desire for recovery has to be genuine, authentic, and deeply felt. It must come from feelings of love, caring, and compassion. Stop and reflect for a moment. Think about your family members, friends, and people with whom you interact. Are your thoughts about them loving and encouraging, or are they limiting and critical?

Directed prayer specifies a particular outcome. In her book, *The Healing Light*, Agnes Sanford, a spiritual healer, identified three steps of directed prayer: to feel a connection to the mind of God that is in all things; to see the result of prayer as already accomplished; and to give thanks. She believes that if our prayers are not in accordance with the divine will, nothing will come of them. Non-directed prayer is what the researchers at the Spindrift Foundation in Lansdale, PA call a "pure and holy qualitative consciousness of whoever or whatever is being prayed for." It is a prayer for the highest good or for the best potential to be made manifest.

Calling on Your Guardian Angels

Many women believe that guardian angels constantly surround them. When these women are in difficult circumstances or uneasy situations, they call on their angels for guidance and protection to help them through trying moments or periods in their lives. Belief that one's angels are with you at all times provides a feeling of safety and security, and releases you from fears.

Max Highstein and Jill Andre produced a CD titled *Visiting Angels* that may assist you to learn how to call upon your guardian angels. The following lines are adapted from this recording.

Angels are all around us. They are here to assist us in every walk of life.

Whenever you strive to be more loving, or who you truly are, the angels gather,
whether you choose to acknowledge them or not. They bring you protection.
Angels are naturally attracted to your openness and peace.

Feel your heart open to them and expand with feelings of joy and loving
communication. Trust that you will receive their love, support, and inspiration.

All things are possible. If there is anything you would like assistance with,
call on your loving angels to help you. Their unconditional love surrounds you.

Give loving thanks for the gifts your angels bring, and feel the joy in your heart,
knowing they are always with you to guide and protect you.

The Healing Consciousness

Dr. Meltzer asserts that healing your soul, the spiritual part of your being, is very important to your health because the soul is the center of your life. The light of your soul is the creative, life-giving energy vibrating and circulating within you, which the Chinese call 'chi.' Your soul has the inner wisdom and power to heal your mind and body through the healing consciousness. The Healing Consciousness is illustrated as a triangle with three spiritual muscles—love, faith, and peace of mind–that need to be exercised daily to enrich your soul's power. Both Ornish and Meltzer believe that heartfelt love is the most powerful healing force in the universe and that it can make you whole. The deeper your love, the more meaning and fullness you will experience in your life. With love in your heart and the courage to sustain you, you can achieve all your dreams.

Faith is trusting in your higher power or God's will for your life and believing in the fulfillment of your dreams—that your life will work out for the best. Faith requires that you relinquish control over your life, which is frightening. Many people resist giving up control because they don't believe that God's will for us and our own inner dream can coincide. Faith is the belief that with God you have the inner power to be whole and happy, no matter what befalls you. It is the union of belief, trust, and spiritual conviction that grounds your soul to the possibility of miracles.

The Healing Consciousness is the dynamic state of being, dominated by divine light and pure love, filled with emotional awareness and spiritual sensitivity. It uplifts your perceptions, thoughts, feelings, and experiences to feel infinite heartfelt love, emotional fulfillment, and spiritual prosperity. The healing consciousness is a creative, inspirational love energy that purifies your soul and allows a clear channel of light and love to purge negative thoughts and feelings and generate positive thinking, heartfelt love, and insight.

Health Benefits of Prayer and Religion

Spiritual fatigue leads to being easily distracted, confused, or anxious. Also, you may feel you are not doing what you want to do in life and become drained. You may lack the will to love, to improve yourself, and to live life to the fullest. Prayer can significantly affect your mental, physical, and spiritual health in a variety of beneficial ways. For many women, prayer offers a dimension of inner peace that cannot be achieved in any other way. Dr. Meltzer says that through prayer you can express the deepest yearnings of your heart for guidance, meaning, healing, and wholeness. In prayer, one's personal problems can be held in a spiritual context of faith, love, compassion, and forgiveness. Healing your soul is a process that gets you in touch with your unique self and gives you the wisdom to seek the truth in your life.

Dr. Mathews and his associates describe the healing power of prayer and cite studies showing that people who pray are less likely to get sick, more likely to recover from surgery and illness, and are better able to cope with their illnesses than people who do not pray. They also reported that religious commitment was consistently associated with better health, fewer psychological symptoms, lower blood pressure, longer survival, and improved quality of life. The religious practices of some groups promote healthier lifestyles and behaviors among their members. Those who are less actively religious are likely to abuse drugs and alcohol, to divorce, and commit suicide. Religious people consistently report greater life satisfaction, marital satisfaction, well-being, altruism, and self-esteem than do nonreligious people. Healing your soul enlivens your heart and exerts a very positive influence on your immune system. Recent studies at Duke University have found that people who are religious or attend church or synagogue regularly tend to have lower blood pressure and to live longer, possibly due to social support and improved mental health. If you don't relate to organized religion, reconnect with your inner spirit through meditation to lower your blood pressure, relieve anxiety, and even reduce chronic pain. Some physicians also report that people who are prayed for often do better even if they don't know they are being prayed for.

Religion serves as a supplement to traditional healing methods. Religiosity seems to affect health, though we don't know exactly why. Prayer has been shown to help people with anxiety, depression, and aggression, to improve self-esteem and self-awareness, and to stimulate mental abilities such as learning, memory, and concentration. Faith in God seems to influence healing because God is considered the almighty protector. We believe in an almighty power to heal us when our health is threatened and fear we may succumb to illness. Your faith may reflect your hope for a healthier future.

The new holistic approach to health and healing supports both the belief in the art of healing and the science of medicine. Whatever you believe in, whether it is God, a higher power, prayer, angels, or medicine, the healing influence of your belief affects your body and produces the same physiological changes. Your belief enhances the effects of your self-healing process.

In his book, *Timeless Healing*, Dr. Herbert Benson noted that the fellowship people experience in their religious communities is also restorative. Some studies suggest that the social support, sense of belonging, and convivial fellowship of various religions may buffer the adverse effects of stress and anger and trigger a chain of physiological processes leading to better health.

Prayer seems to have a positive effect on emotional and physical problems alike, according to Dr. Dorsey. And Dr. Meltzer strongly believes that when you heal your soul, you enjoy substantial peace of mind and feel serene and joyful. The benefits of spiritual health are love, peacefulness, gentleness, and blissfulness. You feel prepared to improve yourself and fulfill your visions, and may feel more lively, bold, forceful, and glowing with a vital spirit which energizes your soul power. Those with a spiritual soul are jubilant and cheerful, and have an inner strength, balance, and calmness. Their faith allows them to believe that even though bad things happen to good people, God may have a purpose and a good outcome will occur. Strong religious beliefs encourage hope, optimism, and positive attitudes that influence good health and longevity.

Web Site
>   www.healingmindbody.com

Affirmations
Morning Affirmation
>   God, let me be loving, kind, caring, sharing, nonjudgmental of self and others, forgiving of self and others, accepting of self and others. Let me be peaceful, calm, joyful, hopeful, courageous, confident within myself and with others. Let me be humble, giving from abundance, nurturing of self and others.

>   Let me be passionate for life, clear on my path, and have clarity of mind and soul. Help me to balance my mind, body and spirit, and let me be receptive of your guiding light, sharing this light with others. Let me be able to ask for and be receptive of any guidance and healing from You when needed, whether for the past, present, or future.

>   Teach me to be thankful for being, striving to be the best I can, and have compassion for others. Let me be comfortable with the knowledge that God is endless and can freely give endless gifts, that all is forgiven and Heaven is there for us when our work on earth is done. Finally, let me thank you for all the positive things in my life.

Daily Affirmation
>   *Lord, make me an instrument of thy peace.*
>   *Where there is hatred, let me sow love. Where there is injury, pardon.*
>   *Where there is doubt, faith. Where there is despair, hope.*
>   *Where there is darkness, light. And where there is sadness, joy.*

O, Divine Master, grant that I may not so much seek to be consoled,
   as to console;
to be understood, as to understand; to be loved, as to love;
for it is in giving that we receive, it is in pardoning that we are pardoned,
and it is in dying that we are born to eternal life.

—St. Francis of Assissi

Loving-kindness Blessing

May I be at peace, May my heart remain open,
   May I awaken to the light of my own true nature,
   May I be a source of healing for all beings.
May you be at peace, May your heart remain open,
   May you awaken to the light of your own true nature,
   May you be healed, May you be a source of healing for all beings.
May there be peace on earth,
   May the hearts of all people be open to themselves and to each other,
   May all people awaken to the light of their own true nature, and
   May all creation be blessed and be a blessing to All That Is.

—Joan Borysenko

I Love Myself Just the Way I Am

I Love myself the way I am, there's nothing I need to change,
   I'll always be the perfect me, there's nothing to rearrange.
   I'm beautiful and capable of being the best I can
      and I Love myself, just the way I am.
   I Love you just the way you are, there's nothing you need to do,
   When I feel the Love inside myself, it's easy to Love you.
   Behind your fears, your raging tears, I see your shining star
      and I Love you, just the way you are.
   I Love the world the way it is, 'cause I can clearly see
   All the things I judge are done by people just like me
   So 'til the birth of peace on earth that only Love can bring
      I'll help it grow, by Loving everything.
   I Love myself the way I am, and still I want to grow
   But change outside can only come, when deep inside I know
   I'm beautiful and capable of being the best I can
      and I Love myself, just the way I am.

—Rev. Lynn Davies

22

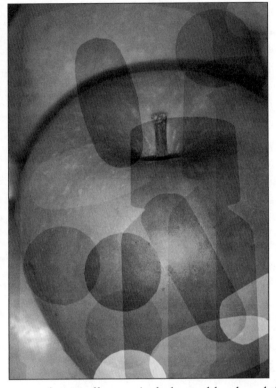

NUTRITION

The rules of good nutrition seem to change daily. Since world scientists can't agree on what's good or bad to eat, it's hard to know what to eat unless your have a scorecard. We used to read that all fats, red meats, highly sugary foods, eggs, salt, and butter were unhealthy for us. Recently studies have shown that although high-fiber diets may have some health benefits, they do not reduce the risk of colon cancer; that most fats and eggs probably do not affect one's cholesterol level; and that for most people, salt does not contribute to high blood pressure, strokes, or heart disease. With these constant changes, it is no wonder that many women have problems choosing the right foods and eating a balanced diet.

A varied, well-balanced diet is the cornerstone of healthy living and functioning at your optimal level. Although there will always be controversy over exactly what makes up a well-balanced diet, it is generally accepted that eating too much animal fat or refined and processed products high in fat and sugar are hazardous to your health. Likewise, there is general agreement that eating plenty of fresh fruits and vegetables is good for you. More recently, scientists have identified how certain foods can affect your mood and stress level.

Knowledge of healthy and unhealthy foods and those that can help you cope better with life's stresses will help you live longer and have less stress in your life.

One way to improve your nutritional health is to learn how food works in your body and how to balance the foods you eat. Another method is to try to make intelligent decisions based on the information available to you that pertains to your age group. There are some general guidelines that will help you establish healthy eating patterns: use *moderation*, *balance*, and *variety* to guide your eating. A healthy diet provides the required energy, and essential nutrients—vitamins, minerals, some amino acids, and certain fatty acids—that the body can't produce. It also protects against disease and supports your overall health.

The Food Pyramid

The American Dietetic Association developed the Food Pyramid to guide adults' eating patterns.

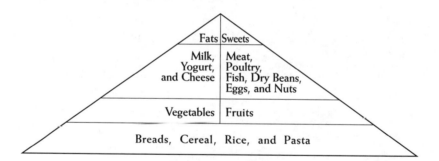

Servings for women: the number of servings from each food group depends upon your total energy (calorie) requirements, which are determined by your age, body build, activity level, and environmental conditions. Generally, older women are less active, require fewer calories, and should have fewer servings.

Food Group Servings
Breads, Cereal, Rice, and Pasta: 6 to 11 servings of grains per day
    1 slice of bread
    1 oz. ready-to-eat cereal
    ½ C cooked cereal, rice, pasta

Vegetable Group: 3 to 5 servings per day

    1 C raw, leafy vegetables

    ¹/₂ C cooked/chopped raw vegetable

    ³/₄ C vegetable juice

Fruit Group: 2 to 4 servings per day

    1 medium piece of fruit

    ¹/₂ C chopped, cooked or canned fruit

    ³/₄ C fruit juice

Meat, Poultry, Fish, Eggs, Beans: 2 to 3 servings per day

    2–3 oz. cooked, lean meat, poultry or fish

    ¹/₂ C cooked dry beans

    1 egg

Milk, Yogurt, Cheese: 2 to 3 servings per day, preferably low-fat

    1 C milk or yogurt

    1 ¹/₂ - 2 oz. cheese

Fats and Sweets: Use sparingly

    30 grams or less of fat per day

Carbohydrates

Your main source of energy is from foods containing carbohydrates, such as grains, fruits, vegetables, dry beans, and peas. There are two kinds of carbohydrates, simple and complex. Simple carbohydrates, which can enter the blood stream easily and provide quick energy, contain sugars like fructose and glucose, found in fruits and vegetables, lactose in milk, and sucrose in sugar cane. Complex carbohydrates are starches and dietary fiber found in potatoes, bread, vegetables, beans, and grains, which are converted to simple sugars through oxidation and take longer to provide energy. It is generally recommended that between 55 to 60 percent of your total daily calories should come from carbohydrates, with no more than 15 percent from simple ones. Many carbohydrates like potatoes, pasta, and rice are not high in calories, and they are bulky fibers which reduce hunger and total caloric intake. Some women were seduced into thinking that they could eat as much low-fat food as they want, yet many low-fat foods are high in calories, and excess sugar turns into fat.

Stress can increase the body's basic caloric needs by as much as 200 percent. Because the stress hormones increase production of body heat, this energy is unavailable for cell metabolism. Caloric inefficiency, induced by stress, contributes to an increased need for energy intake.

For moderation, balance, and variety, try different types of white and brown rice, couscous, polenta, kasha, cornmeal, or grits. Dried beans also are a complex carbohydrate with a rich source of vitamins, minerals, and protein. Almost 70 percent of adults do not eat the recommended five servings of fruits and vegetables a day. Some tips for adding vegetables to your meals are to chop carrots, celery, broccoli, onion, and zucchini in a food processor, then saute to soften them and add them to pizza and spaghetti sauces, meatloaf, hamburgers, soups, or casseroles. Keep baby carrots, celery sticks, broccoli, or red pepper slices in a covered container in the refrigerator to munch on. To increase your fruit intake, treat yourself to some exotic fruits, such as mangoes, papayas, guavas, kiwis, passion fruit, or pomegranates.

Proteins

Proteins are essential for building and repairing body cells such as muscles, skin, hair, and nails. They are constantly broken down in the body and need to be replaced. Proteins are made up of chemicals called *amino acids*, some of which are produced by the body, while others, known as *essential amino acids*, must be obtained from your diet. Essential amino acids are found in fish, meat, poultry, eggs, milk, and cheese. These foods have complete proteins. Other foods, including dried beans and peas, nuts, seeds, and vegetables, as well as some grains, contain some but not all of the essential amino acids.

Soy foods also provide more protein than any other plant-based food. Soy is a rich source of omega-3 fatty acids and is high in calcium, iron, B-vitamins, and zinc. Soy foods also contain isoflavones, antioxidants that keep LDL cholesterol from turning into plaque on artery walls, and may help reduce hot flashes associated with menopause. Soy is cholesterol-free and helps reduce LDL without reducing HDL cholesterol.

Stress may increase the body's need for protein from 60 percent to as much as 500 percent. The integrity of the body's tissues, like the skin and mucosal lining of the mouth, lungs, and nose, depends on adequate protein repair and secretion of protective biochemicals.

The recommended dietary allowance (RDA) for protein is based on a person's age and weight. A healthy 120 pound woman needs about 44 grams of protein, while a 150 pound woman requires about 55 grams of protein, or the equivalent of two 2 to 3 ounce servings of lean cooked fish or chicken. Most Americans eat far more protein than recommended.

Fiber

Fiber is found only in plant foods such as fruits, vegetables, whole grains, and dry peas and beans, but since it is the undigestible part of the plant wall, it is not considered a nutrient. However, fiber plays an essential role in the digestive process. Good sources of fiber include all-bran cereals, lentils, kidney beans, barley, oat bran, apples and pears with skin, prunes, raw vegetables, corn and green peas, dried beans, and whole grains. Raw fruits and vegetables help to keep the colon functioning properly and provide essential nutrients and enzymes that are lost during cooking or processing. Some ways to add fiber to your diet include eating high-fiber cereals like oatmeal, all-bran, or raisin bran, or adding fresh berries, apples, or dried fruit to your cereal; eating whole wheat or whole grain bread with at least 2 grams of fiber per slice; using brown rice and whole grain pasta; adding a variety of raw colored vegetables or garbanzo or kidney beans to pasta, rice, or potato salads; substituting wheat germ, bran, or whole wheat flour for regular flour in recipes; adding dried beans to stews, casseroles, and soups; and adding raisins, grapes, apple chunks, pineapple, zucchini, cucumber, or nuts to coleslaw, chicken or tuna salad.

There are two types of fibers. Water-soluble fibers that form gels to soften the stool are found in oats, legumes, fruits, whole grains, and some vegetables. These soluble fibers help lower cholesterol levels and control blood sugar levels in diabetics. Insoluble fibers, found in wheat bran, increase stool bulk so that it passes through the intestines more readily and help prevent constipation, hemorrhoids, and diverticulosis, or pockets in the intestinal wall. According to Jean Carper, an award-winning health journalist and author of *Food—Your Miracle Medicine*, a recent British study found that high-fiber diets cut the risk of heart disease in women nearly in half, and a Boston study found that high-fiber foods lower LDL cholesterol, blood pressure and triglycerides, which are risk factors for heart disease. Women who ate 23 grams or more of fiber a day, mostly from cereal, were 23 percent less likely to suffer a heart attack than those who ate less. However, a recent Harvard study suggested that there are no significant anti-cancer benefits of fiber for women. Fiber, especially wheat bran, increases stool bulk and moves foods through the digestive tract faster, decreasing exposure of carcinogens to the intestines. Many experts suggest that women eat between 20 to 35 grams of fiber daily, but most women eat half that amount. Don't eat more than 50 grams as this decreases the absorption of calcium, iron, and zinc.

Fats

Fats are a critical nutrient because they can boost metabolism and stimulate or depress other cellular and immune functions related to stress. They also help transport and store other nutrients, insulate the body and protect internal organs from injury, maintain healthy skin and hair, and regulate the body temperature. Fats are a source of energy and, when stored by the body, a source of reserve energy too. The right kinds of fat can also help prevent breast cancer and heart disease if you are genetically predisposed, and lower the incidence of inflammatory diseases like arthritis. But not all fats are the same. Three special families of fats, called the omega fats (omega-3s, 6s and 9s), are considered healthy ones. The omega-3 type in fish oil can enhance brain efficiency, memory, and learning, and may reduce depression and brain degeneration. The omega-3s are found in fatty fish and flaxseed oil, the omega-6s in evening primrose oil, and the omega-9s in olive oil, avocados, and almonds.

Dietary fats are classified as either saturated or unsaturated. *Saturated* fats are found in meat, whole milk, butter, and coconut and palm oil, and are generally solid at room temperature. They are associated with high levels of cholesterol. *Unsaturated* fats remain liquid at room temperature and can be divided into two types. *Polyunsaturated* fats, such as corn, safflower, sesame, and sunflower oils, tend to raise the amount of LDL—bad cholesterol contribute to plaque buildup in the arteries, and also reduce HDL—good cholesterol. *Monounsaturated* fats, such as olive and peanut oil, reduce LDL levels without affecting the HDL levels.

Jean Carper believes that there is no connection between eating foods high in cholesterol and blood cholesterol level, since these foods only slightly affect the blood cholesterol level. However, most nutritionists recommend that you restrict eating saturated fats such as animal fat, fatty meat, cheese, butter, and foods with trans-fatty acids or partially-hydrogenated oils, such as margarine, crackers, cookies, doughnuts, and processed foods. These types of fat may raise LDL cholesterol in genetically-predisposed people, and make the blood more sluggish and likely to form blood clots that constrict the arteries so that less blood and oxygen can get to the heart and brain. Only 25 to 30 percent of your total daily calories should be from fat, and most of those calories should be from unsaturated fats. Some tricks to reduce bad dietary fat are: to use virgin olive oil, which is lower in saturated fat than corn, safflower, or soybean oils; to select lean grades of meat or trim off the fat; to use skim or low-fat milk instead of whole milk and low-fat or part-skim cheeses; to serve fish or poultry instead of meat dishes and broil, bake, or roast meat instead of frying; and to replace fats in recipes for baked goods with applesauce or strained baby fruits. Try to eat a diet rich in plant foods, with lots of fruits, vegetables, nuts, beans, and grains, and more high-omega-3 foods such as mackerel, salmon, sardines, tuna and herring.

Most Americans eat much more fat than is good for them. This contributes to obesity and other health problems such as breast and colon cancer, higher tumor rates, and increased quantity of fecal bile acids, which may be carcinogens or promote tumors. When you prepare low-fat dinners, make enough leftovers for nutritious lunches, or make tuna salad with low-fat mayo and chopped veggies. Also, cooked pasta with tomato sauce or a vegetable-rich stir fry served with rice are good low-fat, high-fiber meals.

For some individuals, a low-fat diet may not be wise. If you replace fats with *sugary* fat-free foods, you just add calories that turn into fat. If you cut out too much good fat, such as fish or olive oil, you may not get enough foods with omega-3, or if your genes create too much bad LDL cholesterol, you may not benefit from a low-fat diet. Restricting fat may save you from a heart attack, but it may increase your chances of having a stroke.

Water

Water is essential to all cells in the body: 85 percent of your blood is water, 75 percent of your brain, and 70 percent of your muscles are made up of water. Water is essential to the digestion, absorption and transportation of nutrients in the body. It carries nutrients throughout your body, helps you digest food, lubricates your joints, protects your organs, keeps you cool, and flushes away wastes and toxins. Most tap water contains many pollutants that you are adding to your system. A filtration system attached to your kitchen faucet or Brita pitchers can remove bacteria and other particulate matter from water. Drink plenty of filtered water, six to eight glasses of water a day, to keep the body well-hydrated, eliminate waste properly, and boost both mood and motivation. Most Americans are marginally dehydrated. Some symptoms of dehydration include loss of concentration or short-term memory, irritability, and fatigue. Water often loses out to coffee, tea, or soda because people don't like the taste. Try using herbal teas, or add a slice of lemon, lime, or orange, or a splash of fruit juice to your water—anything that makes it more appealing. Club soda, seltzer, fruit-flavored or tonic water, and sparkling water are other alternatives.

Gender Differences in Fat Cells and Food Cravings

From her studies, Debra Waterhouse, author of *Outsmarting the Midlife Fat Cell*, found that women have thirty billion smart, stubborn fat cells which are larger than men's fat cells and more often located in the buttocks, hips, and thighs. Women tend to have pear-shaped bodies and the ability to gain weight quickly with a greater amount of fat mass because they have more fat-storing enzymes than men. In addition, women have a slower metabolism, partially due to decreased thyroid production as they grow older. Also, when women take hormone replacement medications, many experience increased weight gain due to increased sodium and fluid retention and reduced metabolic rate. Women are also more likely to use antidepressants than men, and many of these medications slow the metabolic rate, which contributes to weight gain.

The food cravings of women are significantly different from those of men. Women are more likely to crave high carbohydrate foods like chocolate, candy, crackers, and ice cream, while men crave meat, hot dogs, eggs, pizza, and seafood. Women's cravings increase their serotonin levels, while men are more likely to exercise to increase their serotonin 'feel good' levels. Waterhouse recommends that women deactivate their fat cells by engaging in any aerobic exercise for a minimum of forty-five minutes three times a week, that they stop dieting and feed their bodies with smaller, multiple meals during the day. She suggests that women listen to and trust their body's food messages to identify what to eat, why, and when they are hungry, and to avoid skipping meals, overeating, and dieting.

Changes with Aging

Throughout adulthood your metabolism slows down, so it is important to recognize the connection between nutritional intake and activity level. As you move into middle age, you lose 5 percent of your muscle mass per decade. Since a pound of muscle burns 150 calories per day, and a pound of fat burns a mere three calories, you need to either lower your caloric intake or increase your exercise level and strength training as you grow older.

As women enter menopause, their risk for heart disease increases as estrogen levels decrease. Drastically reducing fat intake and eating more carbohydrates is not a good idea. One study found that women on low-fat (25 percent of calories) and high carbohydrate (60 percent of calories) diets increased their triglycerides and decreased good HDL, which increased their risk for heart disease. High-carb diets increase blood sugar and insulin levels, which add to the risk of heart disease. Restrict eating carbohydrates that digest quickly, and choose those which you digest slowly, like peanuts, dried apricots, dried beans, yogurt, or oat bran. Postmenopausal women's iron needs also decrease, so taking an iron supplement is unnecessary and may contribute to heart disease unless you are anemic.

As women near their sixties, their overall caloric needs, appetite, and to some degree, their sense of taste, decrease, but the amount of nutrients needed remains about the same. As you age, your body becomes less efficient at digesting, absorbing, and using nutrients, so older women must eat more nutritionally dense foods. Experts recommend eating at least five fruits and vegetables, generous portions of whole grains and legumes, and lots of dairy products each day. Women should also consider taking supplements of vitamins B6, B12, C, E, folic acid, and zinc to enhance their immune system. Green leafy vegetables, whole grains, seafood, and lean meats are all good sources of these vitamins. To keep your bones strong, you'll need 400 IU of vitamin D, and after age seventy you should increase to 600 IU by taking a supplement. To ensure good digestion, you need to eat 25 to 35 grams of fiber a day, and to reduce your risk of cataracts, consider eating antioxidant-rich foods such as citrus fruits, tomatoes, grapes, carrots, broccoli, soybeans, cabbage, and sweet potatoes.

Older women must also get sufficient protein to guard against decreased strength and enhance their immunity, so 50 grams of protein are recommended per day, along with a multivitamin, and possibly supplements of vitamins D, B12, and calcium. Since liver function decreases with aging, you can reduce the amount of vitamin A in your diet because it is harder for your body to absorb this vitamin quickly. Last, be sure to drink plenty of water because dehydration is common in older adults and contributes to fatigue.

Healthy Eating Habits

Try eating five or six small meals each day and use smaller portions or servings. Small portions of protein between meals at mid-morning and midafternoon are healthier and may aid in losing excess body fat and increase work effectiveness. One trick is to use a smaller plate for lunch and dinner. Another trick is to eat more high-fiber foods which help push fat through your system faster, so that you absorb less. Fresh fruits and vegetables are a great source of high-fiber and low-calorie foods. Forego second helpings, except for vegetables. Take time to enjoy your meal by chewing your food well and focus your attention on the tastes and textures of foods. Remember to eat only when you are hungry, not when you're feeling bored, frustrated, or unhappy. Try to avoid late night snacks, especially while watching TV. Remember that *moderation, balance,* and *variety* should be your guidelines.

The Low-stress Diet

Some nutrition experts claim that eating the right food at the right time can help you live with and even relieve some of your stress. Dr. Judith Wurtman, author of *Managing Your Mind and Mood Through Food,* designed a nutritional program based on eating foods that promote the brain's production of three mood-altering neurotransmitters: *dopamine, norepinephrine,* and *serotonin.* Dopamine and norepinephrine are energizers that your brain manufactures from the amino acid *tyrosine,* found in protein foods. Serotonin acts either as a tranquilizer or aids concentration, depending on the time of day. Carbohydrates such as chicken, fish, milk, bananas, pasta, and rice contain *tryptophan,* an amino acid that increases the brain's production of serotonin and can cause drowsiness. However, protein can impede the production of serotonin. An efficient way to get carbohydrates into your system is to drink them. Warm milk with honey is a good way to reduce insomnia. Carbohydrates such as fruits or starches take longer to digest and will not increase your serotonin production sufficiently to reduce stress. If you're overweight, you may need more sweets because your extra fat cells slow down the conversion process.

When you need to perform under stress, consider eating foods low in calories and carbohydrates. Debora Tkac suggests that you consume low-fat, high protein-foods such as lean meats or fish to ensure a high level of brain-energizing neurotransmitters. Try to eat about two hours before a stressful event so that you will have adequate blood sugar in your brain.

If you are under a great deal of stress, eat high carbohydrates with sugars and starches for the calming effects. Eating carbohydrate-rich snacks can help reduce feelings of impatience or distress. You also are likely to need more of the B-complex vitamins, vitamin C, and the mineral zinc, which the body uses up more quickly when under stress. For fast action, avoid fatty foods which slow down digestion and production of serotonin. You'll find you crave foods like candy, cookies, or ice cream. Nature has a way of directing us to the right food at the right time in the right amount. However, remember that it's the first one or two cookies that initiate the production of serotonin, so don't overdo it or you'll just gain weight. If you are prone to hypoglycemia (a tendency toward low blood sugar), try to eat sufficient protein and carbohydrates every couple of hours.

VITAMINS AND MINERALS

Many people take vitamin and mineral supplements for various reasons. In 1998, Americans spent $6.8 billion on vitamins and dietary supplements. Some people believe that supplements provide a form of dietary insurance, while others think that supplements will prevent various diseases or even treat specific conditions. While eating a well-balanced diet daily is the best way to get the necessary vitamins and minerals, only one person in ten regularly consumes sufficient fruits and vegetables to achieve this. Therefore, most health professionals recommend taking a good multivitamin to help preserve and improve your physical and emotional health, along with intellectual functioning. Some medications interfere with vitamin and mineral absorption, so check with your physician before starting a supplement program. Supplemental vitamins and minerals are absorbed best and are less likely to upset your stomach if you take them with food.

Most packaged foods list the vitamin and mineral contents of the product as the percentage of daily values (DV). Daily values are essentially the recommended amounts needed by adults in the general population to ensure adequate nutrition, but are less than the exact recommended dietary allowances (RDA). The RDA serves as a guide to determine the nutritional needs of adults to avoid nutritional deficiency: they are adequate to prevent deficiency, but numerous studies suggest that women may need higher doses of vitamins and minerals to maintain optimum health. According to Dr. Michael Janson, author of *The Vitamin Revolution in Health Care,* higher doses than recommended by the RDA can help women prevent and treat many common health problems.

The following section describes the action, benefits, and consequences of deficiencies of the most important vitamins and minerals, and the best food sources. The RDA is listed for each, along with recommended higher doses (Rec). Some vitamins and minerals interact with various medications, so you should consult with your physician before taking high doses. Vitamins and minerals with antioxidant properties are starred (*).

Vitamin A*—carotenoids   RDA 5,000 IU   Rec: 20,000 IU
Beta-carotene   RDA 10 mg   Rec: 10–20 mg

Vitamin A is an antioxidant that enhances immunity and promotes normal vision. It keeps the skin moist and is needed for skin repair and maintenance, plus bone and tooth formation. It helps promote healthy hair, teeth, and nails, and maintains the mucous membrane linings of the nose, throat, lungs, and intestines. It may aid in prevention of some cancers. Beta-carotene is a precursor to vitamin A: it converts into two molecules of vitamin A in the intestines, and protects against tumor development. Signs of vitamin A deficiency are dry scaly skin, dry brittle hair, itchy eyes, poor appetite, photo-sensitivity, night blindness and recurring infections. Deficiencies can increase susceptibility to carcinogens and immune problems. People with liver disease, diabetes, or hypothyroidism have problems converting beta-carotene to vitamin A.

Vitamin A is a fat-soluble vitamin whose absorption is also affected by the amount of protein in your diet. Abundant sources are found in egg yolks, whole milk and dairy products, animal liver, and fish oils. Beta-carotene is found in green, red, orange and deep yellow vegetables and yellow and orange fruits: carrots, papayas, sweet potatoes, collard greens, spinach, and other dark-green leafy vegetables. Other sources include apricots, asparagus, beets, broccoli, garlic, kale, parsley, peaches, red peppers, yellow and winter squash, and turnip greens.

Vitamin B1*—thiamine   RDA 1.5 mg   Rec: 10 mg

Vitamin B1 contributes to nerve function and is beneficial to circulation, blood formation, learning capacity, and muscle tone for the heart, intestines, and stomach. It aids in hydrochloric acid production and carbohydrate metabolism. Insufficient vitamin B1 may lead to forgetfulness, fatigue, beriberi, insomnia, digestive problems, and muscle wasting.

Vitamin B1 is found in kidney beans, brown rice, lean meats, peas, soybeans, wheat germ, brewers' yeast, oatmeal, plums, prunes, raisins, egg yolks, and seafood.

Vitamin B2—riboflavin   RDA 1.8 mg   Rec: 10 mg

Vitamin B2 is required in the formation of red blood cells, cell respiration, growth, and metabolism of carbohydrates, fats, and proteins. It facilitates use of oxygen in the skin, hair, and nails. Together, Vitamins A and B2 are needed to metabolize food and maintain mucous membranes in the digestive tract. Inadequate amounts of vitamin B2 in the diet may contribute to eye fatigue, cracks and sores in the mouth, dandruff, and carpal tunnel syndrome. High doses may reduce migraine headaches.

Good sources of vitamin B2 are milk, cheese, eggs, fish, poultry, meat, spinach, and yogurt. This vitamin is also in asparagus, avocados, broccoli, brussels sprouts, and nuts.

Vitamin B3—niacin   RDA 13 – 15 mg   Rec: Niacinamide 100 mg

Vitamin B3 supports nerve function and enhances appetite and digestion. It aids circulation of blood by preventing plaque formation in the arteries, and contributes to healthy skin. It is required for enzymes to convert food into energy. It helps balance cholesterol levels and may be used to treat some forms of mental illness. Deficiencies in vitamin B3 may lead to dermatitis, depression, diarrhea, pellagra, loss of appetite, and mouth sores.

This vitamin can be found in lean meats, poultry, tuna, halibut, swordfish, broccoli, carrots, potatoes, tomatoes, cereals and fortified whole grain breads, nuts, cheese, and eggs.

Vitamin B5—pantothenic acid   RDA 10 mg   Rec: 50 mg

Vitamin B5 is essential for converting food to available forms by the body and is manufactured in the intestines. It is required by all cells of the body, especially organs. It aids in production of adrenal hormones and antibodies and is necessary for steroid and cortisone production in the adrenal glands. Inadequate amounts of vitamin B5 may contribute to depression, fatigue, poor coordination, heart trouble, headaches, and cramps.

Good sources of vitamin B5 are beans, beef, eggs, saltwater fish, whole wheat, fresh vegetables, yeast, wheat germ, and peanuts.

Vitamin B6*—pyridoxine   RDA 1.4–1.6 mg   Rec: 20 mg

Vitamin B6 is essential for protein metabolism and absorption and red blood cell formation. It helps to promote immunity and maintain balance of sodium and potassium. Vitamin B6 is also required for normal brain function, the nervous system, and RNA and DNA synthesis. It is a natural diuretic and reduces symptoms of premenstrual syndrome. When this vitamin is taken with B12 and folate, it may reduce the risk of heart disease and other vascular disorders by decreasing homocysteine levels. Deficiencies may contribute to anemia, depression, irritability, fatigue, confusion, diarrhea, inflamed mucous membranes in the mouth, convulsions, blindness, and loss of appetite.

Vitamin B6 can be found in carrots, spinach, peas, eggs, meat, fish, poultry, brewers' yeast, grains, cereals, avocados, bananas, prunes, potatoes, walnuts, and wheat germ.

Vitamin B12—cyanocobalamin   RDA 1.7 mg   Rec: 3 mg

Vitamin B12 is important for building genetic material (nucleic acid), blood cells, and nerves. It is required for red cell development and helps with digestion, absorption, and protein synthesis. Also, this water-soluble vitamin aids in fat and carbohydrate metabolism, prevents nerve damage and promotes normal growth. A recent study found that 80 percent of American adults were deficient in vitamin B12. Inadequate amounts of vitamin B12 may lead to malabsorption, common in the elderly. Deficiencies can lead to memory loss, one of the first symptoms, along with confusion, depression, blood disorders, hardening of the arteries, and pernicious anemia. Severe deficiencies contribute to fatigue, dementia, and progressive nerve damage.

Vitamin B12 is found mostly in animal products, such as lamb, beef, liver, poultry, eggs, crabs, clams, herring, mackerel, and other seafood. Other sources with small amounts include dairy products, cheese, tofu, and most grains, or a multivitamin supplement from which B12 is absorbed better than from foods such as meat.

Vitamin C*—ascorbic acid   RDA 75 mg   Rec: 500–1,000 mg

Vitamin C is water-soluble and helps to prevent infection and maintain healthy gums, teeth, bones, and connective tissue. It acts as an antioxidant, especially when combined with vitamin E, to reduce the risk of heart disease and strokes. Jean Carper claims that high doses of vitamin C (1,000 to 2,000 milligrams) help block the artery-destroying effects of homocysteine, an amino acid linked to clogged arteries, heart attacks, and strokes. It also helps prevent cataracts and declining cognitive abilities in old age. Vitamin C can enhance your immunity, heal wounds, promote antibody production and tissue repair, and aid in the development of red blood cells. Women with emotional stress, which reduces ascorbic acid blood-levels, need more vitamin C to protect against immune suppression of cortisol during stressful times. Recent studies found that taking a high dose (500 milligrams) of vitamin C regularly can help reduce mildly to moderately high blood pressure. Smokers require more vitamin C than the RDA, about 110 milligrams. High doses (2,000 mg) may prevent the transformation of nitrates into cancer-causing nitrosamines. Deficiencies may contribute to depression, irritability, fatigue, and malaise. Inadequate vitamin C can lower one's resistance to infections, colds, and flu, slow healing, and contribute to tooth decay, gum disease, anemia, thyroid insufficiency, premature aging, and deterioration of collogen. The consumerlab.com web site identifies which pharmaceutical brands contain adequate levels of vitamin C.

Vitamin C is best obtained from fresh fruits and vegetables and is abundant in citrus fruits such as oranges, tomatoes, grapefruit, and limes. It is also found in strawberries, watermelon, cabbage, broccoli, peppers, and plantains. Small amounts are found in some green vegetables, asparagus, avocados, beet greens, cantaloupe, mangoes, papayas, green peas, and spinach. Since vitamin C is neither stored nor synthesized in the body, it must be taken every day, preferably in divided doses. Excess amounts are excreted in the urine.

Vitamin D—calciferol   RDA 400 IU   600 IU after age 70

Vitamin D helps maintain healthy strong bones and teeth by aiding absorption and utilization of calcium, phosphorus, and other minerals to reduce bone mineral loss. Magnesium is required to convert vitamin D to an active form for use. Inadequate amounts may lead to rickets, tooth decay, pyorrhea, osteomalacia, osteoporosis, and premature aging.

Good sources of vitamin D are fortified milk, butter, fish-liver oils, fatty saltwater fish, egg yolks, sweet potatoes, and vegetable oils. Vitamin D is also produced under the skin during exposure to sunlight.

Vitamin E*—tocopherol   RDA 12 IU   Rec: 200 – 400 IU

Vitamin E is an essential antioxidant that prevents red blood cells from clotting and clumping together. It is the only fat-soluble antioxidant, and it works synergistically with selenium to protect fats in the cell walls and blood from free radical destruction (lipid peroxidation). It also improves circulation, boosts the immune system, and promotes normal wound healing. It may help reduce leg cramps and cataracts, slow progression of Alzheimer's disease, and increase resistance to toxins. High doses of 400 milligrams are recommended to reduce the risk of coronary heart disease and atherosclerosis by reducing oxidation of LDL (bad) cholesterol. Zinc is required to maintain the proper levels of vitamin E in the blood, and it works with selenium to protect the body from free radicals. Insufficient amounts of vitamin E may contribute to anemia, difficulty walking and maintaining balance, easy bleeding, "liver spots," and muscle cramps. Major deficiencies in vitamin E contribute to heart disease, diabetes, cancer, arthritis, and premature aging.

Most women do not obtain sufficient amounts of vitamin E in their diets, so a supplement is usually required. Foods rich in vitamin E are vegetable oils (safflower and palm oil are best), and margarine products, along with cottonseed, corn, and soybean oils, and wheat germ, barley, and other grains and nuts. Small amounts are found in soy, egg yolks, green leafy vegetables, legumes, brown rice, and sweet potatoes. Women need to take more vitamin E if their diet contains too much polyunsaturated fat from processed foods.

Vitamin K   RDA 55 – 65 mcg   Rec: 100 mcg

Vitamin K is required for blood clotting, contributes to bone formation, and helps prevent osteoporosis. It also helps convert glucose to glycogen, which affects the liver. A deficiency in vitamin K may lead to nosebleeds, hemorrhages, and premature aging.

Good sources of vitamin K are brussels sprouts, broccoli, cabbage, dark green leafy vegetables, soybeans, liver, and blackstrap molasses. Since vitamin K reverses the effect of blood thinning drugs, it should not be taken by individuals on these medications.

Essential Minerals

Calcium   RDA 1000 – 1200 mg   Rec: 1,000 – 1,500 mg

Calcium helps to build strong bones and teeth and is important for nerve and muscle function. It is also essential for stabilizing blood vessels, regulates heart rhythms, and may lower your blood pressure and risk for strokes by lowering your cholesterol. It also aids in preventing muscle cramps, helps with blood clotting, and plays a role in acid-base balance. Sufficient amounts of Vitamin D and phosphorus are essential for the body's absorption and metabolism of calcium. Deficiencies may lead to osteomalacia, osteoporosis, depression, brittle cracked nails, muscle cramps and spasms, tooth decay, hypertension, and sore joints.

Foods high in calcium are milk and milk products such as cheese, yogurt, cottage cheese, and foods fortified with calcium, like orange juice. Other sources are canned salmon with bones, oysters, broccoli, seafood, tofu, and calcium-enriched soy milk. Calcium is most effective when taken throughout the day with small amounts of fat, rather than all at once. To increase your calcium intake, try sprinkling low-fat shredded cheese on salads or pasta, or add to sauces. On packages, to convert percentages of calcium to milligrams, drop the percent sign and add a zero.

Chromium   RDA 120 mcg   Rec: 200 – 400 mcg

Chromium is required to metabolize glucose and is important in the synthesis of cholesterol, fats, and proteins. It helps to maintain stable blood sugar levels and prevent hypoglycemia. It may also reduce the buildup of arterial plaque. Deficiencies in chromium may contribute to adult-onset diabetes, hypoglycemia, atherosclerosis, and heart disease. Over 60 percent of Americans are deficient in chromium because of the depletion of this mineral in the soil and from diets high in refined sugars and flours.

Good sources of chromium include raw sugar, brewers' yeast, naturally mineralized water, corn and corn oil, cheese, whole grains, and fortified cereals.

Copper*   RDA 2–3 mg   Rec: 3 mg

Copper aids in the production of RNA, which facilitates healing, and is required for the absorption of iron. It maintains natural hair color and skin, and benefits the nervous system. Copper also helps the body produce a potent antioxidant, superoxide dismutase, which aids the body in fighting off illnesses more easily. Inadequate amounts of copper may contribute to anemia, loss of hair and hair color, and possible heart damage.

Copper can be found in almonds, avocados, barley, beans, green leafy vegetables, mushrooms, pecans, and soybeans.

Folic acid—Folate   RDA 400 mcg   Rec: 800 mcg

Folic acid is required for the formation of red blood cells and is necessary for DNA synthesis. Recently scientists found that folic acid can reduce the production of homocysteine, a protein that contributes to blood clots and increases your risk of heart disease, strokes, and LDL oxidation. It is also important in cell division and reproduction of cells and may be helpful in treating anxiety, depression, and cervical dysplasia, which is usually linked to the human papillomavirus (HPV). High doses of folic acid may mask symptoms of B12 anemia, so check with your physician before increasing your folic acid. Inadequate amounts of folic acid in a pregnant woman's diet have been linked with fetal neural tube defects, spontaneous abortion, low birth weight, and growth retardation. Use of oral contraceptives and certain antiseizure medications may increase the need for folic acid.

Good sources of folic acid are barley, beans, brewers' yeast, lentils, dates, chicken, pork, whole grains, wheat germ, root vegetables, spinach, salmon, tuna, milk, and oranges.

Iodine   RDA 150 mcg

Iodine is very important for good thyroid production and aids in physical and mental development. An iodine deficiency can cause an enlarged thyroid, weakness, fatigue, lethargy, decreased libido, and possible mental retardation.

Iodized salt provides most of our iodine, but other sources are seafood or vegetables from iodine-rich soils or the sea, such as kelp, seaweed, or dulse. Small amounts can be found in garlic, pears, pineapple, and artichokes.

Iron   RDA 18 mg

Iron is essential in the production of hemoglobin, which carries oxygen from the lungs to red blood cells. It is also beneficial to the immune system and to normal growth patterns. Inadequate amounts of iron contribute to anemia, hair loss, brittle nails, fatigue, dizziness, light-headedness, shortness of breath on exertion, and headaches. Iron supplements interact with certain prescription drugs (thyroid) and may prevent their absorption.

Good sources of iron are red meats, liver, oysters, blackstrap molasses, shellfish, chickpeas, fortified breads and cereals, and from cooking in cast-iron pans. Other sources include prunes, raisins, brewers' yeast, spinach, beets and beet tops, potato skins, and dried fruits, along with sunflower and sesame seeds. Iron is also found in supplements with sulfates and gluconates and is absorbed best when taken with foods high in vitamin C.

Magnesium   RDA 350 – 400 mg   Rec: 400 – 600 mg adults
700 – 800 mg seniors

Magnesium enables your body to absorb and form new calcium, which promotes growth of healthy bones, teeth, and muscles. It activates enzymes to release energy, yet may act as a tranquilizer. Insufficient magnesium may lead to muscle cramps, weakness, and heart rhythm disturbances. High alcohol or caffeine intake, diarrhea, or diuretics may deplete your magnesium level. High daily doses of calcium without sufficient magnesium can create a magnesium deficiency, which may increase your risk of osteoporosis and heart disease.

Most American women's diets are deficient in magnesium. Good sources of magnesium are whole grains, buckwheat, whole wheat, rye, legumes, beans, nuts, leafy green vegetables, scallops, oysters, soybeans, figs, apples, avocados, and brown rice. Magnesium competes with calcium for absorption. Some researchers recommend a 2:1 ratio of calcium to magnesium, while others believe you should consume equal amounts of calcium and magnesium—up to 600 milligrams taken throughout the day.

Phosphorus   RDA 800 – 1200 mg

Phosphorus converts food to energy to form healthy bones and teeth, helps repair tissues, and maintains proper kidney function. It also contributes to a healthy nervous system, mental activity, and heart contraction. A proper balance among calcium, magnesium, and phosphorus should be maintained. Deficiencies in phosphorus are rare, but may interfere with calcium absorption.

Most foods contain some phosphorus. Good sources are dairy products, egg yolks, red meat, poultry, and fish, along with whole grains, nuts, legumes, apricots, and avocados.

Potassium   RDA 1600 – 2000 mg

Potassium is required for proper muscle contraction, for maintaining normal fluid electrolyte balance, a healthy nervous system, blood pressure, and essential hormone secretions. It is found with sodium in the body's fluids and regulates the transfer of nutrients to cells and cellular impulses. Deficiencies in potassium can result from diarrhea, use of diuretics, diabetes, or kidney disorders and can contribute to heart damage, hypertension, and nervous system disorders. Stress can cause an imbalance in the potassium-sodium ratio.

Potassium sources are bananas, potatoes, apricots, blackstrap molasses, brewers' yeast, oranges, raisins, winter squash, and yams, wheat bran, and nuts.

Selenium*   RDA not established   Rec: 200 mcg

Selenium is an excellent antioxidant which maintains the immune system, and works synergistically with vitamin E to reduce oxidation in the tissues and to prevent fat-soluble oxidants in the watery realm of the cells. It may reduce the risk of various types of cancer, heart disease, arthritis, and degenerative changes in your liver, kidneys, and pancreas. In her book, *Antioxidants: Your Complete Guide,* Carolyn Reuben says that selenium prevents heavy metal toxicity and stimulates the anti-cancer power of glutathione peroxidase. Deficiencies may lead to muscle pains, heart muscle deterioration, premature aging, intestinal and colon cancer, along with liver, kidney, and pancreas damage.

Selenium is found in good soil and is taken up by plants and animals that eat those plants. Good sources of selenium include seafood (oysters, swordfish, tuna), kidney, and liver. Lesser sources are cereals and grains, poultry, non-organ meats, and brewers' yeast. Also, most vegetables such as broccoli, mushrooms, and asparagus, are good sources, depending on where they were grown.

Sodium   RDA 200–600 mg

Sodium is essential for normal cell and nerve function and fluid balance. It maintains proper body fluids and electrolyte balance and is required for hydrochloric acid production in the stomach. Deficiencies cause seizures and weakness, along with dehydration, heart palpitations, confusion, and possibly low blood sugar. Excess sodium contributes to high blood pressure, water retention, and heart disease.

Sodium is part of the salt found in most processed foods and in vegetables from the sea, such as kelp and seaweed, along with celery and asparagus. Most Americans consume too much sodium from table salt and from eating large quantities of processed foods like potato chips, pretzels, pickles, canned foods, and microwave meals.

Zinc*   RDA 15 mg   Rec: 30 mg

Zinc is essential for maintaining healthy bone growth and density, digestion of protein, and metabolism of energy through its action on thyroid hormone conversion and insulin. It works with red blood cells to transport waste from tissues and can boost a compromised immune system by increasing and restoring lymphocyte function. It aids wound healing, maintaining adequate levels of vitamin A in the blood, and overcoming anorexia. Zinc lozenges can also shorten the duration of a cold. Inadequate zinc is associated with cancer of the thyroid and may lead to poor growth and development.

Zinc is more readily absorbed when it is obtained from meat, but it is also found in wheat germ, peas, and lentils.

ANTIOXIDANTS AND PHYTOCHEMICALS

During normal metabolism, as the body burns oxygen, byproducts known as free radicals are produced. Free radicals are unstable because they contain an unpaired electron molecule that reacts by stealing an electron from another molecule to stabilize its own structure. This causes a chain reaction that creates more free radicals and also causes structural damage to the ravaged cells. When this oxidation process occurs, antioxidants are created to surround, control, and destroy free radicals. The body's antioxidant defense system protects us at four levels, according to Bloomfield and Cooper, authors of *The Power of 5*. First, it helps keep free radicals or oxidants from forming. Second, it intercepts those that form and tries to stop the chain reactions from creating other oxidants. Third, it repairs damage caused by the free radicals, and fourth, it eliminates and replaces damaged molecules and removes undesirable substances generated by its activities.

Free radicals are highly active oxygen molecules that build up in the body from exposure to cigarette smoke, X-rays, air pollutants, environmental chemicals, inhaled fumes, herbicides, asbestos, smog, ultraviolet radiation, chemotherapy, and as a by-product from consuming alcohol, cured meats, artificial colorings, and other chemical-ridden, artificially processed, and fast foods. In addition, exercise, emotional stress, physical trauma, and some drugs create free radicals in the body. During aerobic activity, the need for increased oxygen seems to produce free radicals, which can damage muscle cell membranes, making cells more susceptible to disease and aging. Usually, the body has ways to neutralize these free radicals on its own, but when free radicals set off chain reactions that convert fats to peroxides, more free radicals are produced than the body can neutralize, and health problems may occur. Side effects of having too many free radicals and insufficient antioxidants are fatigue, stiffening of the joints, and hardening of the arteries. An excess of free radicals can cause tissue damage that occurs in many degenerative brain diseases, premature aging, and chronic diseases, depending on which tissues are attacked. When free radicals attack DNA molecules, they can cause cancer; when they attack the pancreas, they can cause diabetes; and in blood vessels, they can cause cardiovascular disease.

Scientists have identified four nutrients that are strong and effective antioxidants, which may help reduce the effects of free radicals. These are vitamins A, C, and E, and the mineral selenium, called "The Four ACES." Their interaction is absolutely essential for the successful control of oxidants. Reuben writes that these nutrients protect the immune system by neutralizing free radicals before they damage cells and organs. Vitamins C, E, and selenium enhance the production and function of white blood cells or stimulate antibody activity. For example, vitamin C fights free radicals in watery areas of the body and beta-carotene handles free radicals where oxygen levels are low. Vitamin C also regenerates vitamin E, which protects the lipids in the bloodstream, and fights free radicals where oxygen levels are high. Selenium defends lipids in the cells.

Antioxidants are found in various vitamins, minerals, and enzymes. Along with "The Four ACES," they include carotenoids such as beta-carotene, lycopene, vitamins B1 and B6, lecithin, zinc, isoflavones, flavonoids, indoles, and other substances. These antioxidants strengthen your circulation, enhance cellular vitality, enrich your immune system, and help defend your nervous system from the damage of free radicals. In addition, they protect your body from the ill effects of alcohol, caffeine, sugar, and many drugs.

Bioflavonoids are antioxidants which protect vitamin C from being destroyed. They strengthen capillary walls and therefore help prevent stroke, varicose veins, nosebleeds, bruising, and bleeding gums, help reduce inflammation, and help fight viruses and infections. They also detoxify carcinogens and inhibit cancer from developing, possibly by protecting DNA from damage, and reduce the risk of cataracts in diabetics. A deficiency is characterized by bleeding gums, varicose veins, hot flashes, easy bruising, and small pinpoint red blotches under the skin and nosebleeds. They are found in most citrus fruits, and vegetables such as peppers, broccoli, grapes, and red wine. Blueberries and purple foods like eggplant, currants, purple onions, prunes, and plums also have flavonoids. In general, 500 to 1,000 milligrams of bioflavonoids a day will enhance your body's use of vitamin C.

The more antioxidants you eat, and the fewer free radicals in your body, the better your nutritional balance. Some of the best food sources high in antioxidants are fresh orange fruits, blueberries, green vegetables, whole wheat bread and grains, legumes and beans, fresh-squeezed juices, sprouts, high-fiber raisins, nuts, and seeds. Jean Carper states that antioxidants work together to balance each other, so a combination is more effective than a single high dose of any one and prevents any one from becoming depleted.

Our body also produces millions of enzyme helpers, called coenzymes or cofactors, many of which are nutrients. Antioxidant cofactors include selenium, copper, riboflavin, glutathione, coenzyme Q 10, manganese, zinc, and bioflavonoids. These nutrients are found in diets rich in fruits, vegetables, and whole grains. Enzymes serve as a second line of defense by keeping existing oxidants in low enough concentrations that they can function properly without causing an uncontrolled, damaging chain reaction.

Phytochemicals, or phytonutrients, are substances in plant foods that were recently discovered to block some steps leading to various types of cancer, and that may help prevent cardiovascular disease and delay aging by repairing damaged cells. These chemicals give colorful fruits and vegetables their hue, plus they boost energy and ward off disease. Each phytochemical works in a different way to slow down or reverse steps leading to cell breakdown. One phytochemical helps cancer-causing chemicals bind to take them out of the cells. Another keeps two harmless compounds in the body from joining to make a potentially harmful carcinogen. Many phytochemicals work as powerful antioxidants. They are not essential nutrients, like vitamins and minerals, but they may keep you healthy longer.

Types of Phytochemicals

Allylic Sulfides—may activate anti-cancer enzymes and lower cholesterol and blood pressure. They are found in garlic, onion, leeks, and chives.

Flavones—act as anti-aging, anti-disease chemicals. They are found in dried beans and in soybean products such as tofu and soy milk. Ginkgo biloba is an herbal flavone.

Indoles—may aid production of enzymes that inactivate a cancer-causing form of estrogen, and boost enzymes that may stop carcinogens from damaging the DNA in cells. They are found in cruciferous vegetables, such as bok choy, cauliflower, red/green cabbage, broccoli, brussels sprouts, collards, mustard and turnip greens, and watercress.

Isothiocyanates—are considered anti-carcinogens and may be found in kale, leeks, spinach, broccoli, brussels sprouts, cauliflower, and cabbage.

Lignands—are phytoestrogens that may help protect against breast and possibly other cancers and heart disease. They may lower the risk of colon cancer by adding bulk to your diet and removing toxins from the bowel. Good sources include whole grain products, flax and flaxseed oil, sunflower seeds, bean sprouts, and green teas.

Limonene—may protect against breast cancer by decreasing cell proliferation, inhibiting the growth of abnormal cells, and stimulating anti-cancer enzymes. It is found in citrus fruits, the bright peel of oranges, lemons and limes, or the white membrane of other citrus fruits, which can be grated and added to breads, muffins, or salads. Mint, caraway, thyme, and coriander also contain limonene.

Lycopene—is a carotenoid and has a stronger potential for fighting breast and cervical cancer than beta-carotene. It is found in red fruits and vegetables, mostly tomatoes, and some in watermelons, pink grapefruits, guava fruit, and red peppers. It is more abundant in cooked foods which concentrate lycopene, such as tomato-based sauces, than in raw vegetables.

Polyphenols—are associated with the cancer-preventing indoles which may help prevent skin and esophageal cancers. They are found in green vegetables like broccoli and brussels sprouts, and in green tea, blueberry membranes, grapes, and cauliflower.

Quercertin—helps protect against heart disease by discouraging plaque formation in the arteries. It is similar to the isoflavonoids in soy and can be found in pear and apple skin, bell peppers, kohlrabi, onion, wine, and grape juice.

Reservatrol—may aid in reducing cardiovascular disease, cancer, and the effects of aging. It is found in wine, grapes, and grape juice.

Terpenes—may aid in preventing lung cancer, and are found in oranges.

Eat a Rainbow of Fruits and Vegetables

To improve your intake of antioxidants and phytochemicals, think about eating a rainbow of colors in your fruits and vegetables. Red foods like tomatoes, watermelon, and pink grapefruit contain lycopene. Orange foods like cantaloupe, sweet potatoes, yams, and carrots are full of beta-carotene. Yellow foods, such as squash, lemon and grapefruit peels, and peppers, contain lots of carotenes, along with limonene. Green foods are associated with polyphenols, found in broccoli, brussels sprouts, and artichokes. Blue and purple foods, like blueberries, purple grapes, and plums, have lots of phytochemicals and flavonoids.

A GUIDE TO USE OF HERBS
Coauthor, Peter A. White, RN, M.S.

Many different herbal supplements are used as alternative therapies for a variety of preventive or treatment purposes. The World Health Organization estimates that 80 percent of the world's population uses some form of herbal therapy. Herbal products come in either standardized or nonstandardized forms. Herbal *extracts* contain the chemicals believed to be primarily responsible for specific effects or actions in the body, and are usually standardized to maintain the same amount of an ingredient in every batch. *Whole herbs* have all the ingredients found naturally as part of the herb, but may have some variability in ratios of potent ingredients from batch to batch because various factors such as soil composition, weather, or harvest date influence the herb profile, so they are not considered standardized. However, the effectiveness of most herbals is determined by the part of the plant used to create the therapeutic agent. For example, the root of ginseng is the most potent source of this herb, so extracts made from other parts of the plant may not be therapeutic at all. Check to be sure you purchase the most potent part of the plant of any herbal or extract. Many products contain lower levels of key ingredients than the package claims. Supplements with the letters "CL" in a laboratory beaker indicate that they have been test-ed by the experts at Consumerlab, and provide the exact contents listed on the package.

Many herbs have no solid research to support their claims of effectiveness or to determine their long-term effects on the body. Since herbal products are considered dietary supplements in the United States, they are not subject to the same rigorous standards as drugs, nor are they regulated by the FDA. Dosages may vary and labels may not contain guidelines for proper use. Manufacturers are prohibited from giving you specific information about the remedial benefits of their products. They can only make claims for structure and function of the product, not for specific action and uses. The following advisory (usually in small print) must appear on their product: These statements have not been evaluated by the FDA and therefore this product cannot claim to diagnose, treat, cure or prevent any disease. Some herbal manufacturers may greatly exaggerate the benefits of their products, because herbal/botanical sales were expected to reach *three billion dollars* in the year 2000. While some herbs have been studied extensively in other countries and have been approved by their regulating bodies, their regulating groups do not have the same strict standards for testing drugs and herbals as are required by the FDA in the United States. Therefore, women who decide to use herbal supplements as an alternative or complementary therapy should understand how each herb or supplement acts and know the contraindications and potential side effects. Consider using the following guidelines.

Do not use any herbs or supplements if you are considering becoming pregnant, are pregnant, are breast feeding, or have a serious health problem, without first consulting with your health care provider.

Do not assume that "natural" is always safe. Even though an herb or product may be labeled natural, it may interfere with some medications you are taking.

Inform your health care provider (doctor, nurse practitioner, pharmacist, and/or herbalist) about your use or desire to use an herb or supplement because some of them may have a synergistic effect that intensifies or reduces the effect of the medications you are taking and thus be detrimental to your health. It is your responsibility to ask if your provider is adequately knowledgeable about herbal and botanical remedies.

Read the labels and contents of any supplement carefully. Make sure that the product contains the right plant part in the appropriate amount. Manufacturers often use different formulas and concentrations. Many manufacturers use upbeat generic claims of the benefits of their product, such as anti-aging. If the claims sound too good to be true, they probably are.

Do not assume that taking more is better for you. Exceeding recommended dosage of some herbals and supplements may disrupt your normal physiology, cause health problems, or interfere with the action of prescribed medications.

Review information about the safety and efficacy of each herbal product to understand the contraindications and potential for overdose and toxicity. Do not rely on the manufacturer's information or a store clerk's sales pitch. Check in a reliable book, such as *Tyler's Honest Herbal: A Sensible Guide to the Use of Herbs and Related Remedies,* by Foster and Tyler.

Choose "standardized" one-ingredient herbal extracts, tablets, or capsules to ensure a consistent dose each time, and check the expiration date. You may wish to consult the independent web site, consumerlab.com, which tests the potency of many supplements, to learn which products contain lower levels of key ingredients than the package claims.

Add only one new herbal or supplement to your regimen at a time, so that if you experience an undesired effect or adverse reaction you will know which one caused the problem.

Keep a symptom diary to help you evaluate the effectiveness of any herb or supplement you take. If offered a thirty-day guarantee, and the product has not helped you within two weeks or you had a bad reaction, return it to get your money back. However, some herbs take as long as eight to twelve weeks for their effects to be noticed.

Be sure to keep all medications, herbal products, or vitamin supplements away from children because some of these products may *look, smell,* or *taste* like candy.

Discontinue using an herb, if you have taken it for the recommended amount of time and believe it is not working.

The following herbs are among those used most often by women. The Environmental Nutrition identified the drugs with an asterisk (*) as cited in many research studies for their specific effects.

Bilberry *

This natural herb is a form of European blueberry whose active ingredients are flavonoids. It has been reported to promote both day- and nighttime visual acuity, prevent and treat cataracts, glaucoma, and macular degeneration. It strengthens capillaries to prevent bleeding under the skin surface and increase strength and flexibility of blood vessels in the legs and gums. It aids in protecting red blood cells from clumping, which may prevent heart attacks and strokes. Bilberry helps relax smooth muscles, promote circulation, and maintain healthy blood sugar levels. For prevention of eye conditions, 60 to 180 milligrams a day is recommended; to treat chronic conditions, use up to 300 milligrams a day.

While research supports the benefits of bilberry, little is known about its potential toxicity to humans. Although bilberry is available in 500 to 1000 milligram dosages from some manufacturers, do not exceed 480 milligrams/day as research has shown that more than this amount may be dangerous to your health, according to Feltrow and Avila, authors of *The Complete Guide to Herbal Medicines*. Doses of 1.5 grams of bilberry per kilogram of body weight may cause death. Do not take bilberry to treat diabetes. Drug interactions are likely if taken with blood thinners such as coumadin or aspirin. Consult with a health care professional who is knowledgeable about herbals before taking this herbal with *ginkgo biloba, ginger, garlic,* and *ginseng,* to name a few, as these all affect bleeding tendencies in some way. The German Commission E (GCE) has approved bilberry for the treatment of nonspecific, acute diarrhea and as a local therapy for mild inflammation of the mucous membranes of the mouth and throat, write Blumenthal, Goldberg, and Brinckmann, editors of the *Expanded Commission E Monographs*.

Chamomile

This herb is derived from a flower and contains anti-inflammatory and antispasmodic substances, namely terpenoids and flavonoids. It is an effective remedy for stomachaches and other gastrointestinal upsets, and also has calming and pain-relieving properties. German chamomile is preferred when a mild calming effect to help digestion is desired. Roman chamomile is preferred for relief of severe muscle spasms or pain and sedative effects. Chamomile tea can be strong enough to treat adult insomnia, rheumatic pain, and depression.

The GCE has approved chamomile for internal use to treat GI spasms, inflammatory diseases of the GI tract and for external use for skin and mucous membrane inflammations and bacterial skin diseases, including those of the oral cavity and gums; as an inhalant to treat respiratory tract inflammations and irritations; and in sitz baths for anogenital inflammation, especially hemorrhoids. The GCE did *not* approve chamomile for sleep disorders for lack of scientific evidence, according to Blumenthal and associates. Robbers and Tyler, who wrote *Tyler's Herbs of Choice*, recommend use of the whole flower head with less than 10 percent stems as the best source for therapeutic use of this herb, as it is easily adulterated, which greatly compromises its effectiveness. Don't take chamomile, say Feltrow and Avila, if you are currently taking coumadin, or have a history of asthma or allergic dermatitis. Possible side effects include allergic conjunctivitis, skin irritation, anaphylactic reactions, and vomiting.

Coenzyme Q 10

This enzyme is a powerful antioxidant and free radical scavenger. It helps the body use oxygen and generate energy. It is found in every cell in the body but is more abundant in certain organs, especially the heart muscle. Coenzyme Q10 may increase your metabolism, improve physical endurance, strengthen muscles, and enhance your immune system. The pioneering researcher, Karl Folkers, found that Coenzyme Q10 decreases with age, and that people with cardiovascular heart disease had severe deficiencies, which improved with supplements. Research suggests that high doses of Coenzyme Q10 re-energize heart cells and strengthen heart function. Also, age-related degeneration in the gums, muscles, skin, organs, and immune system may be attributed to inadequate Coenzyme Q10. The usual dose ranges between thirty and sixty milligrams daily.

Echinacea * and Goldenseal

Echinacea has been shown to boost the immune system and possibly fight bacterial and viral infections. It may also lower a fever and calm an allergic reaction. The actions are similar to those of antibiotics and anti-inflammatory agents. Echinacea fights initial germ invasion to help reduce symptoms of infections and stimulates the synthesis of fighter T-cells to reduce the duration and severity of colds, flu, and other viruses. It is most beneficial for colds and flu if taken when you have that intuitive feeling, "I think I'm coming down with something." Walker and Brown, who wrote *Nature's Pharmacy*, say that after you have a cold or flu for more than a day, echinacea may be of no value and may actually extend the time you have a virus. The liquid form is considered to have greater efficacy than powdered forms, according to Robbers and Tyler, especially if held in the mouth for a brief period before swallowing. It should not be used for more than ten to fourteen days, since research has shown that continued use has produced lung infections. In addition, Feltrow and Avila caution that *anyone with a suppressed immune system (TB, HIV, AIDS), or suffering from an autoimmune disease such as lupus, leukosis, collagen disease, multiple sclerosis, or ragweed allergies, should not take echinacea.* The *PDR for Herbal Medicines* warns that you be aware of which type of echinacea you take (E. purpurea herb or root, E. pallida root, E. augustifolia herb or root), as each has received different indications for approval by the GCE, if any approval at all.

Goldenseal has antimicrobial properties to protect against gram positive and gram negative bacteria. It raises the white blood cell count, which may be harmful to those with autoimmune diseases, but is effective in treating gastrointestinal infections. Goldenseal is not recommended for pregnant women (it can stimulate uterine contractions), or for anyone with low blood sugar or hypertension. Together, echinacea and goldenseal reduce general body aches and fevers and stimulate the immune system to respond to minor infections.

Feverfew*

Although this herb was not reviewed by the GCE, Robbers and Tyler report that many excellent studies have found it useful in reducing chronic and migraine headaches before they start, by decreasing serotonin levels so that blood vessels are less likely to dilate. It can prevent or reduce the number and severity of migraine and tension headaches when taken daily, and may reduce vomiting associated with headaches, according to the *PDR for Herbal Medicines*. Feverfew should not be taken by anyone using a selective serotonin re-uptake inhibitor (SSRI) for treatment of depression, or anticoagulants, thrombolytics, and platelet aggregation medications.

Typical doses are 300 milligram tablets, one leaf of fresh herb, or forty drops of fresh plant tincture in 1:5 part solution. Remission of headaches should begin after two months of use, and this herb can be used indefinitely, although some people no longer find it necessary after two years. However, if there is no improvement after four months, Feltrow and Avila suggest that you slowly discontinue using the herb to prevent post-feverfew syndrome, which may include headaches and painfully stiff muscles and joints. Unwanted side effects from feverfew include mouth ulcers, and inflammation and swelling of the tongue, write Williamson and Wyandt, authors of *Herbal Therapies: The Facts and the Fiction.*

Special note: Feverfew without removal of the thujone component is not approved for use in the United States, and has been shown to cause convulsions in normal range doses.

Garlic

New evidence suggests that garlic is effective in reducing risk factors for coronary heart disease and arteriosclerosis by preventing and reducing plaque blockages in the neck and leg arteries. Some researchers also believe that garlic pills reduce LDL cholesterol's ability to promote plaque buildup, thus lowering "bad" cholesterol, but more studies are needed to support this claim. Others believe that garlic may help treat digestive problems, bacterial and fungal infections, and high blood pressure, but this may require eating lots of raw garlic cloves daily because some of its action is lost when cooked.

The effective forms of garlic as a therapeutic agent are: the whole cloves (four daily), or 600–900 milligrams of dried garlic powder if the pill is enteric coated, write Foster and Tyler. The helpful agents in garlic are the amino acids, allicin and ajoene. Allicin is a potent antibacterial, antifungal, and antiviral agent found to enhance natural killer cells. Ajoene provides lipid-lowering and fibrinolytic and platelet-lowering effects that lead to the cardiovascular benefits of garlic. Garlic in oils is not considered very effective because the therapeutic agents are unstable and lost.

The GCE has approved garlic as a dietary supplement to reduce lipids in the blood and to prevent atherosclerosis. However, Feltrow and Avila claim that there are potential drug interactions with aspirin, coumadin and nonsteroidal anti-inflammatory drugs (ibuprofen, etc.), which could lead to increased bleeding time. And Brinker writes in *Herbal Contraindications and Drug Interactions* that garlic will decrease the effect of hypothyroid medications and increase the effect of insulin and other diabetic medications. The *PDR for Herbal Medicines* indicates that adverse reactions to garlic include body odor, halitosis, dizziness, irritation and gas in the stomach, nausea, irritation and burning of the mouth and esophagus, and a rash when rubbed on the skin. And garlic is contraindicated in pregnancy, according to McGuffin, and associates in *American Herbal Products Assocation's Botanical Safety Handbook,* as it can stimulate uterine contractions. Fresh garlic should not be given to children.

Ginger *

This ancient herb is used to treat motion sickness and dizziness with nausea, especially from seasickness. It has a calming effect on the digestive system and helps expel gas from the intestines and soothe the intestinal tract. Ginger may be helpful in reducing migraine headaches and menstrual cramps because it is an antispasmodic, and may be used to prevent and treat flu and colds. While ginger is often mislabeled a root, Walker and Brown say that the therapeutic part is the *rhizome*, or underground stem of the plant. When it is ground up, it is a natural alternative for aspirin in the prevention of heart attacks.

The GCE has approved ginger for treatment of upset stomach, loss of appetite, and prevention of motion sickness. Ginger is contraindicated for people with gallstones, those at risk for hemorrhage (it thins the blood), and use by pregnant women with morning sickness is controversial. When taken in excessive amounts ginger is a central nervous system (CNS) depressant which can lead to drowsiness, so exercise caution if driving. Alcohol or any other CNS depressant greatly increases this effect.

Ginkgo biloba *

This is one of the oldest herbs and has been studied and used extensively in China and Germany to improve cognitive abilities and general well-being. Both the leaves and seeds appear to offer therapeutic benefits. Studies have shown that this antioxidant protects the brain cells from destruction by two very virulent free radicals, and increases circulation of oxygen and glucose to the brain. Gingko is effective in improving short-term memory, reaction time, concentration, and in accelerating learning. The *PDR for Herbal Medicines* says that it helps prevent age-related memory loss, diminished concentration, confusion, depression, dizziness, and tinnitus of vascular origin. It may delay onset of dementia and Alzheimer's disease in older people. Typical doses range between 120 to 240 milligrams daily. If you do not notice a difference after four weeks, increase your dose to 300 milligrams per day. Some people develop headaches, digestive upset, and skin reactions, and bruise easily while taking ginkgo. Brinker reports that ginkgo should not be taken with aspirin, any anticoagulant medication (blood thinners), or some types of antidepressants (MAO inhibitors). It should also be avoided by those with systematic arterial hypertension, as it could lead to a stroke. If you are expecting surgery, check with your doctor before taking gingko. The consumerlab.com web site shows which ginkgo products have adequate amounts of key ingredients to enhance memory. Two ginkgo products, EGb 761 by Dr. Willmar Schwabe GMBH & Company, or LI1370 by Lichtwer Pharma GMBH, have demonstrated beneficial effects, while other manufacturer's products have not established efficacy. Store gingko out of children's reach, since consumption of ginkgo seeds may cause seizures.

Glucosamine and Chrondroitin

Glucosamine is a natural substance that stimulates creation of collagen, the protein found in cartilage and connective tissues. It may stop or reduce the underlying cause of osteoarthritis, deterioration of cartilage, and may even help restore the body's ability to manufacture normal cartilage and connective tissues, if taken for several years. Glucosamine also provides symptomatic relief for inflammatory joint disorders. It is sometimes combined with chrondroitin, a natural substance, which enhances its effectiveness, may increase cartilage synthesis, and reduce joint pain as well as nonsteroidal anti-inflammatory drugs (NSAIDs) like ibuprofen (such as Advil or Motrin). The typical dose is 500 milligrams glucosamine and 400 milligrams of chrondroitin taken three times daily. Check consumerlab.com to learn which products contain adequate levels of key ingredients.

Hawthorn *

This herb is derived from a combination of the flowers and leaves of the plant, as neither alone may be beneficial, write Blumenthal and associates. It is predominantly used to relax the smooth muscles of coronary blood vessels, which increases blood flow to the heart and may reduce angina. In *Stress and Natural Healing*, Christopher Hobbs says that it has a normalizing action on the heart and circulation and acts as a mild sedative with lavender or lemon balm, when mild heart disease is accompanied by nervousness. Favorable effects of hawthorn may not be noticed for several weeks. Although it is considered a safe substance, some precautions are important. Hawthorn can enhance the effect of cardiac medications (digitalis, digoxin, digitoxin), nitrate-based drugs (nitroglycerin), and drugs used to lower blood pressure, and should *never* be used to treat acute angina because it acts too slowly. Brinker recommends that you consult a medical professional familiar with the effect of herbs and interaction with any cardiac drugs before using this herb. And Feltrow and Avila warn that high doses may cause hypotension and other side effects, including fatigue, nausea, and sweating.

Kava Kava

The major benefits of kava kava are to reduce anxiety and nervousness, increase relaxation, and for insomnia. It was approved in Germany as an over-the-counter treatment for nervous anxiety, stress, and restlessness. It may also decrease the need for other sedatives to improve sleep. Tests have shown that it is equally as effective as some minor tranquilizers such as Valium in relieving stress, but lacks the tolerance, dependence, and withdrawal symptoms associated with most tranquilizers. Unlike similar drugs, there is no mental slowing or fogginess associated with kava, although some people become psychologically dependent on it. It is best to take kava with food before bedtime.

Kava should not be taken in large doses, as it may cause over-sedation, or for more than one to three months, as it may cause severe yellow, itchy, scaly patches to form on the skin, as well as reddened eyes, which clear up after it is discontinued. The *PDR for Herbal Medicines* states that kava should be avoided by women who are pregnant or breast-feeding, have Parkinson's disease or endogenous depression, or who take any depressants such as alcohol, barbiturates, Xanax, or psychoactive agents.

Milk Thistle *

This herbal extract can help protect and support the liver in handling the accumulation of internal metabolized toxins, by-products, and the creation of free radicals caused by stress. It helps to strengthen and regenerate the liver so that it can more readily eliminate fats, alcohol, prescription drugs, chemical pollutants, and other toxins. Hobbs says that it is used extensively in Europe to treat hepatitis, cirrhosis, and fatty liver diseases due to alcohol and drug abuse. Check with your health care practitioner before using milk thistle for hepatic cirrhosis, since it is not advisable for treating decompensated cirrhosis. According to Blumenthal and associates, the GCE has approved milk thistle for supportive treatment of chronic inflammatory liver disease, toxic liver damage, and hepatic cirrhosis.

The active ingredient in milk thistle is silymarin, which is very water-soluble and not very effective as a tea: only about 20 to 50 percent of milk thistle is absorbed in the GI tract. Feltrow and Avila write that there are relatively few side effects, mainly a potential laxative effect, and possible uterine stimulation and initiation of menstruation.

St. John's Wort *

Studies in Germany have found that this herb, also known as hypericum, often relieves mild to moderate depression—as effectively as antidepressant drugs—fearfulness, and/or nervous disturbances. Hypericum affects the production of dopamine, norepinephrine, and serotonin, which have a positive affect on mood, although the exact action remains unclear. Today, St. John's wort is one of the top-selling herbs in the U. S. and Germany, since the GCE approved its use for depressive moods, anxiety, and nervous restlessness.

According to the NIMH, St. John's Wort may reduce levels of interleukin-6 (IL-6), a protein involved in communication among cells in the immune system, and it has a positive effect on mood and helps ease depression. Minor side effects of this herb include allergic reactions, dizziness, restlessness, nausea, upset stomach, fatigue and constipation. These adverse effects are usually fewer than those of prescription antidepressants, and may be prevented by taking it with meals. Also, those with fair skin may sunburn more easily.

Do not take St. John's Wort for depression or anxiety without consulting a health care professional with knowledge of herbal actions and interactions with other drugs. Feltrow and Avila caution that this herb was recently found to cause severe drug interactions with both prescription and over-the-counter drugs such as cold and allergy medicines, pseudoephedrine decongestants, and flu medicines. And the PDR for Herbal Medicines warns that this herb should never be used with any MAO inhibitors or antidepressants, and also causes untoward reactions with iron pills, Indinavir, some oral contraceptives, theophylline, and digoxin. It should not be taken during pregnancy, or if breast feeding.

The usual dose is 300 to 350 milligrams two or three times a day for six to eight weeks, and may take up to eight weeks for relief of symptoms. If it causes insomnia, do not take it after 6:00 PM Also, you should not discontinue it abruptly, but wean yourself off by gradually decreasing the daily dosage.

Valerian *

This herb is well known for its sedative effects. The root of this plant is the source for a natural mind/body relaxant. It has been approved by the GCE, and helps reduce stress and anxiety, relax muscles, and reduce the time it takes to fall asleep and improves sleep without producing a morning hangover. It also helps calm a nervous stomach and may relieve tension headaches. Valerian is a mild herb, with few adverse reactions. The *PDR for Herbal Medicines* states that it is a potential substitute for synthetic sedatives like Valium and Xanax, but should not be used when taking barbiturates and benzodiazepines or alcohol, due to the additive effect with these drugs. However, it is not intended for long-term use, write Feltrow and Avila, because it may cause headache, blurred vision, excitability, restlessness, insomnia, nausea, or irregular heartbeats. The typical dose is two to three grams of dried herb infused to make a tea, or a 400 to 900 milligram tablet at bedtime.

Melatonin

This is a hormone released from the pineal gland. It is a derivative of the amino acid tryptophan and the neurotransmitter, serotonin, which appears in the blood in a recurring daily cycle, with nighttime levels as much as ten times higher than during the day. It is an efficient, powerful free radical scavenger that removes toxic hydroxyl molecules from the circulation during sleep. There is considerable controversy as to whether melatonin levels decline with age. Recently a study sponsored by the NIH reported that older people produce as much melatonin as younger ones, so there is no point in replacing something that is not missing. Some people use it to help overcome jet lag or for short-term sleep disturbances. Since it may cause constriction of blood vessels, those with hypertension or cardiovascular problems should avoid using melatonin. The typical dose ranges from 1–3 milligrams at night.

Web Sites

www. consumerlab.com—product-testing reports of accuracy of labeling and potency; whether product meets standards of quality.

www.medherb.com—a herbalist offers anecdotal reports from consumers along with his comments.

www.supplementwatch.com—dedicated to educating people about the pros and cons of dietary supplements.

Figure 1. Vitamins, minerals, and herbals that strengthen the body's systems.

BRAIN
Vitamins B1, B6, C,
Gingko biloba, Magnesium,
Iodine, Kava Kava

BONES & TEETH
Vitamins A, D, E, K,
Calcium, Magnesium,
Phosphorus, Zinc

CARDIOVASCULAR
Vitamins B1, B2, B3, B6, C, E, K,
Calcium, Chromium, Iron,
Magnesium, Folic acid, Bilberry,
CoQ-10, Garlic, Hawthorn

EYES
Vitamins, A, C, E,
Beta carotene,
Bilberry,
Gingko biloba

DIGESTIVE SYSTEM
Vitamins A, B1, B2, B3, B5, B6, B12,
Chromium, Phosphorus, Sodium, Zinc,
Ginger, Chamomile tea

NEUROMUSCULAR
Vitamins B1, B3, B12,
Calcium, Copper,
Magnesium, Phosphorus,
Potassium, Sodium,
Kava Kava

KIDNEYS & ADRENALS
Vitamins B5, B12,
Phosphorus, Potassium,
Siberian ginseng,
Garlic, Selenium

SKIN
Vitamins A, B2, B3,
Copper, Selenium, Zinc

ANTIOXIDANTS
Vitamins A, B1, B6, C, E,
Copper, Selenium, Zinc,
Bilberry, CoQ-10,
Green tea

IMMUNE SYSTEM
Vitamins A, B5, C, E,
Copper, Iron, Selenium, Zinc,
Echinacea, Siberian ginseng,
Beta carotene

〜◎〜

23

Positive Self-talk and Self-esteem

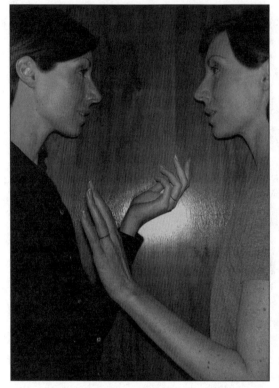

‿◍‿any women were raised in families and social settings where unkind messages of blame, shame, criticism, and punishment were used to control them. Their young receptive minds were imprinted with negative statements such as: "You're stupid, dumb, not as smart as your brother. You're not keeping your grades up. You're too fat or too skinny." From these messages, many young women believed that "something is wrong with me," as they were growing up. These earlier derogatory messages later often became negative "automatic thoughts" which occur almost outside your awareness. Negative self-talk consists of any and all thoughts that are critical of your abilities, assets, and prospects. It often revolves around thinking that you are not good enough, or that you're at fault. A basic fear of women is that they will be judged by others, found unworthy, and abandoned by their loved ones. If you assume you're inadequate, you may begin to feel like a helpless victim, especially when you can't explain your problems away.

According to Domar and Dreher, authors of *Healing Mind, Healthy Woman*, these negative thoughts increasingly enter women's minds when they're having problems, only now they have become unconscious self-talk, such as: "I'm not living up to my parent's or husband's expectations. I'm a failure at everything." Automatic thoughts tend to be very fast, unconscious, and highly believable. They have a great influence over your feelings, emotions, self-esteem, behavior, and health. You may experience feelings of self-doubt, anxiety, and depression if you believe these unconscious thoughts.

Even though you were born into a generally loving family, your sensitive ears and eyes may have picked up your parents', relatives', or peers' negative feelings mixed in with their loving expressions. Along with their positive feelings, parents often have anger, fear, sadness, unfulfilled wants, and other feelings toward their children. As a child, you may have sensed these unspoken feelings, and thought you were the cause of them. If you believed that you were unlovable at any age, the quality of your life could be affected even now.

POSITIVE SELF-TALK

Most women frequently carry on an inner monologue of self-talk or mind chatter inside their heads, interpreting who they are, how well they're doing, and whether people like them or not. Usually they're unaware of most of this self-talk, but occasionally they are aware. This monologue often includes a kind of self-berating mind-talk, which was part of the criticism and attitudes heard during their younger years. Dr. Miller, author of *Deep Healing: The Essence of Mind/Body Medicine*, believes that our minds have a way of bringing up old belittling messages and applying them to present situations. Something in the present situation "pushes your buttons" and triggers negative self-talk from your past. Your reaction to the current situation is often a conditioned response rather than a logically thought-out one.

Definition of Positive Self-talk

Positive self-talk is a great strategy to give yourself powerful, strong inner messages—sometimes called affirmations—about how you want to feel and think about yourself. Since your mind can react to only one message at a time, you can deflect negative self-talk by instilling positive thoughts to change your mind, feelings, and behavior.

How to Develop Positive Self-talk

Most women are usually somewhat aware of their own negative self-talk, but they don't know how to stop the negative mind-chatter and substitute positive messages. You might ask yourself whether your

322 Women's Stressors, Personality Traits and Inner Balance Strategies

thoughts contribute to your stress and where you learned them. Examining your negative emotions can help you understand your reactions to situations and to other people. Before you can change negative self-talk, you must first consider whether your thoughts are logical or true. If your self-talk reflects reality, there's no problem, but make sure that is the case. Too often women's negative self-talk goes far beyond reality and leads to problems. Try to stop negative self-talk before it wears down your confidence and well-being.

If you frequently blame yourself for your problems even though they are not your fault, you may be using negative self-talk. Try using positive coping thoughts that reflect the true situation and help you see possible options for solving your problems. You can also use disputing thoughts to change your negative automatic thinking. Tell yourself what a good job you did, or that you handled that tough situation well in spite of difficulties. The author of *Stress Management for Dummies*, Allen Elkin, provides some good examples of positive coping thoughts which you can say repeatedly to yourself:

- I have accomplished many great things and will continue to do so.
- I will focus on solving my problems rather than crying about them.
- Since I can't predict the future, I'm better off being optimistic.
- I won't take this problem personally.
- I will stay calm and cool and not let this upset me.

Establish basic patterns of positive thinking and leave yourself open to a variety of possibilities. Zilbergeld and Lazarus suggest that you not only need to use positive statements, but statements that directly counter the negative ones you've been saying to yourself. The more directly your positive statements address the criticisms, doubts, and complaints you've made against yourself, the more effective they will be. Gradually, using positive self-talk will become an automatic response to criticisms.

Another technique recommended by Elkin is called "thought stopping." It can rid your mind of worries and negative self-talk. It is also effective in weakening automatic thoughts and making them less likely to return. The five steps are described below:

1. *Notice your negative, automatic self-talk.* Recognize any unwanted thought that increases your stress, whether it is a worry, regret, or nagging concern.

2. *Imagine a stop sign.* In your mind, picture a large and vivid traffic stop sign.

3. *Shout STOP.* Silently in your head yell STOP—several times if you need to.

4. *Do it again.* Shout STOP silently every time an unwanted thought returns.

5. *Find a replacement thought.* Use it as a substitute for your distressing thought. Since your distressing, unwanted thoughts will probably return, you may have to repeat this technique several times to weaken or eliminate them.

Dr. Miller believes that emotional healing depends on your becoming more aware of negative self-talk, then replacing it with positive, strong self-affirmations. Your negative self-talk can be restructured by uncovering the errors in your thinking and the distortions of long-accepted beliefs. When you recognize your errors, you will see new possibilities for viewing a situation. Then you can change your negative, derogatory self-talk by using positive affirmations to uplift your spirits and empower you. Affirmations are also powerful tools for replacing negative self-talk with positive, empowering statements. They are a form of autosuggestion that can effectively counter the vicious cycle of negative self-talk. You can say your affirmations out loud or silently to yourself, or write them down. Quietly repeating the affirmations has a powerful effect on your mind and emotions. Since your mind can hold only one statement at a time (selective awareness), if you repeat positive statements to yourself, they will gradually become part of your reality.

Accentuating the positive can improve your attitude toward yourself and the world, and enhance your ability to achieve your fondest dreams. Think uplifting thoughts first thing in the morning and then again before going to sleep at night. Remember not to use any negative words while practicing an affirmation. Some examples of positive affirmations to say throughout your day are:

- I love and accept every part of myself.
- My body feels strong, healthy, and full of energy.
- Today I will listen to my body and meet its needs.
- I will feel happy and optimistic about whatever happens today.
- I am confident that I can do whatever I am asked to do.
- I will change whatever I can today, and accept everything else.

Health Benefits of Positive Self-talk

In *Minding the Body, Mending the Mind*, Joan Borysenko says that self-depreciating thoughts without sufficient evidence to back them up are like a mind trap which lessens your personal power and freedom of choice. Sometimes you realize that these negative thoughts are false and cruel, but other times you feel vulnerable and ruminate about them. Zilbergeld and Lazarus say, in *Getting What You Want: Mind Power through Mental Training*, that the more you put yourself down, the worse you'll feel and the worse you'll do. And conversely, the more often you tell yourself you'll succeed, the more you dramatically improve your chances of succeeding and feeling good about yourself.

Domar and Dreher believe that about 90 percent of women's automatic thoughts are negative. Negative self-talk can become a self-fulfilling prophecy and increase the likelihood of the personal failures you fear, as well as leading to illness. Dr. Miller believes that negative self-talk can create inner stress, depress your immune system, cause painful sensations, and reduce your resistance to infections. It can make your stomach uncomfortable and your muscles tense, and you may develop a headache, all of which may cause a cascade of more negative thoughts. Some scientific studies suggest that negative self-talk and "toxic" emotions produce toxic chemicals and hormones that can lead to anxiety, fear, and depression, poor mental functioning, fatigue, and lack of enthusiasm.

Studies have found that those who accept their problems as normal occurrences and use positive self-talk to cope with difficult situations have higher self-esteem and much lower stress levels. Successful women learn from their failures and let go of them to avoid negative self-talk. They focus only on past successes and on what they need to accomplish. Positive self-talk can generate good feelings and facilitate successful reactions to your problems. When you tell yourself that you'll succeed, you greatly improve your chances. As the unconscious levels of your mind begin to believe positive affirmations, you will find your inner beliefs, attitudes, and thoughts about yourself changing.

Positive affirmations, says Dr. Miller, lead to greater confidence, well-being, and enthusiasm. Affirmations can help you develop positive emotions, which create feelings of openness and expansiveness. Your body feels relaxed, even joyful, and sometimes energized. Joan Borysenko believes that positive feelings invite unity with others, while negative emotions create a tight, constricted feeling, so that you may seek isolation and push the world away. Therefore, you need to recognize your own emotions so that you can make a conscious choice between love and unity or fear and isolation. In their wonderful book, *The Power of the Mind to Heal*, the Borysenkos emphasize that you always have a choice about what you think and experience. When you think about using the power of your mind, remember that thoughts of peace open your heart to love and close your mind to fear. Thoughts of peace and love can help you discover the true power of your mind. When your mind is flooded by belittling self-talk, tell yourself that you could choose peace instead of these abusive thoughts.

POSITIVE SELF-ESTEEM

Your self-esteem, or the way you see yourself, greatly depends upon the way you *assume* that others see you—how you interpret signals from others. However, your interpretations can be faulty, based on past experiences such as how you were raised and how comfortable you felt around teenage peers. If your parents were loving, you probably have a high self-esteem: if they were punitive and authoritarian, your self-esteem is likely to be low. Many women have feelings of low self-worth and low self-esteem and lack a deep sense of self-respect. Some health professionals believe that being female is a risk factor for a poor self-image because we live in a society that values males more than females. Low self-esteem is especially high among women whose lives and happiness have been constricted by strong feelings of inadequacy.

Domar and Dreher wrote that some women *think* they deserve love, care, and compassion, yet in their hearts they often don't *feel* worthy of others' love. Other women appear self-confident and convince themselves and others that they are strong, worthy individuals. The Borysenkos found that some people wear a mask for fear that others may not accept them for who they really are. Some women who want to protect themselves from losing the love and respect of others pretend they are someone others will like. If you are authentic or genuine, and believe in yourself, you generally feel confident, open-hearted, and loving. If you wear a mask to protect you, you may need to become more aware of the times when you feel the need to put your mask on. You might examine your fears or things that upset you. When a healthy self-esteem helps you to be your true self, you can decide what you want from life, establish your goals, and pursue them.

Definition of Positive Self-esteem

Self-esteem, as defined by Judelson and Dell in *The Women's Complete Wellness Book*, is having a strong sense of self-worth, valuing oneself, and having the confidence and integrity to be your true self. Women with healthy self-esteem feel good about themselves, relate well to all kinds of people, and believe that they are competent to cope with life's challenges. Women with high self-esteem love and respect themselves. They have a positive self-image, know their strengths, and accept their shortcomings. Self-love means that you accept yourself every day and trust your judgments, and are able to view your shortcomings without criticism or comparison to others, and without conditions.

Steps to Develop Positive Self-esteem

One of the first steps to feeling good about yourself is to realize that while you are not perfect, you're a normal person with insecurities and failures. The foundation of good mental health and happiness is unconditional, nonjudgmental self-love and self-acceptance. You are the only one who can create your happiness: others can be supportive and inspire you, but they can't make you happy. Because happiness comes from within, you need to be warm, understanding, compassionate, and vulnerable, and forgive yourself for your imperfections. Unconditional love for yourself is the basis of emotional health and the most essential nutrient.

Sometimes you may feel that you can't trust people. To simplify your world and make it safer, you may find a little protected place where no one can hurt you and you do not feel as much pain. But remember, if no one can reach you, you will not feel the joy of life either. To be free and easy to love, you have to open up that safe place and breathe in fresh air.

Set yourself free from belittling negative self-images. According to Gay Hendricks in *Learning to Love Yourself,* you may have learned so many negative things from childhood that you see the world upside down. Your task then is to set your vision straight again. If you can identify some basic attitudes, you may begin to set yourself free and learn to love yourself. These attitudes may include:

- I have learned to see the world the way it isn't.
- I have done this for my survival.
- I am now interested in much more than survival.
- There is nothing outside myself that can save me.
- I have everything I need inside me.

- All the love I have been searching for is here within me.
- I can give it to myself.
- My very nature is love, so there is no need to search or work for it.
- Love is the only thing I need to change.
- I am now willing to love myself.

Ignore negative thoughts about yourself. Change your attention to something positive. Try to forgive yourself and forget past mistakes. Remember that nobody is perfect all the time. Since you only get one shot at life, make the best of it. Occasionally, you'll feel down or oppressed by the world when you fall short of what you are striving for. If your self-worth is dependent on some outside standard of how well you are doing, any failure can easily lead to a feeling of helplessness. When you feel stuck in your mind or habits, consciously choose to do something to nourish yourself. Dr. Miller feels that taking action is a good way to love yourself and raise your self-esteem, and that self-nourishing acts have positive side effects. A healthy self-esteem should enable you to survive such challenges and even thrive. It could be both protective and healing.

Accept who you are and be true to yourself. Acknowledge yourself as a good and unique person. Be proud of who you are. Dr. Meltzer, author of *The Ten Rules of High Performance Living*, recommends that you accept and love yourself—know that you are worthy and deserve the best. Faith in yourself comes naturally when you accept who you are. You can't depend upon pleasing others all the time. People who love you for who you really are will support your full self-expression. Don't compare yourself to others—you're you, so enjoy your strengths and uniqueness. When you're true to yourself, you can stop pretending to be someone else.

One mistake you may make is thinking that you have to change something before you can love yourself. Women often have negative thoughts about their bodies and self-worth. Over 50 percent of American women overestimate the size of their bodies. Joan Borysenko suggests that you think about all that your body does for you instead of focusing on how it looks. Your legs and feet get you around, your arms hold those you love, your eyes view the world around you, and your ears hear music, voices, and sound. Women who can't accept and respect their bodies often experience feelings of blame, shame, guilt, or fear. They also have lower self-esteem due to distorted images of their bodies. Accept yourself as you are, fat thighs, a big nose, physical limitations, and all. This means more than a grudging acknowledgment that you'll never be the same again, or wish to be.

In their book, *Women's Encyclopedia of Health and Emotional Healing*, Foley and Nechas describe how some women spend years struggling to 'fix' themselves to earn acceptance and affirmation from others that they are good enough. Acceptance means actually valuing yourself as you are now—loving and cherishing your inner self—so that you'll be free to be your true self. When you stop thinking about yourself negatively, you'll reduce your anxiety, tension, and stress. While most women have skills and competencies they're satisfied with, they tend nevertheless to measure their worth by all the imagined things they're not.

According to Hendricks, love is the only thing that needs to be changed in any situation. You don't have to get better before you love yourself. It is the experience of loving yourself that has the power to change everything. But in the experience of loving yourself, *now* is the moment that counts. Love makes life very simple—you have numerous opportunities to learn to love more. Part of learning to love yourself involves undergoing a radical transformation in how your mind sees things, so that you can see the world as a place where you are in total control of the amount of love you are willing to experience. You may give yourself reasons why you are unlovable. Reasons are positions the mind takes when under stress. Whenever it is confused or in too much pain to look at what is really going on, the mind will make up a reason to make things fit a little better. Reasons are a retreat to a safe position, which is an illusion, because reasons are not true and real. You will always have the opportunity to go beyond the false safety of reason into the real safety of love.

Practice putting yourself first—if you don't, no one else will. When you have a healthy level of self-esteem, you'll feel comfortable meeting your own needs, even when others demand your time. Loving and respecting yourself are not the same as being selfish. You must treat yourself with kindness and acceptance before you can give to others. You can't give to others what you don't have. Selfishness is the opposite of self-love—it arises out of an unfulfilled hunger for self-respect and love. It occurs when you feel empty and need to grab for anything you can. When you have plenty of love, you can share your love with others and feel more love for yourself.

Learn to love yourself for how you feel at the moment. One of the hardest things about learning to love yourself is to remember that all you have to do is love yourself one moment at a time. Hendricks and others believe that first you must be willing to love yourself, after having spent years not being willing to love yourself. The big decision to be willing sets you free to begin the journey to your center. It gives you energy and passion, so that you can become a little more open each step of the way. All you have to do is catch the way you actually feel and love it. When you rely on others' feelings and experiences, you cannot take credit for them, or blame them when things go wrong.

Learning to love yourself and developing a healthy self-esteem does not mean that you will never be unhappy or that you will have eliminated all your weaknesses. Rather, it means that you have a healthy self-respect and sense of purpose for your life. You'll know your strengths and weaknesses, and with knowledge of both you will take realistic actions.

Focus on your successes and don't dwell on your mistakes. Believe in yourself and expect the best. Have faith in your ability to succeed in all your endeavors. Learn to feel comfortable accepting praise from others. Accept compliments and acknowledge your strengths with humility. This can help build your self-esteem and improve your self-image, say Judelson and Dell. Unfortunately, many women have been taught that taking credit for a job well done is immodest or self-centered. Some women find it difficult to accept praise, and need to learn that a simple acceptance and the response, Thank you, is all it takes. Have pride in your accomplishments and don't underrate them. During the inevitable moments of self-doubt, remind yourself that you are a capable woman.

Foley and Nachez say that to improve your self-esteem, you need to shift some of the things you do well into the core of your self-concept, and reduce your focus on areas where you're less than perfect. They suggest that you consider mistakes and failures as learning experiences, and rather than becoming upset about them, just think about what you learned from the experience.

Use positive short affirmations to enhance your self-esteem. Positive affirmations of your strong aspirations, beliefs, and feelings can help you develop and strengthen your self-esteem. Repeat affirmations to yourself frequently, especially during moments of doubt, until they become part of your reality. Positive affirmations can help counteract the negative or troublesome thoughts that diminish your self-esteem. Affirmations can be any positive statement, but they should not become a selfish "wish list." Lynch and Bell, authors of Dr. Lynch's *Holistic Self-health Program*, recommend that your affirmations be short, clear, always positive, and framed in the present tense. As you say affirmations, try to let your self-doubts and negative judgments vanish. Focus on believing your affirmations, even if they don't reflect your present reality.

Examples of some loving affirmations are:

- I love myself deeply.
- I love myself no matter how I act.
- I am completely lovable.
- I am willing to give and fully receive love.

Along with affirmations, the use of imagery that reawakens good memories, where you felt the joy and success of being yourself and were living your truth, will help your self-esteem. Affirm your right to be who you are and trust in your goodness.

Health Benefits of High Self-esteem

Many psychoneuroimmunology studies found that your immune system can be profoundly affected by your self-image and beliefs about yourself. Dr. Meltzer writes that how you perceive yourself and the world around you is based on your past experiences, your sensitivities, values, and especially your own self-worth and self-respect. When you have a poor opinion of yourself, you feel unworthy of love. An underlying lack of self-esteem may gradually lead to anxiety and depression, along with feelings of rejection and failure, which may contribute to physical illness. Low self-esteem is a leading contributor to the high incidence of depression among women.

Changing your view of yourself and valuing who you are will lower your stress. How you view things determines your physical and emotional response. According to Dr. Meltzer, if you see yourself as a victim of circumstance or situations, you create unhealthy stress patterns. If you view stressful situations as threats to your relationships with loved ones or your job security, you may overreact. Emotional stress can lower your immune system and cause disease. With positive self-esteem and self-confidence, you're less likely to distort the situation and overreact. When you take responsibility for yourself and hold yourself in high regard, you will learn to handle life's challenges with dignity and humor.

As you learn to love and accept yourself as you are, then you will take good care of yourself with healthy actions. You'll take actions to enhance self-healing and to maintain your well-being, according to Drs. Lynch and Bell. You need self-love, discipline, and faith to act on what you know. Hendricks believes that loving yourself is physical. The idea may start in your mind, then you'll feel it connect and happen in your body. It feels like an expansion of space. There is no limit to how good you can feel. You may feel relaxed, comfortable, and safe—the only true safety is being willing to expand beyond your limits.

Accepting life as it is not only restores your sanity, but guides you toward higher experiences of life—the willingness to be the source of love for yourself and others. You are no longer striving for love—you are love. When you are fully open to love, you can provide an endless supply of it. All that is required is being willing to experience all of life. This opens you up to what is actually happening to you and sets you free. With positive self-esteem, you'll be able to meet stressful situations with dignity, humor, and enthusiasm, and increase your chances for health, happiness, and fulfillment.

24

Relaxation, Yoga, and Sleep

Make quiet time for yourself each day to think and relax. —Joan Lunden

True relaxation—the kind that relieves you of daily pressures, stress, and obligations—isn't easy. Most women seldom take time to slow down and appreciate their surroundings. They tend to think of relaxation as a luxury—something to do on vacation. Some women feel that they don't deserve mental respite and physical rest, while others give up relaxing whenever their schedule gets full. Before you can learn relaxation techniques, you must sincerely believe that you deserve to take at least twenty minutes daily for some form of mental and physical relaxation.

Some people tend to think of deep relaxation and meditation as techniques that involve leaving a normal state of mind and entering an unnatural one. On the contrary, relaxation is a feeling of being in harmony with yourself. In *Deep Healing: The Essence of Mind/Body Medicine,* Dr. Miller describes deep relaxation as a kind of remembering in which you enter a more natural state, one that is balanced and healthy for your body. It is the most normal mind/body state that you can experience.

Within each person is a still quiet center that is always present, even though you don't always experience it. Because of what you have been trained to believe—the tasks you think you should be doing, your fears about what might happen, or your obsessions and compulsions—you may find that appreciation of your gentle, peaceful, loving nature is overwhelmed, so that this quiet place within you becomes invisible.

RELAXATION
Definition of Relaxation
Relaxation occurs any time you sit down, close your eyes, and do absolutely nothing at all. Real relaxation is effortless: you are centered, peaceful, and able to cope with everything in your life. You just listen to your breathing—nothing else—and gradually your muscles relax. Dr. Meltzer believes that relaxation is a way of life and a state of mind, as well as a state of wellness. It is the joyful feeling of being completely free, the art of being calm in mind and body, without stress, strain, or expectations. Whenever you focus your attention within your body, you can become more relaxed. The goal of deep relaxation is to release body tension, relieve stress and anxiety, and create a peaceful, receptive, focused frame of mind. Relaxation is a physical and mental letting-go at the core of your being, a loosening and releasing of the ego-centered limitations that create stress for you.

How Relaxation Works
During relaxation the body operates more slowly than the mind. By focusing on breathing or a word/phrase, you bore the mind into relaxing. It doesn't matter which technique you use, as long as it is rhythmic and breaks your normal train of thought. Deep relaxation simply requires freeing your attention from distractions in your mind and environment. Relaxation must precede any serious form of concentration. In deep relaxation, you reach a state of profound tranquility with a sense of safety, comfort, and freedom. This is a natural state, not one of altered consciousness.

Progressive muscle relaxation is based on controlling each muscle group by tensing and holding it for five to ten seconds, until you can easily identify it by a slight discomfort. As you learn to tense and then relax each major muscle group, you become attuned to the differences in feeling when your muscles are tensed or relaxed. As you learn to discern the difference between tension and relaxation, you can begin to break the vicious cycle of pain related to tension, such as in your neck, back, and shoulder muscles.

Steps to Practice

In his book, Dr. Miller describes several steps for entering into deep relaxation. First, you must make a conscious decision to enter the state of deep relaxation and believe that it is the most important thing for you to do at this time. It helps to have a designated mental place meant especially for your relaxation, which allows you to escape daily stresses. This is a quiet place—an attitude and a spiritual outlook—where you can retreat anywhere, anytime. You'll want to be able to loosen your clothes, set your worries aside, and assume a comfortable position.

You begin by simply taking a deep breath in and out, and assure your mind and body that it is safe to relax so that they do not interpret any environmental sounds as requiring your attention. Turn off the phone and use the answering machine to avoid distractions. Next, choose a method to induce first physical then mental relaxation, such as floating through space or relaxing on a tropical beach, in a garden, or in a safe quiet room. You may increase your relaxed and peaceful state with guided imagery by imagining that you are walking along a seashore, riding gentle waves in a boat, or floating on a raft. To enhance your relaxation, you may add mental affirmations, such as silently repeating, "I am at peace with myself and others," or "I feel completely relaxed in body, mind, and soul." Last, when you are ready to return to reality, gradually and slowly imagine coming back to the room you are in. You may focus on parts of your body and move each slightly, breathing more deeply, and finally opening your eyes. Then stand, stretch, and resume your activities gradually.

There are several different relaxation methods. Try any method that appeals to you for several days or weeks. Dr. Benson at Harvard University, author of *The Relaxation Response,* also believes that "the more comfortable you are with a relaxation technique—the more you believe in it—the better it is going to work for you." Practice at least ten to twenty minutes once or twice each day. Commit yourself to a regular time for practice: you may glance at the clock occasionally, but do not set an alarm. A cassette recording or CD with soothing music may help you relax. It is easier to develop relaxation when you attain self-acceptance. Consistent practice is required to achieve the best performance and highest level of health. When you practice regularly each day, you will benefit more and may notice that you feel more calm, comfortable, and confident in general. By taking a few minutes each day to relax, these wonderful, uplifting experiences will become a regular part of your life.

Benson's Relaxation Response Method

1. Select a focus word or short phrase, such as love, peace, serenity, shalom, or the Lord is my shepherd.

2. Sit or lie quietly in a comfortable position and close your eyes.

3. Relax your muscles from the top of your head to the bottom of your feet.

4. Breathe slowly and naturally, repeating your focus word or phrase silently as you exhale.

5. Assume a passive attitude—don't worry about how you're doing. When other thoughts cross your mind, let them pass and return to your focus word.

6. Continue for ten to twenty minutes. You may open your eyes to check the time. When you finish, sit quietly for a minute or so with your eyes closed, then wait a few minutes after you open your eyes before standing.

Once you become familiar with one exercise, experiment with others to see how they affect you. A variety of different relaxation techniques are described below. You may modify any of them to suit you. Some exercises are more useful in certain states of mind. For example, one exercise may calm anxiety and restlessness, but may not be useful for depression. Another exercise may provide energy when you feel exhausted.

Experienced health professionals can be valuable guides to learning exercises correctly. They can give you feedback and let you know when you have reached an optimal level of relaxation. Some teachers will record your private sessions on a tape recorder so that you can play the recording at home, or you may wish to purchase a professionally prepared cassette. For some people, it is best to work in a group setting with a qualified professional guide.

Variations of Relaxation Techniques

Whole-body Relaxation. While sitting comfortably or lying on your back with your eyes closed, lift up one leg as you inhale and hold a deep breath while tightening every muscle in that foot and leg. Really tense those muscles as much as you can and hold for about ten seconds. Then, as you release your breath, gradually release the muscles in your leg and foot and lower it to the floor. Next, lift the other leg as you inhale. Tighten the muscles as hard as you can and hold for about ten seconds, then release and lower your foot as you exhale. Repeat this same process as you move upward toward your head by tightening the muscles in your buttocks and pelvis, then abdomen and chest, arms and hands, and finally your face and scalp. Finally, tighten the muscles of your entire body as you inhale, hold for ten seconds, then release as you exhale. Now, relax your entire body and breathe normally.

Progressive Relaxation of the Body. In progressive relaxation, you systematically scan each part of your body by tensing and then relaxing each major muscle group. (See the description of a body scan in Chapter 14.) Study the tension and notice the difference between how each muscle feels when it is tensed and when relaxed. This helps you recognize the slightest muscle tensions, so you can release them, and achieve better muscle relaxation. Begin by lying down on a firm comfortable surface (not a bed) with your arms at your sides, or sitting upright in a comfortable position with both feet on the floor and your hands in your lap. Loosen any tight or restrictive clothing and remove your shoes. Close your eyes and take a very deep cleansing breath, filling your abdomen like a balloon. Then take in more air to fill up your chest, hold this a moment, and gently let your breath go.

Now, take an even deeper breath, deeper and deeper. Fill your abdomen and entire chest with air. As you release the breath, let go of any tightness or tension in any part of your body. Take a third, much deeper breath and release your tension as you exhale. Then, take one more very deep breath and gently let it go. When you feel calm and tranquil, you may breathe normally.

Begin with your jaw muscle. Open your mouth slightly and let the jaw muscles relax, then pause. Next, let the muscles around your eyes and forehead relax—feel them become smooth, then pause. Focus on your eyebrows and scalp, let the muscles relax and feel light and calm, then pause. Now, let your neck and shoulder muscles become loose—feel them relaxing and loosening, then pause.

Let the muscles in your arms, hands, and fingers become heavy as you relax and feel the increased blood flow into them, warming and soothing them. They may tingle and pulsate slightly as they relax and become warm. Pause and enjoy the sensations. Next, feel the movements in your chest, back, and abdomen with each breath. As you exhale, relax each of these muscles more and more, feel the tension give way, then pause. Now, feel the muscles in your pelvis and buttocks relaxing more as you exhale, then pause.

Note the feelings of relaxation in your legs, calves, knees, thighs, and feet. Sense an increased blood flow creating a soothing warmth which may cause them to tingle and slightly pulsate, then pause. Your body now feels calm and peaceful with all your muscles relaxed, so pause and enjoy the sensation. Visualize a quiet, calm, restful place in your mind and savor the sensations. When you have sustained sufficient rest, gradually return to the present, visualize the room you are in, and slowly open your eyes.

Guided Relaxation. With this method, you use inspirational audio tapes to facilitate relaxation. The tapes may offer suggestions and use soothing background sounds of nature, such as water flowing, ocean waves, or gentle melodies, as described in the section on music in Chapter 16.

Cue-controlled Relaxation. After mastering the basic relaxation skills, you may try using cue-controlled relaxation. This technique can be used in conjunction with relaxed breathing or alone. You choose a cue to signal the relaxation response. Usually the cue is a verbal signal which you say quietly to yourself, such as relax, breathe, or a short prayer. Another cue may be when the phone rings, or you stop at a red light. With practice, simply saying or seeing the cue can help your body to relax almost automatically and to stay calm.

Health Benefits of Relaxation Techniques

According to Dr. Benson, the relaxation response creates several physiological changes: it decreases oxygen consumption, reduces heart and breathing rates, and lowers blood pressure, metabolism, and muscle tension. Some people have a shift from normal waking brain wave patterns to slower brain waves. These physiological changes can effectively protect people from the harmful effects of stress. In addition, relaxation may empower you to let go of anxiety, restlessness, and hostility, and you may experience feelings of peace and tranquility.

Relaxation exercises also provide several psychological benefits. When your body relaxes, your mind relaxes and helps you let go of that awful "mind chatter." Individuals who practice relaxation regularly report that they are able to focus and concentrate better, improve their memory, and achieve a higher level of mind/body awareness. Researchers have found that relaxation can resolve or lessen negative effects of stress on the body and heal some diseases by enhancing the production of healing neurochemicals and hormones. Because the nervous system also feels more balanced and rejuvenated during relaxation, you can endure more stress without adverse consequences.

During relaxation, as your breathing slows, you may feel as though you have stopped breathing for a short period. By the end of a session, as your muscles become relaxed, their aches and pains may disappear. You may feel a sensation of warmth in your hands or feet. And most people report feeling a greater sense of control over their life, rather than moving with the chaos of their environment. Another benefit is a greater sense of self-assurance.

The immediate benefits of even a single deep relaxation experience are a dramatic lowering of your perception of stress. Along with this comes a sense of comfort and clarity of your mind, as though annoying thoughts have drained away. Your obsessions and compulsions diminish, and you may experience an increased feeling of serenity. When your body and mind are relaxed, your organs, body chemistry, and nervous system are harmoniously invigorated and rejuvenated.

Meditation and deep relaxation offer ways of accepting each thought, each experience, each feeling, and each event as it occurs, free of the need to do anything or change anything. You feel more comfortable with who you are and are better able to deal successfully with your life. You become more centered and can live more in the present moment and stay in touch with your inner guides. As new awareness occurs, you begin to see and perceive things that were previously invisible when you were so busy questioning and calculating.

Making time to practice relaxation is essential to establishing wellness in your life. It requires discipline, but the results are remarkable. It induces deeper, more restorative sleep and reduces insomnia and fatigue. You'll have more energy and a calmer approach to life. Relaxation exercises nourish your soul so that you can achieve a higher level of mind/body awareness. Benson believes that using the relaxation response regularly for several weeks or months may reduce or eliminate stress-related symptoms and health problems.

When deep relaxation is combined with meditation and you earnestly look within yourself to uncover the wisdom of life and love as it flows within you, a profound sense of loosening, widening, and opening inwardly may arise, leading to a deep, real relaxation. Dr. Miller believes that with deep relaxation, your mind learns to be more open and flexible in ways of being, which create new behaviors that become part of your life.

You may notice yourself unconsciously and automatically achieving your chosen goals. And light begins to shine through your whole being from an inner spirit when you feel true harmony, balance, and peace within.

YOGA

Yoga is a philosophy of living that originated thousands of years ago in the Hindu and Buddhist traditions of India. It is the oldest and most holistic form of the mind/body systems, uses a combination of internally directed mindful awareness of the self, breath, and energy. In Eastern traditions, health is seen as the balance and harmony of the mind, body, and spirit.

Definition of Yoga

Yoga is the simple, healthy discipline of bringing the mind, body, and spirit together in perfect harmony. Translated literally, "yoga" means union—to unite one's physical, mental, and spiritual health. Yoga, which has many different forms, includes physical postures, breathing awareness, and meditation techniques. In Western society, Hatha yoga is the form most commonly used. The aim is to free the body of physical limitations and restore balance to the right and left sides, front and back, internal and external, and passive and active parts. You focus on body awareness to correct physical alignment in postures, using internal sensations and experiences as your movement changes. It is not necessary to understand the philosophy completely or master difficult postures to obtain a mind/body harmony and inner calm.

How Yoga Works

The goals of the ancient tradition of yoga are to still the restless mind and to unite the mind, body, and spirit in search of health, self-awareness, and spiritual balance. By unifying the physical body, breath, and concentration while performing the postures, blockages in the energy channels of the body are cleared and the body energy system becomes more balanced.

More than two thousand years ago, the Indian sage Patanjali identified eight steps or basic principles to spiritual enlightenment. Both the postures and breathing exercises prepare the mind and body for meditation and spiritual development. These eight steps include:

Yama—universal ethical principles for living, including non-violence, truthfulness, chastity, and absence of greed

Niyama—purification of self through discipline and study

Asanas—physical postures that focus on development of strength, flexibility, and endurance

Pranayama—breathing practices to regulate the breath, balance life energy, and promote concentration

Pratyahara—freeing the mind from domination of the senses and distractions from the outside world

Dharana—deep concentration

Dhyana—meditative practices

Samadhi—the state in which the soul is supreme

Steps to Practice Yoga

In the typical yoga routine, you clear your mind, breathe deeply, and gently ease yourself through a series of body postures. Most westerners learn Hatha yoga to promote relaxation, enhance flexibility, or heal an injury. Ideally, it is the path to a greater realization of God through mental and physical control. Hatha yoga enhances the physical body through an extensive series of body postures, movements, and breathing techniques that are performed while standing, sitting, or lying prone or supine on the floor. The physical exercises stretch, strengthen, and balance each joint in the body. One simple modified yoga position is to stretch like a cat. Sit on the edge of your chair, with your palms on your knees. Exhale slowly and round your back, dropping your head forward between your knees. Then as you inhale, lift your head up and gently arch your back. Repeat this sequence several times to relieve tension and stretch your back muscles.

In Hatha yoga, the breathing techniques focus on consciously prolonging your inhalation to receive life energy, retaining the breath to hold the energy in, and exhaling to empty all thoughts and emotions. There is no mental focus or repetition of a mantra or prayer. Practitioners concentrate on their breathing while synchronizing a series of physical postures, moving between them slowly and with concentration.

Although different forms of yoga offer hundreds of poses, most routines contain about twenty postures, with specific ones for certain health problems. The postures you use depend on your purpose in doing them. If you plan to study yoga seriously and practice regularly, you should train with an experienced instructor and plan to practice at least three times a week. Yoga works to stretch and tone the back, stomach, chest, and lungs, so that stiffening from inactivity, tiredness, incorrect posture, and aging can be reversed.

A basic yoga session includes the fundamental postures that form the core of all yoga practice. These postures encourage suppleness of the spine and joints, enhance muscular tone, and tone the internal organs. When practicing yoga, it is important to follow a sequence of postures specially developed for you, because the stretches of one position are balanced by counter-stretches in the next posture. The postures are practiced slowly without pushing or jerking the body, so there is no risk of strain or injury. Each pose can be adapted to allow for any physical injury or weakness.

You need a quiet room, free from interruptions. Wear loose, comfortable clothing and practice barefoot. Make sure the room is warm because warmth helps relax and stretch the muscles. Begin with preliminary exercises to limber up your muscles for more strenuous poses. Start with a few minutes of rest in the *corpse pose*, then slowly stand up and do all twelve positions of the sun salutation slowly and gracefully, with each movement flowing into the next. These bending and stretching poses warm up and flex the entire body. Hold each position for as long as you can to obtain the fullest possible stretch, and use slow deep abdominal breathing. Keep your mind focused on the movement to help you relax and develop a sense of mind/body harmony. Other exercises you may choose are the *headstand*, the *shoulder-stand*, the *plough*, the *windmill pose*, the *forward bend*, the *head-to-knee pose*, the *spinal twist pose*, the *cobra* or *bow*, the *seated sun*, the *triangle*, or the *butterfly pose*. Yoga postures have their best effect if practiced regularly for fifteen to thirty minutes a day. Although instructional books and videotapes on yoga techniques are available for all levels of students, learning yoga from an experienced instructor who will help you develop the teacher within yourself is the most beneficial.

Health Benefits of Yoga

The regular practice of yoga can induce deep relaxation and promote physical strength, endurance, and flexibility through gentle stretching and postures which decrease muscle tension and stiffness. Yoga is unique because it stretches all the body parts, especially the spine, loosens the back, and aids in developing correct posture. It also massages the internal organs and glands, and through its coordinated breathing and postures, the mind and body relax. In addition, yoga can lower your blood pressure and helps to alleviate a wide range of health problems, including arthritis, rheumatism, back problems, circulatory, and digestive disorders.

Loecher and O'Donnell, authors of *Women's Choices in Natural Healing*, believe that the mental attitude of calmly looking inward can minimize the effects of external stressors and enhance a sense of tranquillity, concentration, clarity, and well-being. Yoga can also counteract negative emotions such as anger, anxiety, and depression. A sequence of postures is specifically designed to relax, relieve dullness and depression, and reduce insomnia. Yoga may also improve memory, concentration, learning ability, and self-confidence, and increase energy and contentment. It helps clear the body's energy channels, improves circulation to vital body organs, and promotes the same physiological changes as the relaxation response does. For some people, yoga is a system of ridding the body of tension, toxins, and tightness: it helps release tight muscles where you often experience stress—the neck, shoulders, and back. Some long-term practitioners report that yoga has increased their spiritual awareness and led to changes in their perspective of life, producing greater harmony between their inner and outer worlds.

Women can benefit from yoga because of its stress-reducing effects, especially those with autoimmune diseases, arthritis, and migraine headaches. In studies of healthy women who practiced yoga regularly, the women reported greater life satisfaction, felt less irritable and more congenial, and showed higher levels of well-being and health than women who did not practice it. Individuals who experience stress-related physical and emotional problems are likely to benefit from yoga, which may reduce their symptoms and increase their flexibility, strength, and serenity.

PEACEFUL SLEEP AND NAPS

Sleep is as important to your health as good nutrition and exercise is. Your body likes routines, regularity, and predictability. Sleep is necessary to restore your mind and body: it is critical to mental alertness and overall energy. The amount of sleep adults require varies: while eight hours of sleep is recommended, some people consider seven hours a blessing. Although women need more sleep than men, they actually get less. As women get older, they tend to sleep fewer hours, take more naps, and wake up often during the night. Women's hormonal changes, such as low estrogen at the beginning of the menstrual period and during menopause, along with hot flashes, all may contribute to disrupted sleep patterns. Many women feel overloaded with responsibilities, and report more stress than men, which may interfere with their sleep. Your daily cycles of sleep and body chemistry, along with your circadian rhythm, determine how well you think and move. Getting enough sleep and rest affects both your physical and mental health. If you change your sleeping hours or patterns from one day to the next, your internal physiology works overtime to compensate for the change.

Many people suffer from restless or frequently interrupted sleep as a result of daytime stress or external factors such as loud noise. Sleep deprivation—inadequate sleep—affects more than thirty-five million Americans, or 36 percent of adults. Many women are chronically sleep-deprived, and about one in six Americans has chronic insomnia. They may have difficulty falling asleep, or awaken several times during the night and be unable to get back to sleep, or sleep only a few hours each night. Sleep deprivation affects your mood first: you may feel irritable and have difficulty concentrating and staying alert. Your short-term memory is impaired, as is your reaction time and your ability to think clearly. You may have difficulty making decisions, which can lead to making mistakes. If you miss three or more hours of sleep, your immune system activity decreases by as much as 50 percent. Inadequate sleep leaves you feeling chronically tired and depressed, and often impairs your ability to cope with stress and daily problems. Sleep-deprived people eventually snap when faced with small stressors such as snarled traffic or being late for appointments.

Napping is one way to compensate for lack of sleep: it provides some rest for the body during the day. In most European countries and Latin cultures, an afternoon nap or siesta is an established routine where all work ceases and stores close for two hours. The demands of work, especially intense mental effort, can create an inner tension that impairs the vital functions of your body. Napping can restore energy and help release your inner tension in an enjoyable way. Fifteen to twenty minute naps in the early afternoon are okay. Longer naps may cause sleepiness the rest of the day or interfere with sleep at night.

Definition of Sleep

Sleep is actually considered an active state during which the body and mind repair themselves. It is a state of suspended consciousness in which the body can respond to external stimuli, but much less readily than when awake. During sleep the muscles are relaxed and the brain pattern is different than when awake.

Stages of Sleep

Researchers have identified several stages through which people progress during sleep. These stages include a transition period from waking to sleeping, four stages of non-REM (rapid eye movement) sleep, and REM sleep. During a typical night, you go through this cycle four or five times and each cycle lasts about ninety to one hundred minutes.

There are two stages of relaxation before sleep occurs, first a quiet period before you fall asleep, then drifting feelings called drowsiness or pre-sleep. During these stages, your muscles begin to relax and your brain waves decelerate as concentration, memory, and other cognitive processes slow down.

Non-REM sleep, the second stage, consists of four substages. You progress forward through the four substages of non-REM sleep, then go in reverse through substages 3, 2, and 1 before entering REM sleep. During substage 1, your muscles relax, breathing and pulse rate decrease, and your brain waves slow down. Gradually you lose consciousness over a period of several minutes. In substage 2, your metabolic activity, blood pressure, heart rate, and brain waves decrease even further as you go into a deeper sleep. Bursts of electrical brain activity occur during this time and last between fifteen ands thirty minutes. During substages 3 and 4, called "delta sleep," your body temperature drops and your blood pressure and heart rate further decrease. This is the restorative period in which the body starts to repair and rejuvenate cells. Infection-fighting cells are produced to aid the body's immune system, and toxins are filtered out of the body. These substages usually last thirty to forty minutes during your first sleep cycle, but are shorter as REM sleep increases.

REM or active sleep is a period of rapid eye movements, when dreaming may occur. During REM sleep, increased blood and oxygen flow to the brain, the pulse rate increases, and breathing becomes irregular: your muscles twitch and move. Electrical activity in the brain increases most often with dreams and intensely during REM sleep. This stage lasts eleven to twenty-five minutes, and occurs at the end of a full sleep cycle. While REM sleep increases in frequency throughout your sleep at night, with aging your amount of REM sleep may diminish significantly. Elderly women may lose REM sleep entirely.

A short nap of twenty minutes or less between 2:00 and 4:00 in the afternoon is ideal because you do not engage in REM sleep and awaken feeling refreshed. It can increase alertness, revive memory, and reduce symptoms of fatigue. During naps the human growth hormone (HGH) is secreted. The effects of HGH are complex, but it generally helps the body adjust to stress, increases immunity, restores depleted energy, and enhances the action and efficiency of other neurotransmitters like serotonin, which can uplift your mood.

Methods to Enhance Your Sleep

The quality of your sleep is as important as the quantity. You should awaken feeling refreshed and energized if you had sufficient quality sleep during the night. You can improve the quality of your sleep by using some relaxing rituals before bedtime. The following tips are recommended to help you sleep.

Each day, get some regular exercise such as walking, aerobics, bicycling, or gardening, to ease muscle tension. But avoid strenuous exercise three hours before bedtime.

In 52 Simple Steps to Natural Health, Dr. Mayell recommends that you get adequate amounts of B-vitamins along with calcium and magnesium in a two-to-one ratio during the day, and at bedtime for their relaxing effect. A deficiency in these nutrients is associated with insomnia. Some experts believe that eating low-calorie carbohydrate foods which contain the amino acid tryptophan, a precursor of serotonin, has a calming effect and helps you fall asleep. A glass of warm milk with honey, or pretzels, toast, bagel chips, graham crackers, or other low-fat, complex carbohydrates an hour before retiring may help you feel drowsy, but avoid eating large meals close to bedtime.

Develop some regular nighttime rituals to prepare your body for sleep. The best sleep comes from having a regular sleep routine to stabilize your body's internal clock. This means getting ready for bed at the same time every night and getting up at the same time every day. Ideally, you should establish a set of habits that promote an effective sleep routine. When a ritual becomes a regular part of your preparation for bedtime, sleep may come more easily.

Start to relax and unwind an hour before your bedtime. Rituals to help you unwind include a warm bath, meditation, gentle yoga exercises to soft music, light stretching exercises, stargazing, or light reading. Working on repetitious hobbies, such as knitting, needlepoint, sewing, or playing solitaire, may help you relax. Try to do the same things every evening so they become cues for your mind and body to settle down and prepare for sleep.

Journal writing in the evening is a quiet, relaxing way some women use to review their day, while others prefer to list tomorrow's activities before retiring. If you often lie in bed thinking about what you should have done today or planning for tomorrow, try writing a to do list early in the evening, so you won't stay awake worrying that you'll forget some things.

Some women like to relax by listening to soothing music on a stereo or headset. Choose gentle, instrumental music to help you unwind from a stressful day. You relax better when your mind is centered on the music rather than thinking about problems that occurred during the day. The Hallmark Music collection features albums to help you de-stress, such as *Music for a stress-free day*, or *Music to comfort the heart*.

If possible, use your bedroom only for sleeping. Your bedroom should not be a work room, exercise gym, or a place to watch television. Create a restful environment in your bedroom, which should be dark, quiet, and at a comfortable, cool temperature. Keep your bedroom as dark as possible at night to increase your natural sleep-inducing melatonin level. Darkness increases the production of melatonin. You might use room-darkening shades or wear an eye mask. You may use subtle background noise, such as a fan blowing or soft music, to drown out other noise.

Try to get to bed at the same time every evening, even during the weekends, and wake up at the same time each morning. If you feel you are not getting enough sleep, try going to bed twenty minutes earlier and see if the quality of your day improves. Oversleeping in the morning can make you feel sluggish during the day.

Lie down to sleep only when you feel drowsy. Avoid trying to sleep, because the harder you try, the more awake you'll become. Be sure you have a comfortable, supportive mattress since you will spend almost one-third of your day on it. If you aren't sleepy at your usual bedtime, turn the lights down and read something dull.

There are several things to *avoid* which may interfere with regular sleep patterns:

Avoid engaging in anything that increases your alertness before bedtime, such as strenuous exercise, watching stimulating television programs, or reading a mystery thriller.

Avoid alcohol, caffeine, and nicotine before you sleep. Although alcohol is a sedative and may initially cause sleepiness, it eventually leads to arousal and awakening as your blood alcohol level decreases and metabolic activity increases. Alcohol also blocks REM sleep, causing frequent awakenings. Caffeine in coffee, tea, cola, and chocolate is a stimulant, which may increase your adrenalin level for up to six hours and interfere with sleep. Some people refrain from any caffeine products after 4:00 PM because of their long-lasting stimulating effects that interfere with sleep. Nicotine products, such as cigarettes, cigars, and chewing tobacco, are also stimulants that affect how well you sleep. Nicotine may cause problems similar to sleep apnea (inadequate oxygen) and smokers may not sleep as deeply during the non-REM delta sleep stage. Also, avoid eating foods and drinks that are high in sugar and fat, as the calories may boost your energy and fatty foods are difficult to digest while trying to get to sleep.

Sleeping pills are among the most frequently used drugs in the world. An estimated 24 million prescriptions for sleeping disorders are written for Americans annually. These sleeping pills, such as Ambien, Restoril, and Sonata, can relieve all kinds of insomnia, but should only be taken for a couple of weeks: they can become psychologically addictive and later may impair sleep. For anxiety-related sleep problems, the sedative Xanax or Remeron may be prescribed and can be taken for a few weeks.

Using over-the-counter (OTC) sleeping pills like Sominex or Sleep-Eze for more than a few nights can also create problems. You can build up a tolerance to them, and after a couple of months may not be able to sleep without them. Sleeping pills, nighttime pain remedies like Tylenol PM, and antihistamines like Benadryl can be useful for less than two weeks, but their side effects range from dry mouth to constipation.

Prescription or over-the-counter medications may have side effects that interfere with sleeping. Check with your doctor or pharmacist about any sleep-related side effects of all medications you take. Some common cold and allergy remedies such as Sudafed, Actifed and Robitussin CF cause insomnia. Medications for high blood pressure, heart disease, and asthma can also compromise your sleep, as well as diet pills with stimulants.

Use Herbs to Induce Sleep

Several herbs and other natural remedies are effective at inducing mild relaxation and sleep. Compared to sleeping pills, these remedies are generally milder, safer, and less addictive. However, herbs and nutritional supplements, including melatonin, are not regulated by the FDA, although many of them have been studied and approved by European regulatory commissions. Herbs such as catnip, hops, poppies, lemon balm, and passion flower are known for their calming and sedating effects. For more information on herbs and supplements, you may wish to read Chapter 22, or Foster and Tyler's book, *Tyler's Honest Herbal: A Sensible Guide to the Use of Herbs and Related Remedies*, or check the references at the end of this book.

Melatonin is a hormone made by the pineal gland and can be safe when used within the body's normal range. Supplements of 1 to 3 milligrams can be a good remedy for insomnia, but should be taken with caution. If you get headaches, dizziness, or nightmares, stop taking melatonin.

Valerian root is another popular natural sleep aid. It helps relieve anxiety and nervous tension by depressing the central nervous system and relaxing smooth muscles. Taking 180 to 360 milligrams of valerian root has a calming effect which enhances sleep. It should be taken thirty to sixty minutes before bedtime. However, about 10 percent of people are energized by this herb and it may keep them awake. When combined with 80 to 160 milligrams of lemon balm extract (Melissa), valerian may improve deep-stage sleep.

5-Hydroxy-Tryptophan (5-HTP) is what your body uses to make serotonin, a neurotransmitter that helps improve the quality of your sleep. Take 100 to 400 milligrams at night, unless you are taking medications with serotonin, in which case limit your amount to 200 milligrams, because you can develop a rare, life-threatening reaction caused by too high a level of serotonin.

Calcium and *magnesium*, in a two-to-one ratio, such as 600 to 800 milligrams of calcium and 300 to 400 milligrams of magnesium, can be taken at bedtime for their relaxing effect.

Chamomile is an ancient and widely used herb usually taken as a tea to treat anxiety and insomnia, as well as digestive problems. It is among the mildest of herbal sedatives.

Kava kava is a well-known herb which aids in reducing anxiety and promoting calmness. Use a 30-percent extract and take anywhere from 200 to 750 milligrams at bedtime. If a rash occurs, stop taking this herb, or try taking 50 milligrams of a B-complex vitamin and decrease the amount of kava kava if the rash continues.

Passion flower is another herb that can reduce anxiety during the day and help with sleep. Take between 100 to 200 milligrams at bedtime.

Health Benefits of Sleep and Rest

Your mind and body are restored when you get sufficient sleep and rest. During sleep, several major changes occur in your body. Your muscles relax, your blood pressure falls, and your heart and respiratory rates decrease. The production of hormones increases and damaged tissues and cells are repaired. Gradually your brain waves slow down and in REM sleep, your dreams allow your mind to work on unresolved problems and fears. Several studies have shown that adequate sleep and napping can prevent illness and relieve stress and tension. A short nap may boost your performance and productivity.

Videos

Lilias Yoga for Beginners—a three volume set in color—90 minutes.

25

Self-nurturance, Joy, and Laughter

Do something fun as often as you can get away with it. —Joan Lunden

Many women view life as a serious business, full of responsibilities to their spouse, children, parents, employers, and sometimes to friends. Life in the fast lane often consists of over-crowded schedules with numerous changes, sensory overload from multiple incoming messages, and frequent interruptions. Women often focus on their responsibilities to others more than on responsibilities to themselves. Some women get so wrapped up trying to juggle their multiple roles and responsibilities that they become emotionally drained and physically exhausted. They seldom take time for their own pleasures, and often feel guilty when they do.

When women take life too seriously and become so caught up in their chaotic lifestyle and problems that they cannot see any way out, they often lose perspective. Severe stress from an unhealthy balance of multiple responsibilities and too little pleasure can lead to emotional distress and physical illness. Disturbing thoughts, feelings, and attitudes affect women's mental and physical health, rendering them more susceptible to illness. Health professionals know the importance of self-nurturance, joy, and humor to help women handle stress better and enhance their physical and emotional well being.

SELF-NURTURANCE AND JOY

Definitions of Self-nurturance and Joy

Self-nurturance is frequently indulging in enjoyable leisure activities for your own personal pleasure and enjoyment. The goal is to enjoy these pleasures without feeling guilty or asking anyone's permission.

Joy is an attitude of the mind which fulfills the heart and soul. There are close relationships between joy, happiness, laughter, and serenity. Robert Holden, author of *Laughter: The Best Medicine*, believes that pleasure and joy are different forms of happiness. Pleasure is temporary happiness that is attained through physical, emotional, and material objects, pursuits, and achievements. Joy is usually found through spirituality of the heart and soul and self-realization. Joy leads to inner peace and serenity which transcend time and may last forever.

How to Develop Self-nurturance and Joyful Living

How you engage in self-nurturance is an individual choice. Indulge yourself in the activities that bring you the most joy and pleasure. Listen to your inner voice to learn who you really are and what you love to do—the activities you truly enjoy. Then strive to do them—no excuses. Self-nurturance should never feel like another obligation. Open yourself up to the numerous activities available around you. Your choices should emphasize pleasure, joy, and fun that nourish your mind, body, and soul. Domar and Dreher, authors of *Self-nurture: Learning to Care for Yourself as Effectively as You Care for Everyone Else*, suggest that if you are overloaded with intellectual stimulation, consider spiritually rejuvenating activities such as meditation or nature walks. If you spend too much time on mundane tasks, think about stimulating your unused senses with a relaxing massage, listening to soul-enriching music, or attending a concert. If you spend your days sitting or standing for long periods and would enjoy more physical activity, consider getting some form of exercise, such as dancing, aerobics, or hiking.

Robert Holden recommends that you choose a special treat, a well-deserved reward, or a little luxury—whatever it takes to make you feel special or pampered. Some women enjoy soaking in a scented bath, spending an evening with friends, attending a theater event, walking in the park, or watching a sunset. Others enjoy shopping during sales, reading good books or novels, getting a new hair style, having a manicure or pedicure, or taking a dance class. Remember that self-nurturance is a way of traveling through life, not just a momentary destination.

In *The Ten Rules of High Performance Living*, Dr. Meltzer states that we all need to lighten up our lives and take ourselves less seriously. When you focus on being lighthearted, fun-loving, and easygoing, you calm your mind and lighten your thinking. This involves letting go of the unresolved emotional stress and tension that burdens your heart, dampens your spirit, and drains your mind. Although we all experience tragedies and problems, you can act appropriately to keep your emotional life in balance. Joyful living can help you create a positive inner spirit, no matter what is happening in your life. You can feel empowered and learn to appreciate and enjoy life.

Adopt a happy, healthy philosophy about life. Your beliefs about life often influence how you live your life. If you believe in Murphy's Law—if anything can go wrong, it will—then you live your life expecting bad things to happen. Many people tend to focus on what went wrong instead of what went right. Happiness is a balance between making life go your way and accepting what has come your way. Even when you don't feel joyful and happy, try to fake it. Smile in spite of your problems, and you'll soon find that faking happiness can actually make you feel better. Don't suppress your sadness—feel it, but act happy anyway. Begin your day by looking forward to some pleasure you expect to occur, even if it is just reading a book. If you talk as though you feel positive and optimistic, you can actually begin to feel that way. Acting more like the person you'd like to be brings you closer to your pursuit of happiness.

What goes on *around* you does not need to influence what goes on *inside* you. You are responsible for your reactions to all you encounter and experience throughout life. The way you respond to life's ups and downs is your decision. No one else can give you joy; they can only encourage, and possibly help you find your own love for life. Those who believe in the joy of life use their energy, effort, and enthusiasm to enjoy life thoroughly. Holden suggests that as you go through your day, try to notice which things bring you joy and which upset you. When you find yourself in a negative mood, take a break or go for a walk to think about things that make you happy, and then carry those thoughts with you. When good things happen, whether large or small, share your joy with others so that they can see your happiness.

Today is the beginning of a new life. The past is over, the future awaits, so the present is like a gift—it is all we have. Part of the art of joyful living is to capture, celebrate, and make the most of each moment. When you awaken, ask yourself, "How can I celebrate the wonder of life today?" Take time to look, listen, taste, touch, and smell everything around you with appreciation for the experience. Be thankful and express gratitude for all you experience and you will feel blessed. Seek to transcend everyday experiences and become more aware of special moments. Work with, not against, everything that occurs, so that all your experiences will work for you. Empower yourself with a spirit of adventure and a heart full of love and gratitude. Smile and send sincere and generous love and joy to all you meet. Holden encourages you to strive for harmony and balance to become one with whatever you choose to do, wherever you decide to go, and whomever you choose to be with. Those who develop a deep love for life possess the spiritual outlook, appreciation, and understanding of things that transcend everyday experiences. They become one with the true essence of all things.

Health Benefits of Self-nurturance and Joy

Sometimes a woman's responsibilities seem to take up all her time and energy, and she forgets to find ways to maintain her own happiness. Domar and Dreher believe that it is very important to meet your needs for nurturance to replenish your physical, emotional, and spiritual self. Self-nurturance sends a healthy message to your psyche that you like yourself well enough to take good care of your mind/body needs.

Every emotion experienced in the mind creates a corresponding reaction in the organs, systems, and chemicals of the body. And all body systems react adversely to negative emotions during stressful encounters. PNI studies have found that happiness, joyful emotions, and appropriate humor can enhance one's immune system and possibly ward off physical and emotional illness. Holden believes that by engaging in self-nurturing or joyful activities, women can strengthen their emotional and physical reserves before they reach desperate states from stress overload. Stress reduction strategies help women maintain their inner balance, lighten their view of events in life, and remind them that they just may be doing okay.

Joyful living is both an art and a philosophy known as *joie de vivre*. When you adopt a happy, joyful view of life, and focus on what is good and right about your life, you can create such a life. If you go through life expecting bad things to happen, then they probably will happen because you are focusing on what can go wrong. Become an optimist and expect good things to happen, and remember not to postpone joy—you can always cry later. People with a true joy for life recognize that the art of living joyfully is a skill that requires continual practice. Holden feels that joy in your soul can release negative thoughts such as anxiety, over-seriousness, and anger. Feelings of joy encourage the positive expression of fears, hope, optimism, and love that support your health, happiness, and well-being. Those with joy for life find their lives are enriched, and their spirit of wonder and enthusiasm for life are contagious. If you radiate joy, happiness, and love for life, you are likely to attract others who respond in kind. Your health will flourish in this atmosphere. When your life is fulled with joy, it supports your constant growth, renewal, and fulfillment—you experience a sense of wonder, excitement, and zest for living.

Enjoy Life's Journey

Live in the moment. Tell those you love that you do. Smile and laugh often.
Let your light shine. Nurture yourself. Strive for serenity and inner peace.
Make new friends. Appreciate and love yourself as much as you do others.
Enjoy the beauty of nature. Express your feelings, don't bury them inside.
Discover your purpose and fulfill it with a passion. Have realistic expectations.
Take your work, but not yourself, seriously. Grow through change
and challenges.
Love what you do and do what you love. Celebrate life and enjoy the scenery.

—Adapted from Enjoy the Journey, *by Patty Berens*

HUMOR AND LAUGHTER

Your feelings about life's problems are influenced by your personality and previous experiences. Much of your stress and suffering may be due to how you perceive and interpret your problems. You can view any situation as a serious or laughing matter. Which perspective you choose depends on your attitude.

Sometimes women focus so much on their problems that they forget to see the bigger picture or potentially positive outcomes. Also, they may get so caught up in their dilemma that they forget to see the absurdity of the situation or their actions. Although accepting some problems in your life in a positive manner is difficult, it can be done. When you can find some humor in your problems, they may not seem as big or as important as before. Holden believes that when you laugh and joke about your problems, your perspective may change and you'll see things differently. Humor expands your narrow view of a problem. Sometimes circumstances change and problems work out better than expected. The use of humor and laughter makes these changes possible.

Definitions of Humor and Laughter

Humor is the ability to perceive, appreciate, enjoy, or express what is comical, absurd, or funny. It is the ability to perceive what is amusing and be delighted.

Laughter is the act of expressing delight or hilarity with vocal sounds, with the mouth open in a smile at something amusing, improbable, or ridiculous.

How Humor and Laughter Work

In the 1970s, Norman Cousins suddenly developed a mysterious collagen disease called ankylosing spondylitis, which caused severe inflammation of his spine and joints. His body rapidly degenerated so that he had difficulty moving his limbs, his sleep was constantly interrupted by pain, and he could barely speak. Cousins knew about the connection between chronic stress and illness, and thought that positive emotions might help him recover. He chose repeatedly to watch humorous motion pictures which made him laugh, and discovered that ten minutes of genuine belly laughter had an anesthetic effect which gave him two hours of pain-free sleep.

In 1979, Cousins wrote *Anatomy of an Illness*, which described how he used laughter to help heal his body. He referred to laughter as "internal jogging," an exercise in which all the major body systems, including the heart, lungs, muscles, and circulation, get a good workout. His book helped inspire more research into the therapeutic effects of humor and laughter. Science has since demonstrated that humor and laughter improve physical and emotional well-being. Chronic daily stressors often cause major illnesses. Many studies have shown that a happy outlook and sense of humor toward stressful situations can prevent them from leading to physical and emotional problems.

How to Develop Humor and Laughter

Humor and laughter should be a part of everyday life, not just an occasional experience. Any day that you have not laughed is a wasted one. Although some days it is harder to laugh than others, you should make an effort to laugh anyway. Unfortunately, some people believe that laughter is spontaneous, and think that there is nothing they can do to make it happen. Your desire to laugh more, even when you feel like crying, can change your life. When you can laugh through your tears, you may unconsciously be telling yourself that although your problems seem immense, perhaps you'll be able to handle them.

Humor can help you maintain your sanity in an insane world. One way to deal with stressful situations is to look for any absurdity in them that you can laugh about. The world is filled with absurdities—just look for them at work, home, and in your relationships or in anything that upsets you. Allen Klein, author of *The Healing Power of Humor*, thinks that nothing is funnier than the unintended humor of reality, as long as you laugh at yourself or *with* others, not at someone else. When you encounter one of those tough times, try to come up with an amusing line. For example, when my mother worked as a school secretary, she had this sign over her desk: "If you're looking for someone with a little authority, I have as little as anyone." Other examples of absurdity include a sign at a local gas station which read, "Courteous and efficient self-service" or a sign on the ladies room door, "Please wait to be seated."

Sometimes bad things happen to good people—life isn't always fair. Laughter can sometimes help reduce the stress you feel from mistakes, tragedies, and traumas. Although laughing at your problems or mistakes is often difficult, it can take away the sting, so that they have less power over you. Learn to recognize the humor in your errors and crises. You relax and momentarily forget your overriding anxiety, worries, and fears when you laugh. Klein believes that laughing at yourself enables you and others to accept the situation in a more comfortable way, and indicates a healthy ego, confidence, strength, and inner balance. Stephen Covey says that by using humor you imply that "You're off track—but so what?" Those who can laugh at their problems and mistakes get back on track much faster. It puts things in the proper perspective so that you don't sweat the small stuff, and helps you realize that most stuff is small.

Because none of us is perfect, we all need to remember not to take ourselves too seriously. Laughing at yourself may prevent you from taking yourself too seriously and becoming uptight, overreacting to upsetting situations, and becoming unbalanced. The key to maintaining balance is to take your work seriously, but yourself lightly. Try to act like someone who sees the lighter side of things. If you act like a person who can laugh during difficult times, you will find that you can overcome life's crises more easily and enjoy life more. Humorous reminders and amusing notes may help you see the lighter side of life. For example, you might place a note on your mirror that reads, "This person is not to be taken seriously!" When my teenage daughter kept forgetting to flush the toilet, I stuck a smiley-face note on her toilet which read, "Please flush me!"

Everyone's sense of humor is different. It reflects individual personality and personal preferences. Every time you laugh, others learn a little bit about who you are, what you think, and how you feel. Determine what makes you laugh, seek it out, and try to maximize the things that help you laugh. Actively try to become more humorous and inspire humor in those around you. When something strikes you as really funny, laugh out loud. Ask others to share humorous incidents with you, and share yours with others. For some it's like learning a foreign language or looking at the world upside-down, so be persistent. You may need practice to see the funny side of things. You might begin with a smile, then a giggle or chuckle before you're comfortable with a good belly laugh.

Klein suggests that a simple technique to make your painful moments humorous is to use exaggeration. You simply embellish your difficulties and disappointments by describing them in highly dramatic or overinflated ways. When you can see the ridiculousness of your situation, it sometimes hurts less.

Most people like to be around happy, cheerful folks who enjoy good humor. Those with a sense of humor have a natural way of being lighthearted and fun-loving. Seek the company of those who make you laugh and feel better about yourself. They'll add happiness to your life, especially during moments of laughter. Shared laughter creates a feeling of belonging and being connected to others. Fear, loneliness, and isolation disappear when you share laughter. Happy people can make you feel comfortable and relaxed and help you forget your problems during laughter.

Health Benefits of Humor and Laughter

Humor and laughter offer several psychological advantages. Holden believes that they can produce smiles, amusement, hopefulness, and joyful feelings toward others. Laughter is a letting-go experience which helps you connect with your natural, unrestrained self and express your emotions, thoughts, and feelings. If women can find some comedy in their chaos, so that they are no longer caught up in it, their problems may become less burdensome. Klein claims that humor, laughter, and a positive attitude can diffuse stressful events, and release the built-up tension and anxiety that can lead to fear, hostility, rage, and anger. In his book, Allen Klein asserts that through humor and laughter you can transcend some of your personal problems. Humor and laughter can help you rise above feelings of fear, discouragement, and despair, and maintain your inner balance when the world seems to be falling apart. Humor can reduce your suffering by giving you power in what appears to be a powerless situation. If you can laugh at your troubles, you will feel uplifted and be able to handle them with less stress. When you can laugh at yourself and your personal dilemmas, you may feel empowered and view your problems with a new perspective. A happy, relaxed attitude toward life also promotes emotional and spiritual harmony and balance. Laughter may also generate the following physiological changes:

- Enhance circulation of blood in the body.
- Oxygenate the blood and ventilate the lungs.
- Increase the number of natural killer cells.
- Boost functioning of the immune system.
- Lower the blood pressure afterwards.
- Activate the release of endorphins which give a sense of pleasure.
- Reduce muscle tension and help muscles relax, thus reducing pain.
- Trigger the release of catecholamines, hormones that Increase alertness.
- Decrease the output of stress hormones, such as cortisol.

Those who radiate good humor and a happy disposition have healthy personality traits that may protect them from illness or hasten their recovery. According to Holden, your greatest health resources are humor, happiness, hope, optimism, and positive self-worth. Humor, laughter, and happiness are some of the most effective ways to reduce stress. They act like catalysts that promote physical, emotional, and spiritual health. Through laughter you learn to accept life as it is, not as you'd like it to be. By laughing frequently and taking a basically humorous approach to life, you can cope more easily with stress. Laughter is a celebration, a victory, and a triumph over your problems. The best laughter comes straight from the heart. It makes you feel truly alive with joy.

References

Achterberg, Jeanne, Barbara Dossey, and Leslie Kolkmeier. 1994. *Rituals of healing: Using imagery for health and wellness.* New York: Bantam Press.

Albert, Catherine A. 1996. *Getting a good night's sleep.* New York: Simon & Schuster.

Antoni, M. H. 1993. Stress management: Strategies that work. In D. Goleman and J. Gurin, eds. *Mind/body medicine: How to use your mind for better health.* Yonkers, NY: Consumer Report Books.

Arnot, Bob. 2000. *Biology of success.* Boston: Little & Brown.

Bassman, Lynette, ed. 1998. *The whole mind: The definitive guide to complementary treatments for mind, mood, and emotion.* Novato, CA: New World Library.

Beck, Martha. 2000. Love-your-life guide. *Redbook,* June, pp. 84–89.

Bendick, A., M. Phillips, and R. Tengerdy. 1989. *Antioxidant nutrients and immune function.* New York: Plenum Press.

Benson, Herbert and M. Klipper. 2000. *The relaxation response.* New York: Avon.

Benson, Herbert. 1996. *Timeless healing: The power and biology of belief.* New York: Simon & Schuster.

Bloomfield, H. H. and R. K. Cooper. 1995. *The power of 5: 5 seconds to 5 minute shortcuts.* Emmaus, PA: Rodale Books.

Blumenthal, M., A. Goldberg, and J. Brinckmann, eds. 2000. *Expanded Commission E Monographs.* Austin, TX: American Botanical Council.

Borysenko, Joan. 1987. *Minding the body, mending the mind.* Carlsbad, CA: Hay House.

Borysenko, J. and M. Borysenko. 1994. *The power of the mind to heal: Renewing body, mind and spirit.* Carlsbad, CA: Hay House.

Brinker, F. 1998. *Herb contraindications and drug interactions.* Sandy, OR: Eclectic Medical Publications.

Buchanan, G. M., and M. E. P. Seligman, eds. 1995. *Explanatory style.* Hillsdale, NJ: Erlbaum.

Burns, David D. 1985. *Intimate connections.* New York: William Morrow.

Cameron, Julia. 1993. *The artist's way: A spiritual path to higher creativity.* New York: G. P. Putnam's Sons.

Campbell, Don. 1997. *The Mozart effect.* New York: Avon Books.

Carlson, Richard. 1997. *Don't sweat the small stuff.* New York: Hyperion.

Carlson, Kristine. 2001. *Don't sweat the small stuff for women: Simple and practical ways to do what matters most and find time for yourself.* New York: Hyperion.

Carper, Jean. 1993. *Food: Your miracle medicine.* New York: HarperCollins.

Charles, Leslie. 1999. *Why is everyone so cranky?* New York: Hyperion.

Chopra, Deepak. 1991. *Perfect health: The complete mind/body guide.* New York: Harmony Books.

Chopra, Deepak. 1991. *Restful sleep: The complete mind/body program for overcoming insomnia.* NewYork: Harmony Books.

Chopra, Deepak. 1993. *Ageless body, timeless mind: The quantum alternative to growing old.* New York: Harmony Books.

Chopra, Deepak. 1994. *Journey into healing: Awakening the wisdom within you.* New York: Harmony Books.

Chopra, Deepak. 2000. *How to know God: The soul's journey into the mystery of mysteries.* New York: Harmony Books.

Christensen, Alice. 1996. *The American yoga association wellness book.* Sarasota, FL: American Yoga Association.

Clark, C. C. 1999. *Encyclopedia of complementary health practice.* New York: Springer Publishing Co.

Cooper, Kenneth H. 1994. *The antioxidant revolution.*
Nashville, TN: Thomas Nelson.

Cousins, Norman. 1979. *Anatomy of an illness.* New York: Norton.

Covey, Stephen R. 1997. *The 7 habits of highly effective families.*
New York: Golden Books.

DiDomenico, David. 1998. Message and mental health. In
L. Bassman, ed. *The whole mind: A definitive guide to complementary treatments
for mind, mood, and emotion.* Novato, CA: New World Library.

DiGeronimo, Theresa F. 1997. *Insomnia: 50 essential things to do.*
New York: Plume.

Domar, Alice D. and Henry Dreher. 1996. *Healing mind, healthy woman:
Using the mind-body connection to manage stress and take control of your health.*
New York: Henry Holt & Co.

Domar, Alice D. and Henry Dreher. 2000. *Self-nurture: Learning to
care for yourself as effectively as you care for everyone else.* New York: Viking.

Donsbach, Kurt W. 1985. *Acupressure and electro-acupuncture for pain relief.*
Huntington Beach, CA: The International Institute of Natural
Health Sciences, Inc.

Dossey, Larry. 1990. *Recovering the soul: A scientific and spiritual search.*
New York: Bantam Books.

Dossey, Larry. 1993. *Healing words: The power of prayer and the practice of
medicine.* San Francisco: HarperCollins.

Dossey, Larry. 1996. *Prayer is good medicine.* San Francisco: HarperCollins.

Dreher, Henry. 1995. *The immune power personality: 7 traits you can develop
to stay healthy.* New York: Dutton.

Duke, J. A. 1997. *The green pharmacy.* Emmaus, PA: Rodale Press.

Eliot, R. S. 1994. *From stress to strength: How to lighten your load and save
your life.* New York: Bantam Press.

Elkin, Allen. 1999. *Stress management for dummies.*
Chicago, IL: IDG Worldwide Inc.

Flach, Frederic. 1988. *Resilience: Discovering a new strength at times of stress.*
New York: Fawcett Columbine.

Feltrow, C. W. and J. R. Avila. 2000. *The complete guide to herbal medicines.*
Springhouse, PA: Springhouse.

Fleischman, Gary. 1998. *Acupuncture: Everything you ever wanted to know.*
Barrytown, NY: Barrytown, Ltd.

Foley, Denise and Eileen Nechas. 1998. *Women's encyclopedia of health and emotional healing.* Emmaus, PA: Rodale Press.

Foster, S. and V. Tyler. 2000. *Tyler's honest herbal: A sensible guide to the use of herbs and related remedies,* 4th ed. New York: Haworth Press.

Frankl, V. E. 1978. *Man's search for meaning.* New York: Pocket Books.

Fuch-Berman, A. 1996. *Alternative medicine: What works.*
Tucson, AZ: Odonian Press.

Gach, Michael R. 1990. *Acupressure's potent points.*
New York: Bantam Books.

Gach, Michael R. 1995. *Basic acupressure.*
Berkeley, CA: Acupressure Institute.

Gary, D. and D. Dinkmeyer. 1994. *How you feel is up to you.*
San Luis Obispo, CA: Impact Publishers.

Glaser, R. and J. Kiecolt-Glaser, eds. 1994. *Handbook of human stress and immunity.* New York: Academic Press.

Golan, R. 1995. *Optimal wellness.* New York: Ballantine Books.

Goleman, D., P. Kaufman and M.L. Ray. 1991. *The creative spirit.*
New York: Dutton.

Goleman, D. 1998. *Working with emotional intelligence.*
New York: Bantam Books.

Goleman, D. and J. Gurin, eds. 1993. *Mind/body medicine: How to use your mind for better health.* Yonkers, NY: Consumer Reports Books.

Goodman, Ellen and Patricia O'Brien. 2000. *I know just what you mean: The power of friendship in women's lives.* New York: Simon & Schuster.

Goodman, Saul. 1990. *The book of Shiatsu.* Garden City Park, NY: Avery Publishing Group, Inc.

Gordon, Rena, B. Nienstedt. and W. Gesler, eds. 1999. *Alternative therapies: Expanding options in health care.* New York: Springer Press.

Gray, John. 1992. *Men are from Mars, women are from Venus.* San Francisco: HarperCollins.

Guttman, Monika. 1999. Resilience. *USA Weekend* March 5–7, pp. 4–5.

Hafen, B. Q., K. J. Karren, K. J. Frandsen, and N. L. Smith. 1996. *Mind/body health: The effects of attitudes, emotions, and relationships.* Boston: Allyn and Bacon.

Hendricks, Gay. 1987. *Learning to love yourself.* New York: Prentice Hall.

Hobbs, Christopher. 1997. *Stress & natural healing.* Loveland, CO: Botanica Press.

Holden, Robert. 1993. *Laughter—the best medicine.* Hammersmith, London: Thorsons—An Imprint of HarperCollins.

Inlander, Charles B. and Cynthia K. Moran. 1996. *Stress: 63 ways to relieve tension and stay healthy.* New York: Walker and Company.

Jahnke, Roger. 1997. *The healer within: The four essential self-care methods for creating optimal health.* San Francisco: HarperCollins.

Janson, Michael. 1996. *The vitamin revolution in health care.* Greenville, NH: Arcadia Press.

James, M. and J. James. 1991. *Passion for life.* New York: Dutton.

Janov, Arthur. 1996. *Why you get sick, how you get well: The healing power of feelings.* West Hollywood, CA: Dove.

Jarmey, Chris and John Tindall. 1991. *Acupressure for common ailments.* New York: Simon & Schuster.

Jeffers, Susan. 1992. *Dare to connect: Reaching out to others in romance, friendship, and the workplace.* New York: Fawcett Columbine.

Johnson, Spencer. 1998. *Who moved my cheese: An amazing way to deal with change in your work and your life.* New York: G. P. Putnam's Sons.

Judelson, Debra R. and Diana L. Dell. 1998. *The women's complete wellness book.* New York: Golden Books.

Jwin-Ming, Yang. 1994. *Chinese Gigong massage.* Jamaica Plains, MA: YMAA Publication Center.

Kabat-Zinn, Jon. 1991. *Full catastrophe living: Using the wisdom of your body and mind to face stress, pain, and illness.* New York: Delacorte Publishing.

Kabat-Zinn, Jon. 1994. *Wherever you go, there you are: Mindfulness meditation in everyday life, meditation for daily living.* New York: Hyperion.

Kenney, Janet W. and Ano Bhattacharjee. 2000. An interactive model of women's stressors, personality traits and health problems. *Journal of Advanced Nursing* 32(1):249–258.

Kiecolt-Glaser, J. K. and R. Glaser. 1993. Mind and Immunity. In D. Goleman and J. Gurin, eds. *Mind/body Medicine: How to use your mind for better health.* Yonkers, NY: Consumer Reports Books.

Kirsta, Alix. 1986. *The book of stress survival.* New York: Simon & Schuster, Inc.

Klein, Allen. 1989. *The healing power of humor.* New York: Penguin Putnam, Inc.

Knaster, Mirka. 1996. *Discovering the body's wisdom.* New York: Bantam.

Kobasa, S., S. Maddi and S. Kahn. 1982. Hardiness as health: A prospective study. *Journal of Personality and Social Psychology* 42:168–177.

Koenig, H. G. 1997. *Is religion good for your health? The effects of religion on physical and mental health.* Binghamton, NY: Haworth Press.

Kunz, Dora. 1995. *Spiritual healing: Doctors examine therapeutic touch and other holistic treatments.* Wheaton, IL: Quest.

Lamb, Sandra. 2000. How to be a positive person. *Family Circle* pp. 24–28.

Lasater, J. 1995. *Relax and renew: Restful yoga for stressful times.* Berkeley, CA: Rodmell Press.

Lerner, H. G. 1985. *The dance of anger: A woman's guide to changing the patterns of intimate relationships.* New York: Harper and Row.

Liberman, Sandy M. 1998. Dance therapy. In Lynette Bassman, ed. *The whole mind: The definitive guide to complementary treatments for mind, mood, and emotion.* Novato, CA: New World Library.

Loecher, B. and S. A. O'Donnell. 1998. *Women's choices in natural healing.* Emmaus, PA: Rodale Press, Inc.

Lopez, Suzanne. 1999. *Get smart with your heart: The intelligent woman's guide to love, lust, and lasting relationships.* New York: G. P. Putnam's Sons.

Lukeman, Alex. 1999. *Sleep well, sleep deep.* New York: M. Evans and Company, Inc.

Luks, Allan and Peggy Payne. 1992. *The healing power of doing good: The health and spiritual benefits of helping others.* New York: Fawcett Columbine.

Lunden, Joan and Laura Morton. 1997. *Joan Lunden's healthy living: A practical inspirational guide to creating balance in your life.* New York: Crown Publishers.

Lynch, James P. B. and Anita W. Bell. 1994. *Dr. Lynch's holistic self-health program.* New York: Dutton.

Maciocia, Giovanni. 1989. *The foundations of Chinese medicine.* New York: Churchill Livingston.

Magnum, Alice. 2000. Walk your way to great health. *Prevention* July, pp. 122–29.

Manning, George. 1999. *Stress: Living and working in a changing world.* Duluth, MN: Whole Person Associates.

Matthew, Lyn. 2000. *Moxibustion Manual.*
Mesa, AZ: Matthew Enterprises, Inc.

Mathews, D. A., D. B. Larson and C. P. Barry. 1994. *The Faith Factor:*
An annotated bibliography of clinical research on spiritual subjects. Vol. 1.
Lansdale, PA: John Templeton Foundation.

Mayell, Mark, and editors of *Natural Health* magazine. 1995.
52 simple steps to natural health. New York: Pocket Books.

McGuffin, M., C. Hobbs, R. Upton, and A. Goldberg, eds. 1997.
American herbal products association's botanical safety handbook.
Boca Raton: CRC Press.

McKay, Gary D. and D. Dinkmeyer. 1994. *How you feel is up to you.*
San Luis, CA: Impact Publishers.

Meltzer, Barnet. 1998. *The ten rules of high performance living.*
Naperville, IL: Sourcebooks, Inc.

Miller, Emmett E. 1997. *Deep healing: The essence of mind/body medicine.*
Carlsbad, CA: Hay House.

Mooshing, Ni. 1995. *The yellow emperor's classic of medicine.*
Boston, MA: Shambala Publications.

Moss, Richard. 1995. *The second miracle: Intimacy, spirituality, and*
conscious relationships. Berkeley: Celestial Arts.

Myers, E. 1997. *Yoga and you.* Boston: Shambhala Press.

Naparsteck, Belleruth. 1994. *Staying well with guided imagery.*
New York: Warner Books.

Northrup, Christiane. 1994. *Women's bodies, women's wisdom:*
Creating physical and emotional health and healing. New York: Bantam.

O'Brien, P. 1995. *Yoga for women.* New York: HarperCollins.

O'Gorman, Patricia. 1994. *Dancing backwards in high heels:*
How women master the art of resilience. Center City, MN: Hazelden.

Ornish, Dean 1998. *Love and survival: The scientific basis for the healing power of intimacy.* New York: HarperCollins.

Page, Susan. 1994. *Now that I'm married, why isn't everything perfect.* Boston: Little, Brown, and Company

Pageley, Marlene J. 2000. How to talk so people will listen. *Family Circle,* July, pp. 36–39.

Passwater, Richard. 1993. *Getting the most out of your vitamins and minerals.* New Canaan, CT: Keats Publishing.

PDR for herbal medicines, 2nd ed. 2000. Montvale, NJ: Medical Economics.

Pearsall, Paul. 1993. *The 10 laws of lasting love.* New York: Simon & Schuster.

Pearsall, Paul. 1998. *The heart's code: Tapping the wisdom and power of our heart energy.* New York: Broadway Books.

Pelletier, Kenneth. 1994. *Sound mind, sound body: A new model for lifelong health.* New York: Simon & Schuster.

Pennebaker, James W. 1990. *Opening up: The healing power of confiding in others.* New York: William Morrow.

Pennebaker, J. W. and H. C. Trake. 1993. *Emotion, Inhibition and Health.* Seattle, WA: Hogrefe & Huber Publishers.

Pennebaker, J. W., ed. 1995. *Emotion, Disclosure, & Health.* Washington, DC: American Psychological Association.

Pert, Candace. 1997. *Molecules of emotion: Why you feel the way you do.* New York: Scribner.

Peterson, C. and L. M. Bossio. 1991. *Health and optimism.* New York: Free Press.

Pirog, John E. 1996. *Meridian style acupuncture.* Berkeley, CA: Pacific View Press.

Quellette, S. C. 1993. Inquiries into hardiness. In L. Goldberger and S. Breznitz, eds. *Handbook of stress: Theoretical and clinical aspects.* New York: Free Press, 77–100.

Reuben, Carolyn. 1995. *Antioxidants: Your complete guide.*
Rocklin, CA: Prima Publishing.

Robbers, E. and V. Tyler. 1999. *Tyler's herbs of choice: The therapeutic use of phytomedicinals.* New York: Haworth Press.

Robertson, J. C. and T. Monte. 1996. *Peak performance living.*
San Francisco: HarperCollins.

Sandford, Agnes. 1990. *The healing light.*
Lansdale, PA: The Spindrift Foundation.

Schaef, Anne W. 1990. *Laugh! I thought I'd die (if I didn't): Daily meditations on healing through humor.* New York: Ballantine Books.

Schaef, Anne W. 1990. *Meditations for women who do too much.*
San Francisco, CA: Harper & Row.

Schaef, Anne W. 1998. *Living in process: Basic truths for living the path of the soul.* New York: Ballantine Books.

Scheier, M. F. and C. S. Carver. 1985. Optimism, coping, and health: Assessment and implications of generalized outcome expectancies. *Health Psychology* 4: 219–47.

Schiffmann, E. 1996. *Yoga: The spirit and practice of moving into stillness.*
New York: Simon & Schuster.

Seligman, M. E. P. 1994. *What you can change & what you can't.*
New York: Knopf.

Seligman, M. E. P. 1998. *Learned optimism: How to change your mind and your life,* 2nd ed. New York: Pocket Books.

Siegel, Bernie. 1993. *How to live between office visits: A guide to life, love, and health.*
New York: HarperCollins.

Sills, Judith. 1997. Emotional resilience is a muscle you can build.
New Women August, pp. 103, 128–129.

Sills, Judith. 2000. Sweet security—joy of long lasting love.
Family Circle July, pp 28–30.

Simonton, O. Carl and Reid Hudson. 1994. *The healing journey.* New York: Bantam.

Singer, I. 1992. *Meaning in life.* New York: Free Press

Sobel, D. S. and R. Ornstein. 1996. *The healthy mind, healthy body handbook.* Los Altos, CA: DRX.

Spiegal, David. 1993. Social support: How friends, family and groups can help. In D. Goleman and J. Gurin, eds. *Mind/body medicine: How to use your mind for better health.* Yonkers, NY: Consumer Reports Books.

Steinem, G. 1993. *Revolution from within: A book of self-esteem.* Boston: Little & Brown.

Sternberg, R. J. and M. Hojjat, eds. 1997. *Satisfaction in close relationships.* New York: Guilford Press.

Sutcliffe, Jenny. 1991. *The complete book of relaxation techniques.* Allentown, PA: A People's Medical Society Book.

Temoshok, Lydia and Henry Dreher. 1992. *The type C connection.* New York: Random House.

Thondup, Tulku. 1996. *The healing power of mind: Simple meditation exercises for health, well-being and enlightenment.* Boston: Shambhala.

Tkac, Debora, ed. 1988. *Everyday health tips: 2000 practical hints for better health and happiness.* Emmaus, PA: Rodale Press.

Walker, L. P. and E. H. Brown. 1998. *Nature's pharmacy.* Paramus, NJ: Prentice Hall.

Warshaw, Tessa A. and Dee Barlow. 1995. *Resiliency: How to bounce back faster, stronger, smarter.* New York: Master Media.

Waterhouse, Debra. 1998. *Outsmarting the Midlife Fat Cell.* New York: Hyperion

Wiedman, John. 1999. *Desperately seeking snoozin': The insomnia cure.* Memphis, TN: Towering Pines Press Inc.

Weil, Andrew. 1995. *Health and Healing.* New York: Houghton Mifflin Co.

Weil, Andrew. 1995. *Spontaneous healing: How to discover and enhance your body's natural ability to maintain and heal itself.* New York: Alfred. A Knopf.

Weil, Andrew. 2000. *Eating well for optimum health.*
New York: Alfred A. Knopf.

White, L. B. and S. Foster. 1999. *The herbal drugstore.*
Emmaus, PA: Rodale Press.

Williams, Redford and Virginia Williams. 1993. *Anger kills.*
New York: HarperCollins.

Williams, Tom. 1996. *The complete illustrated guide to Chinese medicine.*
Rockport, MA: Element Books, Inc.

Williamson, J. S. and C. M. Wyandt. 1997. Herbal therapies: The facts and the fiction. *Drug Topics LXXX.*

Wurtman, Judith. 1986. *Managing your mind and mood through food.*
New York: Rawson Associates.

Xmnong, Cheng. 1996. *Chinese acupuncture and moxibustion.*
Beijing: Foreign Languages Press.

Zammit, Gary. 1997. *Good nights.*
Kansas City, KA: Andrews and McMeel.

Zilbergeld, Bernice and Allen Lazarus. 1987. *Getting what you want through mental training: Mind power.* Boston: Little, Brown & Company.

About the Author

Janet Kenney, RN, Ph.D., retired in 1999 after teaching Women's Health nursing for over thirty years at several universities nationwide. With a passion for her work, during this time she conducted several major funded research studies on women and stress, and published numerous articles on women's health problems in various nursing journals. Additionally, Dr. Kenney served as editor and coeditor of many nursing textbooks including Contemporary Women's Health. In 1998, Dr. Kenney was recognized by the medical community for her contribution to women's health and received the highly prized Spirit of Women award.

Taking full advantage of her retirement, Dr. Kenney enjoys writing books, visiting and playing tennis with friends, reading mysteries, attending stretch and relaxation classes, dancing, and spending time with her teenage daughter.